REVOLUTION,
RESISTANCE,
AND REFORM
IN VILLAGE CHINA

"The Agrarian Studies Series at Yale University Press seeks to publish outstanding and original interdisciplinary work on agriculture and rural society — for any period, in any location. Works of daring that question existing paradigms and fill abstract categories with the lived-experience of rural people are especially encouraged."
James C. Scott, *Series Editor*

Christiana Payne, *Toil and Plenty: Images of the Agricultural Landscape in England, 1780–1890* (1993)

Brian Donahue, *Reclaiming the Commons: Community Farms and Forests in a New England Town* (1999)

James C. Scott, *Seeing Like a State: How Certain Schemes to Improve the Human Condition Have Failed* (1999)

Tamara L. Whited, *Forests and Peasant Politics in Modern France* (2000)

Nina Bhatt and James C. Scott, *Agrarian Studies: Synthetic Work at the Cutting Edge* (2001)

Peter Boomgaard, *Frontiers of Fear: Tigers and People in the Malay World, 1600–1950* (2001)

Janet Vorwald Dohner, *The Encyclopedia of Historic and Endangered Livestock and Poultry Breeds* (2002)

Deborah Fitzgerald, *Every Farm a Factory: The Industrial Ideal in American Agriculture* (2003)

Stephen B. Brush, *Farmer's Bounty: Locating Crop Diversity in the Contemporary World* (2004)

Brian Donahue, *The Great Meadow: Farmers and the Land in Colonial Concord* (2004)

J. Gary Taylor and Patricia J. Scharlin, *Smart Alliance: How a Global Corporation and Environmental Activists Transformed a Tarnished Brand* (2004)

Raymond L. Bryant, *Nongovernmental Organizations in Environmental Struggles: Politics and the Making of Moral Capital in the Philippines* (2005)

Edward Friedman, Paul G. Pickowicz, and Mark Selden, *Revolution, Resistance, and Reform in Village China* (2005)

Michael Goldman, *Imperial Nature: The World Bank and Struggles for Social Justice in the Age of Globalization* (2005)

Arvid Nelson, *Cold War Ecology: Forests, Farms, and People in the East German Landscape, 1945–1989* (2005)

Steve Striffer, *Chicken: The Dangerous Transformation of America's Favorite Food* (2005)

Lynne Viola, V. P. Danilov, N. A. Ivnitskii, and Denis Kozlov (editors), *The War Against the Peasantry, 1927–1930* (2005)

REVOLUTION, RESISTANCE, AND REFORM IN VILLAGE CHINA

Edward Friedman

Paul G. Pickowicz

Mark Selden

Yale University Press

New Haven and London

Published with assistance from the foundation established in memory of Philip
Hamilton McMillan of the Class of 1894, Yale College.

Set in Galliard type by Keystone Typesetting, Inc.
Printed in the United States of America.

The Library of Congress has catalogued the hardcover edition as follows:
Friedman, Edward, 1937–
Revolution, resistance, and reform in village China / Edward Friedman, Paul G.
Pickowicz, and Mark Selden.
p. cm. — (Yale agrarian studies series)
Includes bibliographical references and index.
ISBN 0-300-10896-6 (cloth : alk. paper)
1. Hebei Sheng (China) — Rural conditions. 2. China — Rural conditions.
3. Communism and agriculture — China — Hebei Sheng. 4. Government,
Resistance to — China — Hebei Sheng. 5. China — Politics and government —
1949– I. Pickowicz, Paul. II. Selden, Mark. III. Title. IV. Yale agrarian studies.
HN740.H66F74 2005
307.72'0951'52 — dc22

                                                            2005043966

ISBN 978-0-300-12595-5 (pbk. : alk. paper)

A catalogue record for this book is available from the British Library.

10 9 8 7 6 5 4 3 2 1

For my mentors, Barrington Moore Jr. and Herman Epstein (EF)
For Li Huai (PGP)
For my mentors, Leo Marx and Mary C. Wright (MS)

❈ CONTENTS

✤ ACKNOWLEDGMENTS

A project spanning a quarter of a century and extending from across the United States to China, Hong Kong, and beyond entails the accumulation of large personal debts.

We have been fortunate in having the guidance, suggestions and support of faculty and graduate student colleagues, including Jeremy Brown, Uradyn Bulag, Anita Chan, Joseph Esherick, Feng Chongyi, David Goodman, Peter Ho, Li Huai, Liu Dong, Liu Yigao, Lu Aiguo, Roderick MacFarquhar, Richard Madsen, Elizabeth Perry, Stanley Rosen, Michael Schoenhals, James Scott, Tao Heshan, Jonathan Unger, Andrew Walder, Wang Liping, Xiao Zhiwei, Yang Yanshu, and Zhang Xianwen.

Thomas Bernstein and an anonymous reader for the Press twice provided perceptive critical readings of the manuscript. We thank them for pulling no punches, and we fully credit their contributions to delaying publication of a work that was already long overdue.

We particularly express our appreciation to Cheng Tiejun, native of Raoyang county, Ph.D. in sociology, specialist on China's countryside, professor of social science at the University of Macau, and author of two forthcoming books on Macau society, for his wise counsel over many years.

Others who assisted in our research are Cai Dongqing, Chen Peiqi, Chen Shidong, Bestor Cram, Luo Lin, Sue Williams, Han Peng, Natasha Pickowicz, Ruan Ruoshan, Ed Settles, Shih Chi-lin, Sarah Smith, Judith Vecchioni, Wang Zhiqiang, Yang Xiaowen, Yu Shaohua, and Zhao Zhida.

We thank the University of Wisconsin-Madison Cartographic Laboratory and Marieka Brouwer for the preparation of the maps.

We have been the beneficiaries of the dedicated professionalism of staff at our three universities, including Donna Andrews, Susan Brenneke, Angela Finnerty, Betty Gunderson, Lisa Rhodes, Alexandra Ruiz, Susan Taniguchi, and especially Nancy Hall and Diane Morauske, who typed and retyped drafts of the manuscript over many years.

Binghamton University, the University of California, San Diego, and the University of Wisconsin, Madison, supported our work over the decades, making possible more than 30 trips to Raoyang and China that provided much of the information for this study. We thank the National Endowment for the Humanities for a research grant that facilitated our research and accelerated the writing.

Our deepest debts are to the people of Wugong, Raoyang, Hengshui, and Hebei whose words and deeds are recorded here, and who shared with us their knowledge, hopes, and dreams for the future of their families, lineages, and neighborhoods.

1 ✤ PRELUDE

This book explores an epoch of clashes between forces of rural revolution and reform from China's Great Leap Forward at the end of the 1950s through the Cultural Revolution to the new millennium. Our study centers on Wugong, a North China plain village 120 miles south of Beijing in Raoyang county, Hebei province. We locate that village in a matrix of power relations and resource conflicts spanning county, province, region, and center, examining contrasting and intertwined experiences of communities that enjoyed none of Wugong's benefits as a state-endowed model village.

Together with our earlier volume, *Chinese Village, Socialist State,* this study reveals the centrality of model villages in Chinese rural development of the Mao era. Models were vanguards in a strategy of political theater and resource allocation that emphasized political mobilization and self-reliance. Their roles would change, but not disappear, in a subsequent era of market-oriented reform. *Revolution, Resistance, and Reform in Village China* also offers new perspectives on hierarchy, power, welfare, and structures of inequality in successive epochs of revolution and reform in China's countryside. Together, the two books introduce three generations of villagers, their experiences, their hopes, their fears, and their engagements with state, collective, and community.

In contrast to numerous anthropologically inflected studies that present village communities as isolated microcosms, we pay close attention to the political, military, and cultural networks that shaped the lives of villagers and are shaped in turn by the values and actions of villagers. This book shows, too, the ways in which successive political campaigns, such as the four cleanups, the Cultural Revolution, the four goods, the campaign to criticize Lin Biao and Confucius, and campaigns to learn from Dazhai reverberated through village China. We explore not only the profound consequences for local people of political campaigns but also the ways in which locals sometimes appropriated campaigns and used them for their own purposes.

In the late Mao era, while little noted by international observers, signs of rural social discontent were legion. They pervaded the mock-

1

ing rhythms of *shunkouliu* (slippery jingles that circulated throughout the countryside by word of mouth) in which the rural poor, the powerless, protestors, and pariahs offered pungent opinions on the privileges of the powerful. During the Great Leap famine of the early 1960s, villagers raged at a corrupt system that forced people to pander to power to survive: "Flatter shamelessly — eat delicacies and drink hot stuff. Don't flatter — starve to death for sure." At critical moments, intra- and intervillage clashes erupted, sometimes spilling over into violence. Violence peaked throughout the countryside during the Cultural Revolution. Armed factional struggle, with militia tied to military units, soared when the leadership fragmented, particularly in the years 1966–70. These struggles constituted critical forms of resistance to the party center or to regional or local authorities.

Most often, however, resistance took indirect, at times even invisible forms. Villagers long remembered the throng from Gaoqiao village, north of Wugong, that marched to the township headquarters in 1959 as famine loomed, demanding grain. One hungry villager, Zhou Minchao, carried a lit lantern to help leaders see the pain of the people. Zhou was jailed as a new class enemy and a foe of socialism. In poorer villages, young men tried, often at great risk, to beat the command economy by turning to the household and the market to find some way to earn money. Villagers maneuvered to protect themselves as policy torrents cascaded down, promoted by officials whose careers hinged on campaign achievements that frequently flouted local preferences, cultural values, and consumption needs. Official pronouncements articulating a revolutionary fundamentalism could carry deadly consequences. Many villagers quietly subverted the revolution's war against locally meaningful ways of marrying, celebrating the New Year, and mourning. Others joined illegal religious sects rooted in Buddhist or heterodox millennial traditions.

The Wugong resident who most eloquently articulated the plight of villagers was Geng Xiufeng. A lifelong enthusiast of socialism, he returned to his home village in the early 1960s. Once known as the Collectomaniac, in the course of four decades he recorded a litany of criticisms of the failure of the Communist Party to deliver on the central promise of assuring mutual prosperity. Xiufeng criticized and opposed, at times openly, practices that sacrificed villagers to the interests of brutal and corrupt officials.

In 1943 Xiufeng had initiated a four-family coop that caught the attention of local wartime resistance leader Lin Tie, who eventually became Hebei's provincial first party secretary and Wugong's patron. The successful coop allowed higher officials to present the village as showing the way to socialism. Coop leader Geng Changsuo, Xiufeng's kinsman, won national fame for turning the original four-family coop into a villagewide unit in the early 1950s. That story is told in *Chinese Village, Socialist State,* which chronicled Wugong's rise as a market-oriented coop in the 1940s and as a mechanized collective in the mid-1950s, ending with the Great Leap from 1958 to 1960. *Revolution,*

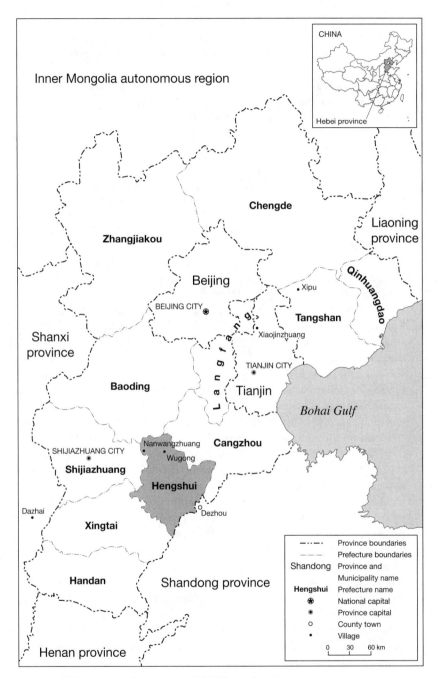

Locating Hengshui prefecture, post-1966 boundaries

Resistance, and Reform in Village China continues the story from the Leap famine in the period 1960–61 through the traumatic upheavals of the Cultural Revolution to post-Mao reforms that both enriched the countryside and gave rise to jarring inequalities.

Wugong was not simply a better-off village in Raoyang county, situated in the chronic grain deficit province of Hebei that surrounded the great cities of Beijing and Tianjin. Because Geng Changsuo's village was promoted by Hebei party secretary Lin Tie, a member of the political network of Beijing mayor and Politburo member Peng Zhen, the careers of county, prefectural, and provincial officials were intertwined with the fortunes of Geng Changsuo, Lin Tie, Peng Zhen, and ultimately President Liu Shaoqi. The ability of local leaders to maneuver was sorely tested by the vicissitudes of Chinese politics. The book details how the fate of peripheral villagers, both those in model villages and in less favored communities, was intertwined with that of higher party, military, and state leaders.

Wugong's early promoter, Lin Tie, had not been alone in backing the village. As Wugong gained prominence, groups tied to such revolutionary fundamentalists at the state center as theorist Chen Boda, who had praised Wugong as early as 1951 and again in the 1955 collectivization drive, also sought leverage by linking up with the village. Indeed, every major leader with a stake in the North China countryside bid for Wugong's favor and sought to shape Wugong in his preferred image. These included Liu Zihou, who would succeed Lin Tie as Hebei first party secretary, Li Xuefeng, who headed the North China Bureau, and Chen Yonggui, China's leading model peasant, who would eventually rise to become vice premier. Each group highlighted qualities that made the village a model from that group's perspective. Wugong reshaped the village's historical narrative with each lurch in the party line and the requirements of successive patrons. To retain model status required agility in adapting to the priorities of momentarily victorious power holders at local, regional, and national levels while maintaining a support base in the village.

Most villages lacked Wugong's pipeline to state resources. When anti-market collectivism and state strictures that prevented labor migration trapped villagers in stagnant misery in the aftermath of the Leap famine, many poorer villagers, at times with the support of local officials, turned to market, mobility, money, and maneuver to survive. This book details repeated clashes, covert and overt, between villagers and the ruling party over successive revolutionary and reformist policies. It examines lineage and religion, which persisted in the face of revolutionary campaigns that branded them as feudal. It highlights the wide-ranging and sometimes violent role of the military, legitimated by popular patriotism, reaching across the countryside and penetrating the villages through the militia. It traces repeated efforts by disgruntled villagers to improve their livelihood by breaking through state controls on household production and the market. Indeed, we show the consequences of pressures from below for market-oriented reform in the early 1960s and early 1970s, long before Mao's death and the triumph of a reform agenda at the center.

In the reform era, patriotism would persist, while lineage and religion would move out of the shadows to assume powerful visible manifestations in local communities and reshape grassroots politics. With the rise of Deng Xiaoping in the late 1970s, a reform agenda directly challenged the collective system that had restricted market activity and locked villagers within local communities. New forms of social and economic organization then spurred economic growth and a more relaxed political climate. But reform also gave rise to new kinds of social inequality and official corruption that among some produced nostalgia for bygone days.

This book draws on field research involving more than 30 research visits to Wugong village and Raoyang county dating back to 1978. These visits made it possible to re-interview informants and family members on numerous occasions in the wake of changing policies and outcomes, and armed with information derived from print and interview sources. To chart evolving village-state relationships, we have made use of a wide array of print sources and informants tapped both throughout China and abroad. Examples include access to six volumes on Wugong village published in China over the years since 1963, the complete run of the *Hebei Daily* since 1949, and sporadic access to the *Hengshui Daily*, the prefectural newspaper. The various unpublished, handwritten memoirs and protest letters compiled by Geng Xiufeng provided a gold mine of vivid, critical, no-holds-barred writing, assessing village history and party policies from the original four-household coop of 1943, by an observer who was resident in Wugong for nearly four decades until his death in 1999. Interviews with former political prisoners who served time in Raoyang county, in the Hebei capital, Shijiazhuang, and in Beijing provided another bird's-eye view of local life. So too did interviews with intellectuals, artists, historians, writers, work team leaders, and university faculty who were sent to Wugong for periods of weeks or months to several years. Following our practice in *Chinese Village, Socialist State,* information obtained from interviewees and confidential sources are not cited in the notes.

Dynamics of revolution, resistance, and reform were played out with regional variations throughout village China over the long twentieth century that is the subject of our two volumes. Bringing villagers in their rich specificity into the pages of history and attending both to their agency in the historical process and state attempts to curb their autonomy, we try to put a human face on conflicts that punctuated rural life. In the reform era, as earlier, villagers offer alternative, value-based understandings of China's future. Now, as earlier, the success of villager initiatives rests in part on finding support in the ranks of sympathetic officials and intellectuals. Comprehending the complex human agency of villagers in a centralized authoritarian China is a major goal of this study.

2 BACK FROM THE BRINK

The calamities of the Leap initiated in 1958 spread alienation. But the desperation of villagers rarely caused officials to question whether the party dictatorship could achieve revolutionary goals. Party leaders had lost touch with policies that had won the allegiance of patriots and the poor during the 1937–45 resistance war against Japan. In contrast to Jacobins and Bolsheviks, who attacked the market, thereby harming villagers, from the late 1930s to the early 1950s China's communists achieved a nearly silent revolution by combining limited redistributive policies with freeing the market and permitting money lending, land rentals, and the employment of hired labor.[1] Economically rational policies, resting on a mixed economy incorporating family farms and small-scale mutual aid, reduced poverty and inequality and expanded the number of owner-cultivator households.[2]

The institutions and policies that were imported from Stalin's Soviet Union and then intensified in the Great Leap to promote revolution had, by contrast, plunged the nation into famine. Committed to a communism defined by the negation of the bourgeoisie and the extirpation of money, property, and markets, the late Mao came to view the successes of the 1937–52 period as courting the danger of normalizing bourgeois evil. Nevertheless, as Lenin turned in the 1920s to the New Economic Policy to end the famine caused by war-communism policies, so, in the wake of the Leap famine, Mao expediently accepted reform to get through the crisis.

Chaos

At the nadir of famine, central and provincial governments were paralyzed. In 1960, with mortality soaring, the state actually exported 41 times more grain than it imported.[3] To make matters worse, in early 1960 Mao pushed for a renewed Great Leap, thereby intensifying the disaster.[4]

Administrative chaos hampered recovery. In December 1958, the Hebei provincial government had dissolved Raoyang county as an administrative entity. Its four gigantic units of nearly 50 villages each, dubbed communes (Red Star, Red Flag, Red Light, and Iron and Steel), were grafted onto an enlarged Xianxian county to the east. Wugong, which had long cultivated contacts in Raoyang town, had to deal with an unfamiliar Xianxian, a Roman Catholic stronghold. Then, in April 1960, three of the former Raoyang communes, including Wugong's, were reassigned to an expanded Shenxian county to the south. One year later, in April 1961, the four communes were reallocated to Anping county to the west. Village leaders hardly knew where to turn to defend local interests.[5]

County-level disarray was exacerbated by reorganization of the prefecture, the next highest rung of state power. In March 1958 Raoyang was shifted from Shijiazhuang prefecture to the west to Cangxian prefecture to the east. Three months later it was placed under Tianjin prefecture to the northeast. In December 1958 Raoyang came under the control of a greatly expanded Tianjin municipality. Between April 1960 and April 1961 Raoyang was administered once again by Shijiazhuang prefecture. In short, from 1958 to 1961 Raoyang was administered by five different prefectures.[6]

Not every administrative change resulted from revolutionary giantism. Hebei party chief Lin Tie's lobbying got the Hebei provincial capital moved to Tianjin in 1958. Baoding was unsuitable as a capital, Lin found, because it lacked industry. Baoding promoted an agrarian socialism in which industrialization was not a prerequisite for socialism. By contrast, Lin wanted metropolitan Tianjin's industry and its educational and cultural resources to help modernize the countryside. In 1956, after the Eighth Party Congress put modernization high on the political agenda, Lin asked Premier Zhou Enlai to approve moving the Hebei capital to Tianjin. Zhou arranged for Lin to put the idea to Mao Zedong. During meetings in Hangzhou and Shanghai, Lin chased after Mao, finally securing his assent. In 1958 the Hebei capital moved to Tianjin in line with Premier Zhou's and Lin Tie's modernization policies, which were immediately undermined by the revolutionary Leap.

Hunger

Although model Wugong village remained a privileged place, it disappeared from party propaganda when Geng Changsuo resisted pressures grossly to inflate Leap-era yield claims. Liu Zihou, who assumed the governorship of Hebei in April 1958, had personally pressed the agricultural labor model to send up five production satellites, that is, to proclaim stratospheric output

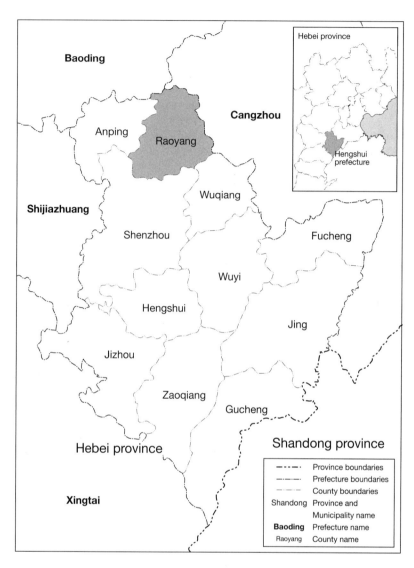

Counties in Hengshui prefecture, 1963 and after

figures for five different crops. When the 58-year-old Geng diplomatically declined, Governor Liu dropped Wugong as a model.[7] The promethean outputs reported by other villages better served the governor's propaganda purposes.

Wugong commune was similarly pressured. In fall 1958, commune party secretary Yin Yubo searched for a sorghum satellite. Some fields in Wangqiao and Wodi villages looked pretty good, he said. If there was not enough in those fields, grain could be moved in from other fields. No one would know. But his staff balked, and Yin scuttled the plan. That winter Yin called for a cabbage satellite. Officials were urged to bring enough cabbages together in a single field to substantiate a claim for yields of 100,000 catties per *mu*. (A mu is one-sixth of an acre.) When an aide protested, Yin exploded, "If I'm a fake, then who's real? In Anguo county a mu of wheat is getting more than 3,000 catties. Is that real? Xinli village in Tianjin is getting 100,000 catties of rice. Is that real? They're all fake." (A catty is 1.5 pounds.) Yin reluctantly abandoned the cabbage satellite.

Commune officials did not resist a provincial agricultural official in fall 1959. Having estimated yields at 270 catties per mu, they were aghast when the high-ranking visitor projected yields of 400 catties. Zhang Fengbin, responsible for the commune budget, screamed on hearing the bloated estimate. "Are we going to leave the common people any grain at all?"[8] Since taxes and compulsory sales to the state at low fixed prices were levied as a percentage of yield, the inflated number pumped up the commune's grain requisition quota from four to eleven million catties. Commune budget chief Zhang protested to no avail at a meeting in Xianxian, Wugong's new county seat.

In late fall 1959 Wugong commune turned over four million catties, and then another five million. Still, the phone kept ringing with demands for two million catties more. "Aren't you still for socialism?" the callers asked. Recently appointed commune party secretary Chai Rui delivered the grain. In January 1962, when Raoyang was restored as a county, Chai was named county magistrate.[9]

When news of the high grain requisitions spread, an old-timer fumed. "Who's kidding whom? During the war we helped you guys make it through. We took care of your food and clothing. But you haven't paid us back." The "we" of the anti-Japanese resistance was turning into "us" against "them." Villagers regarded the requisitions as theft.

As household grain reserves disappeared in late fall 1959, villagers resisted. No one came to meetings. Angry about low state prices, tillers abandoned the cotton fields. Draft animals died of hunger. Stillborn piglets were thrown away. Plowing for the winter wheat crop was half-hearted at best. Villagers grumbled that the destructive power of those above was greater than the atom bomb. Some muttered that officials were greedier than the old class enemies and counterrevolutionaries.

By spring 1960 many villagers were too weak to prepare the land for planting. In Wugong commune's Dongsongjia village, famished people lay down in the fields and refused to work. Commune budget chief Zhang shouted angrily, "Get up and work!" One victim responded, "How can we work on an empty stomach?" To intimidate him, Zhang demanded, "What is your class status?" Intentionally misunderstanding the query, which in the local argot sounds a bit like "What do you use to carry shit?" the protestor responded, "I use a basket to carry shit!" Zhang stalked away.

Lower-level officials in Raoyang who hid grain from the state and distributed it to villagers during the Great Leap famine of the early 1960s were jailed. Villagers vividly remembered He Shouchen from a community just west of Wugong, who put up a poster during the dearth saying:

> Grain is as scarce as beans made of gold;
> The state gives the word and we have to fold.
> They squeeze out our grain from the east to the west;
> It feels like they're cutting the flesh from my chest.

The state's grain-requisition work team branded the incident a "counter-revolutionary action." Before activists could organize a public struggle meeting against him, He Shouchen caved in, posting a final political poem:

> Poster, poster on the wall:
> A sword to make the dragon fall?
> A modern rocket to pierce the pall?
> No. The work team doesn't forgive,
> And the masses won't live and let live.
> So there!
> Placard, placard on the tree,
> No more posters for me!

Commune officials estimated that villagers needed two million catties of grain to survive to the next harvest. Commune party secretary Chai Rui petitioned Shenxian county. He secured 800,000 catties. Later deliveries of 800,000 and 400,000 catties barely got villagers through to the June 1960 wheat harvest.

That summer, rains brought water logging. Corn, millet, sorghum, and peanuts rotted. In Wugong commune 50,000 mu of crops were destroyed. Shenxian county then cut grain rations to but seven ounces a day, starvation rations. One old man protested to a commune official, "I thought that when I got old I would see the richness of socialism. Who could imagine that life would be worse than before?" With household grain supplies depleted and rations low, villagers with precious cash sought black markets. Officials pretended not to see. Prices in the black market soared. In 1960 corn was three yuan a catty, wheat five yuan a catty, more than 30 times the state purchasing price, and eggs were .25 *yuan* each. One local official estimated that Wugong

Locating Villages in Raoyang county

12   BACK FROM THE BRINK

commune, whose deaths in 1960 were twice those of a normal year, was far better off than most.

Commune-level salaried employees, including workers in collective enterprises not entitled to state grain rations, found their pay too little for black-market prices. In the Wugong commune machine-repair shop, eight workers quit. Once sinecures, such jobs no longer provided a living wage.

Shenxian county authorities informed Shijiazhuang prefecture in fall 1960 that many had starved to death in Duzhuang and Ningjin villages.[10] The prefecture blamed subordinates. Local leaders were ordered to oppose the "five winds" of exaggeration (fukua), communism (gongchan), official privilege (ganbu teshu), issuing blind commands (xia zhihui), and resorting to force (qiangpo mingling). Officials were told to "smash walnuts" (za hetao), that is, to target small fry, to find county, commune, and brigade officials to blame for famine deaths. A Shenxian county party vice secretary singled out as a struggle target committed suicide.

The campaign to smash walnuts peaked in late 1960 when higher authorities scapegoated village officials. Wugong village party secretary Zhang Duan, known as the Ox, erupted when told he should not have "blindly obeyed." "We have to obey the commands of our superiors," Zhang proclaimed. "It is wrong to tell us to oppose the party!"[11]

The prefecture ordered villages to run struggle meetings. In Wugong commune the effort was half-hearted. Party secretary Hou of hapless Yanggezhuang, just north of Wugong, and the village head of Xichangbo, east of Wugong, were the two leading targets. They were corrupt and incompetent, but everyone knew the devastation was not their fault.

While other localities were far harder hit, in 1960 Wugong commune members ate wild grass and ground corn cobs mixed with a bit of corn flour, a fodder normally reserved for pigs. Bellies swelled, and people got sick. Chronic constipation was so severe that villagers inserted their fingers into their rectums to extract rock-hard feces.

In fall 1959 provincial party secretary Lin Tie sent Hu Kaiming to Zhangjiakou in Hebei's northwest. Hu ended policies that brought famine and restored officials who had resisted those policies.[12] The prestige of Wugong's Geng Changsuo rose in Tianjin, the provincial capital, because he had resisted the murderous winds of the Leap. Lin Tie's allies, who had opposed Leap excesses, praised Geng for trying to report something close to actual grain production.

By late 1960 malnutrition and edema so weakened Geng that one arm hung uselessly at his side. He was cared for in the bare-bones commune clinic, where he was joined by commune officials Xu Xiangqian and Geng Xiufeng. The three were fed a bland famine recipe of *kangtangmian,* made of fine chaff, some noodles, and a bit of sugar, food not available to others. The three agreed that villagers were poorer than ever and that the system forcing silent obedience to irrational orders was responsible. They decided to send a letter to higher officials.

The letter, dated December 30, 1960, said that output in Wugong commune was down 50 percent in 1960 and that there was not enough food, fuel, and fodder. More than 460 head of livestock had died, crops had been sown in inappropriate locations, and too much grain had been requisitioned. They urged recruitment of officials who would "seek truth from facts," that is, people who would plant crops in suitable places and report yields accurately. Second, units should devise a rational requisition "contract" based on normal output, rather than on-the-spot estimates by visiting higher-ups. Wugong had pioneered such a contract system in the precollectivization 1950s. Third, authorities should stimulate trade and allow livestock to carry collective goods across county lines as had been the policy before the annihilation of the market.[13]

Geng Xiufeng went to commune headquarters to affix an official seal to the letter. A deputy commune secretary warned, "To write a letter to the center is no joke; the advantages are few, the disadvantages many." The deputy warned Xiufeng, "I can't make such a big decision myself. In truth, if he [commune party secretary Chai Rui] was here, he wouldn't agree. If you insist on going ahead, just sign your own names!"[14] The two Gengs then signed the letter, sending copies to the provincial government, to Tianjin municipality, and to Tan Zhenlin, the top party agricultural official in Beijing.

On his return, Chai exploded. "You sent a letter to the center?! Are you crazy?!" Chai turned on Geng Xiufeng. "It wasn't enough that you signed yourself; you had to drag Changsuo along. He's a red flag in this province. If you make a mistake, it doesn't matter; but if you cause Changsuo to make a mistake, that will be the end of the red flag!" To Geng Xiufeng, it was a struggle for Changsuo's soul between those who knew the real needs of local people and those who knew little and cared less about villagers.

Tan Zhenlin's office in Beijing responded to the letter. Although Hebei grain yields had fallen each year since 1958, Politburo member Tan reminded local officials that the province had promised to supply the grain needs of metropolitan Tianjin within three years and of Beijing within five. The state needed the grain for urban dwellers. Tan urged the commune to experiment with requisition contracts. This would commit the collective to reasonable deliveries to the state and protect villagers against sudden demands for more grain. If the reform worked, others could implement it. But the state requisition of grain stood. With Beijing and Tianjin in dire straits in December 1960, the central government told the provinces to do whatever it took to fulfill grain quotas.[15]

Reform

In July and August 1960, the center finally called a halt to the Leap.[16] In October it increased grain imports. In November it allowed greater decentralization, restored household plots and markets, stressed labor incentives, and called for increased income for villagers but retained public dining halls. By spring 1961 rural leaders had a freer hand to stimulate the devastated economy. In March 1961 President Liu Shaoqi, Premier Zhou, Party General Secretary Deng Xiaoping, and Politburo Standing Committee member and economic specialist Chen Yun convened a North China Conference to find a way out, while Chairman Mao met with officials from the southern region to assess the agrarian situation.[17] Mao approved a short-term recovery program that stressed material incentives.[18]

In May 1961 central leaders fanned out to gauge the crisis. Deng Xiaoping and Beijing party secretary Peng Zhen went to suburban Beijing, and Premier Zhou visited Handan county, south of Wugong commune, where even dried potatoes seemed a delicacy. Talks with local leaders and villagers convinced Zhou that the public dining halls exacerbated hunger and demoralization. His 3 A.M. phone call to Mao on May 7, 1961, is said to have been critical in convincing the chairman to abolish the mess halls.[19] In June 1961, collective mess halls were dropped.

In 1961 and 1962 the center reduced the burden on rural producers. Compulsory grain quotas were sharply cut and the agricultural tax lowered. In summer 1961 prices paid to villagers for grain delivered to the state rose 27 percent, with similar increases for pigs and chickens.[20]

Reforms also reduced the size of rural production units and transferred authority to the production team. Teams, cut to approximately 20 to 30 households, replaced giant entities as the basic agricultural labor and accounting units. To curb the waste of the Leap, investment was capped at 3 to 5 percent of total income, welfare at 2 to 3 percent. Households retained more grain.

With hungry villagers resisting economic irrationality, the state tolerated household economic initiatives that recently had been crushed. Team leaders could again set aside 5 to 7 percent of collective land for strictly household cultivation, thus restoring some family plots. Villagers were also encouraged to plant food around their homes and on waste land and to raise pigs and chickens. These goods could again be exchanged in markets. Yesterday's counterrevolutionary crime was today's life-enhancing reform.

In some places, farmers and local officials promoted virtual decollectivization. In Anhui and Sichuan, provincial leaders allowed household responsibility systems (zeren zhi) that redistributed collective lands to households. They had to meet state quotas, but otherwise could respond to market demand.[21]

Boss Geng and Wugong commune secretary Chai Rui applauded the sharp cutback in state grain requisitions, the reduction in agricultural taxes, and the increase in state purchasing prices for grain. They supported decentralization to the brigade (village) and team levels. They also endorsed the state's tripling of the percentage of budget outlays for rural projects in 1962 when expenditures for rural development reached the highest levels of the People's Republic, 17 percent.

The reforms forced down black-market prices. Grain prices in Raoyang fell by five-sixths to .50 yuan per catty for wheat in 1961 and to .10 yuan per catty the following year.[22] The economy rebounded, and famine eased as a result of reform. Wugong's revolutionary leadership remained wary, however, of reform proposals that turned away from the collective.

Resisting Reform

During the 1961 lunar New Year, Geng Changsuo, just home from the clinic, heeded party behests to relegitimate socialism by telling youth of the bad old days, recounting the blessings of revolution. Geng said that the collective road guaranteed Wugong a bright future. It was how the village first won the attention of upper levels to become a richly rewarded model. Clean Geng had local credibility not only because he lived simply, taking last and least, but also because Xu Shukuan, his bound-foot wife, known as the Tigress because she snapped at people who shirked collective work, toiled until she returned home in the evening to soothe the pain of her palpitating feet in a basin of warm water. In many communities, villagers hated corrupt and unaccountable leaders who dined sumptuously, preferentially rewarded friends and family, or built new homes while nonofficials lived in hovels and went hungry.

The county, acting on reform directives, ended the giantism of the communes. Three of the four original Raoyang communes split into twelve smaller ones based on the former township, averaging thirteen villages and 433 party members. A modicum of historic familiarity reduced alienation. But Wugong commune resisted, hewing to the Leap's giantism. It preserved a unit of 36 villages until April 1966.[23]

In May 1961 a North China Agricultural Conference was chaired by Zhang Kerang, a longtime Hebei provincial patron of the original Wugong coop and an ally of Hebei party secretary Lin Tie. Zhang worked in the party's Rural Work Department. The conference recommended nationwide experimentation with contracts to small groups of households or even single households. The idea was promoted by Zhang's boss, Deng Zihui, who headed the Rural Work Department. Deng had opposed premature collectivization. Following the conference, Anping county, Wugong's latest administrative home, urged commune and village leaders to expand household plots "borrowed" by villagers as "land to save lives." Wugong commune and village leaders, however, rejected this reform, insisting that expanding the household sector would weaken the revolutionary model's collective foundation.[24]

In summer 1961 Shijiazhuang prefecture sought to rein in commune-level commandism. It called on local officials to "dismount from the horse" and reduce state-tethered collective activity. Again, Wugong commune resisted. While acknowledging that some communes had built useless enterprises during the Leap, Wugong leaders held that closing its collective enterprises would be like "cutting off one's queue just to cool off a bit." Some suggested circumventing the directive by turning the commune's productive brick factory over to Wugong village to enhance the economy of the region's "red flag." Others proposed breaking up the commune's transportation team, giving one of its two trucks to Wugong and allowing several villages to share the other. No one wanted to disband the commune's machine-repair shop.

Despite Wugong's coolness to reform, the Anping county leadership promoted the village as an experimental site for a grain-distribution reform designed to offer material incentives. The village's fame was a magnet attracting resources. During the 1961 fall harvest, county deputy secretary Du visited and declared, "Wugong is a red flag in this province. Therefore the county decided to start here. Your experience will spread to the whole county!" Geng balked. Du stated that reform was a party decision; no party member could oppose it.

All other commune villages distributed grain entirely according to labor. Wugong alone parceled out just 20 percent according to labor, the remainder per capita. Soon after Du departed, the 35 other commune villages embraced Wugong's leveling 20-80 formula.

Higher levels continued to press reform. Hebei's provincial party committee stipulated that the appropriate size of a production team was 35 households. Accordingly, a work team led by headmaster Qi of the provincial party school went to Wugong. The brigade (village) was divided into three teams. Teams 1 and 2 in the east and center village had about 170 households each, and team 3 in the west had 200. Each was about the size of whole villages in many regions. Village officials would not break up Wugong's three large teams despite Qi's insistence that teams of more than 150 households violated the regulations of the provincial party committee.

Qi called a village meeting. A minority, later labeled antisocialist rich peasants, broke with Geng and backed the provincial directives. But team officials and most villagers supported Geng's opposition to breaking up the large units. Defeated, Headmaster Qi's provincial work team left.

Wugong did implement reforms to allow villagers once again to grow vegetables and raise domestic animals in home courtyards for household consumption. Wugong called its bookkeeping system "democratic accounting." The numbers were open to scrutiny. But leaders hectored villagers seeking cash earnings in the market.

In line with reforms proposed by Deng Zihui's Rural Work Department, some in central Hebei tried out a system of "responsibility lands." Households contracted to meet state grain quotas. After fulfilling a quota, tillers could sell or consume the balance. Geng, however, opposed "responsibility lands," contending that household farming would turn too many into paupers on small strips of land and squander investments in tractors and mechanized wells.

In 1961 and 1962 agriculture recovered. The market also came back to life. Locally made Zhanggang wine, which had disappeared in the early 1950s when the state took command of the economy, reappeared to the delight of older men, who found the 134-proof Hengshui White Lightning too strong.[25]

Wugong households chafed at being kept from tilling "responsibility lands." Many resented exclusion from household sideline and marketing activity. Village party secretary Zhang Duan inveighed that if households used their pig manure on responsibility lands, collective production would suffer.[26]

State command of the economy seemed unfair. Popular or "hot" goods were available to villagers only if the commune bought unpopular or "cold" goods. To get good homespun cloth, a unit also had to purchase fifteen unneeded pitchforks; every straw mat cost an additional cloth bag. To get a belt from the commune, a villager had to buy two bags of tooth powder; a 20-yuan mirror cost an additional and unneeded 20 spare parts for a wagon.

Theft

With decent weather, improved incentives, reduced pressure to reinvest, and a sharp drop in state requisitions and agricultural taxes, the Raoyang food crisis ended in 1961. Team 2 in Wugong village, home of the old elite southern Li lineage, even responded to an appeal by former Wugong residents by contributing 2,200 catties of grain for famine relief to Dezhou city in neighboring Shandong province, where kin had moved.[27] In 1961 corn, millet, and sorghum output rose significantly in the pacesetting village; peanut and cotton production were also up. Although the wheat harvest fell, total grain output passed one million catties, up 300,000 from 1960. Collective vegetable production soared.

Before the 1961 harvest, Anping county contracted to buy 750,000 catties of vegetables from Wugong commune at a set price. But after the bumper harvest, prices dropped. Anping refused to honor the contract. Weeks passed and the vegetables shrunk in size, weight, and value. They began to rot. Village officials pleaded with commune leaders to pressure Anping authorities. The commune kept calling the county, thirty times in one day. For three months, Anping stalled. Brokers in Tianjin, in Yangquan in neighboring Shanxi province, and in other famished regions heard about the vegetables in Wugong. People from northeastern provinces offered to supply carts with rubber tires to facilitate transportation.

The county insisted, however, that regulations precluded moving produce across county lines. While people went hungry in neighboring regions, 20,000 catties of cabbage rotted in Wugong's Dongliman village, and 130,000 catties of radishes rotted in the Xiaodi supply and marketing coop. Finally, villagers illegally transported vegetables to Shenxian county.[28]

In December Anping at last agreed to make some purchases. But the remaining cabbages held only a third of their harvest weight, and the county refused to compensate villagers for the lost weight. That felt like theft. Villagers refused to sell.

Geng Xiufeng protested to the provincial financial committee in Tianjin, the Hebei capital, about the vegetable debacle, lambasting Anping officials. In late 1961 a work team from Shijiazhuang came to investigate. It covered up for the county, finding that vegetable losses were normal. Geng Xiufeng fired off a missive denouncing the coverup.[29] County officials saw him as a loose cannon on the deck of their prized flagship, a model Wugong led by Geng Changsuo.

Restoration

By early 1962 the party center was split. Most leaders, sobered by the famine, advocated reform. But Mao, preoccupied with a specter of capitalism restored in the Soviet Union, rejected the notion that development required greater use of the household and market.[30] He touted class struggle. Seeing conflicting signals, most lower-level officials concluded that the center's policies were "right in economics, left in politics."

In line with the downsizing, on January 1, 1962, Raoyang was restored to its pre-Leap boundaries. A few months later, it was put under Hengshui prefecture, whose party secretary, Zhao Shuguang, was a patron of Boss Geng. Wugong celebrated.

Raoyang's new party secretary, Li Chunyu, had headed the Shijiazhuang prefectural party committee office. Chai Rui, the former Wugong commune leader who arranged the massive Leap-era grain requisition, was appointed county magistrate.[31] Chai briefed Li on Raoyang's and Wugong's recent history.

Political rehabilitations were ordered in early 1962. In Raoyang 2,517 cases were reexamined, many dating from the 1957–58 antirightist movement. They included party and nonparty officials, teachers, technicians, commercial and retail employees, workers, farmers, and students. Reinvestigation found 583 people "completely innocent" and another 501 "partially innocent." The remaining 1,400 were said to have been judged correctly.[32] The rehabilitated victims were expected to thank the party.

In January 1962 the party's North China Bureau met to discuss grain distribution.[33] Wugong's delegate, Geng Changsuo, supported requisition, tax, and price reforms to give villagers more grain, but he resisted strengthening the household economy. He was on a collision course with reformers.

Geng joined other delegates at the Beijing Hotel, the capital's finest. The conference goal was to motivate work by distributing grain according to labor, rather than by head. Some delegates called for "three freedoms and one contract" (san zi yi bao), meaning more household plots, markets, and household sidelines, and also a fixed grain-delivery quota for households. Usually quiet, Geng burst out, "This method won't work." "The households with a large supply of labor will get more grain than they need and will sell some at high prices; households with less labor won't have enough to eat." He predicted polarization between rich and poor. "How can we practice socialism when there is polarization?" he asked.[34] Geng's priority was meeting the food needs of the vulnerable: widows, the elderly, orphans, and military and martyr dependents. Reformers too supported welfare for the needy but insisted that only reward based on performance could spur the dispirited victims of the Leap to work hard.

Stories were told about people like Hu Kaiming, an ally of Hebei's Lin Tie, and about Anhui provincial party secretary Zeng Shisheng, who pressed for reform after famine ravaged Anhui. Hu promoted "responsibility systems" that closely linked labor and income, with the initiative for farming in the hands of small groups of households (bao chan dao zu).

Mao was said to have backed Hu in September 1959 at a meeting in Handan in southern Hebei. However, staff members of Lin Tie, Hu's patron, told us that Mao's comment was more like, "If all it does is the good you say, who could say no?" That is, Mao left himself plenty of wiggle room. Hu wrote to Mao in 1961 urging a reform agenda to restore villager enthusiasm.[35]

Soon after Geng's outburst at the Beijing Hotel conference, Shijiazhuang prefectural secretary Kang told him to go home and remain silent.[36] Two decades later Geng recalled that he had taken a "die-hard" stance at the conference. "All I had to do was agree with them at that time and [President] Liu Shaoqi would have shaken hands with me."

Returnees

In 1961 and 1962 the state ordered more than 20 million first-generation city dwellers back to the countryside.[37] In 1962 Tianjin had a target of 400,000 rural-bound people. The forced population transfer reduced China's industrial workers from 29.8 million in 1960 to 17.1 million in 1962.[38] To go to the countryside was to be sent down (xiafang), excluded from a system of state-distributed and subsidized benefits. By 1963, 84 percent of China's people lived in the countryside, the highest percentage in the history of the People's Republic.[39]

Most returnees hoped the trek would be a sojourn. Once hard times passed, they were told, they would be rehired, restored to urban state payrolls, and provided with subsidized grain. The party's word was law, but its promises were not legally binding. Few ever returned to the cities or their state-sector jobs.

In 1961 and 1962 Raoyang received 6,000 families, far below the regional norm. The military and its dependents were spared from being sent down. Many Raoyang natives served in Tianjin and Beijing, having joined the army during the anti-Japanese resistance or civil war. Perhaps three times as many villagers returned to neighboring Anping county, which had been occupied by the Japanese. It had fewer Liberation Army soldiers but many people employed in urban enterprises.

As part of the effort to cut state payrolls, 20 returned to Wugong from jobs in Shenyang in the northeast to which villagers had fled in the 1943 famine, from factory labor in Tianjin and Qinhuangdao on the Hebei coast, from a construction company in Raoyang, and from a Handan steel mill. Some returned from state farms in Qinghai. Many had held urban and industrial jobs for a decade or more. Wugong embraced its returnees. Much of rural China, lacking Wugong's resources and facing harsher conditions, resented having to feed a flood of migrants.

Zhang Tiedi had worked in the Raoyang commerce bureau. Wugong assigned him to make brigade-run enterprises more efficient and profitable — rope manufacture, rubber products, and repair of carts and irrigation machines. Li Xi had joined the army in 1956. He was stationed in Shijiazhuang, a Hebei railroad center, where he learned of incursions by India in 1959. Li was trained as a communications specialist. Back in Wugong, the 26-year-old demobilized soldier was put in charge of sideline work.

Iron caster Xu Xinyue had worked in a Tianjin factory since 1949. "I must tell you the truth," he recalled, "it was very difficult in the early 1960s. I did not have enough to eat." Xu had earned a hefty 60 yuan per month in Tianjin as a grade 6 worker on the eight-grade scale that governed China's industrial wages. When the price of grain skyrocketed to five yuan for a catty of wheat on the black market, Xu believed his wife and four children would do better with him back in Wugong.

In 1958, during the Leap, west-ender Xu Xiuwen had got an industrial job at the Tianjin Power Turbine Factory. It was a major step up. She loved the independence. Living with other young women, Xu felt camaraderie. She felt sorry for young women stuck in Wugong.

When Xu's urban residency permit was revoked in 1962, her girl friends, in tears, vowed eternal friendship. Many who worked with Xu promised never to marry and lose their independence. Like many returnees, Xu resolved to prove herself by becoming a model youth. She took the hardest jobs. She collected a year's worth of manure in six months. Covering oneself with shit — Mao's symbol of purity — caught the attention of leaders. Xu was honored as a model worker. She stuck close to a group of young women activists, many of them returnees.

Xu resisted pressure for an early marriage. She was 21. Matchmakers asked,

"What are you waiting for? If you wait any longer, all the good ones will be snapped up by others!" Xu felt betrayed when a former co-worker wrote to say she was marrying. To Xu, marriage meant children. "Women with children have to stay at home," she said. "Your life resembles a grinding stone that always turns in circles around a small family. Eventually you shrivel up like so much dried grass."[40] Xu turned her energies to politics.

The Politics of Virtue

The Leap disaster led to heavy cutbacks in education.[41] In 1961 Mao endorsed half work, half study and told students, "Don't ask the state for a penny."[42] The poor would self-finance. In spring 1962 the center cut the number of senior high schools by more than half, and the number of specialized junior high schools even more. A dozen or so Wugong villagers were among millions forced to end their education. Sent home, they were told to help families weather the crisis. The Raoyang high school student body was lined up, each given a number. The odd numbered were sent home. In 1961 the county closed its normal school for teacher training. Hopes and careers were dashed. A bitter ditty circulated:

> Raoyang junior high students, nine years of study squandered.
> High school behind a horse, normal school closed.
> The province sends people down, the prefecture stops recruitment.
> Back home to till the big land, poverty generation after generation.

Boss Geng's daughter, Huijuan, was not among those sent home.

On sighting a former teacher, one Wugong returnee, Li Huiying, feeling like a failure after seven years in an urban school, recalled, "I was so scared he would laugh at me that I hurried into an outhouse to hide."[43] On July 10, 1961, Li Huiying was sent back from the famous Xingji Junior High School, on the outskirts of fast-growing Shulu county, southwest of Wugong. Her dreams were shattered. Parents contacted a relative to arrange a city job, but there were no jobs. In the fields, returnees felt locals mocking their failures, blisters, blood, exhaustion, and ignorance. It was humiliating when a production leader corrected them.

By early 1962 Chairman Mao's concerns about backsliding toward capitalism led to a stress on socialist propaganda. Defense Minister Lin Biao urged young people to emulate selfless martyrs, usually young male soldiers. In January 1962 Mao highlighted a civilian militia under military control. Recruits were ordered to prepare for war, fight crime, and quash enemies. Youngsters, with opportunities lost because of Mao's Leap disaster, were told to focus on their own moral failings and the need to sacrifice for the nation.[44]

The state prodded young people to work beyond their capacity in order to prove themselves. Some were crippled, among them Li Guanghui of Shenxian county, who had trained as a geologist but ended up directing foreign affairs in Raoyang after injuring his back.

Wugong's returnee from Xingji Junior High felt similar pressure. How was Li Huiying to find proper work and a suitable husband? She looked like a failure. Local leaders sometimes helped well-connected returnees. Pepperpot Li, standing well under five feet tall, was made deputy secretary of the village youth league. Excerpts from her diary were published in September 1963 to show that Wugong was full of model youth with socialist ideals. Revolutionary Wugong latched on to Mao's propaganda line. Provincial publishers edited out Huiying's concern for a good marriage and a good job. Still, no matter how focused she was on winning party plaudits, she had little hope of entering an inner-circle reserved mainly for men.

Li Huiying's diary became a fantasy of selflessness, a testimony to "redness." She claimed she was "enthusiastic" about returning to Wugong. She had been studying science, but the party wanted her to do collective manual labor. "It doesn't matter whether one climbs the summit of science or tills the fields," she wrote, "it's all for the party and state."[45] Actually, she did want to continue with science but soon realized it was impossible. The diary hinted at a humiliating fall. On her fourth night home, walking to an outdoor movie, she overheard a mocker say that Huiying's father had scrimped to pay for a fancy school, but now she was back with nothing to show.

Huiying sought party membership, the road to respect and honor, to a good marriage and job, she thought. Less than two weeks after her return, she applied to join the party, noting in her diary that as a returned student she did not "expect to be admitted the first time."

In late summer 1961 her parents learned that a Tianjin transport company was looking for workers and urged her to apply. Responding in the language of war communism, Li noted, "The party asks me to do farm work; therefore, I won't do industrial work. I won't be a deserter." In the diary she criticized her parents' work habits. Model youth could not be seen as easy on kin.

Li Huiying was selected as a "five good youth" in midsummer 1961. "Now I must work even harder in the future," she wrote, "or I'll be letting everyone down." She became skilled in the politics of virtue.

By late 1961 and early 1962 Huiying's diary was full of self-congratulations. On October 4 she wrote that she "no longer felt exhausted doing field work and always worked ahead of others." On October 11 she noted that her clothes were "soaked with sweat." On March 14, firing a rifle for the first time, she felt "vigilant in the face of the enemy." On March 24 she finished "two days of work in a single day." On April 14, when a cart ran over her foot, she kept working. "No time can be lost in bringing manure to the fields," she wrote.

Huiying's girl friend, Shi Guiying, felt similar pressures. Her father, Shi Xishen, an old guerrilla fighter and educated tractor technician from Handan, came to Wugong in fall 1953 to direct a tractor station, one of China's first. Her family was classified as urban. But, as part of the forced exodus of 1961, technician Shi's urban residency and grain ration were canceled; his family was stuck in Wugong. Guiying could not continue her studies in the city after classes ended in July 1961. She declared, "When final exams were over, childhood was over."

Still, there were advantages in model Wugong. A budding writer, dancer, actress, and singer, Guiying was taught by authors, directors, and musicians sent to the state-privileged village, some for months or years. She performed "Song of Our Advanced Coop" during the temple festival in the market village of Zoucun in 1957, the year before Leap policies closed the market and festival because they were "feudal remnants."

Market towns were the sites of opera performances, temple festivals, and holiday galas. In the honeymoon era of the early 1950s most Raoyang townships had opera troupes perform in the market, especially during the long New Year festival. Market-town transactions linked families and villages in marriage; business contracts were negotiated; and both daily consumer goods and ritual and mourning items were available. Villagers blamed outsiders for the loss of the festival.

In 1960 aspiring writer Shi Guiying's poem "The Lights Are Turned On," celebrating Wugong's new power plant, a gift of patron Lin Tie, was published in a Hebei literary magazine. That same year she was a soloist in a Raoyang performance of a modern opera. But the aspiring writer's future was marred by her father's honesty. Having spoken out against the economic irrationality of the Leap, he was labeled a "black element." The whole family was under a political cloud.

Like her friend Li Huiying, Shi Guiying kept a revolutionary diary. In later years she recalled that joining the party was her "daily dream," adding, "Everybody knew that without party membership you had no future."

She realized that manual labor was a "test." Never complain or ask to rest. Always volunteer for the most difficult and dirtiest work. Publicize one's eagerness to collect manure. On August 22, 1961, she wrote, "On the way back from harvesting corn I saw some shit on the road. I remembered that the more manure we have, the more grain we get." Exhibiting the virtues that would earn her a "five good youth" citation, Shi proclaimed, "It's not shit, it's gold, the cleanest of all things."

According to the diary, when a commune official asked her a trick question about taking an urban job, Guiying replied, "I already have a job; farming is my job." "But what if you were needed to do another job?" the official asked. Guiying responded, "I'll do whatever the party wants me to do!" Only then was she told she had been picked for a mobile film-projection team that covered 36 villages. She coolly recorded in her diary, "The party tells me where to go and where to fight."

Villagers laughed at Guiying's Beijing accent. She developed a passion for movies, especially those featuring female socialist heroes. Monitoring her own political thought was like keeping an eye on a film projector, she wrote. "If I inspect and keep it clean every day, I can correct problems in a timely way."

In early 1963, with war communism propaganda pervasive, Guiying's hero was martyred soldier Lei Feng, then lionized in the media. He was said to have sacrificed his life for the revolution. At night in bed, she fantasized about the handsome Lei Feng. "Life is worth living, and I love my life," she wrote, "but if it is necessary to sacrifice it for the happiness of the people, I'll rush forward without hesitation." She hoped to become a "glorious" party member.

Guiying kept her most intimate dreams out of the diary. In 1960 she had warmed to junior high classmate Li Mengjie. Orphaned since the age of eight, he lived with his sister in the east village. The Geng coop had cultivated their land, providing the children with income. State propaganda called Mengjie and his sister a second set of orphans adopted by Geng's coop in the late 1940s.[46] The tale made Boss Geng and Tigress Xu, his wife, seem like selfless saviors. Years later, Mengjie's sister, Xiuying, skewered the myth that wrote her sacrifices for her brother out of the story. "People can say whatever they want, but the truth is that old Xu never served us a single meal!"

Aspiring writer Shi saw herself as the savior of the orphaned Mengjie, three years her senior. Mengjie, who saw little point to school, towered over classmates. Guiying thought of herself as the goddess in the popular movie *Tian xian pei,* who lived on earth as an ordinary villager because she had compassion for a poor man. In the movie, the lovers married and lived happily ever after in an idyllic mountain village.

Shi's teacher told her she was dreaming. Guiying and Mengjie had little in common. But by marrying a poor villager, a living symbol of the Wugong myth, Guiying would be saving Mengjie and Mengjie would be saving her. In 1960, as the famine deepened, the two began secretly exchanging notes.

Guiying's diary said nothing about the difficulties she and Mengjie faced during the Leap. He was always famished. He quit school in the hungry summer of 1960 and joined the army to secure food. He won a prized posting in Beijing. Village conditions were tougher. With Guiying's father a political target and the household ineligible for state rations, the family was desperate. The small pot of gruel that Guiying brought home from the public mess hall held little millet for the family, consisting mainly of discolored rotten vegetables. An ironic village verse went:

Day before yesterday ate rice gruel,
Yesterday ate millet gruel,
Today ate corn gruel,
Tomorrow I'll have sorghum gruel,
Day after tomorrow there'll only be cabbage gruel,
After that what kind of gruel can we expect?

One day Guiying joined malnourished classmates in stealing cabbage leaves and carrots. Caught, they were publically humiliated for "failing to stand up to the test of temporary material difficulties."

When Mengjie left for the army, the two corresponded. No stigma was attached to young people writing, particularly a soldier. They exchanged letters for three years. Correspondence, usually by hand-delivered note, was part of rural courtship in the 1960s and 1970s. Junior high students built relationships by exchanging poems and notes. The risk of embarrassing discovery added excitement. A Chinese author noted that reading and writing letters was "the most important thing in the life of young people with secondary school education."[47] Eager to avoid ridicule, intimates could not even hint at relationships. Strict gender divisions meant that there were few opportunities to be alone. In summer, however, when ten-foot-tall sorghum crops created a green curtain, young people could share moments alone. In the early 1960s, with education cut short, many young returnees married as soon as possible. A very few, like Xu Xiuwen, the returned worker from Tianjin, said that old-fashioned marriages meant a loss of independence.

Resurrection

In 1962 Wugong reaped a second consecutive bumper harvest. A grain yield of 482 catties per mu was the best ever. Cotton also set a record. Wugong's economy boomed.

The state requisitioned 73,000 catties of grain in 1962, a fraction of the 180,000 catties delivered in the famine year of 1959. Income in cash and kind increased for the second straight year. In 1961 each collective member received a record 68-yuan income, including the value of grain and other crops. The 15 yuan paid in cash nearly doubled the previous high of 1955, prior to state-imposed collectivization. In 1962 per capita distributed income shot up to 130 yuan based on a labor day that paid 1.42 yuan, by far the highest daily pay in the history of the collective.[48] Reform initiatives won the highest distribution since the creation of Boss Geng's big coop in 1953.

Grain distribution soared from a low of 270 catties per person in the famine year of 1960 to 362 catties in 1961 and then to a record 500 catties in 1962. The 1962 grain distribution record would not be surpassed for a 19-year span during which reform was again negated by revolution. The extraordinary

130-yuan average per capita distributed income in 1962 also represented a settling of accounts as the village moved from villagewide (brigade) accounting to accounting by customary neighborhoods, the east, center, and west, designated as teams 1, 2, and 3.

Good weather, vastly reduced state requisitions, lower agricultural taxes and collective investment, good sales of collective sidelines in timber, rope, and fruit, and improved incentives boosted Wugong's net collective income from 114,000 yuan in 1960 to 334,000 in 1962. With the state relaxing its grain-first and antimarket policies, and with collective sidelines and commerce no longer treated as exploitation, sidelines surged.

Revolutionary logic had sidelines blocking agriculture. In fact, sideline income allowed farmers to view low-priced labor for grain as famine insurance, while cash was earned elsewhere. Sidelines also provided consumer products. In 1962 village sidelines accounted for 38 percent of collective income, the highest share since 1950, when the state first began to squeeze out the rural market in the name of socialism.

What distinguished Wugong from other recovering villages was that its gains came from *collective* enterprises. Having been burned in the Leap, most poor North China villages would not invest in collective sidelines. Some that did failed. In Fengyang county in Anhui province, which Chairman Mao had proclaimed a model of revolution, but which suffered grievously in the Leap famine, villagers ordered to reinvest in the collective instead consumed all they earned, saying that sacred custom demanded it. In Marxist terms, one might say that the more the state pushed socialism, the more villagers embraced feudalism. Leap disasters destroyed for poorest villagers trust in distant collectives. Faith grew in local bonds, sacred mores, and working for the household economy and the market.

Wugong heeded the reform call to invest less, distribute more, diversify, and strengthen the team-level unit to win back disenchanted people. Resilient villagers did the rest.

In spring 1962 the reform-minded Zhang Kerang, head of Hebei's Rural Work Department, invited Boss Geng to a North China meeting of rural models. The conference encouraged further rural reforms, including the "three guarantees and one reward" (san bao yi jiang) system of household and small-team responsibility. Village leader Chen Yonggui came from Dazhai, a fast-rising Shanxi village just across Hebei's western border. Geng had met Chen for the first time in January at the Beijing Hotel Conference. From Wang Guofan's Paupers' Coop in Xipu, another Mao model of revolution, came Du Bao, the younger brother of Du Kui, who ran the village. Boss Geng built personal ties to leaders from better connected villages.

In July 1962 Hebei party secretary Lin Tie further prioritized economic work. Lin was buoyed by reports from North China Bureau party secretary Li Xuefeng that Mao had approved small-group farming as a means to break the famine. Lin encouraged reformer Hu Kaiming to send letters to Mao explaining that Leap policies had lost touch with reality and documenting how the rural economy rebounded when villagers were allowed to act on their own perceived interests. Mao ordered that the letters be circulated. What Lin did not know was that Mao told his confidants that Hu's agenda of having villagers "go it alone" negated the promise of revolutionary socialism.[49]

A Hebei party committee resolution designated agriculture, not politics, as the main responsibility of the party secretary at every level, reemphasized the role of the smaller team as the critical level of production, and initiated an experimental program in 30,000 production teams to "combine sidelines, animal husbandry, and agriculture," a key reformist plank. Another experimental program in twelve Hebei counties stressed animal husbandry, sidelines, and handicrafts, with emphasis on household production. It focused on the particular strengths of localities in contrast to the revolutionary emphasis on growing grain everywhere.

In late 1962 Hebei catapulted Wugong to the fore as a leading model of "socialist modernization." In early 1963 Hebei secretary Lin Tie invited Geng Changsuo to a provincial Agricultural Work Conference in Tianjin. Geng liked what Lin said about the mechanization of collective agriculture. At the Tianjin meeting Geng met Premier Zhou Enlai. While shaking hands, Zhou guessed Geng's age at 50 or so. Geng was actually 62. The premier commented, "Good. You are very healthy."[50] He was not. But his resurrected village was close to achieving national prominence.

With Lin Tie again promoting Wugong, visitors flocked to the red-flag unit. Village leaders again pledged to attain high yields. In September 1962 they boasted that in 1963 Wugong would harvest 550 catties of grain per mu and 240 of cotton, up 14 and 5 percent, respectively.[51] One month later, after the party's Tenth Plenum, Geng upped the ante, proclaiming that Wugong would bring in a six, three, three harvest, 600 catties of grain and 300 each of cotton and peanuts.[52] Collective sideline income was projected at 400,000 yuan. To meet the targets, the grain harvest would have to jump 25 percent and cotton more than 40 percent above 1962 bumper levels. More land would be leveled, more wells dug, more pig manure applied, more labor mobilized for collective projects. But even before nature interrupted Wugong's smooth sailing, revolution roiled stormy seas.

3 ✿ MEMORY
AND MYTH

As the 20th anniversary of the original 1943 coop neared, Hebei party secretary Lin Tie sought to involve Mao in legitimating Wugong's achievement. When some of Mao's personal guards visited Nanwangzhuang, a Hebei village whose leader, Wang Yukun, the chairman had once received, Lin got the leader of the guards to convey an invitation to Mao to visit Wugong (as well as Nanwangzhuang) to celebrate its pioneering of socialism. Lin's effort to win Mao's blessing failed, but Lin believed that Wugong best displayed the superiority of socialism: a productive, redistributive collective economy in contrast both to a polarizing market economy and to fundamentalist economic irrationality.

Wugong's 1953 tenth-anniversary gala had represented socialism as large economic organizations and constriction of markets. Since the famine, however, gigantism had been criticized and the household economy encouraged. The party's line after September 1962 tolerated some economic reforms but simultaneously touted class struggle to prevent capitalist restoration. Lin Tie then promoted Wugong as emblematic of socialist modernization — mechanization, electrification, and water control — advancing material interests through diversification via flourishing collective agriculture and sidelines.

Memory Wars

From his provincial capital, Tianjin, Lin commissioned a volume hailing Wugong's 1943 four-family coop, choosing as editor the writer-official Wang Lin, vice chair of the Tianjin Writers' Association. Wang had attended Qingdao University, where he met Jiang Qing, later Mao's wife. In the late 1930s, they were classmates at the Lu Xun Academy of Literature and Art in Yan'an, the party's wartime capital. A native of nearby Hengshui, Wang hid in Raoyang during Japan's 1942 military offensive and worked in Wugong during the 1948 land reform. In 1955 he wrote an article on the Wang Guofan paupers' coop that Mao featured in his *Socialist Upsurge in China's Countryside* anthology to promote collectivization.

In fall 1959 Wang took Tianjin writers to Wugong to gather materials for a book. But Wugong's refusal to accede to gargantuan production claims and the collapse of the Leap doomed the project. In 1962, in preparation for the gala 20th-anniversary celebration of the original four-family coop, Lin Tie proposed sending twenty writers led by Wang Lin to Wugong to produce a book highlighting the achievements of a modernizing village.

Helped by his old Wugong friend, Geng Xiufeng, Wang prepared a 68-page overview. He cut a section dealing with the provincial government's failed effort in 1953 to reduce the size of the nearly 400 household Wugong coop. Xiufeng complained, "That section is very important, and it's true." Wang explained that the provincial party committee had asked, "Why do you want to expose the dark side of the provincial committee?" Saying he was "scared stiff," Wang dropped the sensitive material on this conflict between provincial and village leaders.[1]

Wugong leaders presented the village as a model of collectivism. The media featured feisty Xu Shukuan, Geng Changsuo's wife. A picture of the Tigress with a new radio appeared in *Hebei Daily* in late 1963. Two orphans the coop adopted in 1948 were by her side. "Xu Shukuan, who fiercely loves the collective" was the caption. At 53, Xu helped lead east village team 1 and was deputy head of the women's association. Xu felt that socialism had saved her from being an object of ridicule, a child sold into marriage. She dismissed mutterings against her for prying into family affairs in order to prod villagers into collective efforts. Socialism, in her view, was the public good replacing familism.

She liked the rhetoric of the heaven-storming leap into communism. "Some people say I mind too many things; they call me a busybody. I say, just so! I am a busybody. Some people, noting my true concern for the collective and my strong character, say I want to be a heaven stormer. I say, just so! I will storm the heavens."[2] Villagers who had been publicly shamed by her itched to get even.

When Wang Lin arrived in early 1963, he knew the story the Hebei party wanted. Wugong would not be praised in the language of the Leap, in which wealth sprang from the spirit of everything for the public.

Wang's team included Liu Xi, a deputy head of the Tianjin Writers' Association who had visited the village a decade earlier with her husband, screenwriter Hu Su, to help orchestrate the coop's tenth anniversary. Another writer, Ge Wen, came to Wugong after researching a book on the Mao-favored Wang Guofan village. Aware that in 1955 Mao had approved helping two Hebei villages, one led by Wang Guofan and the other by Wang Yukun, she wanted to see how Wugong did with far less state aid.

Interviewing went on throughout spring 1963. Villagers were wary. Yang

Guan, the head of the brigade forestry team, answered in monosyllables. The party secretary, Zhang Duan the Ox, who stuck close to the outsiders, was embarrassed. The writers were told whom to see.[3] Activists accompanied them as minders every step of the way. The writers heard of oppression and hardship in the "old society" and during the Japanese invasion. Elders and orphans vouched that only the collective cared for the weak and vulnerable. Young militants embodied Chairman Mao's view of the redness of the next generation. A heroic mythos presented Boss Geng Changsuo as a lesser version of the worshipped Mao.

Women's leader Qiao Wenzhi told how senior lineage member Qiao Damei prostrated herself whenever she saw Boss Geng or Wenzhi herself, because the party had helped Damei in her old age. When Geng explained that credit belonged to Mao, Damei walked three times a day to commune headquarters to bow to a portrait of Mao.[4]

Before publication, a draft manuscript had to pass inspection by the commune and county party committees. The commune party secretary approved. But county party secretary Li Chunyu was troubled by the chapter on the outspoken Geng Xiufeng, which noted that the original 1943 four-household coop was initiated by Xiufeng several months *before* Mao's instruction to "Get Organized!" County boss Li asked Wang, "Are you saying that Geng Xiufeng went to organize peasants before Chairman Mao published 'Get Organized'? Can he be smarter than Chairman Mao? This is a mistake of principle. We can't have this chapter!" Wang responded that the order of events had been verified. No one was suggesting that Xiufeng was smarter than Mao. Writer Ge Wen agreed with Li that the chapter should be cut because Xiufeng was an undisciplined self-promoter. After the writers left, Li Chunyu sent aides to the Tianjin publisher to get the chapter on Xiufeng deleted.[5] The publisher refused.

Tensions between county leaders and Geng Xiufeng surfaced again when a Beijing film crew highlighted Wugong in a documentary on communes. The film featured Geng Changsuo, members of the original coop, scenes of everyday life, pictures of wheat fields, and images of roads that carried grain to the state. Because it also showed Xiufeng, county secretary Li charged that Xiufeng was trying to steal Changsuo's glory.[6] Xiufeng believed that few in the village had done more than he had to dramatize Changsuo's contributions.

Back to Fundamentals

Word spread that in 1962, at the seaside resort of Beidaihe, Mao had commented that he felt "oppressed" (ya) by a deluge of reports on Hebei reform pioneer Hu Kaiming's program in Zhangjiakou. Hu was placed under house arrest. Reform was in trouble.[7]

Because of restrictions on commerce, the only way to get spare parts was to send agents to distant warehouse centers. In early 1963 Li Changhai trekked six hours from Wugong to the railroad crossroads city of Shijiazhuang to buy parts for team 2's equipment. A former co-worker urged Li to buy a kiln that would sell for a much higher price near Wugong. With money so precious, people were conscious of the price of almost everything. Li wrote to Geng Changsuo about his profit-making plan. Boss Geng snapped back, "No!"

On his return, party secretary Zhang Duan lectured Li that buying for profit was the capitalist road. Mao's emphasis was on defeating capitalism. In March a campaign began to emulate the communist values of the martyred soldier Lei Feng, followed two months later by a socialist education movement.[8]

Geng Changsuo's antimarket zeal was shrewd politics. After reining in the kiln deal, he got the village party branch to agree "not to promote sideline industries of a commercial nature." Sidelines must promote agriculture, not lead toward commerce or speculation.[9] Villagers hurt by the economic irrationality of revolutionary policies either resisted by maneuvering around the constraints or suffered.

Wugong, whose postfamine recovery relied on a rapid expansion of collective sidelines, endorsed four economically self-wounding principles: no participation in activities contrary to party policy on sidelines, no commercial sidelines, no sidelines involving materials that are not available locally, and no sidelines involving raw materials needed by the state.[10] While villagers elsewhere expanded household sidelines and market activity, Wugong even shrank collective sidelines, whose earnings sank from the 1962 peak of 164,000 yuan to just 81,000 yuan in 1963 and 57,000 yuan in 1964. Sideline employees fell from 139 in 1962 to 113 in 1964.

Geng pressed villagers into land reclamation in early 1963. Sixty-two-year-old Geng tried to lead by example. Youth would be shamed if they did not outdo their senior. Women were prodded by Xu Shukuan, Geng's wife. As popular enthusiasm for state-imposed toil dwindled, leaders imposed discipline.

The economic price of political virtue seemed high to most villagers. Geng Xiufeng recalled that Wugong villagers chafed at being denied the opportunity to earn cash by selling crops from household plots as some villages to the west did. "Those people are going it alone," a villager complained, "so there's no record of how much grain they produce. Our village is collective, and grain requisitions are done strictly by the book. There's not even a catty left over. It's useless to produce more grain. All you get is an empty bag."[11]

The young, looking for mates, mobility, and material progress, were not pacified by tales pitting preliberation landlords and savage invaders against poor peasant heroes who provided the revolutionary army with grain, shoes, and recruits. Some villagers wondered if Geng Changsuo and his family were scoring political points at the expense of their families' ability to get by in hard times.

Neighboring villagers arriving in early 1963 to learn from the red-flag unit concluded that Wugong fared poorly. At lunch, villagers hid their coarse grain. With Wugong curbing market activity and Boss Geng delivering the best grain to the state, neighbors found little to emulate. Outsiders, however, repeated the standard criticism of models: privileged Wugong officials dined sumptuously.

In 1963 Hebei modernizers saw revolutionaries locking villagers into stagnant misery, thwarting socialism's promise that the poor would prosper. Silent on the reform issues of household sidelines and commerce, Hebei party secretary Lin Tie, a modernizer, publicly pushed mechanized and diversified collectives. In early 1963 Hebei lieutenant governor Yang Yichen went a step further. Visiting Wugong commune, he touted the market as a means to jumpstart the economy. Boss Geng sat in. Yang urged Wugong commune party secretary Huang to raise income via sidelines and commerce. Geng prevailed upon Huang to see such measures as neither revolutionary nor rewarding manual labor. While Geng's 1940s coop had risen on a union of sidelines and commerce, he now viewed the market as exploitation. Wugong would promote collective sidelines while cracking down on the household economy and the market.

When the commune party secretary reiterated his stress on collective enterprise, the lieutenant governor offered the usual carrot. The province would guarantee 300,000 catties of scarce chemical fertilizer at subsidized prices and buy back a grain surplus equal in value to the chemical fertilizer. Commerce, production, and profits would soar without risk. Wugong would not, however, take the bait.

By the next day the visitors were gone. Geng Changsuo redoubled his commitment to the collective, assuring that labor's fruits would meet the basic needs of villagers and fulfill the state's grain and cotton sales quotas. He claimed that collective labor helped Wugong get through the dearth better than others. Some villagers were not persuaded.

In 1963 Lu Guang, an adviser to Wugong in the period 1953–56, was attacked. A Lin Tie subordinate, Lu served in the North China Bureau's organization department tied to the network of Politburo member Peng Zhen, the party secretary of Beijing. In an innerparty campaign that preceded the socialist education movement, Lu was targeted by revolutionary Li Xuefeng, the first secretary of the party's North China Bureau, who challenged conservative modernizer Peng Zhen. Lu was demoted two grades and removed from the organization department, which controlled appointments.

The purge seemed a portent. Members of the Hebei party apparatus linked to Lin Tie, Lu Guang's patron, worried when Lu was accused of being a capitalist roader and the reform pioneer Hu Kaiming was arrested. Who else might fall in attacks on Peng Zhen's subordinates?

The Great Flood

From August 2, 1963, rain fell for a week. Water rose knee deep in the fields. Wugong commune members built embankments to keep the flood from their fields. Worst hit were Nahshan and Beishan villages; all crops and most homes were destroyed.[12] Fortunately, the June wheat harvest had been good. In Wugong it was excellent: 356 catties per mu, even better than in 1961 and 1962. The state took its wheat share before the rains. But corn, sorghum, and cotton were threatened, and villagers worried again about hunger.

Wugong villagers toiled for seven days and nights using lights first strung up in the Leap. As with the 1956 flood, retaining walls and drainage ditches allowed some grain and cotton to be saved. Boss Geng's east-end team 1 was hard hit. Twenty-five inches of water sat in the fields. Draining those fields would require releasing the water into neighboring Zoucun. Geng said no, and his team suffered.

Young activists won commendations for working in the rain through the night singing a song of Lei Feng, the lionized martyr soldier.[13] Fed up with elders' tales of revolutionary heroism, teenagers strove to prove their mettle. The women's association leader, Qiao Wenzhi, won praise for leading a team of women into flooded fields.[14]

It was Hebei's worst flood since 1939. The rain of August 2–8 was more than three times the mean annual precipitation.[15] The same ruinous torrents struck Dazhai village in Shanxi province west of Hebei. A refusal of proferred state aid — in the form of grain, funds, and relief materials — became the foundational myth of a Dazhai path of self-reliant development. By December, Shanxi would call on all party organizations to emulate Dazhai and its leader, Chen Yonggui.[16]

Boss Geng's east-end aide, Qiao Liguang, who headed village administration, allowed team 3 in the west end to store the cotton it had already picked, while the cotton of the other two teams still stood in the fields. Geng was furious. He forbade unloading the cotton. West enders protested, saying the cotton would be lost. Geng insisted that not a boll be unloaded until every village field was picked. He then sent the west-enders to help bring in what was left in the east and center. Later he blasted Administrator Qiao for threatening village unity.

Tensions between east and west were electric. Team 1, home to Boss Geng, was the village's political center and media focus. But team 3, dominated by the Xus and the Zhangs, economically outperformed Geng's team. Collective income in team 3 was significantly higher in every year from 1961 to 1978. West-enders were suspicious when Boss Geng kept them from salvaging their cotton.

When disaster struck, villages had to forecast probable yield so the authorities would know what to expect in taxes and sales to the state. Team 3's Steady

Xu Mantang would not accept Boss Geng's high forecast. It augured high state crop requisition, a cause of hunger. Xu bemoaned irreparable damage. Geng countered, "This grain can still be saved and yield 200 catties per mu." "It can't be done," Xu replied. "One hundred would be a lot." "I guarantee 200," Geng shot back. "Don't talk like that," Xu pleaded, trying to get Geng to accept relief. "How much state grain can our collective expect this year?" Xu asked. But Boss Geng refused to file a report that would lead the state to send relief. "You mean," Geng snapped, "how much grain will we supply to the state."

Everyone in hearing distance giggled with nervous embarrassment. Fears about surviving the winter were rife. Later, at village headquarters, party secretary Zhang Duan, also from the west end, offered a compromise, a token offering to the state to make Geng's firm stand for local self-reliance harmonize with the needs of villagers.

"We've been hit by a disaster," Zhang pointed out. Extra grain should stay in the village because "the commune has not said we have to fulfill our [remaining] grain quota. The party branch has studied it a bit. Based on total income from sidelines as well as crops, we'll have enough to eat and then some. We plan to send the state a bit of cotton and grain. What do you say?"

Geng then appealed to villagers to join him in sending more grain to the state. "Others were hit far harder than Wugong. In some villages, houses collapsed. In some nothing could be harvested. If we give the state a bit more grain and cotton, then there will be more for state industrial construction and to support disaster areas. Think it over. Should we or shouldn't we send a bit more?"

"Go hungry to give more to the state" is how Geng's message was remembered. Locals countered, "The villages just north of us were hit more lightly than we were. How much are they sending?" Geng responded, "Don't look at others. Just look at ourselves. If we hurt the state, we only hurt ourselves." But many households could not accept that political logic. They sought to help hungry kin.

Boss Geng told us he remembered how much the socialist state had done for him and his family, far more than as a destitute youth he had dreamed possible. He had built a new house in 1962.[17] As a child, his dirt-poor family could not even afford meatless dumplings to fool the gods at the lunar New Year to win an auspicious future. To Geng, China was not so much suffering scarcities as it was sacrificing to maintain its independence and its national honor. Identifying with relatives who died in war, Geng embraced the state's claim that sacrifice was the price of not surrendering to Khrushchev's Soviet Union, which cut off aid and demanded food as repayment for loans. Patriotism and military ties made many villagers responsive to patriotic appeals for sacrifice. The government sought high grain deliveries. A model village helped achieve this goal if it kept relief demands to a minimum. If Wugong requested relief, than it served only its short-term needs, jeopardizing its special connection to the socialist state.

Zhang Duan moved to Geng's position. "Our leader is right. We have to consider the living conditions of our members, but we also must remember the needs of the state. Tomorrow we'll call a meeting so everyone can discuss it."

The next day Zhang the Ox silenced villagers who could not see enough food to satisfy both state demands and villager hunger. Some conceded, "All right, in the past the state took care of us. . . . Who did our Wugong rely on to prosper if not the party and the state?" "We'll have enough to eat. It's nothing to give another few thousand catties of grain."

Flooded Wugong, whose 1963 grain yield was the lowest since the 1960 dearth, and whose cotton yield was the lowest since the 1956 flood, sent the state 85,000 catties of grain, including the 40,000 catties delivered before the flood. The sale was second in size only to 1959, when Leap zealotry emptied reserves. Wugong also sold 15,000 catties of ginned cotton, referring to it as 45,000 catties. That was prior to ginning. The exaggerating method was standard, and few would be fooled.

In late 1963 Wugong took in draft animals from distressed communities in two neighboring counties that lost their fodder. It cared for them all winter, presenting newborn calves to their original units in the spring. Wugong also sent 60,000 catties of fodder and 50,000 of vegetables to harder-hit neighbors.[18] Numbers were politics. In Wugong's socialist narrative, it sacrificed for the common weal.

The village accountant told us that Wugong trucked 12,000 catties of cabbage to chronically poor Yanggezhuang. In that low-lying community, water rose to rooftops. With wretched soil and the loss of historic market earnings, the impoverished village was perennially dependent on state relief. Whereas 250 to 300 catties of husked grain per person is a subsistence minimum, in 1963 Yanggezhuang produced only 17 catties for each of its 1,844 people.[19] During the flood Yanggezhuang villagers traveled about by shallow-draft boat. Its leader recalled no trucked-in relief aid from Wugong. Trucks, after all, cannot swim.

No published account of Wugong's generosity mentioned the huge pipe between Wugong and Zoucun that siphoned off flood waters. As a result, though 1963 harvests were reduced, high-lying Wugong (which had a bumper winter wheat crop in June) was far better off than its neighbors.

Twenty-eight-year-old county official Xu Fu was dispatched to Shandong province to the east to secure grain, oil, and thousands of tons of cabbage to relieve Raoyang hunger. The grain and cabbage went by train to Qianmotou in neighboring Shenxian county. Raoyang had no railroad. More than 100 trucks worked around the clock delivering food.

Higher levels of government provided short-term, interest-free loans of a few yuan per household to hard-hit communities. The Chinese nation pitched in to help flood victims. Inner Mongolia sent oats, lamb, and beef. Shanxi villagers living along the Hutuo and Fuyang rivers, upstream from Raoyang, provided beancurd. Such root vegetables as taro came by ship from South China.

To save Tianjin, the provincial capital, the dikes of central Hebei were opened, as in 1956. In 1963 Tianjin residents contributed more than eight million yuan in disaster relief, in addition to ten million catties of grain and 669,000 articles of clothing, bedding, and shoes.[20] The most memorable aid was camels from Inner Mongolia sent to replace drowned draft animals.

In one poor north Raoyang village, the state provided a 1,000 yuan subsidy to help flood victims. The party secretary skimmed off 800 yuan, leaving only 200 for the needy. That pittance was restricted to martyr families who lost a son in the anti-Japanese war. Hungry villagers grumbled about corruption.

Since the reorganization of 1962 made Raoyang part of Hengshui prefecture, the county was less likely to receive generous aid. In the early 1950s Raoyang had been the poorest county in Dingxian prefecture. It was now the second-most prosperous county in a poorer Hengshui.

The floods strengthened Hebei party secretary Lin Tie's commitment to technological modernization. Searching for support to control the Hai River system, Lin contacted an Anping county native serving on Chairman Mao's secretarial staff, asking him to use his connections to get Mao's support for controlling the Hai River. Mao complied, offering eleven items of calligraphy declaring "Control the Hai River" (genzhi Hai he). On November 17, 1963, Mao's word launched a water-control campaign. Lin used it to promote well-drilling, electrification, and agricultural mechanization. Resources were mobilized to tame the regional river system.

Living standards, however, could hardly rise. Rural underemployment was endemic, and villagers were prevented from leaving poor communities to find work. Grain-first policies precluded wealth from diversification. Off-farm employment, a resurgent household sector, rural industry, modern transportation, and the market were anathema to revolutionaries. In the atmosphere of rising class struggle, Hebei secretary Lin Tie urged only very conservative modernization.

Beginning in 1963, as in the Leap, thousands of laborers mobilized through the militia toiled on two big reservoir projects in Pingshan county in the Taihang Mountains. Water-conservancy projects initiated during the Leap continued, sometimes involving entire militia units carrying rifles with bayonets. Reservoirs and dams built upstream on the Hutuo River in 1963 and 1964 did eliminate flooding in Raoyang. But the river dried up. The county lost river travel and commerce and its only above-ground water source, propelling feverish work to drill deeper for water without the benefit of ecological-impact analysis.

The Book on Wugong

In September 1963, as Wugong recovered from the flood, the book prepared by the Wang Lin writing team was published. It was entitled *The First Flower*, and 25,000 copies were printed. The book exaggerated suffering in the first half of the twentieth century and was silent on the state policies that caused starvation in the early 1960s. *The First Flower* argued that collective efforts had saved people during natural disasters in 1943, 1952, 1956, and 1960. If Wugong leaders had followed the lead of those who wanted to profit from the market, life-saving collectives, the book claimed, would have been undermined.

Highlighting Mao's notion of class struggle, the book presented evil landlords, rich peasants, and local despots as predators stalking innocent and defenseless people, until the Communist Party won power. One chapter introduced 58-year-old Li Duolin, a leading member of the Wugong militia. Li's job was to keep a close eye on "class enemies." He can't tell you the theory of class struggle, but he's clear about one thing: the enemy hates us!"[21] Li always carried a rifle. Class enemies, Li said, were like sly foxes that made off with chickens and pigs; they had to be hunted down and eliminated.

The First Flower told how 500 cotton plants were cut down in July 1955. Another 1,600 cotton plants were destroyed in July 1956. Rather than explain that villagers resented the state-imposed low price that made raising cotton profitless, antisocialist class enemies were blamed. Pigs were poisoned by "middle peasant" Li Qingyun, and protest leaflets were distributed by "middle peasant" Li Can in spring 1958. Both were incarcerated.[22]

A hastily prepared "postscript" described Wugong as a model of revolution. "In the course of the great socialist education movement, and in the struggle resolutely to combat modern revisionism," editor Wang Lin asserted, "factory histories, commune histories, and village histories are instruments for allowing us to give young people and the broad masses a class education and an education in revolutionary traditions." Wugong exemplified the path to be taken in the "two-road struggle" between socialism and capitalism.[23] *The First Flower* was silent on the special resources given to models. It did not record how ordinary villages resented model units. Wugong's neighbors, constantly exhorted to "catch up with Wugong," believed that it was state subsidies that allowed Wugong to increase production.

In 1963 Hebei party secretary Lin Tie presented Wugong as a model of modernized, collective farming. But just as Lin Tie was making Wugong a model of how materially to improve life and mechanize and modernize agriculture, Mao promoted a class struggle agenda that stigmatized an economic emphasis as counter-revolution.

Celebration

Despite the flood damage, Lin Tie pushed ahead with the Wugong coop's 20th-anniversary celebration. He cleared the event with President Liu Shaoqi, who said that the praise should be lavish but the cost and size of the event limited.[24] In fact, the scale far exceeded that of the 1953 celebration. In fall 1963 Hebei sent an official to prepare a fancy exhibition, and Hengshui prefecture sent someone to arrange the public meetings and official speeches.

Villagers swept up for the thousands expected by November 25. The celebration was held in an open space at the north end of the village. In order to house guests, the county upgraded a small hostel into a reception station. In the early 1950s the hostel had received a work team led by Lu Guang (the recently targeted member of the Peng Zhen–Lin Tie network), who had helped make Wugong a pioneer on the road to Soviet-style socialism. Built with county funds, it could accommodate 32 people in 16 rooms. Benefits would flow from a facility where higher-ups, technical specialists, and guests could eat and stay.

The small rooms had bare cement floors and two narrow wooden beds with colorful quilts but no mattresses. Each room contained a wooden chair, a table, a desk lamp, a wash basin, and a comb. Rats and lizards scrambled overhead on the beams. The final squawks of chickens being slaughtered in the swept-earth courtyard could be heard in the predawn hours. Cook Liu Zikui, a comic and amateur magician, was more than passable.

Two mat structures were built. One doubled as the official meeting site and a venue for after-hours film and regional opera presentations; the other housed the exhibition set up by the province. The gala was presided over by the Hebei party secretary, who arrived from Tianjin in a grand motorcade. Never before had so high an official visited. Lin Tie wore an elegant coat and Russian-style fur hat. He had first visited the Wugong coop in May 1945 as party secretary of the Central Hebei Military Region.

On the eve of the celebration, while preparing to show a film, aspiring writer Shi Guiying was called aside. Waiting nearby was orphan Li Mengjie, with whom she had corresponded for three years. Annual home leave for soldiers applied only to married men. Mengjie was given his first visit since enlisting in the army in 1960 to attend the coop's anniversary.

Among the official guests were 62 provincial-level labor models from Hebei and surrounding provinces, 337 model workers from Hengshui prefecture and Raoyang county, 109 representatives of the 36 villages in Wugong commune, 500 ordinary villagers, and 82 journalists and art workers. Including officials, there were 1,237 guests. Telegrams arrived from bureaus of the State Council.

Wugong was alive with color and noise. Village men wound customary white cloths around their heads. Each honored guest presented Wugong with a banner, and each was greeted by fireworks. A historic producer of pyrotechnics, Raoyang put on a spectacular display. Representatives from other model villages stayed in homes. Wang Guofan's Hebei village, blessed by Mao himself, sent a representative of the Du lineage, deputy party secretary Du Zhenyu. The class-struggle line had sharpened the tension between the Du and Wang lineages.

Li Shunda, an agricultural-labor model from Shanxi who had traveled with Boss Geng to the Soviet Union in April 1952 to study collectives, was greeted by Geng at the bus stop. Surveying a wide road lined by poplar trees, a supply and marketing coop, a restaurant, a post office, and a branch of the Bank of China, Li took Geng's hand and averred, "We're in a city now!" Geng, mocking flattery, joked, "What city?"

Visitors were greeted by the Wugong drum corps, with four men pounding each of the big drums. No celebration was complete without those rhythmic beats. Firecrackers exploded as guests passed beneath Mao's five-character Leap slogan: "The people's communes are good!" To the left of the entrance was the slogan "Long live the Great Leap Forward!" But the content that Hebei party secretary Lin gave to what was "good" was not revolutionary mass campaigns of unpaid labor, ever larger collective units, or class struggle. The entrance way to the meeting tent featured the slogan "Carry through mechanization" and, opposite it, "On to agricultural modernization." Above the tent it said "Long live the general line."[25] But it was the collective modernization line that Lin celebrated.

The exhibition featured statistics, photos, and displays about Wugong's modernization, patriotism and loyalty to the collective. More than 2,000 mu of village land were said to be irrigated. Almost 90 percent of the fields were tilled by machine. Grain production in 1962 was 482 catties per mu, up from "150 catties" per mu three to four years earlier. (Actually, Wugong's grain production was never that little in the collective era.) Cotton production, 229 (unginned) catties per mu, was more than four times greater than in 1953. Peanut output was 300 catties per mu.[26]

The exhibition trumpeted Wugong's "patriotic" deliveries to the state. From 1953 to 1962 the village had delivered 660,000 catties of grain, 970,000 catties of unginned cotton, and 720,000 catties of peanuts. The average income of individuals was said to be 446 catties of grain and 120 yuan.

Model units had to make ambitious future projections. The commune announced a Ten Year Plan to reach 400 catties per mu for grain, 200 for unginned cotton, and 400 for peanuts. These four, two, four targets represented increases of 115 percent, 202 percent, and 110 percent, respectively. Commune irrigated land was to increase from 8,000 mu to 62,000 mu, or 43 percent of the total. Wugong village aimed higher than the commune of which it was a part. It promised 800 catties of grain per mu, 400 of sorghum, and 500 of peanuts by 1973.

The November 25 keynote address by Lin Tie emphasized technological advance, party leadership, and ideological mobilization but did not neglect the theory of class struggle. The real political conflict that had already victimized two of Lin Tie's lieutenants, reform pioneer Hu Kaiming and Wugong adviser Lu Guang, was not even hinted at.

Lin depicted modernization in technological terms. "Old Wugong" had suffered from unfavorable natural conditions and poor technology. "Twenty years ago," Lin recalled, "Wugong had drought in the spring, waterlogging in the fall, dusty winds blowing in every direction, thin top soil, and unending natural disasters. If it wasn't drought, it was flood, dust, storms, or insects. In those days there were practically no irrigated fields, and a shortage of draft animals and farm equipment. Thus, a mu of land produced only about 100 catties of grain."[27] Lin made a passing reference to the "exploitation of landlords and rich peasants" as a cause of suffering.

The provincial party secretary praised Wugong for tractor plowing and electrified irrigation. Exaggerating, he said that villagers had replaced "backward hand labor" with "modernized" and mechanized production.

Lin's script starred Geng Changsuo. Although Lin well knew that Geng was not a founding member of the original 1943 coop, he referred to Geng as a founder, "a model soldier who should be studied by everyone, including the commune heads of the whole province."

Lin's second theme was party leadership. Geng was a model because he always managed affairs "strictly according to the policies of the party." Lin cited Geng's refusal to "distribute responsibility land" or to make "the family group the basic unit of account" as evidence of loyalty to the party. In the wake of the Leap famine, Geng actually resisted reformers who urged household plots. With Mao promoting class struggle and a socialist education movement, Geng's resistance to reform was touted as party loyalty. "Under the party's leadership" in fighting natural disasters, Lin continued, villagers "planted trees to combat the winds, remained frugal and self-reliant, enthusiastically pushed agricultural mechanization and electrification, engaged in various types of scientific experiments, and tried out new seed strains, thereby constantly transforming agricultural technology and raising production levels."

Lin's third theme, militant class struggle and mass ideological mobilization, was a revolutionary one, at odds with his central theme of modernization. Lin alluded to "monsters and demons" who opposed socialism in a "two-line struggle" between capitalism and socialism. Rural revolutionaries should "tighten control of the weapons of class struggle" and "always follow Chairman Mao's instructions."

In contrast to Lin Tie's praise for a Geng Changsuo who could "draw in well-to-do middle peasants to take the collective road" and modernize Wugong so that tractors and not humans pulled plows, county party secretary Li Chunyu singularly stressed class struggle. Inveighing against "class enemies" and "reactionaries," Li declared, "We want revolution, we want socialism, and we want communism, . . . but the class enemies . . . want counterrevolution. They want to destroy socialism. On the road of socialist construction, it's impossible to forget class, it's impossible to forget our dependence on the poor and lower-middle peasants, and it's impossible to forget socialist class education."[28]

Geng received banners from Lin Tie, prefectural secretary Zhao Shuguang, and county secretary Li Chunyu. Lin Tie's banner read, "Rise in greater vigor and self-reliance, manage the economy with thrift, aim high, and struggle to complete the modernization of agriculture."[29] Ten years earlier, at the 1953 celebration, provincial authorities had presented a banner inscribed "The flower of socialism." The challenges and slogans of 1963 seemed more complex.

Geng Xiufeng, the drafter of the 1960 letter protesting Leap policies, next read two telegrams written to Chairman Mao and the Central Committee. As at the 1953 celebration, friends of Wugong wistfully hoped for support from Mao.

The next day, November 26, Lin Tie and the more than 60 provincial labor models, each presented with a copy of *The First Flower,* gathered for a symposium entitled "Learning from Wugong and Geng Changsuo." Reporters from *Hebei Daily,* Radio Hebei, and *Hengshui Masses* recorded the session and edited the minutes.

Most speakers offered uncritical praise. From nearby Houtun, Yao Fuheng, a former guerrilla fighter who had turned himself into a competent agronomist, said he was impressed with how Wugong managed its large, complex economy and how it nurtured seed strains for the local climate and soil. Another village leader said Wugong was a model because it "gives priority to state interests." "Wugong produces enough to meet the state's agricultural needs," declared another. "Wugong will forever be our model," was yet another vacuous contribution to the litany. One person said Boss Geng had succeeded because he put the public first. Absolute power generated absolute sycophancy.

Some speakers blew their own horns. Wei Rong, party secretary of Yaotou brigade in Shulu county proclaimed village grain production of 690 catties per mu. This was far higher than in Wugong! Similarly, Zhang Benlin, the head of Nanhetou brigade in neighboring Xianxian county, a Roman Catholic bastion, after saying that Boss Geng "has always been my teacher," noted that Nanhetou grain yields surpassed Wugong's.[30]

Others sought help. Song Xingru, head of Chang'an brigade in Liuchu commune in Raoyang county, was at first drowned out by the men. She said she respected those who promised to catch up with Wugong, but, truthfully speaking, her brigade could not. "Chang'an brigade," she reported, "is a village of drought, sand storms, and frequent flooding. We are still like the Wugong of old."

Hebei party secretary Lin Tie was moved. "Your conditions are different," he agreed; "you should do what is best for your village." The national media reported neither the comments of those who felt superior to Wugong nor the painful words of those mired in poverty. Not one village representative mentioned class struggle, class enemies, or two roads.

Finally Geng responded: "Everyone says emulate Wugong, emulate me. Please excuse me. But what do I have worth studying? Many fraternal brigades do better than Wugong and are worthy of our emulation. In collectivization, our 20 years is a short experience: to sum up, it's rely on the masses, participate in labor, manage the commune frugally and economically — all of which are the instructions of the party and Chairman Mao." Ignoring his own resistance to party instructions both during and after the Leap, Geng concluded, "If you want to discuss our experience, it's just 'listen to the party.'"

Geng acknowledged that many villagers experienced statist command and collectives as locking the rural poor into poverty. When he refused to become further involved with peanut wholesaler Li Hengxin in 1951, people mocked Geng as a "simpleton" who "won't eat meat-filled dumplings put in his mouth." Members of the small east-end coop of 1952 who opposed a big unit, since their income would decline, called him a "dummy." There was much anger at Geng in his own end of the village. Invectives were hurled when he insisted on high grain sales to the state at a time when villagers had less to eat. Geng argued that one had to be willing to seem stupid to people who only saw short-term gains. He echoed Mao, "Everything for the collective, forget self-interest."[31] Geng summed up his views in four principles informed by revolutionary perspectives. Stress agriculture, not commerce. Profit is exploitation. Work to eat. Take the socialist road.

That evening younger Wugong leaders joined the visitors and chatted in the informality of cheap cigarettes and home-brewed whiskey, seated on brick beds with doors closed to the ears of the more powerful.

Model of What?

In 1963 Wugong won national recognition. On November 26 the full text of Lin Tie's November 25 speech was published in the party's top paper, *People's Daily*. Soon after, on December 7, the paper carried three items on Wugong, including two detailed features and an editorial extolling Geng and the village. "History has shown," the editorial proclaimed, "that the road taken by these four Wugong peasants 20 years ago later became precisely the road to follow for the nation's entire peasantry."

Geng Xiufeng and Geng Changsuo fantasized that Mao himself had written the editorial, proving that Wugong was finally a national model.[32] A day later another leading national paper, *Guangming Daily,* carried a lavishly illustrated tribute. Immediately, *Hebei Daily* in Tianjin, *Zhongguo xinwen* in Guangzhou, and *Dagong bao* and *China Youth Daily* in Beijing jumped on modernizer Lin Tie's Wugong bandwagon.[33] The New China News Agency's international wire service and *China Reconstructs* ran lengthy features in English for overseas readers. The party presented Wugong as a model of revolution, class struggle, and socialist education.

The new line was tied to a cult of Mao. Although no villager had heard of it when Wugong's first coop was established, Hebei party secretary Lin Tie described Mao's 1943 talk "Get Organized!" as inspiring them.[34] Illiterate Tigress Xu Shukuan supposedly said she would have had to do more begging and sell more children but for Mao's inspiration.[35] In this cult, Mao was the source of all good. Boss Geng identified with and exemplified that cult. Villagers, however, combined reverence for Mao with cynicism about local powerholders.

Mao, supported by Defense Minister Lin Biao, pushed class struggle. In 1963 Raoyang set up a preparatory committee to establish poor-peasant associations. Suddenly, Wugong's backing for mechanized, modern agriculture seemed less than revolutionary. The book about Wugong was already out of date as a propaganda tool.

Wugong and Geng Changsuo rode high in December 1963. But to be visible was to be vulnerable. Villagers knew that "the biggest trees catch the most wind." What sort of model was Wugong? To some revolutionaries, who thought the Soviet system was a capitalistic revision of socialist doctrine, Wugong looked too much like a Soviet collective. To some modernizers, however, Wugong was too antimarket.

There was also discord within the model village. Boasting about grain sales to the state in the flood year of 1963 hid hunger. After the celebrants left, many Wugong households spent the last of their savings and borrowed from relatives. Only primordial bonds seemed reliable. The savings of Wugong residents in the local credit coop fell 90 percent in 1963, from more than 100,000 yuan to just 10,000.

Lin Tie had hailed the village's modernization, but critic Geng Xiufeng observed that the heavy stone rollers still pushed by women to grind flour symbolized an actual lack of progress. Oxen still pulled plows. Carts still lugged barrels of water to the fields. And why? It was, Xiufeng found, because of the dictatorial behavior of higher-ups. They expected villagers to act like stupid pigs, incapable of remembering who it was that kicked them. Xiufeng worried that Geng Changsuo was becoming the voice of such officials instead of representing suffering villagers.

Relief finally arrived in Wugong commune early in 1964 in the form of cabbages as well as taro and lotus root, recalled hard-drinking Li Lu, a skilled west-end stone mason who had been sent back to Wugong in 1962 from the Raoyang Construction Company. Gao Guixin, head of women's work in team 3, remembered that after the 1963 flood "people in other places assisted us with rice and flour." In the wheat- and millet-eating north, the provision of rice, identified with the rich south, was memorable.

Li Mingxiang, 35 years old, had been working at the commune grain station since the start of the Leap. He vividly recounted the state relief that winter — grain and vegetables, mostly turnip and cabbage. It came to the commune, he said, in a continuous caravan of trucks that dropped off their load, immediately turned around, and headed back for more. He unloaded them day after day. In short, while model villages publicly declined aid, Wugong commune actually received substantial state assistance. Some villagers even insist that aid was dropped by parachute to Wugong.

There is disagreement between the official rendering of the selfless village sending food to the state in 1963 and helping neighboring villages get through the disaster and the contrary early 1964 reality of relief, however belated, coming to the commune from the state. The conflict exemplifies why model villages and their leaders are so vulnerable to attack both from locals and from above when a state leader sets out to discredit a previous policy line and an earlier model. Inevitably there is "evidence" of falsification; invariably there is popular dissatisfaction. These are the consequences of villagers trying to meet impossible requirements to win the praise of the center. To do what a model should do was also to expose oneself to being undone. Yet it seemed crazy to reject patronage.

There was, after all, political gain in Boss Geng's calculus. If he had requested immediate state relief after the August 1963 flood, could the November celebration have resulted in national praise for Wugong in *People's Daily?* If Geng had immediately asked for aid, could Wugong have won the rich fruits of model status? The village of Dazhai, devastated by the 1963 flood, presented in the press as the premier model of self-reliant development, eventually, and without mention in the media, received great state help to solve its water crisis.

Throughout the countryside, villagers mocked hypocrisy by the wielders of corrupt and unaccountable power:

Relief from all over the country, commune members happy at heart.
Never saw a penny in cash, only new houses for office holders.

Villagers seethed at local tyrants who grabbed much of the relief, leaving little for the needy. The integrity of Geng Changsuo and his conciliationist leadership group that worked to unite villagers had deeply impressed members of the Wang Lin writing team. But virtue would soon be defined by the center as class-struggle revolution.

Right after the twentieth-anniversary celebration, Boss Geng hit the road to return the courtesy of visits paid by prominent village model leaders, to touch political bases, and to study the experience of more successful units like Chen Yonggui's Dazhai and Wang Guofan's Paupers' Coop that Mao had personally blessed, sites whose myths seemed more appealing to revolutionary power holders.

4 ❀ SOCIALIST EDUCATION

In early December 1963, just after Wugong's 20th-anniversary gala, Geng Changsuo attended an award ceremony in Tianjin hosted by Hebei governor Liu Zihou, a proponent of class struggle. Hebei party secretary Lin Tie was not present. Participants included representatives of all Hebei prefectural and county party committees and more than 1,000 provincial labor models.

When Lin Tie was in charge, Geng was often the top labor model. But with Governor Liu, Geng was twenty-fifth. A provincial official commented, "Just because we give someone an award doesn't mean he deserves it!" Geng and his aides worried that their village was considered "rightist," insufficiently revolutionary because it had refused to send up fake production satellites during the Leap.[1] Talk in Tianjin focused on socialist education.[2] Wugong leaders scurried to prove themselves revolutionary.

Socialist Education, Survivalism and the Third Front

Inspiration for the socialist education movement (experienced as overlapping with a four-cleanups campaign) came from Hebei. Revolutionary North China Bureau party secretary Li Xuefeng and Hebei governor Liu Zihou nurtured a model in Xingtai prefecture, just southwest of Wugong. An Ziwen, an official in the party's Organization Bureau, cultivated a model near Shijiazhuang, a Hebei railroad center. In early 1964 Wang Guangmei, the wife of President Liu Shaoqi, visited Hebei party secretary Lin Tie in Tianjin to find a rural spot for her model. She wanted it near the Hebei seaside resort for party leaders in Beidaihe. Wu Qingcheng, a Lin aide, suggested Taoyuan village and took care of her there.

Mao Zedong's "First Ten Points," a major policy statement promoting the socialist education movement, was drafted in spring 1963 and drew on events in Hebei's Baoding region, where people resented Lin Tie's role in the 1958 transfer of the provincial capital from Baoding to Tianjin. Baoding officials had even tried to block supplies to Tianjin, forcing direct intervention by Premier Zhou.

In early 1963 Mao praised newly founded poor and lower-middle peasant associations in Baoding for preventing a landlord comeback.[3] Mao would mobilize the poor to unseat corrupt officials supposedly plotting a capitalist restoration. The party told villagers to choose between violent class war or a return of vengeful landlords. Mao's ten points argued that the socialist education movement in Baoding was "like a magic mirror [that reveals monsters]. Whether one is a just or false official becomes immediately clear. . . . If the cadres sincerely review their errors and actively make compensation, they are forgiven by the masses — except for a few bad elements."[4]

Mao praised Hebei governor Liu Zihou as a vanguard of socialist education.[5] Renewed class struggle would prod villagers to eliminate household production and marketing and instead embrace collective grain and cotton production, thus blunting the reforms that made possible the post-Leap recovery. Revolutionary theorist Chen Boda and security chief Kang Sheng attacked capitalist economics and feudal culture and demanded redoubled efforts to raise communist consciousness.

By contrast, President Liu Shaoqi saw the socialist education movement as an internal party matter. He traced the rural crisis in the wake of the Leap-era famine to corrupt grassroots officials who abused power and alienated villagers. General Secretary Deng Xiaoping emphasized that, whether struggling against capitalist speculation or corrupt officials, no campaign should hurt production or cut precarious village incomes. Deng and Liu agreed with Premier Zhou on the need for household plots, family sidelines, and rural markets to stimulate the economy and boost rural living standards. While sobered by the Leap-era catastrophe, reformers dared not directly challenge the economic irrationalities of the command economy or the class-struggle agenda.

Hebei province, leading the socialist education movement nationwide, assigned 100,000 officials to work teams bound for the countryside. The campaign reached Hengshui prefecture and Raoyang county in early 1964. In January, Raoyang party secretary Li Chunyu ordered 232 officials to form teams and go to every county village. Work teams propagated both Mao's "First Ten Points" and the "Later Ten Points" spelled out by Deng Xiaoping and Peng Zhen.[6] It was the first of several phases of the socialist education movement. The message seemed to be that lax and corrupt village leaders needed rectification. But the teams merely lectured, urging village leaders to read the documents.

Wugong's leaders thought they had been promoting socialist education since spring 1963. To foreground the political purity of village youth, Wang Lin's Tianjin writing group had been introduced to activist Xu Xiuwen, aspiring writer Shi Guiying, and pepperpot Li Huiying. Wang Lin's book showed how Wugong fostered "socialist education."

Mao's Baoding class struggle was not pursued in most of rural Hebei in January 1964. Provincial secretary Lin Tie, like President Liu, emphasized overcoming post-Leap disaffection by curbing corrupt officials and helping the economy regain momentum.

Anxiety over food shortages had spread in the wake of the Leap famine. Facing isolation by both Moscow and Washington, Chinese patriots legitimated a military that grew its own food and emulated Lei Feng, who gave his life so China and its revolution could live. Likewise Dazhai villagers, said to work selflessly to assure grain self-reliance, promoted the survivalist motif.

Survivalism legitimated a third-front (da san xian) initiative. In May 1964 Mao prevailed in prioritizing national survival in the face of a potential foreign invasion. His third-front program, proposing three lines of defense, placed immense strains on the still fragile economy.[7] In the next eight years, as China prepared for war, major industries and hundreds of thousands of workers on the Soviet border and in coastal areas deemed vulnerable to attack were relocated inland or to mountain zones in southwest China. In addition, each province, prefecture, and county was to become militarily self-reliant to survive invasion. That precluded economic exchange. Hebei province, until 1964 almost devoid of military industry, invested heavily in armaments factories, becoming a national leader in military production.

Rural counties, including Raoyang, began building nitrogen fertilizer factories that could contribute to food self-reliance and be convertible to munitions production. Phosphate fertilizer factories that could not convert were given low priority, resulting in an economically irrational imbalance of fertilizers. Moreover, in many counties, small factories produced low-grade fertilizer.

The authorities in Tianjin moved provincial records to a cave in a "small third front," Xinglong county in the mountains of northwest Hebei, where dampness eventually destroyed them. To make state leaders safe, work began on a War Preparedness Highway from Beijing to southern Shanxi, just west of Hebei. Building roads to third-front regions, like investment in distant factories lacking inputs or end users, did benefit some places. It brought a good road right by Wugong, easing transport to Beijing, Baoding, and Tianjin. But, with commerce illegal, the roads brought few real benefits.

Revolutionary Successors

Geng Changsuo responded to the socialist education campaign by promoting red successors, drawn mainly from his team 1 in the east end and team 3 in the west. As with his marriage to Xu Shukuan, Geng's power base linked the east and west. Team 2 in the village center, home to the old southern Li elites, was marginalized. Its children were seldom groomed for higher office.

Geng nurtured his east-end neighbor Li Shouzheng, a northern Li lineage member who headed the village militia. Mao and Defense Minister Lin Biao urged militia activists to teach red successors to welcome hardship. Sturdy and broad faced, Macho Li was fond of quoting his father, an army veteran: "After I'm dead, do things as you do now; carry on the family tradition of us 'poor people.'" His militia job won Li his first trip to the rich metropolis of Tianjin. The system privileged its own, whatever the rhetoric about overcoming greed.

A backbone militia looked up to demobilized veterans. Active-duty soldiers from commune headquarters provided special training with live ammunition. Men with connections to the army tended to be tougher and more xeno-phobic. Many found self-reliance a matter of ethical purity. Veterans not only transmitted a survivalist message of an encircled China, they also enjoyed toughening soft youngsters. The soldiers spoke of a world full of dangers and enemies. The militia policed the village, keeping an eye on class enemies and watching crops at night.[8]

The militia took orders from the commune armed-forces committee, made up of active-duty soldiers appointed by the county armed-forces department.[9] The county armed force fell under the prefectural military district, which belonged to the Hebei military region. In 1965 General Ma Hui became commander of the Hebei military region. He held this job, later combining it with top provincial party and government posts, for some two decades.

The militia line on training revolutionary successors embodied Defense Minister Lin Biao's views: selflessness and everything for the state, nothing for oneself. Boss Geng's fourth daughter, Huijuan, was a budding revolutionary successor. In 1964 she became the first Geng family member to graduate from senior high school. A lackluster academic record prevented her from moving up in a system based on competitive exams. But she scored high in politics. Huijuan was named deputy head of the village militia led by her neighbor, Macho Li Shouzheng.

Huijuan said that she might have been sold were it not for socialism. Her older sister was sold in the 1943 famine.[10] Chairman Mao, she proclaimed, therefore merited primary allegiance, more so than parents. With the center calling on educated youth to serve in the countryside, Huijuan declared she would not seek an urban job; she would merge with poor peasants. Locals scoffed at the heroics of the offspring of the powerful, knowing that nepotism propelled the wellborn.

The socialist education movement in part reflected Mao's concern that China's educated might stray onto the path of Hungary's Petofi Club students, who in 1956 helped lead a democratic revolution against communist dictator-ship, or, as Mao termed it, a counterrevolutionary restoration. Huijuan, re-sponding to Mao's concerns, denounced her education as bourgeois. She insisted that schools had almost turned her into a petty-bourgeois intellectual fretting over book learning instead of a revolutionary successor committed to class struggle. She mastered the lyrics of the fundamentalist chorus. Averring oneness with the poorest and vigilance against class enemies, she won the nickname Xiao Beng, little pump, for spouting off. Others called her "Xiao Bang," meaning ear of corn, a word that also means "to club" or "to cudgel."

In early 1964, returning from the fields, Huijuan chanced upon two young east-village women pouring human excrement into a manure pit. She saw an opportunity to prove herself a red successor covered with shit and thereby politically cleaner than a parasitic bourgeois. She moved toward the women, who were joking while working. Shit, Huijuan then noticed, had splattered on their hands and eyelids. She faltered. Her heart was not in dirty farm work.[11]

A young successor from the west village was handsome and articulate 18-year-old Li Zhongxin. He was a member of the southern Li lineage. But when the three production teams were demarcated, his home fortuitously fell into the west end, not the politically tainted center, home of the southern Li. Zhongxin was able to rise in a village leadership controlled by east- and west-end neighborhoods dominated by the northern Li, Geng, Qiao, Zhang, Xu, and Yang.

Like east-enders Macho Li Shouzheng and daughter Geng Huijuan, west-ender Li Zhongxin played a leading role in the 1964 militia and socialist education movements. In 1935 Zhongxin's veterinarian father, like millions of other North China residents, had fled to the economically dynamic, Japan-dominated northeast, accompanied by his wife from neighboring Gengkou village. Zhongxin was born in the northeast in 1946. He and his mother returned to Wugong in 1949. An elder brother became an elementary school teacher in Gengkou and later in the Wugong junior high. Zhongxin's father wanted the son to take an exam to get into a good school in the northeast. His mother wanted him to enter an agricultural college. But the Leap famine left education in shambles and Li too weak to study for exams.

Zhongxin experienced the closing of his school during the post-Leap depression as a denial of a career and a tragedy for country people. He identified with the promise of the Leap into communism. Returning to labor, he worked with large carts. His uncle, hard-drinking builder Li Lu, taught Zhongxin the building trade. He excelled in the campaign to "learn from Lei Feng," the selfless, martyred soldier loyal to Mao.[12]

Simmering Resentments

Despite Wugong's fame, many grievances simmered. Geng's commitment to revolution hurt villagers seeking cash. Villagers, to be sure, were patriots devoted to Mao. But humiliating poverty caused by selling scarce and under-priced basic crops to the state and forgoing cash crops was infuriating.

Young people craved the blessings of modernity. They wanted to be drivers, factory hands, administrators, anything providing a stepping stone out of village dirt and up to urban jobs on state payrolls that promised cash incomes, pensions, prestige, and a chance to travel. Young women hoped to be teachers, nurses, technicians, factory workers, performers, and artists. They too wanted to get out of the muck and mire. Collective labor producing grain for subsistence seemed like a dead end, earning a bare subsistence, the lot of losers, of unskilled illiterates.

In Raoyang, primary school students had increased only slightly, from 19,000 in 1949 to 23,963 in 1962. Junior high students had risen to 1,727. But fewer could advance to high schools or normal schools than in the 1950s. The Leap catastrophe, moreover, had forced many students to leave school. What future could they dream of?

To youth who enjoyed hitching rides to Raoyang town on Sunday, the "bad old days" were the early 1960s, when bellies grumbled, educational bubbles burst, dreams of better jobs went unfulfilled, and the newly implemented *hukou* system of locking families into villages barred all but the officially favored from leaving the countryside. There was a growing gap between a dissatisfied younger generation and elders for whom resisting Japanese aggression and restoring peace, order, subsistence, and national independence seemed achievement enough. The formation of poor and lower-middle peasant associations beginning in June 1964 held little promise for those hoping to rise through education or entrepreneurship.[13] Younger people chafed at hearing they were soft and selfish.

Villagers tended to a jaundiced view of ambitious activists held up as models of selflessness. What was called a campaign to foster revolutionary successors looked like feudal lords passing on an inheritance. To ordinary villagers, strutting activists seemed opportunists.

In the wake of the Leap debacle, intimate ties lent significance to daily lives. Daughter Huijuan's closest friends were neighbor Qiao Ban, a daughter of Qiao Wanxiang, a better-off member of the original 1943 coop, along with neighbor Shi Guiying, the aspiring writer, and neighbor Li Changfu, a deputy team leader who was raising five younger brothers following her mother's death. After supper Huijuan and Guiying often strolled over to help Changfu clean up and put the boys to sleep.

The problems of women were not central to a socialist analysis of exploitation. The three girlfriends shared their tribulations and dreams. At times Huijuan did not even go home. She and Changfu kept whispering on the *kang* until they fell asleep next to each other. Whatever Huijuan might have said in public as a red successor, villagers assumed that it was Changfu who knew what was in Huijuan's heart. But friendships with the powerful were suspect. People whispered that Changfu was fawning over Boss Geng's family to win favor.

Villagers worried when the reforms of 1960 to 1962 to energize the famine-stricken rural economy were cut short. Between 1962 and 1965 the state reduced by 6 percent the price it paid for products villagers were required to deliver. State investment in agriculture dropped from a peak of 21.3 percent of total investment in 1962 to 14.6 percent in 1965.[14] Nationwide, grain output in 1965 was no more than the output of 1957, while the population had increased by 80 million.[15] In Wugong, grain output dropped from 482 catties per mu in the reform year of 1962 to 410 in 1963, dipping to 370 catties in 1964, as total grain output fell to just 776,000 catties from 1,254,000 two years earlier. Per capita collective income fell from a high of 130 yuan in 1962 to 85 yuan in 1963 and 61 yuan in 1964. While output and income declined, state requisitions increased. Only 6 percent of Wugong's grain was sold to the state in the reform year of 1962, but the state took 9 percent in the flood-ruined year of 1963 and 7 percent in 1964, which had the worst harvest since the 1960 famine.

Commune officials were jittery about shipping out grain to the state. "If we cannot fulfill the task, we will be criticized by our superiors. If we finish the work, the peasants will curse us," one complained. "We are not afraid of any other work, we only fear grain requisition. It's impossible to express our bitterness."[16] For hungry villagers, of course, the bitterness was far greater. Officials worried about disturbances.

Socialist education was supposed to convince villagers of the virtues of an antimarket, collectivist economy that left field workers without cash income. Boss Geng won fame for telling didactic stories. In one tale a teenager who ran into Geng in the village's poorly run collective orchard remarked, "The apples are really beautiful."

"Do you know what used to be on this piece of land?" Geng asked. "No. Tell me," she answered, "What kind of tree was it?" Geng shot back, "Tree! This was a sand dune. When the wind blew you couldn't even open your mouth. How could there be trees?"

"Why didn't they grow apples then?" the youngster queried. "Who would grow them?" Geng snapped. "The old moneybags of a landlord would not let it be used for food. The poor didn't even own sand dunes. We didn't have enough to eat. Who could think of growing apples?" The girl was confused. "So who grew these trees?" she inquired.

Geng then inveighed against the fecklessness of youth. He asked why it was not enough that youngsters had sufficient food, basic schooling, and guaranteed employment, with time for an occasional movie. Because of the sacrifices of his generation, he went on, youngsters had no anxieties about landlords. Their future was secure. So why, Geng demanded, did they hanker after pretty clothes and the wherewithal to wash regularly and stay neat and clean and out of the shit and dirt?

Activists were told to praise those with the right attitude about hard work and grain requisitions. The youth league and militia collected stories about self-sacrifice. Geng spoke of 77-year-old Li Fengchun. Because Li and his wife were both over 70 and had no children, they were entitled to join the "five guarantee" households whose subsistence would be met by the collective. Notified of his eligibility in 1961, Li rejected social welfare, saying, "I'll work as long as I'm breathing." When the village tried to supplement his earnings, he declined.[17] The goal was to minimize claims on scarce collective resources.

Geng regarded Liu Yuqiao in team 2 as an example of revolutionary self-lessness. Born into a poor family in nearby Sangyuan village, she married into Wugong in 1945. During the recent dearth, Liu heard commune officials urge people to sell more grain to the state. "We have surplus grain," she said. "Come and take it." She went home and waited, but no one came. So she returned with her child to commune headquarters. "We thought you were joking," the official said. A work detail then bagged 1,000 catties of her grain to hand over to the state at low official prices. Neighbors gasped.[18] Villagers who complained about hardships were told to emulate selfless Li Fengchun and Liu Yuqiao. Geng and his wife, Xu Shukuan, mastered a politics of shaming. They prodded loyal old-timers to embarrass complainers.

Geng's socialist education work was recounted in an article, "New Years Past and Present," in the February 10, 1964, issue of *People's Daily*. It told holiday celebrants that in the old days, during the New Year, the children of landlords openly gorged on meat-filled dumplings, a sign that their lineage merited a good year. "Once my boy Delu saw a landlord's kid eating meat dumplings," Geng recollected. "So he ran home to ask the old lady to make him some. We didn't even have a speck of flour at home, so how could we make anything? He started to bawl, angering the old lady, who gave him a couple of backhanders."

It was no use, the article went on, trying to borrow New Year supplies from landlords. They would say, "You base-assed poor people want to eat dumplings!? You want to borrow from us, but how are you going to pay us back? No way!" Geng concluded that villagers now lived in paradise. "If it weren't for the party and Chairman Mao leading us poor people in the struggle for a new beginning [fanshen] in the fight against the landlords and in the movement to get organized and take the collective road, how could we enjoy days like this?" he asked. In the old society, there was a saying, "For families of landlords, New Year went well; for families of the poor, it was pure hell."[19] Despite the economic downturn and local discontent, Geng and Wugong would star in the state-directed drama of socialist education.

Class Struggle Wugong Style

A county socialist education work team arrived in Wugong in early 1964 to promote the revitalization of the poor and lower-middle peasant association. As in 1948, when outsiders wanted proof that the once poor were in power, village leaders manufactured poor and lower-middle peasants.[20] In the 1950s several rising activists, including west-ender Brains Zhang Chaoke, whose families belonged to such less than pure red categories as "prosperous middle peasant," had been reclassified to make it appear that they had more impoverished pasts. In 1964 the Wugong leadership again reexamined the classifications of party insiders and increased the number in poorer categories.

The tactic concealed the broad alliance of independent tillers fostered in the Communist Party's rise to power. By reclassifying politically favored middle peasants as "lower-middle" peasants, the village expanded the ranks of the "poor and lower-middle peasants" by another dozen households. Future party secretary Yang Tong and other west-village Yangs were reclassified from middle peasant to lower-middle peasant, legitimating their claims to power.

Wugong's leaders used the call to class struggle to solidify the position of friends and expand the ranks of the "poor." Many communities took the opposite tack, targeting enemies and manufacturing more rich people. By reclassifying a middle-peasant household as a rich-peasant or landlord household, activists could claim to unmask enemies of socialism. But villages split by party-manufactured vigilantism called "class struggle" were too divided to compete for state largesse.

Most Wugong households were treated according to their behavior, rather than by an ascribed class position. However, Wugong also had official pariahs, stigmatized and outcaste black elements, who, together with their spouses and children, were victimized as ritual scapegoats. Foremost among them was Li Maoxiu, who had served the communist-led anti-Japanese resistance. During the land reform, patriotic teenager Maoxiu, a landlord son, was struggled against as a landlord and in the early 1950s was sent to a labor camp for five years. His wife, Fan Shufang, was publicly shamed and beaten during the 1957 antirightist campaign.[21]

In the early 1960s, however, the Geng leadership urged villagers not to mistreat the children of black elements. Children who suffered discrimination would become troublemakers. Ancient wisdom was cited on behalf of contemporary prudence: "Trees must have bark, people need face."

Li Wei, the only son of Maoxiu, benefited. Wei started school in 1957, at the age of 12, after he and his mother returned to Wugong when Maoxiu was released from prison. On graduating from primary school, Wei was assigned to manual labor. Designated a landlord, he had to work harder. He studied machines and kept silent, eventually becoming an expert at repairing the diesel engines and electric motors that powered team 3's wells.

In 1963, at the age of 18, the six-foot-tall wiry strong mechanic sought to marry when national Youth League leader Hu Yaobang, a reformer, urged that law-abiding children of former landlords should be able to marry freely.[22] Without the reform, children designated as class enemies would either marry each other or see the family line end, a desecration of filial piety.

A go-between from Sangyuan village, two miles west, suggested as a wife for Wei the daughter of a party member and team leader named Zhao Gennian. Just as model villages tried to form links at higher levels, ordinary villages tried to network into model villages. Zhao had married his younger daughter to a member of the Raoyang public security bureau. He knew that marrying his older daughter into Wugong, even into a landlord family, could help him.

The prospective father-in-law went to check up on Wei. Zhao found a solid income earner whose uncle, Li Feng, was a party official in urban Dezhou. Wei did not seem like an endangered victim of discrimination. His parents' house was run down, but it had a sewing machine, a radio, and an antique wooden dresser. For this groom, Zhao need only provide a minimal dowry for his daughter.

As part of the wedding bargain, Wei set off for a five-day visit to his uncle in Dezhou, four hours away by rail in Shandong province. Red Li Feng had not returned to Wugong since 1952, when his younger brother, black Maoxiu, went to prison. A Korean War veteran, Li Feng helped run the newspaper *Dezhou Daily* and headed a junior high.

The bride, Zhao Dian, was a junior high graduate and political activist four years older than Li Wei. It was customary in the region for brides to be older than husbands. The following year, 1964, the first of three children, daughter Li Wenhua, was born. On registering the birth, officials handed the mother a form designating baby Wenhua's class status as "landlord." No one had told Zhao Dian. She had not heard of Li Maoxiu's imprisonment or Fan Shufang's beating. Outraged, Zhao Dian contemplated divorce. She soon learned there was no future for a divorced woman and her baby in a black landlord family. She was stuck for life.

Thinking stereotypically, daughter-in-law Zhao Dian concluded that Fan Shufang was a vicious mother-in-law who had taken advantage of Zhao's simple mother while her father remained aloof. Neighbors smiled as they heard Zhao Dian cursing her mother-in-law. No one told her that the two fathers had arranged the marriage. Neighbors said her father was a man who did not care what happened to a daughter, so long as he benefited and got her off his hands cheaply.

Cultural Connections

Mao Zedong, a poet, and his wife, Jiang Qing, a former actress, believed that cultural circles had become ideologically lax. In December 1963 Mao complained, "Even party members are enthusiastically promoting feudal and capitalist art but ignoring socialist art. This is absurd."[23] Thus, in the early phase of the socialist education movement urban artists and writers were sent to villages to taste bitter rural life. Favored artists went to model villages.

Immediately after the 1964 lunar New Year, 30 members of the Beijing Experimental Drama Troupe arrived in Wugong commune, half settling in

Wugong village, half in nearby Gengkou. Another team of actors from this unit was sent to the pacesetting Anshan steel works. Wugong was recommended by writer-official Wang Lin, who had taken a writing team to the model unit in 1963. Wang's wife, actress Liu Yanjin, was the leader of the group assigned to Wugong. She had spent much time in central Hebei during the resistance war. In 1962 she had starred in a low-budget black-and-white film, *A Blade of Grass on Kunlun Mountain* (Kunlun shan shang yi ke cao), playing a woman working at a desolate truck stop on the Tibet-Qinghai border who helps a frightened female graduate from Shanghai adjust to the rigors of frontier life.[24]

The actors were shocked by the poverty of the "poor peasant" homes in which they lived. Troupe members were told to cleanse themselves by doing dirty farm work. They put on short cultural performances during work breaks or after hours, if villagers requested. Some actors resented the back-breaking field work. "We should have been bringing culture to the countryside," one troupe member recalled, "but, instead, we spent our time adjusting to culture-less conditions."

Working in the fields with youth league go-getters could be humiliating. While some villagers helped them complete stoop labor tasks, others criticized their substandard work, never lifting a hand to aid the strangers. In the evening the city people, all party members, were required to read political documents to villagers.

A cultural gap separated actors and villagers. The urban men were embarrassed by elderly village women, stripped to the waist in the hot summer months, working nearby in the fields. "At first we could not bear to look," one said, "but later, of course, we got used to it."

The Beijing actors were surprised at how villagers openly raged against state grain requisitions. Villagers acknowledged that Geng was honest and did not steal, but they feared his hot temper and hated the meddling and dressing downs by his wife, Xu Shukuan. When actress Liu asked Tigress Xu why she did not visit people's homes to make critical comments quietly, Xu said, "If you don't point out people's shortcomings right on the spot, they'll deny everything later!"

The visitors saw that villagers still suffered from the 1963 flood. The actors had to hand over their urban grain-ration coupons and their cash salaries to the commune. In return, they ate in "poor peasant" households. The food was monotonous. Villagers ate rolls made of wheat flour only during the wheat harvest. "It was a big event," one actor recalled, "to buy a chunk of bean curd." Households slaughtered a pig and ate meat dumplings only during the New Year holiday. The outsiders saw small vegetable gardens in courtyards, but villagers were required to consume all they grew. Marketing was not allowed. The performers were kept from visiting the nearby Zoucun market alone. They could go only when a host family went.

The actors noticed that village youth, especially females, worked to impress leaders. Each morning a young women's "shock team" raced around the village collecting shit from more than 500 family latrines. The motivation of the activists "was to join the party."

On August 1, 1964, Army Day, famed author Yang Hansheng arrived. Writer-official Wang Lin, who sponsored the visit, had been feeding Yang information about Wugong. Yang was introduced as a hero of the Nanchang Uprising of August 1, 1927, that marked the founding of the Red Army. Youth league activists showed Yang their poems celebrating the daily chamber-pot collection. In the early 1960s Yang had written *Jiangnan in the North* (Beiguo jiangnan), a screenplay about a Hebei village during land reform and collectivization.[25] It featured a stubborn party secretary and his activist wife who angered villagers by demanding that they dig wells during the winter slack season.[26] Some bemused Raoyang viewers saw the husband and wife as Boss Geng and Tigress Xu.

The region's most famous storyteller, Sun Li, also visited in 1964. Born in 1913 in neighboring Anping county, he had worked in the central Hebei base during the anti-Japanese resistance.[27] Many of his stories took place near Raoyang. After Sun's visit young people read his novella *The Blacksmith and the Carpenter* (Tie mu qian zhuan). It was set in the early 1950s when the state encouraged small, voluntary mutual-aid teams and cooperatives. Sun's novella was published in 1957 during the Hundred Flowers liberalization. During the 1957–58 antirightist campaign, it was criticized. Sun's work stopped appearing in the literary supplement he once edited for *Tianjin Daily*. The more relaxed cultural atmosphere of the post-Leap reform years had permitted Sun, an early proponent of voluntary coops, to visit Wugong to gather material for a sequel to *The Blacksmith and the Carpenter*.

Village youth-league and militia activists benefited from exposure to cultural luminaries. Liu Yanjin was warmly known by Shi Guiying, the aspiring writer, as Teacher Liu. Village bedroom walls were adorned with charcoal portraits sketched by drama-troupe members. Villagers enjoyed a brightening of daily life made drearier by the state's war on popular culture, which was stigmatized as "feudal." A 1964 performance of *The White-Haired Girl,* a play about hope born in antilandlord struggle, remained a vivid memory for decades. The troupe brought color to dirt-poor lands and harsh toil, a world without television, toilets, running water, refrigeration, or sanitary napkins.

Before the drama troupe returned to Beijing in early fall 1964, an actor taught Handsome Li Zhongxin how to tell stories dramatically. By the end of 1964, Zhongxin was chosen to represent Raoyang at a competition in Hengshui. So well did he recite stories about the bad old days and how revolution brought the present sweet life that party secretary Zhang Duan chose him to represent Wugong at a 1965 competition in Beidaihe, summer home of China's rulers. At the end of 1965 articulate Li went to Hengshui to introduce an agricultural exhibition of Wugong's socialist successes. Accompanying the exhibit all over the prefecture, he did not return home until May 1966.

Shi Guiying was another cultural star. Cited in 1963 as a model worker for her talks at film presentations, her poem "Mengjie's Returned!" (glorifying her soldier fiancé) was published after Wugong's 20th-anniversary celebration.[28] She too had become a dramatic performer of the political script. In early 1965 she sang "In Praise of Our Team Leader" and "Our Team Leader Changed" at a provincial competition in neighboring Xingtai prefecture. She showed slides in the prefectual capital, Hengshui, to Politburo member Li Xiannian, the patron of Hebei governor Liu Zihou.

The patronage ties of Boss Geng helped. Thanks to the visiting luminaries, young Wugong activists were able to form a touring cultural troupe subsidized by the prefecture. It won a peculiarly warm reception in the prefectural capital, where urbanites ridiculed the bumpkinish sounds of an uncultured accent. Shi Guiying sang, performed kuaibar — a rhythmic comic monologue to the accompaniment of bamboo clappers — and dreamed of an acting career. The Wugong troupe also read poetry and put on plays. It was Raoyang's stellar attraction. One singer won admission to the Tianjin Arts Academy and a career in the big city. With household registration and internal passports locking people into their native village, travel was a happy privilege.

Politically astute and well-connected villagers moved ahead as promoters of revolution. But the socialist education campaign kept writer Sun Li from completing his sequel. Revolutionaries attacked the complexity of his characters, insisting on polarized portraits of class struggle, of pure good versus pure evil. In summer 1964 author Yang Hansheng was recalled to Beijing from Wugong. A campaign against *Jiangnan in the North* was under way as part of the socialist education movement.

5 ❖ A WHIFF

Wugong breezed through the start of the socialist education movement. It won fame by sticking to revolutionary fundamentals in agriculture, nurturing red successors, and maintaining its network of influential contacts.

The Taoyuan Model

In most of Hebei, the four cleanups followed the wishes of President Liu Shaoqi and provincial party secretary Lin Tie, rooting out corrupt officials who alienated villagers and slowed recovery. Stories had spread of local tyrants who ate well while villagers went hungry. Villagers bridled at the corrupt and cruel ways of local chiefs.

President Liu wanted party-organized investigative teams to root out corruption. He did not mobilize the poor as Chairman Mao preferred. Wang Guangmei, Liu's wife, investigated Taoyuan village in Funing county, a few hours from Beijing at the eastern tip of Hebei.[1] There, using the pseudonym Dong Pu, she headed a team reporting directly to the Central Committee. Wang was guided to a village notorious for abusive leaders. Lin Tie directed public security operatives to support her incognito work. But it was impossible to hide the entourage accompanying the wife of China's president. Her masked face, her haughtiness, and her large retinue led some to guess her identity. Lin Tie visited Taoyuan several times and addressed a conference on the four-cleanups movement.[2] In an investigation conducted from January to June 1964, the work team uncovered pervasive corruption; 40 of 47 brigade and team officials were publicly denounced for their crimes.

Outsiders do not easily learn about village life. In the wake of the Leap, President Liu found that even in his natal village only his own lineage spoke frankly to him. A senior official who had been with Chairman Mao during the resistance was shocked in the early 1960s when he walked into a rural home in search of reality. An elderly male immediately fell to his knees, groveled, and banged his head against the dirt floor in a traditional *ketou* of subordination. Villagers were terrified of criticizing local tyrants.

early March 1964, before the team completed its work in Taoyuan,
yang officials were ordered by the party's North China Bureau to initiate
ur cleanups," experienced locally as the second phase of the socialist educa-
n movement. County work teams were to bring "clean politics, clean economics, clean organization, and clean thought" to all dirty officials guilty of
the "four uncleans."[3] The emphasis was on cleaning out bourgeois elements in
the economy, that is, cracking down on noncollective activities, "capitalism."

Once the cleansing began, households in eastern Hebei that raised pigs and
chickens on marginal and waste land were no longer praised for overcoming
famine. Those who persisted in household sidelines were branded antisocialist. Local officials who did not ban household sidelines were attacked.

Zhang Kerang, once Hebei party secretary Lin Tie's agricultural specialist,
worked in the Rural Work Department of the party's North China Bureau. In
1964 Zhang was criticized for having pressured Dazhai's rising village leader,
Chen Yonggui, to support market-oriented policies. Raoyang party secretary
Li Chunyu was criticized for allowing some contracting of production responsibility to households. Attacking the policies that sped recovery from the Leap
disaster created a whiff of another catastrophe to come.

During collectivization in 1955 and 1956, the state had approved family
plots. The commune drive in 1958 eliminated them. To get agriculture going
again, in 1960 and 1961 most villages had restored household plots on 5
percent of land and some villages contracted collective lands to households.
Now in a fourth policy lurch in eight years, household plots were again forbid-
den. Having criticized Rural Work Department chief Deng Zihui as a proponent of household contracting in September 1962, Mao demanded action
premised on Lenin's dogma that a peasantry not producing for the collective
was a nascent petty bourgeoisie that would ineluctably give rise to a polarizing
capitalism.[4] Hengshui prefecture ordered work teams to end household plots.

Wugong had rejected the 1961 reform permitting household plots. By
early 1964 its prefecture, Hengshui, had eliminated household plots in one-
sixth of its villages. Even vegetables for household consumption were allowed
only on what were called "collectively cultivated private plots." Households
lost crops that could earn needed money in the market. Work teams were
instructed to stop families from planting vegetables in their courtyards, a
practice hitherto welcome even in collectivist Wugong village. Hungry, cash-
starved villagers bitterly resented impoverishing revolutionary policies.

As leaders warned of the subversion of socialism, Mao drew closer to Kang
Sheng, the public security chief whose files purportedly documented traitors
to socialism within the party. Mao invited Kang to offer ideas to prevent a
rollback of revolution in China.[5]

Chinese were warned that Yugoslavia had restored capitalism. So had the
Soviet Union. Unless China rooted out all seeds of that evil, such as work for
family gain, household sideline production, and marketing to increase in-

come, revolutionaries claimed, capitalist roots would grow into killer weeds and strangle tender sprouts of socialism. Villagers whose livelihood would suffer were told that the alternative to uprooting capitalism was treason, betrayal of all that the poor had won through decades of sacrifice.

In response to a prefectural call for an anticapitalist four-cleanups mobilization, in March 1964, Raoyang county party secretary Li Chunyu organized 335 county officials to lead the second phase of the socialist education movement.[6] For the second time in three months, county work teams visited every commune and village. The party monitored itself. This campaign, like the one in January, was brief and uneventful. In the eyes of Raoyang county leaders, official corruption was not a big problem.

In some counties, the campaign was protracted and bloody, involving thousands of investigators. In Tongxian, in suburban Beijing, it lasted for more than a year. More than 100 people were beaten and 70 attempted suicide, 50 successfully. In suburban Tianjin, a work team that included fundamentalist theorist Chen Boda targeted three so-called counterrevolutionary cliques, led respectively by a rice specialist, a female labor model, and a township party secretary.[7] In Raoyang, token self-criticisms sufficed.

Wugong breezed through the March 1964 investigation, as it had in January. It sent the state lots of grain. Its leaders, Geng insisted, did not pilfer. As for "capitalism," the village had not diverted any collective land. It had instead slashed even collective sidelines and discouraged household sidelines. Geng loved talking about vegetable grower Li Qingxiang, whose wife urged him to plant in the family yard to sell in the market. But Li stuck with the collective vegetable plot.[8] Wugong was clean. Its cohesion and state-supported irrigation facilitated collective work. Eliminating household plots could, however, be disastrous in places where collectives and corrupt leaders were discredited.

Yet, even Wugong had to soften the pain of revolution. Household imperatives had to be met. When cotton shrubs were distributed in winter for fuel, some cotton was left for family clothing. To remain legitimate, leaders both resisted the state's irrational rules and also embraced revolutionary socialism.

Higher levels advised Wugong to abandon its quota system for rewarding labor. Under the 1954 plan devised by the recently purged adviser Lu Guang, workers were credited for tasks. Surpassing quotas won bonuses. The incentive system, suspended at the start of the Leap, returned in 1960 to reinvigorate labor. But revolutionaries charged that quotas encouraged acquisitiveness. In 1964 Hebei province dubbed quotas and bonuses antisocialist.[9]

The four cleanups carried out in Taoyuan village by Wang Guangmei was different. It found that "officials of the brigade openly take things, production team officials steal, and the commune members are forced to sew up the officials' [trouser legs]," that is, pay bribes. She concluded that "the four uncleans exist universally among the cadres. All of them, big or small, have problems and cannot be trusted." When higher levels ratified her findings,

...e party secretary, Wu Chen, charged with 31 beatings and ...vas expelled from the party and branded a "bad element." His ...ed a "major corrupt cadre." Leaders were ousted from office at ...and the militia head became party secretary.[10]

...iited about among Hebei party insiders was that when officials ...Wang introduced a torture known as the jet plane. The body of ...rained to the breaking point by his being made to stand for ...it knees and arms pulled straight back. Confessions were extracted. In August 1964 Mao endorsed Wang's report and supported theorist Chen Boda's suggestion that it be circulated.[11]

That touched off attacks on corruption throughout the countryside. President Liu, drawing on the Taoyuan experience, estimated that no less than 60 or 70 percent of Hebei was "under the control of enemies." Liu ordered work teams to use draconian measures to deal with the crisis.[12] In September he generalized the Taoyuan approach, ordering outside work teams to shake rural power to its foundations. Teams had to stay in villages for six months if necessary and deal severely with offenders.[13]

"We Don't Have Any Problems"

In October, in response to new North China Bureau and provincial directives, Raoyang county party secretary Li Chunyu sent work teams to carry out a third phase of the socialist education/four-cleanups movement. This time teams would not investigate their own county. Raoyang officials went to Hengshui, Jixian, and Gucheng counties in Hengshui prefecture. Altogether Li dispatched 531 officials. The Raoyang contingent was led by Li Chunyu himself and three deputy party secretaries in "a great military campaign" against class enemies.[14]

A temporary Standing Committee of six, led by deputy party secretary Chai Rui and including military representative Li Guoqiang, administered the county. Throughout Hebei the military was rising, as indicated by the appointment of a military representative to the Standing Committee of the Raoyang party. One hundred and twenty thousand provincial officials and intellectuals, organized in small work teams, fanned out across the countryside. Each prefecture received more than 10,000 investigators. Some 18,000 concentrated in the key point county of Xincheng. Many villages were investigated for the first time since the 1947 land reform.

The political atmosphere was infused with patriotic pride and survivalist paranoia. On October 16 China announced the explosion of an atomic bomb. The event swelled national pride but also heightened the danger of preemptive attack. Mao urged Chinese to keep socialism (here meaning anti-imperialist patriotism) alive in every locale.

Hengshui prefectural authorities divided counties into those that would get a "once over lightly" (cu) treatment during a relatively short period and those that would be investigated intensively (xi). The teams led by Raoyang party secretary Li went where the campaign would be intensive. Raoyang villages, however, received only a light going-over.[15]

Hengshui prefecture assigned Yuan Kejian to lead a team of three to Wugong commune. Members were young and inexperienced. Cang Tong, a 30-year-old nonparty member, was assigned to Wugong village. Cang was a Raoyang native, born in Zhaizicun village. His grandmother was from Wugong, and he still had relatives there. A graduate of a Roman Catholic junior high in neighboring Xianxian county and Shijiazhuang Transportation College, Cang held a minor administrative post in Hengshui in 1962.

Cang Tong was not alone in Wugong. Learning that the village was to be subjected to a light "once-over" investigation, Wugong's old friend, writer-official Wang Lin, recommended to Hengshui prefecture that the Beijing Experimental Drama Troupe, led once again by his wife, actress Liu Yanjin, return to Wugong in October to help. A team of 15 had already resettled in Wugong when outsider Cang arrived. Wang Lin meant to protect Boss Geng and Wugong.

Geng, a delegate to the first session of the Third National People's Congress convened in Beijing in December 1964, left the village shortly after outsider Cang arrived. The two met briefly. Cang told us that Hengshui instructed him to isolate local officials, rely on the poor peasants, deal with abuses by mobilizing the masses, and make use of "large crowds and a lot of noise" (da hong da wang). Cang had been warned that most village leaders were corrupt and that powerless villagers would not risk the wrath of the powerful by exposing cruelty and avarice. In the Hengshui version of the Taoyuan model, the corrupt were to be humiliated and then forced to repay all they had stolen. Confiscated property would be put on public display, as during land reform. Justice would be done, the public treasury enriched, leaders cleansed, and the corrupt party and exploited villagers reconciled; collectives would flourish.

During his first meeting with Wugong party secretary Zhang Duan the Ox, Cang explained that he would investigate corruption involving grain, work points, accounts, and other abuses. This required checking the records and regularizing bookkeeping. Zhang explained to Cang that Geng did not even accept collective grain coupons for time spent at the National People's Congress. The warning about honest Geng's power was clear. With the Boss away, Zhang defended the village.

Following the Taoyuan model, Cang and the actors temporarily suspended the village party branch. Cang set up office in the "clubhouse," once the southern Li lineage hall. The investigators contacted the village poor and lower-middle peasant association, encouraging villagers to speak out: "Most people were passive," Cang recalled. "Few were willing to say anything. And the few who spoke up were rarely influential. But gradually the ranks of the outspoken expanded." According to Cang, the actors from Beijing "were very enthusiastic about bringing out the people's criticisms."

The investigators lived with the once poor. Cang moved in with Li Yuqing in team 2, the southern Li lineage team with the weakest bonds to the leadership. As with the 1947 land reform, the strategy was to have the alienated speak bitterness. In 1947 a young Zhang Duan, now village party secretary, had cooperated with an outside work team.

The focus of the campaign in Wugong was not senior brigade leaders like Geng Changsuo or Zhang Duan. It was neighborhood officials. The targeted found that the charges came from malcontents with grudges. Cang and the actors tried to scare the accused leaders at a closed door meeting.[16] "When you're trying to mobilize the masses," Cang acknowledged, "you have to use excessive language." Insisting they were "unclean," Cang demanded that all leaders "wash their hands" and confess to stealing public food and property, violating laws and regulations, and embezzling funds. Critic Geng Xiufeng described Cang's methods as beating "the hell out of the branches regardless of whether there were any dates on them."

Defending Wugong, party secretary Zhang urged leaders to remain silent and admit to nothing. "We don't have any problems," one protested, "but he [Cang Tong] makes us do self-criticisms day in and day out. When will it end? It seems as though you're automatically guilty once you become an official."

Those who failed to confess to corruption in neighboring Zoucun were forced to stand in the cold November air night after night. The targeted party secretary swore that when the campaign was finally over he would quit. "If anyone asks me to work again, I'll kill myself."

In Wugong, Cang Tong told the intellectuals from Beijing they were too soft. "You don't have the stomach for it. In Huanghua we had our own methods of doing things. People were hung up and beaten. The 'shaking balls of coal' (yao mei qiu) torture was used." That is, a target was encircled and smashed by people on one side until he began to fall toward the other side, which then pounded him until he fell in the other direction. It was likened to shaking coal balls in a bamboo sifter. The punishment continued until the victim confessed or lost consciousness.

Cang also referred to the "slow-cooked eagle" torture (au ying), which denied people sleep until they confessed. Known as the "wheel-battle" torture (che lun zhan) in the Soviet Union, this inhumanity reminded villagers of the way eagles were tamed and trained by sleep deprivation. Finally, Cang called attention to the most ruthless torture, a slow burning to death known as "peeling skin off the back" (bo bei tiao). "We have plenty of ways," Cang told the actors. "We're not the least bit afraid they won't confess. Can you handle that?"

Many tortures were creations of the 1940s, the fruit of the brutal war with Japan and the party's 1947–48 terrorizing land reform. The abominations were meted out in darkness so a survivor or his family would not know whom to target for revenge.

Cang suggested to Wugong party secretary Zhang that the village militia tie up some leaders. However, the militia commanded by Macho Li Shou-zheng would not move against Geng allies. Without the militia, Cang could not employ force.

On the night Boss Geng returned from Beijing, Cang called a meeting that included all village officials. Cang proclaimed, "When I arrived at the edge of the village, the peasants told me there isn't one good official in the village." Geng shot back, "Don't invent a lot of rubbish." Geng told officials not to confess to things that never happened. After the meeting Cang went to Geng's home, saying that he was "young and inexperienced." Geng also apologized. "I wasn't in the village and didn't know the situation." Besides, "Young people are naturally daring in thought and action."

Villagers finally began to point to abuses by lower officials. In midwinter Cang called a public meeting to announce charges. Team 1 leaders Li Yantian and Wei Shujuan stood accused of pilfering 90 catties of stored grain.[17] Li, an east-end leader since the founding of a villagewide coop in 1952, was alleged to have kept much grain in reserve for corrupt, personal consumption instead of distributing more to households.

Cang claimed that Li had picked up two cloth sacks for his own use and taken two wooden poles to support a wall of his house. Cang also announced problems in team 1's accounting and work-point system. Team leader Li gave himself 270 work points for 1964 but, Cang claimed, Li had rewarded himself merely for shuffling paper. Cang proposed reducing Li's work points by 200. Moreover, Cang exclaimed, Li was a notorious womanizer.[18] Cang insisted that Li be tied up and put on display. But Zhang the Ox dismissed the charges as empty rumors. Zhang told militia leaders to ignore Cang. Nor would the recently activated poor and lower-middle peasant association rough up the accused Li. Party secretary Zhang's resistance enhanced his stature as a defender of the community.

Cang got a slew of team officials to confess to petty corruption. He expressed shock that Xu Shukuan, Geng's wife, a deputy head of team 1, had piled up more than 300 work points. "An old woman with bound feet cannot be allowed to tally so many work points." It was bad for morale. Who would believe the figures? Cang demanded that 200 points be deducted.[19]

A search of account books revealed that Li Zhimin, team 3 treasurer since 1961, had sold vegetables to a purchasing agent from Hengshui prefecture but had not recorded the money received. Treasurer Li was already suspected for 80 cents worth of reimbursement (a day's wages) with no clear purpose recorded. Li shouted that the 80 cents was repayment for a personal outlay for an office paper cutter. He also insisted that the cash for the vegetables arrived early the next year and was properly recorded. Cang responded, "Your case is not cleared. You are sent upstairs." That is, Li was suspended on suspicion of corruption.

To Wugong leaders, Zhang Duan heroically resisted a meddling outsider. But Cang did discover abuses. Eventually most team-level officials confessed to some peculation. Team 1 leaders had a habit of eating collectively grown peanuts whenever they wanted a snack. They were ordered to reimburse the collective. Xu Yizhou, a pioneer guerrilla leader from the west end who had angered Boss Geng in 1953 when he opposed organizing a villagewide coop as too gigantic to be efficient, and who for the next decade had been relegated to the unproductive collective fruit orchard, had wheeled home a broken cart from the orchard and used that collective property for about a month for light jobs around the house. Xu admitted his unclean act, suggesting a fine of 50 yuan, many months' earnings. The assembled villagers found the sum ridiculously high. The act seemed petty. Xu merely received a warning.

The most serious complaints focused on Xu Lianzheng, the team 3 leader. During the hungry, cold winters of the recent dearth, west enders suffered when Xu forced them to dig out virtually inedible sweet potatoes and peanuts from frozen ground, instead of allowing them to benefit from reform opportunities. They also faulted Xu's favoritism in assigning jobs and bridled at his bullying and beatings. "When he exploded, your blood ran cold," one team member said.

Cang sought proof that Xu stole from the collective and sided with the once rich. West-enders reported that Xu had borrowed an animal from the collective to mill his own flour and given a factory job to Li Zongxian, a son of war hero Li Fengxiang. Xu brushed off the trivial accusations.

Simmering anger at Xu's callousness during the dearth, however, incited a desire to get him. West-enders believed that he got a kickback on a sweetheart contract for 17 team 3 pigs at the Zoucun market. How else to explain his return from the market with a plump porker? Villagers complained that he paid ten yuan below the going price of 40 yuan for average-size hogs. Xu denied it. "I paid 35 yuan and it was market value." Zhang the Ox defended Xu: "Pay no attention. Just continue your work."

Heeding Zhang, Xu refused to mount the stage or criticize himself. His web of local ties, the informal political structure that grew stronger whichever line won at the state center, made him invulnerable to the pinpricks of a junior, nonparty outsider. In the era of war and revolution, Xu had headed the small coop of Xu Zhuan, brother of revered village martyr Xu Dun. Although Xu Lianzheng was not a party member, his wife, Qiao Wenzhi, Wugong's first female party member, had headed women's work for more than two decades. She was a member of the Qiao lineage, Boss Geng's close ally since the first coop in the 1940s, another strand in the web of silklike threads binding the east with the west. Xu Lianzheng's brother-in-law was administrator Qiao Li-guang, Geng's "good aide" whose story was featured in the 20th-anniversary book celebrating the model village.[20] Xu was finally docked five yuan (a few weeks' earnings), the heaviest village fine.

Zhang Duan criticized himself for eating collective fruit, for taking a cucumber from the collective fields, and for twice dining lavishly with dignitaries at village expense. But the party secretary felt it was he who was wronged. After all, he never took gifts. And visiting officials had to be feted. He angrily told his wife that in the future he would make certain he was always above suspicion. No matter how bad the pain in his head and his need for quiet, he would never again walk through the tranquil fruit orchard unless the fruit was not yet ripe and was, therefore, obviously still inedible.

Given its unified leadership and ties to power, Wugong survived unscathed. Petty officials confessed to minor indiscretions. In most villages, work teams unearthed far more corruption, although many troubled units were never inspected. Poor Yanggezhuang, north of Wugong, riven by clique, lineage, and party faction conflict, had thieving, brutal leaders. But it was not investigated in fall 1964.

In an earlier phase of the four cleanups, Liu Zhe, a Red Army veteran from Raoyang and a war buddy of Yanggezhuang party leader Bai Zhongxi, who had joined local guerrillas in 1938 at the age of 16, looked into Yanggezhuang. Bai believed in big collectives. In early 1956 he joined Yanggezhuang with another village in a megacollective that was not broken up until after the Eighth Party Congress in September. He became party secretary in 1963. He attended Wugong's 20th-anniversary celebration but found no way to emulate Wugong, lacking its state-funded access to water. Bai was removed from office for theft in an early stage of the four cleanups. But he was restored to office by his cronies. Entrenched networks of unaccountable power did not easily disintegrate.

In Zoucun, the market village east of Wugong, the work team temporarily removed the entire leadership for preferring to get rich in the market to toiling in low-paying collective agriculture. In fact, Zoucun's economy had stagnated since collectivization. Its market shriveled after a war on commerce began in the early 1950s. Resistance, in the form of black-market activities, seemed a matter of family survival.

One Zoucun tiller began biking to Wugong early in the morning to earn a few pennies cutting hair in a shed near the village crossroads before peddling back to Zoucun for a day of compulsory collective labor. Because people had little cash, the barber had little business. Yet he cherished that small amount of real money. The more the state locked villagers into the stagnant collective, the more they resisted, looking for and legitimizing any other means, legal or not, to earn cash.

In November 1964, just after county party secretary Li Chunyu headed off to Hengshui with a Raoyang "combat brigade" to carry out a thorough cleanup, word came that critical-minded Geng Xiufeng's request for early

ment from his commune job had been granted. In retirement, Xiufeng
close track of the Li Chunyu "combat brigade." It did not return to
ing until spring 1966. Whereas outsider Cang only *talked* about using
e in Wugong, Xiufeng claimed that "when Raoyang party secretary Li
led a team to Hengshui to carry out a 'thorough' four cleanups, in one 17-day
period he caused the death of 18 people." Powerless villagers were fodder for
ambitious officials. "There is a historical pattern here: higher-ups feel they can
squash the peasants under their heels whenever they want and the peasants
will never have an opportunity to strike back."[21]

Politics of Restoration

In late 1964 Boss Geng Changsuo hastened to Hengshui to complain to
prefectural party secretary Gao Jian about "phony charges." Gao had hidden in
Wugong during Japanese raids in the 1940s and had served as Raoyang party
secretary in the mid-1950s. Geng's friend Chen Yonggui, leader of fast-rising
Dazhai village in Shanxi, went to see Mao Zedong to register his own complaints about work teams targeting Dazhai.[22]

Mao soon urged an alternative to the Liu Shaoqi/Wang Guangmei way
of ferreting out corruption in Taoyuan. Mao denounced concentrated inva-
sions as human sea tactics.[23] People loyal to theorist Chen Boda ran the four-
cleanups campaign in Tianjin. Mao pointed approvingly to a Tianjin-area
village experience that had been popularized by Chen Boda in *Red Flag*.

At Beidaihe in late summer 1964 Mao summoned Hebei governor Liu
Zihou and asked what he thought about the Taoyuan experience. Liu replied
that it was helpful. The response angered Mao. He was eager to mobilize class
struggle in order to seize power from enemies and forge a generation committed to revolution. In late 1964, as reports from places like Hengshui
reached the center, Mao complained again that the Taoyuan focus on corruption was too narrow, the penalties on local leaders too harsh. Worst of all,
Taoyuan-style work teams bypassed the masses.[24]

In January 1965 Mao drafted "Twenty-three Articles," inaugurating a fourth
and final phase of the socialist education movement, highlighting revisionism
(capitalist backsliding). Instead of lowly village team leaders, Mao would
attack top leaders, labeled "capitalist roaders." After Mao chided the Hebei
governor for overemphasizing an experience in which lower leaders were
deposed, work teams dared not overthrow local authorities.[25]

In January 1965 Cang Tong left Wugong, derided as a meddler foiled by
heroes. The prefectural party committee immediately sent someone to Wugong to "correct mistakes." Cang returned to Hengshui and rose in the bureau
of communications. Actress Liu Yanjin and the troupe from Beijing left Wugong after the 1965 lunar New Year.

The Raoyang party committee, still headed by Chai Rui in party secretary Li

Chunyu's absence, followed Mao's directions. With the help of 7 provincial and 31 prefectual officials, in early 1965 Chai organized 273 Raoyang officials into small work teams. For the fourth time in 12 months, teams visited every commune in the county, this time to propagate Mao's "Twenty-three Articles."

Thousands of cases of corruption were said to have been exposed in Raoyang during the four cleanups. The offenders included 318 county-level officials, 595 at the commune level, including economic officers and teachers, and 7,889 village- and team-level officials. Fines totaling more than 200,000 yuan in cash and property were assessed and more than 100,000 catties in penalty grain collected.[26] But the old leadership retained its grip on power. In Wugong, the targeted Li Yantian, Xu Shukuan, and Xu Lianzheng resumed office.[27]

Occasionally, however, serious offenders were punished. In Shengli village, five miles northeast of Wugong, party secretary Li Qi was charged with embezzlement and brutality. He was sacked and ordered to repay all his ill-gotten spoils. Since the money had already been spent, Xu Fu, a brash 29-year-old Raoyang county official, ordered Li to surrender his wife's dowry, including a wooden dresser and several big wooden boxes. When this proved insufficient, Xu commandeered the coffin the embezzler had prepared for his elderly mother, then ordered the militia to tear down one room of Li's house and confiscate the valuable beams. Li Qi would repay his debt to the people.

But frightened villagers seldom reported on the inhumanities of tough power holders. In one Raoyang community, villagers told each other, a toppled leader confessed and was then reinstated. Revenge on his accusers swiftly followed. In another place, villagers criticized party leaders but were too terrified and humiliated to turn on the militia chief, a serial rapist. The system was deeply entrenched.

Wugong leaders soon learned that team 3 leader Xu Lianzheng, outsider Cang Tong's main target, had once sent an agent with 7,000 yuan to buy dyes in Tianjin for a team 3 sideline. Four thousand yuan disappeared. The Wugong party, anxious not to alienate villagers or to leave itself vulnerable to ill-willed outsiders, removed Xu as team 3 leader. He was demoted to head a small production group within the team. Another Xu lineage member, an old guerrilla fighter, Xu Mantang, took over as team leader, with Li Wer, a real go-getter, albeit not a party member, remaining as deputy leader, and increasingly the real leader. In Wugong, the leadership remained united.

In many villages investigations degenerated into vigilantism. Factions fought based on old group identities and divisions. In the many localities where the leadership split and the militia incarcerated and tortured accused leaders, village unity unraveled, leaving vengeful leaders and fearful villagers little basis for any future trust.

An unanticipated consequence of sending educated urbanites to clean up villages was the creation of many tens of thousands of young people like Cang Tong who returned to urban homes to spread a story of a reversal of revolutionary gains in the countryside. Their stories pictured a manichean conflict pitting hated entrenched officials against heroic young fighters for the masses. The returned intellectuals reported pervasive cruelty and corruption and a populace too intimidated to attack new oppressors. People were poor beyond belief, the returned youngsters said, because corrupt officials abused their power. It hardly seemed that a revolution had occurred.

Party rulers were said to be greedy and capitalistic, like those in Zoucun. Officials were so deeply rooted, as in Wugong, that people feared disclosing violence and plunder. Villagers suffered silently. A composite picture portrayed idealistic educated youth battling ignorant party authorities taking the capitalist road. When they read of heroic events in Cuba or Vietnam, these young people dreamed of proving themselves true to revolutionary ideals, superior to the older generation that called them soft.

These young, sincere, often humiliated or defeated urban youth returned to cities and towns to interpret societal dynamics in terms of Mao's obsession with preventing capitalist restoration. Mao seemed right in insisting bold action was needed to save socialism.

Similar alienation and anger grew among the children of highest leaders. With access to translations of foreign literature that were off-limits to ordinary people, they read Salinger's *Catcher in the Rye,* Kerouac's *On the Road,* and almost anything else they found that derided suffocating conformity. Such children also had access to the fruits of the Khrushchev-era thaw. They delighted both in the new literature and such movies as *A Soldier's Story.* They also read works showing the evils of fascism and the Soviet system, such as William Shirer's book on the Third Reich and Anna Louise Strong's study of the Stalin era. What they found was that China suffered similarly. Thus, all over China increasing numbers of educated youth concluded that China's socialism negated their ideals. Outsiders like Cang Tong were shocked by their encounters with rural backwardness and entrenched corruption.

That, however, was not how village party elites saw it. Across the countryside, local officials, many of whom had risen in the anti-Japanese resistance and consolidated their positions during land reform, were furious at higher party officials who had scapegoated them and at villagers who pointed fingers at them. Many ordinary villagers raged not because revisionists thwarted revolution but because they were forced to do profitless collective labor and to deliver grain to the state at outrageously low prices. The successor generation of village youth-league and militia activists was also frustrated, having been denied opportunities outside the village during the dearth and been thwarted in their desire to rise no matter how hard they worked. There were great divisions in China. Based on selective memory, each group would respond in its own way to Chairman Mao's subsequent call to "bombard the headquarters" in an all-out struggle called the Cultural Revolution. With the campaigns of 1963 to 1965 there was a whiff of savage violence to come.

6 ❧ RIDING HIGH

The clash between revolution and reform was still not obvious to Raoyang village leaders. Both lines sought to root out corruption and restore confidence in the party. Both supported the experience of the national model village of Dazhai. In Raoyang county, village leaders invoked the language of survivalism and class struggle while attempting to meet practical needs through improved water control, housing, and education.

Learning from Dazhai

In Beijing in December 1964, Dazhai village leader Chen Yonggui, a delegate to the National People's Congress, made headlines by meeting with Premier Zhou and Chairman Mao. Friends with Chen since 1961, Geng Changsuo, also a delegate, went to Chen's room and, fruitlessly, knocked. Geng found Chen in the dining room eating with Xing Yanzi, a female labor model. During the congress Premier Zhou proclaimed that Dazhai embodied "the principle of putting politics in command. That meant self-reliance, hard struggle and loving both the country and the collective."[1]

After the congress, Geng went to Dazhai. For three winter days, Chen escorted Geng by jeep all over the region. Geng invited Chen, who would soon become a vice premier, to visit Wugong. Geng knitted ties with leaders Li Chunyu and Chai Rui in Raoyang, Gao Jian in Hengshui, Lin Tie in Tianjin, and village pacesetters who knew how to tap scarce state resources.

Soon traveling to Dazhai were Wugong production specialist Zhang Chaoke, party secretary Zhang Duan, and administrator Qiao Liguang.[2] In 1965 Wugong leaders announced they had learned from Dazhai the spirit of class struggle and self-reliance. They claimed that back-breaking toil in the winter of 1964–65 to irrigate, level land, dig wells, and expand collective pig production was emulating Dazhai.

Dazhai chose not to chop down a beautiful willow tree, sup-

71

posedly to remind red successors of the lashings and hangings meted out there by landlords. Wugong then proclaimed that it too would preserve a formerly barren piece of land to give youngsters a lesson in class education. The plan would protect the shady cemetery, the loveliest spot in Wugong (a lover's lane, some said), a sacred place for all lineages, the geomantically favored former burial ground of the old elite southern Li lineage. The language of class struggle could protect the sacred. Revolution could also embody resistance.

Water

The 1963 flood dramatized the urgency of water control. After flying over the ravaged area on October 17, 1963, Mao's proclamation, "Control the Hai River," legitimated a claim on state resources for flood prevention.[3] Yet the Dazhai-inspired campaign to expand farmland in Hebei hill regions, to "get grain from rocks," intensified deforestation and increased the risk of flood.[4]

Water conservancy was a central task of the state throughout Chinese history. North China had long staved off famine by combating drought and flood. The Kangxi emperor (1654–1722) placed water at the heart of official tasks and the people's livelihood.[5] Still, the water problem was chronic. From 1964 to 1966 specialists surveyed Hebei water resources, focusing on the Hai River basin. Hydrologists studied sources of sweet and salt water, the rivers, and the weather and then suggested how to optimize long-term use of water with an eye to flooding, agriculture, industry, consumption, and transportation.

Dismissing the scientists, revolutionaries launched a mass campaign to mobilize labor to fight flood and expand irrigation. With help from Beijing, Hebei launched a 15-year project to control the Hai. Each year 300,000 to 500,000 young males were sent to dredge and build reservoirs. Almost a million more worked on local projects with picks, shovels, and wheelbarrows. Without careful geological exploration, without action premised on hydrological science and integrated programs tied to investing in steel and cement, vast labor efforts were wasted. Floods in Raoyang ended, but the water table plummeted, making irrigation ever more costly. River-borne travel to Tianjin for trade, seasonal jobs, and family visits became impossible.

Villages sent young men to water-conservancy projects during the winter slack season. Living outdoors and doing heavy labor for up to three months was seen as immoral for females. The yin-yang cosmology prevailing in North China held that women brought bad luck to water work. A pollution taboo was strong in Raoyang.

The ambitious fought for the honor of working on a project blessed by Mao. Leaders of work gangs were often sons of red families. At the same time, young men not born red and those inheriting political problems were dragooned into the back-breaking toil. For them it was punishment for the sins of sires. From his early teen years, Li Wei, the son of Wugong "landlord" Li Maoxiu, was forced to participate. "My son had to go every year," Maoxiu recalled. "For the ten years of the project, he went there eleven times. Why do I say this was punishment by heavy labor? Because it was very hard work and the food was poor. Nobody really wanted to go and work there." None dared complain. Some hoped service would better family status. Villagers soon realized, however, that behavior was irrelevant. The class designations reified in the 1948 land reform had hardened into castelike strata.

One coerced 16-year-old Raoyang villager failed at pushing dirt-filled carts up steep muddy inclines from dawn to dusk. Unable to fill his quota of moved earth and fearing a whipping, he fled. Those caught escaping were hung from a tree, lashed, and left dangling. This fortunate youth got home safely and was shielded.

In the winter of 1965–66, 270,000 people in 297 Hebei villages were moved to make way for the project. Villages were ordered to evacuate a year before construction began. Officials told villagers they would benefit from relocation. Those who could not move in with relatives were promised comparable land. Some took apart, carried away, and rebuilt their houses brick by brick, beam by beam. Elders dismantled graves and dug up remains for reburial. But villages were rebuilt on marginal land. No good uncultivated soil existed. The state's pledge could not be honored. The dislocated were promised "five-guarantee" treatment so that living standards would stay at the average for the place where they resettled. The buck was passed to team officials, who had the impossible task of squeezing resources from impoverished locals to support destitute migrants.[6]

Beginning in 1964, a well-drilling campaign was launched across North China. Water increased grain production. But as the water fled, deeper drilling required more labor and higher costs. Mass mobilization took priority over cost accounting that could indicate actual economic results.

Fresh water was easily found in Wugong's east and southeast. However, Geng Changsuo insisted that drilling proceed in the northwest whatever the cost, as only with water for high, stable yields for all could the village hope to preserve harmony and meet the high grain deliveries the state demanded of a model. Ignoring prevailing opinion to drill where there was water, in winter 1963 Geng again ordered drilling in the sandy, alkaline northwest. Later, he told us, "Sometimes you need to practice democracy and sometimes to use force."

The first well was dry. So it was with a second and a third. Geng's obstinacy was costly. A fourth hole was sunk near the barn. It too went down dry to 100 meters, to 150, 200, and even 250 meters. The drill hit sweet water at 270 meters. The whole village could soon be irrigated. Drought would no longer intensify intravillage tensions. Geng saw coerced labor mobilization as a fount of unity and bounty.

Starting in the 1950s the press had presented Wugong's accomplishment in tapping water as persuading villagers of the superiority of collectivism. The first primitive wells of the 1950s were soon replaced by ceramic and wood-lined wells, which then gave way to cement and iron pipe, all with great (and unmentioned) state assistance to the model village.

Recovery from the Leap famine had been aided by an electric generator, a gift from provincial party secretary Lin Tie. It ran the pumps that irrigated the fields. Yet even with all the help, grain produciton in 1964 was the lowest since the 1960 dearth. Villagers had to draw down reserves and eat more low-quality coarse grains.

In 1965 Raoyang county began tying into the state electric power grid. Wu-gong's patrons in the provincial capital in Tianjin dispatched a well-drilling team to guarantee it more fresh water. It cost Wugong 4,000 yuan per well and took 10 to 15 drilling days to reach water. Five new mechanized wells were sunk.[7] By the end of 1965 there were 2,000 mu of irrigated land. Villagers dug 40 irrigation ditches, ignoring complaints that partially grown millet was destroyed in the process. Wugong's former sandy soil with gullies and ruts vanished; in spring the village offered a vista of green. The state rewarded greater grain deliveries with more chemical fertilizer, which it monopolized, assuring yet higher yields. Neighboring villages were envious of Wugong's success but cynical about claims of self-reliance. Zoucun villagers muttered, "Give us the fertilizer and our grain will pile up too." Propaganda about revolutionary self-reliance as a source of economic success did not persuade.

The War on Culture

Drums beat the day before lunar New Year when village leaders visited army martyr families. The drums heralded all village celebrations. During the 1965 New Year season the collective provided martyr households in economic difficulties with up to 40 yuan in cash. Such households received 20 yuan regardless of need.

Despite the disappointing 1964 harvest, every household ate pork at New Year. Yet much joy had gone from the two-week festivities. Operas and other market-related cultural events had disappeared. Revolutionaries demanded that superstition be replaced by a scientific "spring festival." The party criticized old-style mourning. County officials tried to get villagers to cremate. But to the day Mao died, no Raoyang household chose cremation. Villagers did not abandon remains when water projects flooded their cemeteries. Raoyang provided households ten yuan to defray expenses. Even Raoyang high officials honored lineage ancestors each spring during the Qingming festival to mourn ancestors. Ceremonies bound society in a moral way through lineages. The socialist education movement's denunciation of the sacred as a feudal vestige sabotaging socialism had little impact on what villagers believed.

Still, village leaders feared being labeled antisocialist. The August 1963 flood had knocked over two ancient stone lions near the Zoucun market. They were left to nature's ravages. No one dared restore a "feudal relic." Cherished culture was attacked as nonsocialist. The socialist education movement treated lion dancing as a stinking old custom. Some iconoclasts welcomed the attacks. But for most people life seemed emptier. It left some cynical and most turning to hidden forms of cultural expression.

Whatever their frustrations, most in Wugong felt a stake in the success of the leaders who had won their village prominence and rewards. Villagers became more intertwined by marriage, reversing an exogamous practice of daughters marrying out.[8] The endogamous tendency was pronounced in models, suddenly richer than marginalized, poorer communities into which progeny had historically married. Parents wanted daughters to enjoy the better life of a model village. By polarizing marriage locales, further separating the state-blessed from others, models did not endear themselves.

The Wugong Way

In summer 1965 *China Youth Daily* asked Boss Geng to write an article in commemoration of the tenth anniversary of a Mao essay that had launched collectivization.[9] Since 1961 Geng had had a commune-assigned aide to help with public relations. Ji Suozhu had long done commune administrative work.[10] He read so beautifully that youngsters in Wugong said listening to Ji was better than reading the book. As Geng's scribe, Ji prepared speeches and articles.

In the *Youth Daily* article, the first major political tract attributed to him, Geng advocated eliminating the "household economy in the countryside so that all rural people will become well off together." Wugong, the article boasted, had been loyally following Mao's lead since 1943 in opposing "individual production" (geti shengchan) and the market.

By taking the collective road, Wugong's "sandy wasteland" was turned into "a sea of cotton and mountains of grain." Tractors and irrigation replaced hand tools and primitive water wheels. "If we hadn't listened to Chairman Mao," the article claimed, "we wouldn't even be able to imagine such bounty in our dreams." But, Geng cautioned, "the socialist road is not smooth. There has been class struggle and two-road struggle every step of the way." There were always people who wanted to "go it alone." In the early 1950s, it supposedly was the coop's mobilization of "vast labor power to do irrigation work" that convinced skeptics to give up household farming.

Dwelling on revolutionary class struggle, Geng said that after Mao pressed for collectivization in 1955, "the poor and lower-middle peasants in our village requested that we form a completely socialist collective," with no payments for land contributions. But class enemies stirred up trouble and spread rumors, encouraging people to drop out of the collective. Bad elements said that surrendering household land and relying entirely on labor for income was "unfair and irrational." Geng falsely claimed that malcontents "were allowed to drop out of the collective and take their land with them."

Echoing Mao, Geng warned that "the spontaneous forces of capitalism have been steadily growing in the countryside in recent years." Nothing was said about the disasters of the Leap, recovery via reform policies, or the recent disruptions of the four cleanups.

Geng portrayed commerce, even collective commerce, as dirty. Everyone should struggle against "the capitalist thoughts in their minds." Each time Geng rejected a commercial project, resisters joked that he "was afraid money had thorns that would prick his hands" (pa qian chi shou). Others chuckled that Geng had everything "abacus backwards." Unamused, Geng insisted that sidelines be cut. Wugong's collective sidelines collapsed from a record high of 164,000 yuan in 1962, at the peak of post-Leap reform, to 57,000 in 1964. Revolution cost villagers income.[11]

Wugong's leaders believed their village was truly Mao's. They wondered why Mao had not recognized that it was China's most socialist. After all, Mao-blessed villages led by Wang Guofan and Chen Yonggui both acknowledged they had learned from Geng, the leader of China's earliest continuous coop.[12] Yet Wugong never won the accolades and resources of Xipu and Dazhai.

What was so advanced about Dazhai where 80 households distributing income at the village (brigade) level was proclaimed a breakthrough to a higher stage of socialism? Wugong long had income pooling in production units of 200 households or more in each of its three teams. Moreover, the limited flood damage in Wugong compared to the disaster suffered by Dazhai proved which village had done a better job at collective work

Wugong leaders concluded that their village had done more with less. Villagers used their hands and backs to dig the first wells and level the land in cold 1940s winters. They created China's first big coop. Mistreated during the class struggle land reform of 1947 and 1948 and again when the state cut its big coop in 1952, Wugong revolutionaries prevailed. The villagers overcame water disasters in 1952, 1956, and 1963. Efforts to smear the village in the four cleanups had failed. Wugong leaders believed their village had made it on its own against great odds. Just as neighbors doubted Wugong's story, so Wugong leaders were skeptical of Dazhai claims. Visitors reported that the military did most of Dazhai's reconstruction.

Education for What?

Geng ended his July 1965 essay by endorsing the revolutionary policy of bashing the educated. He said he constantly reminded daughter Huijin, "You're an intellectual now." He told her, "It is right to return to the village to do manual labor. But you have to be ideologically prepared for this task. To do farm work is to build socialism. Don't be afraid of being dirty or tired. Intellectuals don't have any real experience and haven't been tempered. So it's very easy for them to speak beautiful words that are hollow and empty."[13]

In fact, Raoyang educators had accomplished much, and county residents valued education. Under master teacher Zhang Baochen, the principal, dedicated and accomplished instructors helped Raoyang High School students achieve at a national level of excellence. Principal Zhang had his best teachers prepare the senior class for the college-entrance exam. Education was a way out of poverty.

Some of the teachers were locals returning from colleges and normal schools in Beijing, Tianjin, and Baoding. Some sent down teachers who, with no hope of uniting with their spouses and children in a major city because of regulations locking villagers out of urban areas, brought their families to Raoyang. Yang Duo, a native of Beijing and a graduate of North China University, recalled trekking in from Dingxian in 1948, his belongings on his back. Relishing the blue skies and ripening fields, Yang sang as he crossed the Hutuo River barefoot. People considered Yang the prefecture's best calligrapher.

Educational facilities were spartan. There was no electricity. Many primary schools used earthen desks well into the 1970s. While some teachers won rapport with students and their families, a chasm generally separated locals from outsider teachers. Villagers saw teachers as dressing like city folk and speaking without the authenticity of the regional argot. The inner/outer dichotomy was strong.

In the 1950s the junior and senior high schools were in the county seat. There was intense placement competition, with selection by testing. Youth hiked for miles to take the exam, carrying bedding and three days of food. The event was etched in the mind of one impoverished hiker by the 30 cents his mother gave him, a small fortune. The test-taking hall was a solemn testament to China's long history of examinations. Each student wore an identity badge. On each desk was the name and photograph of the examinee. At the bell, all quietly filed to desks and began writing.

In the 1950s Raoyang had only one high school class, of about 50 students. After increasing to two classes during the Leap, it dropped in the famine years, then increased to four with 200 students in 1965. Principal Zhang fostered educational quality. Many regarded the high school's cook as the county's best. At special events the county requisitioned his services.

Some high school teachers, including mathematicians, Russian-language specialists, physicists, and geographers, won renown. Several students achieved high scores in provincial and national exams. While far greater resources were lavished on model schools elsewhere, from 1962 to 1964, with entrance based on test scores, 90 percent of Raoyang high school graduates moved on to higher education, an extraordinary record for a poor rural county. Top students advanced to Beijing University and Qinghua University in the national capital and to Nankai University and Tianjin University in the provincial capital. Locals praised principal Zhang and his teachers. But the post-1962 stress on class struggle led to a "social-class" criterion for college entrance in 1964. That favored the children of party leaders, people born red. Revolution had a caste component.

Good News

Thanks to the new wells, access to the state's chemical fertilizer, and good weather, Wugong enjoyed record harvests in 1965. Peanut production rocketed from 18 to 316 catties per mu, and cotton jumped from 47 to 92 catties per mu, the results touted as proof of success in emulating Dazhai.[14] Grain sales to the state nearly quadrupled. Villagers, of course, grumbled about selling so much grain for so little. But per capita income jumped by 50 percent to 91 yuan, with 21 in cash, the second highest ever.

Yet, loyally hewing to the revolution caused the percentage of gross income from collective sidelines to fall for three consecutive years. Household sidelines virtually disappeared. Revolutionaries stressed grain and cotton. Wugong's grain harvest of 740 catties per mu was more than four times the county and three times the Hebei average. What explained Wugong's ability to outperform neighboring villages? Was it collectivization, modernization, or privilege? Geng Changsuo said it was the self-reliant Dazhai collective road; Lin Tie said it was socialist modernization; Wugong villagers attributed it to hard work; residents of less favored villages said it was privilege.

In spring 1965 it seemed auspicious that a tomb was discovered that had been built 1,400 years earlier by a Sui dynasty official, part of a line of five officials (wu gong), the first of whom buried his father near Wugong. Glories of the past promised future glories.

Dramatic evidence that Geng was in favor came in the form of an invitation to attend the October 1, 1965, National Day ceremonies in Beijing and join dignitaries in the reviewing stands reserved for guests of honor. He even glimpsed Mao, whose lead Geng had been following in attacking sources of counterrevolution — household plots, lion dances, and marketing. Geng shook hands again with Premier Zhou. "I'm Changsuo," Geng said. Master politician Zhou memorably replied, "I know. I saw you in Tianjin."[15]

Wugong's celebrity status was reconfirmed three weeks later when *People's Daily* published a polemic attributed to Geng.[16] The theme was that officials should listen to the criticisms of the masses. Silent on the traumas of the four cleanups, the article presented Wugong as a place where Mao's mass line was working. "There are people who consider only the opinions coming down from the top, but won't listen to opinions coming up from the bottom. They accept guidance from the top, but they won't accept guidance from the bottom." Geng claimed he had learned his lesson years earlier. Rushing to a meeting, Geng had failed to say a few words of greeting to villagers standing along a path. One elder had shouted, "Look! Big officials are all the same! When they see us they don't even have time to let off a fart!"

Geng noted that some village leaders refused to listen to the good criticisms of a minority. "Sometimes there are things about the opinion of the majority that are inaccurate," Geng ominously warned. It is possible "to blow with the breeze when you see that most people are expressing a view. But it doesn't mean that this view is always right."

Criticism, Geng wrote, was like good herbal medicine: "It's bitter as hell, but it cures you!" In his team 1, Geng claimed, villagers reported on any official who "makes a false step." "Nobody holds back. This is good. It's a way to control officials. When our officials experienced the socialist education movement, they were pleased. They said, 'The commune members like to criticize us, this helps us eliminate our mistakes.' There are even some officials who regret that they didn't get still more supervision after committing errors." In the exhilarating months of late 1965 when Wugong was riding high, Geng portrayed the hated four cleanups as a love fest.

Rebuilding

Villagers wanted something done about housing. They complained that homes were too small or falling apart, courtyards cramped, lanes narrow or rut-filled, blocking carts and goods. "Going out is too inconvenient," locals said, "but staying home is too uncomfortable." Villagers wanted to enjoy the fruits of their toil. Socialist modernization was supposed to make life better. But Boss Geng feared that investing in home building might bring accusations of ignoring class-struggle priorities.

As it had in the case of the preservation of the cemetery, the Dazhai model offered a way out. Geng and administrator Qiao Liguang had recently seen Dazhai's new, two-story apartment-like dwellings. Wugong would present house building as "leaning from Dazhai." It meant allowing families to divide and provide a new house for young couples when a daughter-in-law gave birth.

Geng Changsuo asked the recently retired Geng Xiufeng to join Qiao, party secretary Zhang Duan, and Geng's amanuensis, scribe Ji Suozhu, to plan the housing project. They met in late fall 1965 and agreed on a plan that allowed family preferences. Larger families wanted larger houses. The typical courtyard in Wugong was about .5 mu. But some courtyards were as large as one or two mu, while others, including Boss Geng's, were minuscule. But how much living space should be assigned? How much for storage? Who would get the first homes? Would the vanguard of socialism be favored?

Ji Suozhu presented a preliminary plan to the village party committee. A raucous meeting of the entire community followed. Diverse ideas, including huge common houses, were put forward. The throng agreed that a committee of 20 respected villagers, led by Zhang Duan and Qiao Liguang, should settle on a few basic models. The consensus was that the future should feature order, straight lines, and wide roads lined with trees. The irregular and twisting paths of the old village seemed feudal. The village should look like a grid: three large north-south avenues would intersect with three east-west roads. Every home would open to one of the streets. The two arteries meeting in the village center would be 16 meters wide, while the other four would be 12. The village would be surrounded by willow trees.[17]

Two plans were brought back for discussion. The first, associated with Qiao, was inspired by Dazhai. Wugong would have neat rows of two-story apartment buildings. This urban vision precluded walled courtyards for Wugong's nearly 500 families. Boss Geng thought it madness. The other plan, promoted by Ji Suozhu, Geng Xiufeng, and Zhang Duan, recognized that families wanted spacious walled courtyards and room for storage and raising chickens and a pig or two. A villagewide meeting endorsed that idea. The discussion was the most open since Geng's original coop was founded in 1943.

Families of three would get a big gate, a private courtyard with four large rooms along the north wall, three smaller, lower-quality rooms (pei fang) for storage along a side wall, an outdoor privy, and a pig sty. The courtyard was to be 16 meters wide and 21 meters long and to have ten trees. Village art teacher Kong Guangyu was invited to draw up a master plan. Demolition would begin in the winter slack season in late 1965.

Home building was popular. It continued even through customary rest hours under the blazing summer sun. Even in the busy harvest season it moved ahead so that families with daughters-in-law or grandchildren could divide at the propitious time. Villagers wanted ample courtyards, homes facing south to catch the winter sun, a detached kitchen so soot and smoke from cooking would not soil the dwelling, solid gates and high walls, spirit paintings inside the main gate auguring good fortune and long life, personalized window frames, roofs and doorways, warmth for winter, and enough rooms for all household members. Local tastes had little in common with the apartment-like dwellings of Dazhai.

Some leaders argued that the village should be rebuilt in sections to minimize chaos or favoritism. Wugong chose otherwise. After the fall harvest those in greatest need received priority. Construction went on all over the village. As a result, the whole never fitted together in the planned grid. The dissatisfied faulted the secretive system of power. Some grumbled that brigade administrator Qiao Liguang's parents and son were among the first to get new quarters, and that they seemed to get more indoor living space than allowed.

Historically, home building was a cooperative venture. Friends and relatives, sometimes 40 to 50 people, would help knock down the old house. The collective subsidized half the transport costs for building materials and paid for running electric power into the house. Even after the village's contract system was eliminated as antisocialist, the 17-member construction team was paid piece rates, 80 work points each for a four-room house. That meant at least 12 work points per day, where ten was the normal high for collective work. Building homes was valued labor.

The owner paid for the materials; the collective provided labor. In 1978 the cost of 10,000 red bricks for a three-room house was 289 yuan. The foundation bricks ran 100 yuan. Cheaper sun-dried earthen bricks used for the courtyard wall, storage rooms, kitchens, and outhouses cost about 200 yuan. Flooring cost nine yuan per room. Doors, windows, and frames were 80 yuan, wood for beams and the like added 450 yuan, the roof 150. A solid wooden gate and shadow wall to keep out unwelcome spirits could run 350 yuan. In all, an average three-room house cost 1,500 to 2,500 yuan. The village provided the land. Most 1960s Wugong homes had four rooms and cost 2,000 to 3,000 yuan. That compared with average annual family incomes in 1965 of 500 yuan. Before construction, villagers visited builder Li Lu's west-end courtyard early in the morning to review designs for doors, windows, and kitchens. He was a member of a small group of village artists.

Stone masons on the North China plain are renowned for hard drinking. Li Lu liked a few glasses at breakfast, some again at lunch, and a bottle with dinner. He held a particularly sweet mood most of the day. His preferred alcohol was Hengshui White Lightning sorghum whiskey. The 134 proof drink was already famous in the area more than three centuries earlier. At times, Li favored a stronger brew he cooked up himself.

With Dazhai legitimating home construction, and with rising yields and villagewide irrigation, life in Wugong seemed better. Heavy grinding stones began to be replaced by electric milling of grain, with the village picking up 70 percent of the milling cost. With Raoyang tying into the state power grid, Wugong homes were among the first in Hebei villages to enjoy the glow of a single dim electric light. Families began purchasing radios, sewing machines, and bicycles. Geng Changsuo credited Mao's revolutionary line.

Rumblings

On March 7, 1966, Premier Zhou Enlai's State Council established an agricultural small group for eight North China provinces, including Hebei.[18] Zhou took special responsibility for agriculture in general and North China in particular. The following day, March 8, when a powerful earthquake measuring 6.8 on the Richter scale hit Hebei south of Wugong, the premier flew to Matouli village in Hengshui's Jixian county. Supplies went to the needy in 30 communes and 350 villages. Zhou visited victims, saying that, even with state aid, they had to rely on themselves to rebuild their lives. Inspecting Handan and Xingtai prefectures the next day with his wife, Deng Yingchao, Zhou assured people that the state would act as a virtuous household head should; it would care for the orphaned and the elderly who had lost household bread-winners. Powerful aftershocks on March 12 added to the devastation, including 1,641 dead and more than 20,000 injured.

Culture taught that great changes were preceded by earthquakes and that evils followed when women held power. Jiang Qing, Mao's wife, was emerging. Many would later interpret her rise and the earthquake as bad omens.

The Xingtai earthquake did not cost lives in Wugong, but two homes collapsed. The walls of most homes cracked, roofs split, and chunks of debris littered floors. The state sent bricks, timber, and tar sheets for reconstruction. Boss Geng did not rebuild the earthquake-damaged house he had constructed four years earlier. He said that to fix up his house now would be to work for himself when he should be giving all to the public.[19] The four-cleanups campaign had been a warning of what could befall tainted leaders. With the state partially subsidizing postquake rebuilding, locals sped up work on a new village that would be orderly, convenient, and beautiful.

In April 1966 the prefecture divided the 36 villages in gargantuan Wugong commune into five parts, led by a three-person Wugong Work Committee headquartered in the village to coordinate the five sections.[20] It was the only such administrative unit in the province, and was disbanded one month later.

Not everyone welcomed Boss Geng's way of following Mao and Dazhai. Geng's team 1 had suffered income decline in the 1950s when he merged his coop with the whole village. Villagers with grievances, such as team 1's Qiao Yong, could be unforgiving. Qiao's uncle was village martyr Qiao Hengtai, who had introduced fellow east-ender Geng Changsuo into the party and in whose home Qiao Yong had grown up after Japanese invaders killed his father. Qiao Hengtai, who headed the village resistance during the war with Japan, died in combat in 1945. Qiao Yong, the son of a martyr household with claims to special support, felt that the Geng leadership kept his family poor.

As Qiao experienced it, Xu Shukuan, Geng's wife and a team 1 leader, never treated him fairly. Xu branded him lazy and anticollective and consistently assigned him to back-breaking field labor. No one could prosper on collective work with the state holding farm-gate prices low. So Qiao pressed into commercial ventures. Tigress Xu pounced on Qiao. Humiliated, Qiao was not about to forgive the public dressing-down.

To Xu Shukuan, anyone not devoted to the collective was a thief. Should children nibble on piled-up peanuts while waiting for collective peanut distribution, she scolded them. Calling Xu a "nosey body," shamed parents fumed. But caution dictated silence. Villagers bridled at leaders who protected one another, while intimidating ordinary folk.

The earthquake badly damaged Qiao Yong's home. But, as he saw it, because of low-paying work assignments, he lacked the savings to pay for needed repairs. A final humiliation came when Qiao had to accept ten yuan in charity from Xu Shukuan. Frugal Xu was generous to the needy. To people like humiliated Qiao, Boss Geng's grandstanding built Geng's political credentials at the expense of their households. But, given his success and fame in 1965 and 1966, Geng hardly noticed.

The ranks of the frustrated included youngsters sent back during the dearth. Ambitious, young Li Changfu was upset when turned down for a coveted "five good" designation in summer 1964. He knocked himself out doing good deeds. But villagers complained he was a "fake activist." True, Li rushed to help others, but he then shamed them, saying "You're going too slow! If it wasn't for you, we'd have been done long ago!" Li was furious when Geng told this story in *People's Daily*.[21]

Li joined 11 "young intellectuals who had returned to the village," including Geng's political daughter, Huijuan, styling themselves the Wugong Literary Group. They wrote up their selfless deeds, claiming inspiration from Mao. In a short article published in December 1965 in a Beijing newspaper, they proclaimed: "Read Chairman Mao's works! Listen to what Chairman Mao says! Carry out Chairman Mao's instructions! These words are the compass by which the members of our collective, and especially the members of our literary group, guide our movements."[22]

But what if Chairman Mao's compass pointed to a need to attack people in power, say, Geng Changsuo? Geng had successfully ridden the choppy seas of 1964 and 1965 campaigns dealing with socialist education, the four cleanups, revolutionary successors, and the Dazhai model. He had emerged with his head high above the churning political waters. But a tidal wave lay ahead.

7 ◈ THE STENCH

Geng Changsuo was riding high in early 1966, but, as memory has it, villagers noticed bad omens. In late February an epidemic attacking the central nervous system swept through Raoyang High School, the county town, and several outlying communes, including Wugong. Seventy-six people were stricken. Nine died. The authorities said it was encephalomyelitis. The March earthquake that hit nearby Xingtai and five neighboring counties was followed by two more major jolts. Black lava oozed from cracks in the earth's crust, damaging 197 Raoyang villages. More than 30 aftershocks hit in the next few days; then two more big quakes struck on the evening of March 27. The year of the horse was off to an ominous start.

Mao's Cultural Revolution would reverberate throughout rural China.[1] Since state power penetrated to the grassroots, when higher leadership was overturned, the consequences reached the countryside. The Cultural Revolution involved more than elites, intellectuals, and urban workers.

Hebei in Turmoil

In May 1966 Mao toppled Politburo member Peng Zhen, Beijing's first party secretary. Defense Minister Lin Biao led the charge, accusing Peng and others of plotting a coup against Mao and revolutionaries. Attacks were soon directed at high-ranking officials within the party, state, and army. Revolutionary Li Xuefeng, who had long vied with Peng, replaced him as Beijing first party secretary, adding the post to that of first secretary of the North China Bureau.[2] At Mao's behest, an enlarged Politburo meeting in May created a Cultural Revolution Group to attack enemies of socialism inside and outside the party. The group spearheaded a Cultural Revolution.

A marathon meeting of the North China Bureau from May 21 to July 23 toppled leading figures. Governor Liu Zihou bid for supremacy in Hebei.[3] He wooed Li Xuefeng and denounced Wugong's patron, provincial first secretary Lin Tie, as the top Hebei official "taking the capitalist road." Liu claimed to have opposed market-oriented material incentives in the early 1960s. He acknowledged speaking on behalf of reform in 1962 but blamed Lin Tie for handing "me his manuscript just before the meeting, claiming that he was not well. I just read out what was written down."[4] Lin, who had worked under the ousted Beijing party chief Peng Zhen during the anti-Japanese resistance, was stripped of all positions and confined to a military compound.

Governor Liu turned his back on Hebei war heroes and many of his own associates, ordering or approving jailings and beatings. At least 33 people died. The whiff of revolutionary vigilantism that had been growing stronger since 1963 became a stench of political corpses.

A regional chain reaction ensued. Lin Tie's aide, reform pioneer Hu Kai-ming, under a cloud since criticism by Mao in 1962 and subjected to house arrest in Baoding, was beaten and forced to assume the excruciating "jet plane" position. On August 25 the Central Committee ratified the North China Bureau's dismissal of Lin Tie as Hebei first party secretary and third secretary of the North China Bureau and the appointment of Liu Zihou to both posts.[5] Liu was also made political commissar of the Hebei Military District, consolidating his power over party, government, and army. Liu's accumulated powers made him seem like the monarch of Hebei.

Zhang Kerang, Wugong's longtime supporter and head of Hebei agriculture under Lin Tie, had led rural work in the North China Bureau since 1960. When Lin fell, Zhang was ousted. He spent the period 1966–73 at hard labor in Hanhu village east of Tianjin. Numerous officials were thrown out of the Hebei Bureau of Agriculture and sent to semislave toil called labor reform.

By August 1966, with Mao's blessing and the support of Defense Minister Lin Biao (Mao's heir apparent) and Premier Zhou Enlai, youthful revolutionaries were organized as "red guards" in major cities.[6] The Cultural Revolution projected Lin Biao's military forces as uniquely pure. All other power holders seemed tainted. Lin Biao's army protected Mao, socialism, and the nation. The 63rd Army maintained order in Shijiazhuang. The revolutionary city became a center for studying Mao thought. Red-guard membership allowed China's youth to bask in the glory of the army, historically an attractive pole to village patriots.

China's youth, long alienated from the privileged party apparatus, their aspirations stifled by reduced educational opportunities in the wake of the Great Leap economic decline, and their critical faculties sharpened during the socialist education movement and the four cleanups, joined Mao's crusade against false socialists. When children played out the battles of the Three Kingdoms era, they said that Zhuge Liang, the brilliant strategist, was like Premier Zhou, but no one was said to be comparable to Mao. He was godlike. Young people wanted to prove themselves worthy of Mao and superior to party people in power who had betrayed Mao, mocked the young, and blocked their rise.

Violence in Tianjin

President Liu Shaoqi's enemies dispatched agents to Tianjin, the Hebei capital, to "prove" that in the 1920s Liu had been a counterrevolutionary spy. Hebei lieutenant governor Yang Yichen, a Liu ally, was arrested and imprisoned. Professor Zhang Zhongyi of Hebei Normal University, who was rumored to have once taught Liu's wife, Wang Guangmei, was tortured to death.

Mao's wife, Jiang Qing, like other revolutionaries in the 1920s and 1930s, had had many sexual liaisons. Some in Tianjin knew about her sexual history. Agents were dispatched to silence anyone who might embarrass her.

Red guards belonging to the "beating dogs" faction at Tianjin's Number 99 High School "carried a stick or hammer to destroy, smash and pillage. . . . They burned everything they could and confiscated the rest."[7] A story circulated that red guards had broken into a Tianjin hospital to interrogate a top official who was being kept alive on oxygen. The oxygen was turned off to force the accused to talk. Instead, he died.

Allies of revolutionary theorist Chen Boda established themselves in Tianjin. He claimed that the party in eastern Hebei was a nest of traitors. Three thousand were soon killed. Revolutionaries persecuted Tianjin Writer's Association member Liang Bin, who was a favorite of recently toppled national culture chief Zhou Yang. Some cultural stars in Tianjin jumped to their death.

At Nankai University, red guards focused on a high-level university official who had been transferred recently to a leading position in the Hebei government. He was identified as one of 61 former political prisoners associated with the fallen central government planner Bo Yibo. Treating surviving prisoners as traitors, Kang Sheng, China's public security and secret police czar, sent in agents to ferret out quislings at Nankai. The university was home to allies of Yang Xianzhen, a top theorist in President Liu's brain trust.

Nankai faculty were beaten and publicly reviled. Some were murdered. Factory workers were urged to seize the homes of "black" teachers and kick the stinking struggle objects out of residences superior to those of proletarians. Many faculty families were left homeless. Strangers walked into a home at any hour, took what they wanted, and vandalized what they chose not to take. Intellectuals were targets of a continuous *kristallnacht*, with theft, terror, and thuggery called revolution.

As virtually everywhere, two red-guard factions fought it out at Nankai. The August First group, named for the founding date of the Red Army, vied with the Defenders of Dong, signifying both Mao and the east, the sources of revolution. At Tianjin University, Defenders of Dong opposed a faction called the Paris Commune. In fall 1966 dozens of fresh dead bodies lay unattended in Tianjin's streets following each day's fighting.

High school teachers were targeted by their students. Stories circulated about murdered teachers and principals who were hung in the doorway entrances of high schools. Red guards forced teachers entering the schools to kiss the corpses.

The most violent group, August 25th, came from the Tianjin Academy of Engineering, although some thought Nankai's August 13th even more brutal. The factions at the academy welcomed factory workers to join the struggle. Red guards tortured the Tianjin party secretary until he died. Some said he was tortured into committing suicide. Incited by reports about spies, traitors, and nests of capitalist roaders, youth defended revolution. The 66th Army was unable to maintain order. Blood had to be repaid in blood. Hundreds died in continuous fighting by both high school and college students. After public degradation and torture, suicides proliferated. They seemed more numerous than murders. The military wavered, its ranks divided, uncertain whom to support, whom to suppress.

Xie Xuegong, the North China Bureau leader who had accompanied Mao to the model Xushui commune at the outset of the Leap, took control of Tianjin. Xie, tied to Jiang Qing and her ally, public security head Kang Sheng, became Tianjin's first party secretary and political commissar to the army. In April 1967 the military distributed arms to Tianjin red guards loyal to Xie.

Upheaval in Raoyang

Chai Rui, the former Wugong commune leader, was acting first secretary of Raoyang in early 1966 because Li Chunyu was away wrapping up the four cleanups.[8] Although the Xingtai earthquake struck in early March, promised relief did not arrive until late October. County officials, anxious for their careers, curried favor with higher-ups by ignoring the food crisis and handing over more grain to the state. The resulting hunger forced many Raoyang villagers into illegal begging.

When Raoyang county leaders saw the Politburo's "May 16 Circular" (Wu yiliu tongzhi), which established the Cultural Revolution Group and propelled the Cultural Revolution into high gear, Chai Rui merely ordered officials to study Cultural Revolution directives. The county only denounced Beijing intellectuals said to belong to a "black gang" opposed to Mao. By early June, however, students learned of rebel actions in Beijing and Tianjin and demanded a halt to classes. Students at Raoyang High School pasted up accusatory posters. Factional violence began between the Headquarters, a rebel group that held the allegiance of most students, and May First, a group mainly of children of officials that would eventually be labeled a "protect the emperor" faction. County secretary Li Chunyu, who returned to Raoyang in early July, sent work teams to schools to control and channel student zeal.

But students, hearing how metropolitan red guards were destroying old ideas, old culture, old customs, and old habits, took to the streets on August 24. In response, Li Chunyu had county employees plaster the town with Mao quotations. When students set up the first red-guard organization, Li ordered the county party to set up its own "rebel organization" (zaofan zuzhi).

Violence exploded when red guards "arrested" high school teachers and officials, including Principal Zhang Baochen and the head of the county education department. Zhang was kept in the painful jet-plane position and was denied food, drink, and use of the toilet until he groveled and begged.

Teachers who could claim poor or lower-middle peasant origin sought to protect themselves by organizing as the Red Education Workers and barring those of less than pure-blood origin. Rebel teachers and students attacked the work team sent to the school by county secretary Li Chunyu in July and sought new struggle targets. Those accused of ties to a "black gang" in Beijing were roughed up and paraded with humiliating signs hung around their necks. Wang Shuzhai, a mathematics teacher who had a relative overseas (taken as virtual proof of spying), was brutalized and suffered a heart attack. After assaulting teachers, school officials, and work team members, the Raoyang red guards headed for the villages to destroy the four olds.

County secretary Li convened a three-day meeting in mid-September of nearly 1,500 county officials and staff, four-cleanups work teams, commune officials, village secretaries, village chiefs, militia leaders, heads of poor-peasant associations, and representatives of rebel secondary school students and teachers, urging them not only to "grasp revolution" but also to "promote production." Raoyang was poor, and, coming on the heels of famine, the state's third five-year plan had to be implemented.

By November, tensions eased as many students and teachers left home to link up with rebels throughout the country. One Raoyang youth who hiked to Mao's model village, Dazhai, was shocked to find an army construction unit bivouacked outside. It had been working full time for the preceding year to help tame recalcitrant nature. On its own, he suddenly realized, the national model for self-reliance could not excel. Travelers saw and experienced much that conflicted with the official policy line.

The late 1966 lull was short-lived. By early January 1967 the red guards from Raoyang High School returned home, guided in part by the ancient rhythms of the rural calendar. With the lunar New Year holiday approaching, it was time to be with family. Eager to bring down "revisionist" local leaders before the New Year, the returnees set up more than 40 "combat brigades" (zhandou dui) and renewed attacks on Principal Zhang Baochen. They were soon joined by red guards from Beijing and Tianjin, mostly Raoyang natives returning for the New Year. The urban red guards, led by Lu Donghu, called themselves the Aid Raoyang Rebel Corps (Fu Rao zaofan tuan).

In January 1967, rumor had it that county party chief Li Chunyu would be detained and condemned as ringleader of a "black headquarters" (hei siling). Li and his top aides, Yuan Zijie and Chai Rui, fled to Hejian county, northeast of Raoyang. Red guards from Hebei were searching Hejian on rumors that deposed Hebei party secretary Lin Tie was hiding there. The pursuers, storming into a safe house, found Chai Rui in the privy. Eventually all leading officials were captured. Former Hebei party secretary Lin Tie was beaten and paraded in a truck in Jinxian county.

The red guards chose New Year's day, February 9, 1967, for Li Chunyu's public humiliation. Li and other top officials were paraded through Raoyang streets in dunce caps. They were then dragged to a mass struggle session. Finding that Li had long pilloried innocents, the rebels saw themselves righting wrongs.

In February 1967 more than 90 percent of Raoyang county officials at the level of bureau chief and above were beaten, degraded, paraded, and incarcerated. An internal report described the county as "in a state of anarchy."[9] Li Chunyu's five-year reign came to an abrupt halt. In March 1967, acting on Mao's call for revolutionaries to seize power, rebel groups in Raoyang took over party and government buildings. But they were inept as rulers. For almost a year there was no county governance.

Since magistrate Yuan Zijie was a stickler for style and grammar, his tormentors repeatedly rejected his elegant confessions, forcing him to scrap flowery phrases like "my criminal acts in following the deep, black bourgeois line" and to acknowledge his crimes in plain language. Deputy magistrate Pu Shaoli (nicknamed Lao Huli, or Old Fox, by the red guards) and Zhang He, with close personal ties to Wugong leader Geng Changsuo, were severely attacked. While county secretary Li struggled to maintain his composure, his wife, Wang Yuhua, deputy director of the county party school, collapsed under attack.

In April, heeding appeals from on high to unite, the 40-plus rebel student groups formed the Raoyang High School United Rebel General Headquarters (Rao zhong lianhe zaofan zongbu). After receiving training from army units, the Rebel Headquarters students set up office in the county post and telecommunications bureau.

Rebel groups in party and government organizations also united. The Red Rebel Brigade (Hongse zaofan bingtuan), a party committee group, and the Revolutionary Rebel Brigade (Geming zaofan bingtuan), a government group, united to form the Red Revolutionary Rebel Brigade. The Rebel Brigade interrogated former party Standing Committee members and scoured secret files for evidence that the county leaders had tried to blunt revolution. On May 16, 1967, the first anniversary of the outbreak of the Cultural Revolution, Raoyang rebel leaders summoned disgraced top leaders of Hengshui prefecture and paraded, abused, and repudiated them at a mass rally.

Factional disputes soon split the rebels. A May First Battle Brigade (Wu yi zhandou bingtuan) broke from the Rebel Headquarters. Members of the Raoyang armed-forces department (wu zhuang bu) intervened, but bloody conflict continued. In June the May First faction seized the office of the county education department. In July disgraced officials, including county secretary Li and his top aides, were paraded and confronted in each of Raoyang's 16 communes, sometimes all night long. It was called "people's dictatorship."

Convinced that the military was conspiring with the county party to suppress revolution, the May First group forced its way into the county armed-forces department at the end of July. Comparing the Raoyang military leader to General Chen Caidao, commander of the Wuhan Military Region who fell in mid-July after suppressing rebels in Wuhan, May First rebels called on "true" revolutionaries to "bombard Li Guoqiang and Zhang Shicun," leaders of the Raoyang armed-forces department. With the local military paralyzed and weapons seized by youthful combatants, violence spread.

Renewed Culture Wars

When Geng Changsuo learned of the "May 16 Circular" launching the Cultural Revolution, he assembled villagers to criticize officials and writers under attack in distant Beijing. In August 1966, following Hebei's lead, the village party set up a "Cultural Revolution preparatory committee." West-ender Xu Fulu, head of the poor-peasant association and a Geng loyalist, was named chair. Agricultural production continued by day. Lights were strung up to allow criticism of "bad elements" by night. When listening to broadcasts, the first to hear of a directive from Mao raced from lane to lane with the news. Cymbals and triangles clanged, and the big drums thundered as Wugong people shouted, "Warmly welcome the publication of the latest directive of Chairman Mao!"

Youth league zealots cleansed the village of the four olds, pressuring people to break incense burners, destroy images of Buddhist and Daoist deities, and burn the Confucian classics, lineage genealogies listing male ancestors, religious sutras, and popular ("pornographic") novels. Families were told to hand over paper funeral offerings and to smash devices used for gambling. "Lucky stars," mythical "lion dogs," and other decorative items were stripped off roofs to purify the village.

Activists burned books, even school texts, that did not come from Mao. Zealots said wedding ceremonies were too expensive. Wugong would end bride prices, dowries, and banquets. In the past, brides used a ladle to stir a pot of water filled with grain seedlings, evoking fecundity, a hope for many children. In another fertility ritual, the groom "shot an arrow" toward a corner of the bridal chamber bed to "pin down" the "peach-blossom maiden." Superstitions like these had to end. Weddings were taken away from families and turned into collective rituals. Newlyweds now sat on a platform at party head-quarters, each wearing a single red paper flower. The head of the village women's association presided. Elders particularly found revolutionary wed-dings bereft of meaning.

Youthful iconoclasts railed that funerals were superstitious because incense was burned by the bed of the departed to "illuminate the road to the after-world." The relatives of the deceased went to a small shrine to report a death to the god of the land (tudi ye). Mourners wailed three times: "Forgive his transgressions and care for him!" At home they burned funeral "money" and paper carts for the ancestor's use in the world beyond. Now funerals would be handled by the production team. There would be no funeral master or musi-cians, no visit to the shrine, and no burning of objects and incense. The team simply hung a sign containing the single word *mourning* (sang) on the home. Three days later the body was moved to the collective burial ground.[10]

The war on popular culture intensified in late August when squads of red guards arrived from Raoyang High School. They marched in carrying large red flags. The person in front held a portrait of Mao. Proclaiming that they had come to learn from Wugong, the red guards listened to "poor peasants," including Tian Changru, a former Buddhist nun, speak of "class bitterness" (jieji ku) and anti-Japanese "racial hatred" (minzu hen). The red guards helped take in the fall harvest, plant the winter wheat, and level the land. They joined households for tasteless "remembering past bitterness meals" (yi ku fan). So many visitors poured in that Wugong set up a "red-guard reception station." Village officials began wearing red-guard armbands, proof that they were taking Mao's socialist road.

By late August 1966 Wugong's junior high and elementary schools had closed. In September, junior high principal Zhou Xijia was forced to wear a dunce cap that had a jagged iron base. The only way to keep the cap from toppling, proof of disrespect for Mao and the revolutionary masses, was to pull the iron base down hard over the forehead, where its sharp edges caused painful bleeding. To survive, the victim had to torture himself. Other tragedies followed. A pharmacist at the Wugong hospital drowned himself in a well; a commune doctor leaped to his death.

Local rebels attacked scribe Ji Suozhu, Geng's amanuensis. Ji had written to foreign embassies and kept what they sent to him. Connections to anything foreign was proof of spying. Worse yet, one embassy publication contained a picture of a less than fully clad woman, "evidence" that Ji was immoral. He was tortured intermittently for weeks, forced into the jet-plane position on a rickety table until, exhausted, he lost his balance. Then the table legs were kicked out, sending him crashing, his head smashing on the concrete floor.

Activists proved themselves worthy revolutionary successors by punishing class enemies. "Landlord" Li Maoxiu was beaten and debased before every group that descended on Wugong, proving village determination to continue class struggle and prevent capitalist restoration. Also scapegoated were suspected rapist Xu Jichang, who had been sent home in disgrace from a state job in Raoyang in 1951, Daoist Li Jingzhua, and Provider Li Peishan, who had belonged to a secret society. Struggle sessions humiliating the ritual scapegoats drew crowds to the clubhouse in the north end of the village.

Revolutionary Tourism

In November Wugong red guards joined millions responding to Mao's call to "link up" with other rebels. Some went far south to Mao's birthplace. It was so overrun by people camping out that water and sanitation became problems. Others set off on "Long Marches" to early revolutionary guerrilla bases, shrines such as Yan'an, and the national model village, Dazhai. Many Raoyang youth had never left the county. Now, with travel restrictions lifted, millions of red guards rode the trains for free. For many it was a lark. Some teenagers enjoyed ferry rides across Shanghai's bustling waterfront and were agog at the lush green and surfeit of water in the south. In contrast, the north seemed like a desert. Most went to see Beijing, Shanghai, Xi'an, or Guangzhou, and such famous beauty spots as Suzhou, Hangzhou's West Lake, and Guilin. When the train loudspeaker blared out "The east is red, China has produced a Mao Zedong," travelers snapped to attention and faced north to Mao, the red sun in their hearts. The south was where counterrevolutionary Chiang Kai-shek had fled to be propped up in Taiwan by the American imperialists, whose B-52s were bombing people like them in Vietnam. The red-guard struggle assured that Chinese would no longer be insulted and bullied.

Youth felt a sense of exhilaration as schools closed and a rigid system lost its grip. They declared themselves Mao's good soldiers and felt they were toppling oppressors. Many felt liberated from tight control by Li Chunyu's party, teachers, and family.

Some red guards already knew about official abuse. Others found proof in rifled offices. Revolution seemed legitimate and hopeful, a way to be loyal to Mao, to help victims, and to be patriotic, a way to make China the one true socialist nation.

In Beijing the logistical services of the army fed and housed the visitors until it was time to throng Tiananmen Square and shout themselves hoarse when the great leader appeared and raised his hand in silent greeting. Mao's military uniform and red-guard armband symbolized the purity of the army and the sanctity of the red-guard movement. Actually, peering across the huge square filled with a million or so people, red guards seldom could tell who was Mao and who his defense minister and political heir, Lin Biao. The young people chanted and wept during what many remembered as life's happiest moment. By early December most Wugong youth returned home.

Cultural Revolution Loyalists

In mid-December 1966, following a central party directive, Wugong set up a Cultural Revolution Committee. Geng Changsuo pushed to the fore the loyal youth he had long been fostering. The committee was headed by the youth league leader, 24-year-old, still unmarried, Xu Xiuwen, who had lost her urban life back in 1962. Committee members included Geng's political daughter, Huijuan, and articulate Li Zhongxin. The leaders were known as *toutou,* bandit chiefs. Although each of the three teams set up a Cultural Revolution Committee, the center, home of the old southern Li elite, was excluded, except for a few of the poorest tillers.

The village militia was led by Macho Li Shouzheng. In team 1, Geng's grandson, Zhang Mandun, was rising fast. Mandun's mother, Boss Geng's eldest daughter, had married out of the village. But Geng had arranged her reestablishment of residency in Wugong, where the grandson would be groomed for leadership.

At the suggestion of his daughter, Huijuan, Geng Changsuo went before the young loyalists and asked for criticism. He scolded himself for the slow development of the village. Others defended him and praised village progress. Order reigned. It was socialist theater.

Beijing Red Guards and Village Rebels Target the Boss

In early January 1967 Geng lost control. An "Aid Raoyang Rebel Corps" comprising red guards from Beijing and Tianjin launched a search for class enemies. They were natives of Raoyang who wanted to root out phony reds and to "pull down the black flag" of Wugong. Eighteen red guards from Beijing Normal University and People's University arrived by bus from Raoyang. The Normal University rebels were led by Zhang Xinli, the People's University contingent by Niu Fuqing, a former youth league leader at Raoyang High School. Her father headed village public security in Niucun village, four miles northwest of Wugong. Villagers recall her as wearing ugly thick eyeglasses.

Across the countryside, red guards targeted models to overthrow power holders taking the capitalist road. The Beijing red guards believed that Wugong's success rested on privileged access to the fallen capitalist roader Lin Tie. They ordered the Wugong party committee to stand aside. All were suspect. Any secret meetings — and all party meetings were secret — would be regarded as illegal conspiracies against the masses. The red guards moved in with the formerly poor to find proof.

They sought out villagers with grievances and encouraged them to topple antisocialist elements. Village leaders were warned not to keep a lid on popular forces. Geng Changsuo, his wife Xu Shukuan, and other leaders were dragged out, forced to kneel, and verbally barraged. The tormentors, instructed to avoid using fists to beat victims, kicked them. Wugong was unusual in that the attacks never went beyond certain limits. Geng allies in the militia and poor-peasant association saw to that.

It was still too much for party secretary Zhang Duan, who wore skimpy cotton cloth shoes on the coldest days. Zhang cursed the red guards as chaos yet knew that Mao said chaos was good. The chronic throbbing in Zhang's head worsened. He vigorously shook his head to drive out the pain and muttered about chaos. Neighbors linked his physical malady to political tensions.

Ignoring red-guard orders, party leaders gathered at night in the club-house. The Beijing red guards and some village allies rushed in and denounced the gathering as a "black" meeting. Who, they demanded, had authorized it? Was it the red guards? The poor and lower-middle peasant association? The Cultural Revolution Committee? If the masses had not given authorization, it could not occur. The meeting was terminated.

The Beijing red guards appealed to the village Cultural Revolution Com-mittee led by activist Xu Xiuwen to attack capitalist roaders, including Geng. But Xu and the other village rebels were loyalists. Still, Xu took her work seriously. She coveted the respect of urban red guards speaking for Chairman Mao. But the charges hurled at Geng did not resonate with the gripes of villagers. While the red guards called Geng a Soviet-type antisocialist, dis-affected villagers raged about food and abusiveness.

Wall posters went up, and brooms painted giant denunciations. New Wugong rebels not sanctioned by Geng and the party included both the young and middle-aged. The most militant group called itself Jinggangshan, the site of Mao's original base of revolution. It was led by Li Xin'geng. He was an early member of Geng's coop. Membership came from Geng's east end. Jinggangshan grew to 40 members.

Bad blood between now middle-aged Li and Geng began in the mid-1950s. Geng publicly criticized Li for taking some peanut shells from the coop's grain station. Later, when Li's son broke a collective crop sprayer, Tigress Xu fined him three days' earnings. Li Xin'geng and his wife, both party members, felt "exploited" by the Geng leadership. Jinggangshan denounced the Tigress as the tough fist and sharp tongue that gave force to Geng's softer words. Geng was attacked for "40 errors" and called the backstage supporter of "monsters and demons" (niugui sheshen), officials who preyed on the people. He was labeled the son of a broken landlord family. His dirt-poor father had, it was true, briefly rented out the household's minuscule plot while away in Raoyang town eking out a living making rope.

Geng wanted to fight back. While adult education gave him rudimentary literacy, he doubted his skills. He asked his political daughter, Huijuan, to post a refutation of the rebels. She refused, saying, "You can't do that! That's suppressing the masses!" Instead, she posted Geng's willingness to accept criticism.

When Chief Huijuan posted Geng's "request to be struggled against," a storm of denunciation of the Boss as the tool of the province's leading capitalist roader and as an enemy of Mao followed. "Down with Lin Tie!" "Geng Changsuo is a three-anti element!" The Jinggangshan rebels, backed by the Beijing red guards, mocked Geng's request for criticism. "This is Geng Changsuo's strategy for covering up his mistakes." Posters covered Geng's door. One, with Geng's name upside down and crossed out, graced his outhouse, warning, "Remove this and you'll have your dog's head smashed."

Hard-drinking builder Li Lu, uncle of the rising Li Zhongxin, invited the independent-minded Geng Xiufeng and Qiao Wanxiang, an east-end member of the original 1943 coop, to his west-end home. Two former party secretaries, Xu Chuan and Zhang Zhensheng, both west enders, were there. Xiufeng was startled when told they were "not very clear" on whether Boss Geng had been following a "bourgeois" line. Xiufeng tried to reassure them that while the Boss had shortcomings, the success of the collective proved Changsuo had taken the socialist road.

Among the skeptical was Xu Chuan, a leading party member during the resistance war when the west end was the village's party stronghold. After Geng's coop became famous, party power shifted to Geng's east end. Xu resented how Boss Geng had pulled strings to bring home his oldest daughter, the mother of heir Zhang Mandun. Many wanted to bring married daughters home to favored Wugong, but only Geng's daughter secured an official change of residence.

Geng Xiufeng tried to win over the outside red guards. He told the leader of the Beijing Normal University contingent that Geng Changsuo had always followed Chairman Mao's revolutionary line. The youth replied, "Wugong may once have been revolutionary, but it turned revisionist later." "Look! The young women here wear fancy scarves when they do field work. Some even wear *two* scarves!" Material success was counterrevolutionary.

Xiufeng went to see his neighbor Li Xin'geng, the leader of the militant Jinggangshan rebels. If the banner is black, Xin'geng warned, "we'll have to pull it down." The next day posters railed "Down with landlord element Geng Xiufeng!" "Geng Xiufeng is the backstage black hand managing Geng Changsuo!"

Cultural Revolution Committee head Xu Xiuwen saw the attack on Geng Changsuo for ties to deposed Hebei provincial secretary Lin Tie as bogus. Of course Geng had treated the provincial party secretary well when he visited in 1963. What else was he supposed to do? Xu and west-end leaders friendly to Geng were immediately attacked for protecting the emperor by two east-end groups, the Yan'an Combat Brigade (led by Qiao Yong, whom Tigress Xu had humiliated) and Jinggangshan (which included Li Changfu, whom Boss

Geng had criticized in *People's Daily* as a phony activist). As for west enders, Xu Xiuwen understood that they resented Geng for shipping so much good grain to the state at low prices and distributing earnings regardless of actual work, thereby, as most west-enders saw it, privileging the lazy and incompetent and preventing west-end families from improving their standard of living. By not silencing these voices, east end and west end alike, Xu won support for her leadership. Even in a model, villagers spurned Mao's analysis of what was wrong and aired their own grievances.

In mid-January 1967, 66-year-old Geng stood before the villagers. Li Shuxin, deputy chair of the village Cultural Revolution Committee, escorted him. "Uncle Geng! Be prepared to do self-criticism this afternoon!" he said. A Geng protégé, articulate Li Zhongxin, chaired the meeting. When Geng stood up, he did not know what to say. He finally blurted, "You people criticize me." The first to come forward was Old De, an east-end neighbor. Placing his hand on Boss Geng's shoulder, he asked, "Do you know that people don't have enough to eat?" Geng replied, "Yes, I know. This is the state regulation. Each person gets 420 catties." Old De shot back, "Can't you give people more?" Others criticized Geng for planting too much cotton for the state and blocking household sidelines that could earn cash. While the red guards wanted to bring Geng down for having betrayed revolutionary socialism, villagers criticized him for sacrificing the people in service to the socialist state.

Geng Xiufeng, who vigorously defended Boss Geng from attack, nevertheless felt that the old coop leader had become alienated from villagers. The Boss seemed in closer touch with revolutionary higher-ups than with his neighbors. Xiufeng recalled that in 1966 "many families, especially families with many children, were short of grain. They did not have enough food. Most of what they reaped was sold to the state." According to Xiufeng, "People wanted to do sidelines to make a little cash. He wouldn't agree because the leadership didn't allow household industries. . . . The leadership wanted him to turn vegetable gardens into cotton fields."

Village opinion divided. Li Xin'geng's Jinggangshan — backed by Xu Chuan and team 3 allies — meant to oust Geng. To the Xu Chuan group, team 3 outperformed team 1 with higher yields and higher incomes, but Geng's team got the glory. It was unjust. Yet, a pro-Geng group, the United Headquarters (lianhe zongbu), was also based in team 3. Its leader, builder Li Lu, understood that if Geng were disgraced, Wugong would lose its enriching ties to the state.

At the rally Li Lu tried to put village discontent into perspective. But Jinggangshan rebels unleashed a torrent of criticism. Humiliated Qiao Yong, leader of the Yan'an Combat Brigade, jumped up to respond to Li Lu. Li Xin'geng and Qiao Yong, learning that a camera given to Geng in the Soviet Union was missing, charged that Geng had "sold the camera for 200 yuan and spent the money!" Geng insisted he gave the camera to the commune office.

Someone raced to check, soon returning with the camera. The crowd chuckled, and tension fizzled.

The Tigress Falls

A few days later the same rebels went after Geng's wife, Xu Shukuan. She rejected all criticism of her abusive treatment of slackers, declaring that the collective came first. Daughter Huijuan advised her to "trust the masses." Not to accept criticism was proof that Tigress Xu held the revisionist idea that leaders were superior. Mother suffered, Chief Huijuan insisted, from individualism and egoism.

Allegiance to Mao often required abandoning family. In some families where children denounced mothers and fathers, parents assured progeny that they understood and would always cherish the children. Xu could not understand. She, who had given all for the collective, was everyone's favorite target.

In mid-January Beijing red guards dragged bound-foot Xu to a rally at the clubhouse. Villagers denounced grain-requisition policies. Geng was responsible, but villagers cursed the wife. One grabbed the Tigress by the collar and exploded into her face, "You old hag, you sifted and selected, selected and sifted, until there wasn't a single speck of sand in the grain. You delivered this good grain to the state. You didn't want to leave anything for us, did you?" Another shouted, "You delivered the best grain to the state. We harvested it and we dried it. But you delivered it. We didn't have enough to eat!" Another screamed, "Did you know how little grain we had?" Rebel leaders from her east end, including Li Xin'geng and Qiao Yong, led the tormentors.

The meeting roared approval for ousting Xu. A white dunce cap, symbolizing a descent into hell, was placed on her head. The rebels dragged her forward on her tiny feet and paraded her. Stumbling, confused, 56 years old, worn out, wounded, she still shouted, "Long live Chairman Mao!" People screamed back insults, demanding she be silenced. How dare a counterrevolutionary invoke Mao's name! They pushed her head down and shut her up. Xu tried to shout again, "Long live Chairman Mao!" Someone hit her. She hobbled ahead and tried to raise her slogan again. Enraged, local people pressed forward and beat her.

No one lifted a finger to help her. When the pandemonium quieted, friends comforted the wounded Tigress and took her home. Others joined them. They cried. Their community was being ripped apart. Returning home later that evening, daughter Huijuan exclaimed, "Party members are the oxen of the people. Struggles are good."

It was much easier to attack the wife than the husband, national model Geng Changsuo, just as it was easier, at the national level, to revile first lady Wang Guangmei than her husband President Liu Shaoqi. At work, in part, were the misogynist cultural dynamics of a patriarchal society.[11]

Father and Son Stage a Split

While the Cultural Revolution called for targeting "those in authority taking the capitalist road," red guards repeatedly attacked powerless scapegoats, especially "landlord" Li Maoxiu. Militants led by Chief Huijuan joined the Beijing red guards in forcing 21-year-old Li Wei to repudiate his father. Wei was put on a stage before 1,500 people at the clubhouse. His father, head shaved like a convict, was forced to his knees, then trussed up, tied by the ankles, hung upside down high in the air, and whipped until he fainted. The torture became a ritual. "One afternoon," Li Maoxiu later recalled, "I passed out four times. I stopped breathing. Later they didn't even have to hit me. My breathing stopped when they hung me up."[12]

Li Wei had to prove his father deserved the torture. The son invented a diary that his father had burned, "remembering" passages that hoped for a landlord comeback. Activists told each other about so-and-so having seen this diary, persuading themselves that their barbarous cruelty was just. The son claimed his father sang counterrevolutionary Hebei opera arias, changing the lines to ridicule socialism.

Li Wei had to draw a class line. He, his wife, and his child left Maoxiu's house for a separate building in the same courtyard. The most colorful clothing of Li Wei's daughter was seized by red families to "save the child" from superstitious influence. Years later the father insisted that the son had had no choice in violating filial piety. "For thousands of years in China," Maoxiu said, "according to custom, fathers and sons had close ties. But we had to break it off. We had to say we were no longer father and son."

Rebels broke into the homes of black elements and village leaders, ransacking in search of proof of antisocialist thought, or simply plundering. Children were traumatized by the sight of parents as powerless, debased targets. Eleven-year-old Yang Yuexin, distraught at the degradation of her father, Yang Tong, a rising west-end party stalwart, and his friend, scribe Ji Suozhu, set out on a long march to prove the family's revolutionary credentials. She collapsed and had to be carried home. When red guards ransacked Xu Mantang's home, the old west-end guerrilla fighter nearly lost an eye and had to be rushed to a clinic. Provider Li Peishen had kept the Confucian classics. They were thrown on a pile that was turned into a bonfire.

Guiying Marries a Soldier

Aspiring writer Shi Guiying had sung "Father Left Me a Precious Thing" from the Cultural Revolution model opera *Red Lantern*. But in neighboring Shenxian county, her father was accused of having informed on comrades after being captured by the Japanese. Surviving prison was treated as evidence of treason. Revolutionaries should die for the cause. A fabricated confession was tortured out of Shi Xishen. With her father a traitor, Guiying was ordered not to sing revolutionary songs. She burned her diaries. To survive, people destroyed much that they treasured. Party membership was now out of the question.

Before his fall, county party secretary Li Chunyu urged Boss Geng to protect Shi Guiying's father. The family then hid Shi for more than a year in an underground hideout tunneled beneath the home. Such tunnels honeycombed the village in the 1940s, saving revolutionaries from the Japanese. The more modest hideouts of the Cultural Revolution saved Chinese from revolutionaries. When the frenzied attacks subsided, the father resurfaced. He was sent to years of hard labor in a Shenxian county reeducation camp, then made an ordinary worker at the factory he once directed. His rank was reduced from the fifteenth to the nineteenth grade.

His daughter, Guiying, and soldier Li Mengjie kept corresponding. When Li visited in 1967, they discussed marriage. Both her former teacher and her mother opposed it. The army took a dim view of Mengjie's marriage to the daughter of a black father but did not force the issue. Finally overcoming his own hesitation about career damage, Mengjie proceeded with the wedding.

Guiying had built up savings from her 20 to 30 yuan monthly salary to build the couple a 1,000 yuan house. It had three rooms and was the first in Wugong to use a new horizontal brick structure (wo ban zhuan). Full of ideals, Guiying was proud of having reversed a local practice in which the groom's family provided a home, the most costly item required for marriage. Orphaned Mengjie had no parents to help. His response to the gift was "I know you wanted to do this for me, but it's not much use for a soldier. What use would it be if I died in battle?" Guiying wondered whether Mengjie lacked feelings or whether she expected too much of life.

After the wedding, Guiying tried to please Mengjie by not singing in the house, by not writing in her diary, and by working less outside the house. When Mengjie returned to his post in Beijing, she brought him love poems. He rejected her overtures. Guiying became convinced that because he had no love as a child, he could not love. Guiying told herself that what mattered most was revolution, not personal happiness.

Cultural Resistance

The rebels attacked culture, the so-called four olds. Magic shows were banned. So were unscientific paintings, such as pictures of fairies. The few burial mounds remaining in the fields were proof that Wugong was a false model. Militants forced families to dig up the graves, coffins, and bones of loved ones, sometimes allowing them to transfer remains to the shaded cemetery.

When Li Yunman's mother died in early 1967, her two sons split the funeral costs. Big expenses were banned. But what was big? Yunman still welcomed mourners to his home with cigarettes and sweets at a cost of ten yuan. People wept. Eventually a "simple" wooden coffin, for which the two brothers paid "only" 140 yuan—a year's cash earnings for the household—was carried to the consolidated cemetery. Mourners circled the mound while words of praise were showered on the deceased. A white paper wreath was placed on the burial mound.

Each spring thereafter, during the Qingming festival, the family honored the dead by visiting the burial mound, shoveling fresh earth on it and decorating it with white paper. In attaching themselves to ancestors, survivors bound themselves each to all. Mourning was a portent. Disrespectful reduction in display augured bad prospects; so mourners spent heavily on coffins.

There was a precise relation between who spoke at a funeral and the hierarchal position of the family. Party people were treated better. Boss Geng spoke at the funerals of the few truly elect. Ritual revealed status in the socialist system.

Rebels were more successful in restructuring weddings. In the past, friends of the newlyweds usually gathered at night in the courtyard outside the bedroom, cracking jokes and teasing the couple. This was stopped. Villagers were also ordered not to put money in red envelopes as gifts. No longer could *quanren,* complete persons, be selected to preside at weddings. Quanren were males who had sired a living son and daughter and had living parents, a brother and sister, and an uncle and aunt. Ceremonies alive with historic significance were replaced by empty revolutionary forms.

Just after the lunar New Year Wugong held a collective ceremony with seven couples. Subsequent mass weddings occurred on May Day and National Day, state-chosen days with no auspicious meaning in lineage lore. Expenses were to be kept to a dinner for closest relatives at the groom's house, followed by a similar meal at the bride's home three days later.

Li Qunying, a staunch ally of Geng Changsuo who had joined the small coop in 1949, got his 21-year-old son, Zhongyu, to volunteer for the first mass marriage. Chief Huijuan's group of youth league militants choreographed it. It was held in the clubhouse, and only immediate family were invited. The spartan rite began after breakfast and ended quickly. The gutting of ceremony diluted family joy. Household happiness seemed almost a crime.

The revolutionary changes left women vulnerable to physical abuse. Many young women had worked for ten years before marrying, all the while living at home, doing chores, and turning their pay over to their parents. The effort to eliminate dowries, deemed a degrading feudal custom, felt unjust, increased the difficulty of finding a mate, and lowered one's status in the husband's family. A bride needed a good dowry to buy security in the husband's household. If she brought too little, she risked mistreatment by her in-laws.

Li Zhongyu's wife, Yuma, brought a dowry consisting of a dresser (worth 30 yuan), a clock (20), mirror (five), a teapot, and a thermos flask, all from

Raoyang town. The wedding feast centered, as always, on pork-filled dumplings, symbolizing an intermingling of ingredients that could never come apart. Three days later the couple visited the bride's family in nearby Yanggezhuang, where revolutionary scrutiny was less rigorous. Yuma's parents happily served five courses to a party of 12 guests.

A year later Yuma had a baby girl. Yuma and Zhongyu then divided from his parent's household, built their own home, and bought another 380 yuan worth of new furniture. That large family outlay contradicted official efforts to enforce colorless frugality. Ever more, villagers circumvented revolutionary fiat.

In naming children, families often proclaimed loyalty to revolution. Before the 1967 lunar New Year, Li Huiying, whose education had been cut short by the Leap disaster, gave birth to a son. The child was named Xiangyang, "toward the sun," meaning toward Mao.[13] Names captured changing political priorities variously emphasizing nation, water, and collective. Aspiring writer Shi Guiying's brother, born in the early 1950s, was named Xuesu, "emulate the Soviet Union." During the Cultural Revolution, with the revisionist Soviet Union the enemy of socialism, Xuesu was renamed Pixiu, "criticize revisionism." But the name change did not end the bullying and beating of the boy. In the mid-1940s Wugong had been known as Little Moscow. Leaders now scurried to invent a history of opposition to the Soviet Union.

Many families resisted revolutionary names and stuck with ancient verities. At the peak of the struggle against the four olds, Xu Fenglan in team 3 named her third daughter Sukong, "a simple Confucius." Her neighbor Li Sui called his daughter Su'e, "pretty maiden." Li Kun called his daughter Xinghua, "apricot flower," and Zhang Minxun named his daughter Jingru, "the respectful one."

Resisting political pressures, boys too were given names full of historical symbolism. Pan Luan called his son Junliang, "talented and virtuous," and Li Songxian named his son Yuquan, "jade fountain." Li Luguo, a team 3 official, named his Cultural Revolution–era son Yanbo, "a man of virtue and wealth." Li Wei, beaten and terrorized for his birth ties to his "landlord" father, still named his two Cultural Revolution — era sons Shuangqing ("double purity") and Shuanglong ("double dragon"). Our household survey reveals that nearly half of the children born in team 3 during the high tide of the revolutionary war against Chinese culture were given names sanctioned by custom rather than revolution.

Wugong purged its culture far more rigorously than its neighbors. Burial mounds remained in the fields of surrounding villages. Leading households in other villages still used musicians, parades, and expensive silks in mourning rituals.

Drumming was branded a stinking old custom. The treasured Wugong drums were hung on the gates and roofs of the homes of the once prosperous. The popular was branded feudal. Rain quickly ruined the beloved drums. No one dared save them. Throughout the county, drums and cymbals were silenced, even for political rallies. Similarly, the familiar sound of firecrackers marking major events disappeared.

Young militants demanded an end to incense and to hanging posters honoring gods during the New Year holiday. In the old family residence of Mao Zedong, his mother's images of kitchen gods were stripped from the walls of the house, which had become a shrine attracting millions. Homes were now festooned with images of Mao and words from his sacred writings. Lineage rites were replaced with state worship. One Wugong villager displayed 72 Mao badges. Geng Xiufeng plastered his bedroom walls with posters depicting major events in Mao's life. Landlord Li Maoxiu's home also prominently displayed statues and images of the "great leader." The former nun Tian Ruchang condemned Buddhist prayer, destroyed her religious images, and solemnly announced, "I will only believe in our savior, Chairman Mao." This was called reason replacing superstition.

Defense Minister Lin Biao's army popularized dances of loyalty to Mao that some said were invented by elderly bound-foot women in Shenyang in the northeast. In the military, factories, offices, schools, and politically ambitious villages, people performed loyalty dances to the tune of "Sailing the Seas Depends on the Helmsman."[14]

But political revolution did not obliterate cultural understandings. In Wugong everyone knew exactly where each lineage was buried. The outside lineages had united in 1936 against the elite southern Li lineage and organized the Association to protect west ender Xu Dun in his attempt to keep his lineage whole and later to preserve mourning and marriage rituals. In the 1940s, the small east-end Geng coop held its meetings and elections on the three major feast days. Buddhist analogies flowed from the lips of local leaders. Even the village narratives praising Boss Geng's revolutionary character celebrated venerated cultural practices. It was said that in his years as a rope maker, Geng never collected debts from those too poor to afford a proper celebration of the New Year with dumplings, which augured auspicious futures. This made Geng moral. While outward signs of the sacred, such as temples and household burial, were demolished, customary values persisted in the hearts of resisting villagers.

Tianjin Red Guards Smell Revisionism

In January the Beijing red guards tried to shut down the Wugong Cultural Revolution Committee, denouncing it as a "protect the emperor" faction. Instead, the family ties of invading red-guard leader Niu Fuqing shut her down. In late January 1967 word came that Fuqing's father was under attack. The daughter raced home to help, but the father, a public security chief, was dethroned. That made the daughter a black element. The discredited Beijing red guards skulked away. The Wugong Cultural Revolution Committee resumed its duties, naming Geng Changsuo head of a "production group" (shengchan ban).

In early February 1967, within days of the departure of the Beijing red guards, a contingent of the Aid Raoyang Rebel Corps from Nankai University in Tianjin appeared, led by Li Changjin, a chain-smoking chemistry major. His female assistant is remembered as the toughest of all the red guards, writing down every charge. Their goal was to strip Wugong of its model status in time for the anticipated downfall of county party secretary Li Chunyu in Raoyang at the lunar New Year, a time for settling accounts.

Activist Xu Xiuwen, Chief Geng Huijuan, the Cultural Revolution Committee, and various rebel groups greeted the Nankai red guards. Calling themselves Defenders of Dong (Wei Dong), they settled in the school complex and announced they would root out the source of Wugong's stench, its leadership. Like all rebels, they dragged out the ritual whipping boy, "landlord" Li Maoxiu, for the usual torture. Son Li Wei was viciously beaten and compelled yet again to denounce his father. Maoxiu believed he had saved his son's life by pretending to rupture the father-son bond.

The Nankai red guards continued to torture scribe Ji Suozhu and attacked a recently arrived *Heibei Daily* reporter before turning their attention to the village militia. It was a "headquarters for protecting the emperor," they declared. The militia was demobilized. Nankai red-guard leader Li Changjin charged that Chief Huijuan had been groomed for high office to "protect the Geng household empire." Every adult in Boss Geng's household was a party member, most with good jobs on the state payroll. Was that not feudal, privileged power? The Wugong Cultural Revolution Committee was also attacked for protecting Geng. Declaring they would strip him politically naked before the masses and the truth, the Nankai red guards allied with the Jinggangshan rebels in team 1. Again, big character posters targeted Geng.

The outsiders approached Li Changfu, the close friend of Chief Huijuan. The red guards, believing Li knew all Geng family secrets, offered her a Hobson's choice: reveal the dirt and become a rebel chief or stay silent and face attack as a royalist. Changfu caved in. So did aspiring writer Shi Guiying. Trust shriveled as the community imploded.

In early February the Nankai red guards proclaimed they now had the evidence to prove that Geng Changsuo was antisocialist. Fearing that his allies would block revolution in Geng's team 1 base, they assembled at team 3 headquarters. Leader Li Changjin interrogated Geng. From the time of the resistance war, Li said, the rich had run Wugong. Even now, the team and village accountants were from richer families. "Why did you allow upper-middle peasant Geng Lianmin to serve as accountant?" Li rhetorically demanded. His answer was that Boss Geng had long been in cahoots with Lin Tie, the leading capitalist roader in the province.

As Hebei party secretary, Lin Tie had sent Boss Geng to the revisionist Soviet Union and spent lavish sums on the village. Production statistics had been falsified. Wugong was a sham model.

"When did you become a model?" Li demanded.

"I'm not a model, I'm not qualified," Geng replied.

"Then why were you always in the newspapers?"

"I was in the newspapers, but I wasn't qualified to be a model."

"When did you go to the Soviet Union?"

"In 1952."

"What did you do there?" Li shouted, banging on the table.

"I went there to learn about collectivization and mechanization!"

"They're revisionists! Don't you know that?"

"Not when I went there. Comrade Stalin was the leader then."

"But now they're revisionist. Do you understand?"

"Yes, I do."

"Are you also a revisionist?"

"No, I'm not,"

"You're not? I could smell the revisionism when I arrived at the edge of the village!"

"Don't talk like that. Criticize me any way you want, but if you say our brigade is revisionist, I can't agree."[15]

Villagers pushed their way into team 3 headquarters as word of the confrontation spread. There was shoving; punches were thrown. An old man shouted at outsider Li Changjin, "Our old coop leader is a revolutionary. What the hell are you?"

Li, impassive, kept smoking. His assistant kept writing, inscribing more proof that Wugong's leaders were organizing a handful to suppress the revolutionary masses. "Has Lin Tie ever been here?" Li asked Geng.

"Yes, on the 20th anniversary of the founding of our coop," Geng said.

"What did he give you?"

"Nothing."

"Awards?"

"Yes, but he also criticized some of our work."

"He is a member of a black gang."

"I didn't know that then."

"Did you see him personally?"

"Yes."

"Couldn't you tell from his appearance that he was a member of the black gang?"

"My eyesight isn't so good."

Articulate Li Zhongxin broke in, "Why do you want to know all these things?" The Nankai red-guard leader responded, "We're going to send this material to our people in Baoding," the center of violent revolutionary fundamentalism in Hebei province. Geng supporters in the crowd shouted that they would never allow "black material" out of the village. "Search them! Search them!" a voice rang out. Fearing violence, Geng pleaded with the crowd to back off. Sixty-six-year-old Geng Changsuo was advised to go home, and the meeting broke up.

The next day a poster charged Geng with "stirring up the masses to attack the students!" A Geng loyalist countered by tacking up a cartoon portraying outsider Li Changjin with a huge nose trying to "smell revisionism" in Wugong. Nankai Li cursed the whole village, "These motherfuckers are hard to deal with!" One of the cooks, overhearing Li's remark, shouted back, "Who do you motherfuckers think you're talking about?"

In many model villages "rebel" groups loyal to the old party regulars had faded by the spring of 1967. But in Wugong, loyalists stood firm. The thwarted Jinggangshan faction, afraid the Nankai red guards might abandon them, decided to strike again.

A White New Year

The most memorable assault on Geng Changsuo came on February 8, 1967, the eve of the lunar New Year. The Nankai red guards knew that their allies in Raoyang town would subject party first secretary Li Chunyu to a mass struggle meeting the next day, New Year's day. They determined to do the same to Geng.

That rainy evening Jinggangshan rebels ordered Geng to team 1 headquarters. Li Changjin and the Nankai red guards awaited. Headquarters loyalists rushed over and insisted on inclusion. Fearful of violence, Geng's supporters took him home, telling him to "lock your door and go to sleep!" Although the hour was late, the throng swelled. The meeting had to be moved to the clubhouse.

Geng could not sleep. Slipping and falling in the mud, he returned to face a torrent of criticism. Jinggangshan rebels attacked him and his relatives and associates, giving vent to grievances built up over a quarter century. Once again, however, the criticisms were not what the red guards sought. Li Fuzeng, a wounded soldier and former official, was one of the 70 middle peasants who had been labeled rich peasants and lost houses and land in the terroristic 1947 land reform. Despite the eventual property restoration, Li had vented his anger by posting a sign that read "The sky is dark, the clouds are black!" Punished for this defiance, the demobilized soldier's alienation deepened and he became a critic of requisition policies that sent so much grain to the state. When Li conspired with a team official to provide unrecorded grain to team members in the 1950s, he was arrested and placed on probation for three months. He was also accused of subverting military recruitment by discouraging young people from serving in the army. Soldier Li spoke for many at the New Year's eve meeting: "Why did you sell so much grain to the state when we were hungry? Don't you know that there are still villagers who can only survive by buying [black-market] grain outside?"

But the Nankai red guards could not support village charges that Geng sacrificed household interests to state interests, because those detested policies were indubitably Mao's. When the outsiders snickered superciliously at the supposed ideological confusion of local accusers, a villager snapped, "Don't laugh! This criticism is in the interest of the people. The village and teams store so much grain to supply the state. Shouldn't it be distributed to the hungry?" Villagers also criticized the crackdown on cottage industries, not only household enterprises but even collective enterprises. Such activities could turn a handsome cash profit in the market. The ban kept cash incomes low. The charges reflected popular discontent with a revolution that kept villagers poor.

Throughout Hengshui prefecture officials confiscated the supplies of illegal grain sellers. The crippled market that had been hanging by a thread in poor Yanggezhuang, north of Wugong, vaporized. Since the nationalization of commerce in the early 1950s, Yanggezhuang's external connections had been cut away. Now everything was gone. Miserable soil plus corrupt leaders left a destitute village (whose livelihood had once rested on sidelines and commerce) totally dependent on the state dole. The poor and famished felt vulnerable.

The confrontation in Wugong went on for most of New Year's eve. Geng asked people to go home, saying he would welcome their criticisms the next day. But Jinggangshan rebels shouted him down, telling him they were in charge. Denunciations rained down on the old leader. Suddenly a cry went up that Geng be hatted with a dunce cap and paraded in a degradation ritual on New Year's day together with "landlord" Li Maoxiu and the other "bad elements." Envisioning the enormity of such an act drained everyone's energy. Geng took least and last for himself, his supporters insisted. And he never beat people. The crowd fell silent. Would not the whole village suffer if Wugong lost its model status?

Leaders in other model villages, lacking Geng's virtues and a unified leadership, could not hold back popular resentment ignited by invading rebels. Red guards from violently fundamentalist Baoding burst into Taoyuan, the Hebei village made into a model in 1964 by Wang Guangmei. They reversed the class categories of everyone Wang had promoted. In Nanwangzhuang, red guards unseated Wang Yukun, Mao's model in the 1955 collectivization drive. But the army would not permit someone tied to Mao to fall. It rescued the arrogant Wang. The army also intervened to save Lu Yulan, the ranking rural member of the Hebei party committee, when she was threatened in her home village, Linxi, 100 miles south of Wugong.[16] In Xipu village, home of the Paupers' Coop, which Mao had so warmly praised during collectivization, virtual clan war broke out between Wang Guofan's group and the Du lineage led by Du Kui. The army restored Wang to power. Geng Changsuo was the only prominent Hebei rural model to survive on his own strength.

Wugong loyalists subsequently insisted that Geng was spared because he was clean. He even earned less than others in the village. That self-restraint permitted Geng to bully others into submission when they complained about not getting enough. His leadership style kept Wugong from splintering violently, in contrast to every other major Hebei model village. When the cry erupted to cap Geng, Li Shuxin, the vice chair of the village Cultural Revolution Committee, stood up and shouted, "No!" Neither the Nankai red guards nor the local rebels dared cap Geng. The throng dispersed in silence, adjourning until the next day, the first day of the 1967 lunar New Year.

It would be a while before the visiting Nankai red guards slept. They wrote and pasted up couplets on the homes of leaders. Instead of red paper, the color of celebration and of revolution, they used white paper, the color of death and mourning. Village leaders were greeted on New Year's morning with charges of protecting enemies of Mao.

Geng's house was covered with white paper. Geng's wife, Xu Shukuan, was called a snake and a ghost. On their front gate one slogan read "Ripping down posters is counterrevolutionary!" Tigress Xu announced that this time she would not fight back. Instead, she would invite the rebels to have tea in her home. The couplets remained. The white mourning paper is what many villagers remembered most vividly about the Nankai red guards. They violated people's special time for celebration.

On New Year's day articulate Li Zhongxin got into an argument with the Nankai rebels at the clubhouse where he had slept. Zhongxin asked about the deathlike couplets. He was warned to abandon counterrevolutionary leaders before he too was with the enemies of the people. Nankai's Li Changjin said, "When the tree falls, all the monkeys flee. Wugong is a false model. It was constructed by that revisionist Lin Tie." "No," Zhongxin insisted, "Wugong self-reliantly won its achievements." "You say it's self-reliance," the Nankai leader responded, "we say it's money." "But we never even accepted a state loan," Zhongxin naively insisted. The red guards urged Zhongxin not to be so sure, to wait until all the facts were unearthed. Zhongxin felt great pride in Wugong's destruction of old customs. He certainly was not opposed to a cultural revolution. But Geng a capitalist roader? He could not buy it.

Virtually no one came to the village struggle session that morning. In Raoyang town county party secretary Li Chunyu and other leaders were publicly disgraced, but in Wugong New Year's day was a time for lineage and family. Villagers stayed home. They locked their gates. They would not go out to attack Geng Changsuo. Instead of a mass parade of humiliation for Geng and other party insiders, "landlord" Li Maoxiu and other ritual struggle objects, a handful of "bad elements," were marched back and forth.

The push to dislodge Boss Geng fizzled. By the end of February the anti-Geng Jinggangshan faction in the village's east end began to disintegrate. Still, humiliated Qiao Yong would not give up. He and a few diehards tried to reenergize the Yan'an Combat Brigade. They trekked to neighboring villages to win support for an assault on Geng. But in nearby Gengkou, villagers put up posters saying, "Firmly support Geng Changsuo in the revolution!" In Yuanzi, Zoucun, and Wodi, villagers ignored Qiao's anti-Geng appeals.

Next, Qiao Yong went to Shi Guiying's commune movie-projection team, where a group called "Wei Dong Biao" (Defend Mao Zedong and Lin Biao) had formed. Qiao was pleased when members agreed that Wugong had been "Lin Tie's black experimental site" and that the village had been "stuffed full with state money." The two rebel factions would compile a file on the Geng empire. Qiao took the "black materials" to Beijing but returned empty-handed in a few days. When the rebels ordered Geng to criticize young loyalists who mocked Qiao, he flatly refused.

Boss Geng urged middle-aged Li Xin'geng of the now disintegrating Jinggangshan faction to organize a mass meeting to "see whether people still have criticisms of me." But when only six people showed up and no one spoke, a defeated Li averred, "We never intended to knock you down. We just wanted to help you!" Jinggangshan capitulated.

Geng never had to endure the humiliations forced on Li Chunyu in Raoyang, on Lin Tie in the provincial capital, and on model village leaders throughout Hebei. Soon the national political winds shifted. Unity became the new order of the day. Li Changjin and his Nankai University red guards returned to Tianjin at the end of February. By the end of March 1967, urban red guards in Raoyang and elsewhere were ordered by Beijing to return to school.

Military Factionalism in Baoding

Liu Zihou had risen by deposing Hebei party secretary Lin Tie and his allies. From January 1967, however, Monarch Liu was attacked in Baoding, the temporary provincial capital. The Red Rebel Regiment with 2,000 student members vied with the August First red guards, which eventually grew to 10,000 and included many workers and army veterans. Both denounced Hebei power holders "taking the capitalist road," which now meant Liu Zihou and his associates. Liu lacked a power base in Baoding. Both Baoding groups contained supporters of former Hebei party secretary Lin Tie, the top man in Baoding in the first decade of the People's Republic, when it was the provincial capital.

Soon after Liu arrived in Baoding to administer the temporary provincial capital, the two major red-guard groups, spurred by a seizure of power by red guards in Shanghai's January Storm, united to topple the provincial party secretary. On January 29, 1967, the August First red guards paraded Liu for five hours in the back of a truck, dressed in the gown and hat of a Qing dynasty official. A million people witnessed the spectacle.

In Baoding, Raoyang, and across the land, rebels occupied the premises of the party and government. But in February Mao listened to senior military leaders, people who were not tied to Defense Minister Lin Biao, inveigh against the disorder. Mao ordered a temporary halt to the chaos, disbanded the red guards, and ordered them to return to their schools and units. Throughout China, yesterday's revolutionary sowers of creative disorder became today's enemies of the people.

In most of Hebei, order returned. Restored officials crushed the rebels. But in Baoding prefecture the chaos and killing continued on a scale far worse than anywhere else in the province. The popular view was that Baoding was uniquely rife with enemies of the people. It was known as a city of strangers from elsewhere, a place full of crude and violent people, all made worse by a prolonged Japanese occupation and a secret police war against Chinese patriots, a combination engendering desires for revenge and pervasive fears that the city was full of quislings. With each faction armed by opposing military units, vigilante violence became bloody.

In February 1967, as Mao called for an end to the chaos, two armies, the 69th and the 38th, vied for control of Baoding, which had been designated the temporary provincial capital one month earlier. The 69th was an old Nationalist unit whose 1949 defection enabled the red armies to capture Beijing peacefully. Stationed in Baoding, it reported directly to the Beijing Military District command, which controlled Beijing, Tianjin, Hebei, and Shanxi. The real power of this 50,000 man force was exercised by Deputy Commander and Political Commissar Xie Zhenhua.

The 69th and 38th armies were bitter rivals. Both had fought in Korea. But as officers and enlisted men from the 69th recall it, the 38th, long associated with Defense Minister Lin Biao, was privileged. Whereas the 69th fought with guns of resistance-war vintage, the 38th had sparkling uniforms and modern equipment. The 69th was sent to the front in the most dangerous combat situations. Then, its soldiers insist, with the battle virtually won, they were withdrawn so the 38th could claim the victory and receive plaudits. Model army units, like model villages, were perceived by those in less favored units as frauds.

On February 11, 1967, two days after the lunar New Year, the 69th, backed by the old marshals, restored Monarch Liu Zihou to power in Baoding, jailed 1,000 activists of the August First group, and branded that organization counterrevolutionary. In Shijiazhuang, in a similar development, the 63rd Army under Ma Hui, commander of the Hebei Military District, squashed rebel organizations, including the Madman's Commune (Kuangren gongshe), and arrested its leader, railroad engineer Pan Zhi. The Madman's Commune, a rebel group with local headquarters at Shijiazhuang Normal College, lionized

Chen Lining, whom they hailed as the "madman of the modern age." It was an allusion to "Diary of a Madman" (Kuangren riji, 1918) by Lu Xun, China's renowned writer. Red guards found Chen confined to an insane asylum because he had criticized President Liu. Members of the Cultural Revolution Group "reversed the case" against Chen, whose backers published his pamphlets and speeches and produced a play about his life. The revolutionary rhetoric of the Madman's Commune led locals to joke about changing the city's name from Shijiazhuang (Shi Family Village) to Zuojiazhuang (Left Family Village).

At the end of February 1967 the 100,000 strong 38th Army, bulwark of revolution, was ordered out of Beijing and sent to Baoding. Part of the 69th was then transferred from Baoding to Shanxi province, where General Xie Zhenhua eventually became head of the provincial revolutionary committee.

The 38th had a long revolutionary history from its formation in the late 1920s in the Jinggang mountains. During the civil war in the late 1940s it fought from the north to Hainan in the south as part of the 13th group army under Huang Yongsheng.

After fighting in Korea, the 38th was stationed in Jilin province on the Korean border. General Liu Haiqing, commander of the 38th, had been Defense Minister Lin Biao's bodyguard during the Sino-Japanese war. In mid-1966, in a virtual antiparty coup, the 38th moved into Beijing to help pressure high officials to go along with the Cultural Revolution. The most militant red guards looked to it for support. The 38th's ferocious reputation made Shijiazhuang's Madman's Commune seem like a church choir. Mao wrote in its praise, "Long live the 38th Army!" A song that praised its soldiers as "Steel Troops" spread in popularity. Having spilled their blood for the nation, the 38th was seen as pure revolution. The 69th supported Monarch Liu Zihou, while the 38th backed vigilante groups hostile to Liu.

A directive of April 7, 1967, by Mao and Lin Biao that criticized the suppression of rebels sparked further conflict throughout Hebei, especially in Baoding. The Red Rebel Regiment, backed by the 38th, demanded the release of August First allies arrested in February. In June a meeting billed as the Baoding Red Guard Congress denounced the February suppression of rebels and forged a red-guard coalition called the Workers' General Headquarters. The new rebel formations, helped by the 38th, opposed Monarch Liu.

Baoding red guards tied to the 38th used army trucks to commandeer weapons in Raoyang. Twelve Baoding trucks confronted a Raoyang military force of approximately 30, which was forced to surrender hundreds of rifles and crates of ammunition. Raoyang people were terrified.

Divided over the fate of Monarch Liu, the 69th and 38th distributed arms to their supporters, including high school students. Throughout Baoding prefecture, and especially in Baoding city, the killing continued intermittently until 1976. The death toll was high. Antagonistic armies, paranoia about alien enemies and internal traitors, ultimate faith in Mao, and teenage bravado combined in a savage slaughter.

All across Hebei, recently suppressed rebel organizations struggled to survive in summer 1967. Fleeing suppression, members of the Madman's Commune escaped into Raoyang and neighboring counties, invoking Geng Changsuo's name, since Geng was seen as a follower of Lin Tie, and thus the adversary of victorious Monarch Liu. Geng Changsuo, a former client of the fallen Lin Tie, had survived, but what place was there for him in Monarch Liu's kingdom?

8 ❧ WHATEVER CHAIRMAN MAO SAYS

The hasty departure of the Tianjin red guards in late February 1967 left Geng Changsuo loyalists ruling Wugong. Its "poor and lower-middle peasants" urged that local party leaders be treated fairly and used wisely.[1] The United Headquarters, which had protected Geng, took him in along with party secretary Zhang Duan, administrator Qiao Liguang, and Zhang Chaoke, the production specialist.[2] Geng became "honorary" deputy chair of the village Cultural Revolution Committee.

Jinggangshan rebels were furious. Humiliated Qiao Yong put up a protest poster. "It's a travesty that Geng Changsuo can grab any official post he seeks without us peasants knowing anything about it!" Later Qiao whitewashed on a wall in the east end, "Down with three-anti element Geng Changsuo!" An old-timer disagreed, "What's wrong with you? If Geng Changsuo is overthrown, who's gonna be in charge?" Li Shuxin, vice chair of the Cultural Revolution Committee, grabbed Qiao Yong's bucket of whitewash and dumped it on Qiao's head. A fight ensued. Isolated and degraded, Qiao Yong's mental health deteriorated until he seemed crazy. And Wu-gong was a relatively humane place.

Geng's flexibility in dealing with his critics did not extend to economic policy. Hunger festered. In May 1967, just before the wheat harvest, administrator Qiao reminded Geng of those who borrowed grain to get through the spring dearth. Geng snapped, "People have to return whatever they borrowed." Disgruntled elders discussed getting villagers together to protest, but they dared not.

When Geng noticed dispirited laborers merely going through the motions of weeding, he had the team 1 head assemble them. "If we waste a 600 mu field like this," he warned, "you can forget about getting 420 catties a person to eat. You won't even get 320 catties." Mocking his recent accusers, Geng jibed, "It's not enough to 'grasp revolution,' you also have to 'promote production.'" Geng still put first the demand of the state for grain.

Rethinking Wugong's History

Geng Changsuo and his inner circle reconstructed Wugong's history to prove that they had unfailingly supported Mao's revolutionary line, not that of the fallen Lin Tie, Geng's patron. An old friend showed the way. In early summer 1967 Geng Xiufeng passed on a package from Wang Lin, who had brought the writers to Wugong in 1963. The package contained classified material, "How Liu Shaoqi Sabotaged China's Efforts to Take the Socialist Road," an April 12 speech by public security specialist Kang Sheng to an enlarged meeting of the Central Military Commission.[3]

Kang claimed that President Liu had long opposed socialist transformation. He denounced Liu for nurturing a "rich peasant economy," protecting private property and the rural market, and for blocking collectivization. Kang asserted that Mao had criticized Liu since the early 1950s. The Wugong leadership then convinced itself that the toppled president had persistently undermined them. A new narrative emphasized his responsibility for Wugong's plight. The problem with this view was that Geng's erstwhile patron, Lin Tie, had been labeled Liu's main agent in Hebei.

By late summer 1967, Hebei first party secretary Liu Zihou was consolidating his power. Anti-Liu rebels tied to the fallen Lin Tie were endangered. So Geng attacked Lin. Years later, a magnanimous Lin told us that when people like Geng denounced innocents, they "did not wish to act this way." Politics was a matter of survival.[4]

The new village history highlighted class struggle. Nothing could be said about how the early coop maintained harmony by meeting both the income concerns of more prosperous members and the welfare needs of the most vulnerable. The early history of the party branch could only mention the poor-peasant faction centered on Pioneer Xu Yizhou, not the patriots who rallied around the old elites. Xu's group was presented as heir to the late 1930s Association that joined the lineages of the east and west against the southern Li in the center, although neither "lineage" nor "neighborhood" could be mentioned. The Association was recast as a promoter of class war by the poor against the rich.[5]

It was impossible in this mythos to describe prospering in the late 1940s through commercial sidelines. Support from Hebei party secretary Lin Tie in the 1950s was likewise taboo. Silence prevailed on how the village was harmed both in 1956 and again in the period 1959–61 when revolutionary policies devastated the economy. The Leap, which brought famine, was hailed as a triumph of Mao's line.

The new history had some real appeal. Geng had long wondered why his small coop was attacked as a "rich-peasant" organization in late 1947, why the "big coop" of more than 400 households was drastically "slashed" in size in 1953 and then slighted in 1955 when Mao pushed collectivization, and why the 1962 meeting at the Beijing Hotel advocated a restoration of material incentives. Geng concluded that President Liu, Beijing party secretary Peng Zhen, and Hebei party secretary Lin Tie made up an anti-Mao faction responsible for Wugong's snubbings.

In this narrative, Wugong began in 1943 to mobilize in response to Mao's call, "Get Organized!" While Wang Lin's 1963 book on Wugong acknowledged that the first coop was organized before anyone had learned of Mao's article, a Cultural Revolution pedigree required Mao as the fount of all wisdom. The new narrative claimed that, following land reform in 1947 and 1948, Liu Shaoqi and his agents opposed "agrarian socialism." Liu held that collectivization before mechanization was wrong.[6] In this logic, a black line strangled the attempts of those who supported the expansion of the un-mechanized Geng coop into ever larger units.

In short, Wugong was a pure socialist place victimized by President Liu. Geng now recalled that in early 1951, at a conference on cooperation and mutual aid, he was told that Wugong was a "bad model," a model of "agrarian socialism," and was "reactionary, utopian, backward." He concluded that Hebei party secretary Lin Tie had acted on behalf of President Liu in opposing Wugong. Geng came to believe that an invitation to a 1951 Tianjin exhibit came belatedly after Mao visited the conference, spoke on behalf of big cooperatives, and frightened Liu's agent, Lin Tie, into making room for Wugong. Geng also persuaded himself that Mao must have been behind the 1952 invitation to Geng to join the delegation headed for the Soviet Union to study collectives.

Wugong's leaders learned that in 1953 ruling groups had debated whether to rush to collectivize agriculture. Mao and revolutionary theorist Chen Boda had urged swift action. President Liu and the head of the party's Rural Work Department, reformer Deng Zihui, warned of negative consequences. Early in 1953 Mao conceded to Liu and the Central Committee majority. China would promote gradual, voluntary cooperation to consolidate the gains of land reform.[7] Geng and his advisers concluded that Liu Shaoqi and Hebei party secretary Lin Tie must have dispatched the April 1953 work team that cut back Wugong's big coop. No wonder Mao failed to respond to the letter Geng sent on the coop's 1953 tenth anniversary. Liu undoubtedly blocked it. Like many Chinese, Geng envisioned himself as Mao's ever-loyal supporter, fantasizing that the reversal of the 1953 "slashing" came straight from Mao.

Village leaders concluded that in 1955 Lin Tie had kept Mao from learning that Wugong was an outstanding model of collectivization. Geng denounced Lin Tie's criticisms of the deadly 1958–61 Leap. Although Geng himself had fallen ill because of the Leap dearth, he claimed that communes had allowed

Wugong to mobilize labor to sink 20 wells, raise grain yields from 300 to 600 or 700 catties per mu, and to sell the state far more grain and cotton. Provincial aid that facilitated Wugong gains in yield was not mentioned. Silent about how Lin Tie's gift allowed Wugong to build Raoyang's first electric power plant, Geng credited the commune, Mao's innovation, with building the plant that made possible the first electrically driven irrigation in the region.

From the 1943 drought to the "three bad years" following the Leap, history "proved" that only large-scale collective efforts freed families from nature's scourges. Revolutionary policies that actually locked villagers into misery were perversely credited with the economic recovery of the first half of the 1960s. Successful reforms went unmentioned.

Geng had in fact opposed reforms at the 1962 Beijing Hotel Conference. He now saw his faith in the leveling collective as faith in Mao. The legend was exhilarating. It demonstrated that Wugong's problems came from opponents of Mao's way. Geng reinterpreted the 1963 Wugong visit of Lieutenant Governor Yang Yichen as an anti-Mao plot to pressure Wugong to boost sideline production. With Yang persecuted to death as part of Lin Tie's Hebei clique, village leaders "remembered" that Yang had arrived after dark, met in secret in a small room, and tried to bribe Wugong to abandon collective agriculture. Yang sneaked away when he failed to fool local folk. Wugong had resisted a Liu Shaoqi follower trying to bump it off the socialist road. It stood with Mao.

With the help of his daughter, Huijuan, Geng "wrote" 40 manifestos attacking President Liu and Hebei party secretary Lin Tie, styling them "China's Khrushchev and his agent in Hebei." In fall 1967 these poster letters were sent to woo leaders in Beijing, Baoding, Shijiazhuang, and Hengshui prefecture.[8] Highlighting village history as a struggle against enemies of Mao presented Wugong as an embodiment of revolution.

Raoyang's Revolutionary Returnees

In July 1967 party secretary Li Chunyu and other deposed Raoyang leaders were struggled against in every commune in the county. The May First Battle Brigade, a student group, even broke into the military affairs department and hurled charges at Raoyang military leader Li Guoqiang. But by the end of the summer, the power center in Beijing sought to restore order. Fallen party and government leaders then counterattacked, often in concert with the military.

On the morning of November 3, a poster on the gate of the county party committee compound proclaimed, "Li Chunyu and Yuan Zijie are not three-anti elements! They are revolutionary officials!" A few days later posters plastered the county town. "Welcome the revolutionary officials who have returned!" Li Chunyu, former county magistrate Yuan Zijie, and others were "liberated." Their fall had lasted nine months. Li and Yuan were then whisked to Tianjin to learn the new line in sessions run by the Hebei Military District.

The Raoyang military helped the old party establishment resume power. One night in November a rebel group from nearby Anguo county stole arms from the Raoyang military affairs department. A Raoyang military committee was then set up in early December to take over all county public security units, procuratorial organs, and people's courts. At the county jail, the wardens switched from blue to olive green outfits that resembled the army uniform. Only the insignia affixed to hats distinguished the two. The army cap was adorned with a red star, the security police cap with a replica of Tiananmen gate.

On December 21 when four trucks from Anguo again pulled up to Raoyang military headquarters, leader Li Guoqiang's forces fired a volley of warning shots. The rebels fled. Li contacted military authorities in neighboring Anping county, who put up a roadblock and opened fire, killing one driver. All over Hebei factions fought over arms. Many weapons ended up in Baoding and were used in fierce fighting.

Revolutionary committees were set up in late 1967 and early 1968. Li Guoqiang, Li Chunyu, and Geng Changsuo had won. The first Hengshui prefectural revolutionary committee meeting, held on December 9, 1967, saw Geng and military chief Li Guoqiang representing Raoyang, with Geng a member of its standing committee. On February 2, 1968, a Raoyang revolutionary committee was set up with the approval of the Hebei Military District party committee. Li Guoqiang was named chair and Li Chunyu vice chair. The Standing Committee of 12 included Geng.[9] Rebels who had attacked Geng as an ally of the fallen Lin Tie were introduced to a Geng parading as a consistent opponent of Lin Tie.

On February 10 county military chief Li Guoqiang directed 700 brigade-level officials to attend special courses to "combat self and fight revisionism." These were local versions of the military courses senior county leaders had taken in Tianjin. In late spring 1968 officials returned to set up village revolutionary committees. Rebel organizations were crushed in most villages. In some, rebels received token representation in the new power structures. Defense Minister Lin Biao's military was still the model. In many areas the military dominated revolutionary committees.

Military Virtue

The military's prominence was tied to the rise of Defense Minister Lin Biao. The military seemed uniquely pure.[10] Lin's military protected Mao, socialism, and the nation. Activist youth basked in the glory of the army. They proudly wore military-style uniforms.

In November 1967 Geng's daughter, Huijuan, attended a high-profile meeting of "Mao Zedong Thought Activists" organized by the Beijing Military District. She wrote jubilant letters back to allies about her two weeks of learning to implement Lin Biao's militia policies. On November 13, Mao and Lin visited the group. Huijuan boasted in *People's Daily,* "The great leader Chairman Mao and his closest comrade in arms, Vice Commander Lin, came to see us. It was the most unforgettable day of my life. Think of it! Me, an ordinary girl from a poor peasant family, able to see Chairman Mao, the great teacher of the revolutionary people of the whole world. That's happiness!"[11]

Military recruits from Raoyang and Wugong increased. Wugong's team 3 sent just three recruits to the army between 1949 and 1966, an average of one every five years. Between 1966 and 1974, the number was 16, ten times the prior rate. Raoyang was allowed to conscript 550 new recruits in 1969, a reward for loyalty. When a village youngster was conscripted, parents covered the household's front gate with red paper proclaiming pure red status and signifying eligibility for village support.

Some Raoyang recruits were stationed in the Beijing garrison guarding the capital. Large numbers enrolled in Unit 8341, the armed guard that also served as Mao's personal administrative staff. Ties to Unit 8341 dated from the late 1940s when the party center was headquartered in the west Hebei village of Xibaipo and land-reform work teams came to Raoyang. Over the years, more than 500 of the unit's soldiers were recruited from Raoyang. The county was regarded as especially loyal to Mao.

Villagers in old base areas who had sacrificed to resist Japanese invasion strongly identified with the army. To elders, the militia and army presented the best hope for ending violence and vendettas. Still, vigilantism persisted. Mao disbanded the urban red guards, sending many youth to the countryside. But from this time forward, the most savage violence was top-down and organized, resulting in far more damage than the anarchy of the red guards.

Cleansing the Class Ranks

In early April 1968, as part of a nationwide campaign, a reinstated Li Chunyu initiated a "cleansing of the class ranks" and "dictatorship of the masses" movement in Raoyang. The targets were people with bad class labels, "complicated" family backgrounds, and a "history of problems." "Living targets" (huo bazi) would suffer the "dictatorship of the masses" backed by the army.

Mao's wife Jiang Qing directed red guards to attack people in Tianjin with ties to President Liu, including Song Jingyi of the Tianjin party committee. A "searching for traitors team" comprising Tianjin and Shijiazhuang red guards raced to Song's native village 25 miles west of Raoyang. His relatives were arrested and tortured. Some committed suicide. Murder and mayhem spread.[12]

On April 18 campaign zealots killed Lu Baoyu from Zhengbao village, a biology teacher at Raoyang High School. Party member Lu was an activist in the school's Red Education Workers rebel group. During a raid on personnel files, the militants learned that Lu had disclosed Red Army tunnels to Japanese troops. Actually, back in the 1950s investigators had cleared Lu by confirming that he only revealed abandoned tunnels.

Nonetheless, rebels denounced Lu as a traitor. They shackled his legs and inserted within the shackles a long, heavy log that pulled down his back and neck in a cruel torture. Keeping Lu standing, they stood on each end of the log and jumped. When Lu collapsed, the rebels left. Half paralyzed, he crawled to his room. Teacher Lu's death was recorded as "cause unknown."

Ten days later, in the "cleansing of the class ranks," United Rebel General Headquarters youth joined three Red Education Workers to seize Raoyang High School principal Zhang Baochen in his home village. Before they could drag Zhang back to school, however, club-wielding village resisters from Houpu and Qianpu routed the marauders, smashing their bicycles. The rebels returned to Raoyang town and armed themselves with steel bars. But the military blocked another bloody melee.

Allegations of treachery flew. In mid-May 1968 revolutionary committee leaders Li Guoqiang and Li Chunyu summoned 600 village and 200 county functionaries, "activists in the living study and living use of Mao Zedong thought," to the county seat. That phrase was Lin Biao's trademark. Two weeks later Wei Cunhou of Dasongjiazhuang just west of Wugong proclaimed that his village was the headquarters of spies controlled from Taiwan, the last bastion of the civil war that brought the communists to power. One hundred and eleven villagers were named members of a secret anticommunist Nationalist Party cell led by Communist Party branch secretary Wei Shixin. For 133 days party secretary Wei was tortured by kinsmen until he committed suicide.[13] In Yanggezhuang village north of Wugong, two villagers were accused of harboring Nationalist spies.

Models and the Politics of Production

Maintaining Wugong's red-flag status still required delivering substantial grain to the state. Brains Zhang Chaoke ran the economy. His wife had a mental breakdown, and her body ballooned. She lost control of her senses. Doctors found no organic etiology. The family cared for her at home, sequestered like other disabled villagers.

Brains Zhang went out to study production models. He was impressed by the Shanghai suburbs run by fundamentalists. The industry and flourishing fields made his rural hinterland seem stagnant. Many thought of Shanghai in terms of higher wages, richer culture, and fresh vegetables all year round. Winter in Beijing was cabbages and turnips. But the view from his tenth-floor Shanghai room made Zhang dizzy. The polluted air made white shoes turn black in two days. By comparison, Wugong's shit and mud seemed clean.

In 1966 Wugong village harvested a record 768 catties of grain per mu. The state took 15 percent, the largest amount since the Leap. The percentage of collective sideline income fell by more than half from the reform year of 1962, bottoming out at 17 percent of village collective income in 1967. Neighboring villages were mired in poverty. While Wugong harvested 611 catties per mu in 1968, in Yuanzi and Zoucun it was only 203 and 190 catties, respectively, in miserable Yanggezhuang a mere 81.

Fundamentalists got Wugong households to stop raising cats, a bourgeois affectation. Elsewhere goldfish and flowers were attacked as class enemies. The suppressed rural market left rat poison scarce. So, with cats and poison scarce, rats flourished, taking ever more grain.

Wugong's team 3 kept out-producing the others. In summer 1967 its team head, Li Wer, withdrew the team from the money-losing village rope collective. West-ender Xu Chuan, the former village party secretary who had supported anti-Geng rebels in early 1967, said, "In earlier days all three teams made their own ropes. At that time the income of our sideline group was the same as the income of the other two groups put together! When rope making was unified . . . our team 3 lost a lot. That's why people want to split."[14] Big collectives were costly.

With Geng away at a meeting, Zhang Duan the Ox and Brains Zhang Chaoke, both from team 3, put out the brush fire. They pressured Xu Mantang, party secretary of team 3, to lean on kinsmen Xu Chuan and Xu Yue. East-ender Geng Xiufeng reminded Xu Yue about his father, Xu Dun. "When the rich faction searched your house [in 1936] and threw your father in jail, how did he get out? The people of the whole village got together to form the Association. That's how he was rescued." Finally, Xu lineage members conceded, and team 3 stuck with the money-losing villagewide collective.

Loyalty had its benefits. State-funded projects were still vital. In June 1966 Hengshui prefecture gave Raoyang a 42,800 yuan long-term, low-interest loan to drill mechanized wells. The funds were divided among 83 villages; 92 wells were sunk. In September 1966 a project to place phone wires underground was initiated. Twenty-four kilometers of back-breaking digging was completed in a first phase. Thirty-nine more kilometers, including a line that tied Wugong village to the county seat, were finished by the end of July 1967.

In October 1967, two water-control projects were coordinated by a new Raoyang Flood Prevention Office. The first sought to rebuild the banks of the Hutuo River. Laborers conscripted in Baoding and Shijiazhuang prefectures completed the 18 kilometer project in 1968. Raoyang people then built two drainage canals, totaling 13-plus kilometers.

In late February 1968, as part of the mammoth Hai River project, 30,000 conscript laborers were sent to Raoyang from Baoding and Shijiazhuang prefectures to move earth on the northern bank of the Hutuo River. Raoyang's Flood Prevention Office was told to provide housing and food. This burden was passed on to villages and communes.

Leaders of poor Raoyang villages gathered that winter to discuss why they were still poor. Boss Geng Changsuo pledged that Wugong would help Yang-gezhuang, which had been devastated by revolutionary policies that ruled out suitable economic crops and off-farm employment.

Restoration: The Hebei Revolutionary Committee and the Rise of Geng

In December 1967, alarmed at the chaos and factionalism in the province surrounding the capital, Mao sent revolutionary theorist Chen Boda and North China party secretary Li Xuefeng along with Zheng Weishan, acting commander of the Beijing Military District, to all major Hebei cities. Everywhere except Baoding, where local rebels were backed by the 38th Army, the revolutionary leaders condemned rebels and pressed for an alliance of the military with the forces of Liu Zihou. The way was paved for the formation of a Hebei provincial revolutionary committee led by Monarch Liu.

To expedite Liu's return, the Hebei military smashed the Madman's Commune in Shijiazhuang. Survivors of the Madman's Commune found succor in Baoding. They allied themselves with others opposed to Liu Zihou's power. To avoid the ire of groups associated with Defense Minister Lin Biao and the 38th Army, factions in Baoding that once backed deposed "counterrevolutionary" Hebei party leader Lin Tie now joined factions supporting revolutionary Jiang Qing.

After spending months in chaotic and violent Baoding, a former leader of the Madman's Commune risked returning to his factory. At 7 A.M. he entered the Shijiazhuang Tobacco Factory. When workers arrived, they found him at the factory entrance bowing before a portrait of Mao. Five militiamen immediately dragged him to security headquarters.

Factory revolutionary committee members locked the door and began pummeling and kicking their former rival. One female begged the tormentors to stop. Pleas for mercy fell on deaf ears. Suddenly the victim pulled a gun from his underclothing. Now it was the torturers' turn to beg for mercy. They were shot one by one until only the female and the top leader remained. The leader kowtowed and pleaded with the gun wielder to remember that the leader had a family with children. "Did you ever think about my family and children? Where was your heart?" was the rejoinder. He shot the leader and then committed suicide. When the door was opened, the men lay dead in pools of blood.

The Hebei leadership used deadly class struggle tactics to unearth traitors. Targets were described as members of a May 16th reactionary clique, rightists discrediting socialism in the guise of ultraleft politics. The militia cracked down on those who sought to improve their lot in the market. Some stole. When a miserable soul was apprehended, mass struggle ensued.

Following the January 29 movement of the capital to Shijiazhuang, Boss Geng arrived for the inauguration of the Hebei provincial revolutionary committee. It had been created in Beijing under the aegis of the Beijing Military District in mid-January. A mass rally in Shijiazhuang on February 3 celebrated its founding.[15] North China party head Li Xuefeng chaired it; Monarch Liu, the first deputy chair, was de facto head. Hebei was one of the few provinces whose revolutionary committee was not headed by a military commander. Military representatives numbered only 26 of its 121 members. Still, the army was there in force.[16] Deputy chairs of the revolutionary committee included Political Commissar Zeng Mei and Commander Ma Hui of the Hebei Military District, and Wang Meng, political commissar of the 38th Army. The 38th Army in Baoding, however, continued to challenge Liu Zihou.[17]

According to Geng Xiufeng, the revolutionary committee originally designated Mao-blessed village leaders Wang Guofan and Wang Yukun as members of its powerful Standing Committee, with Geng Changsuo an ordinary member. Mao had never said anything about Wugong. Boss Geng's detractors believed him lucky to be at the meeting, since he had been criticized for ties to the Madman's Commune that had tried to topple Monarch Liu. But the military supported Geng. He was appointed a deputy chair of the Hebei revolutionary committee, listed ahead of both Wangs![18] It was Geng's highest position ever. *People's Daily* praised his 1967 posters denouncing President Liu and his Hebei agent Lin Tie.[19]

The Hebei revolutionary committee members were shuttled to Beijing at night and ushered into a grand meeting room. Geng was escorted to the front. Mao's wife Jiang Qing, revolutionary theorist Chen Boda, and Premier Zhou Enlai spoke. The premier joked that Jiang Qing always worried about the number of women in delegations. Zhou knew them. He called out the names of Hebei women activists. "Is Xin Yanzi here?" "Yes!" "Where is Rong Guanxiu?" "There!" "What about Lu Yulan?" "She's over here!" The group was overjoyed at Zhou's familiarity. The premier then asked, "Is Geng Changsuo here?" Geng jumped up saying, "Here I am!" "You look so healthy," Zhou said, smiling.[20] To 67-year-old Geng, anything seemed possible if he but went where Chairman Mao led.

Hebei, Raoyang, Wugong: After the Storm

By February 1968, Liu Zihou held power all across Hebei except in Baoding. Tianjin, directly under central administration, was run by Xie Xuegong, who enjoyed personal ties to Jiang Qing. Geng Changsuo stayed in Shijiazhuang for most of spring and summer 1968. With Wugong a model of overcoming the evils of President Liu and his Hebei henchman Lin Tie, journalists rushed to Wugong. It was the village's first major publicity since 1965.[21]

Using the mantra of Lin Biao, Mao's political heir, Geng said his policy was "to read the books of Chairman Mao, listen to the words of Chairman Mao, and act in accord with the directives of Chairman Mao." He iterated, "Whatever Chairman Mao says, I will do" (Mao zhuxi zhenma shuo, wo jiu zhenma ban).

Geng echoed all who seemed to speak for Mao. He was cultivated by Hebei Monarch Liu, North China party boss Li Xuefeng, and Gao Jian, a former Raoyang leader who was deputy director of the Hebei bureau of agriculture. The February 6, 1968, issue of *People's Daily* ranked Geng first among Hebei village leaders who excelled in the "living study and living practice" of Mao's thought.[22] Geng said over and over that studying Chairman Mao's words was "life's number 1 need."

Worship of Mao spread. By 1968 four million Hebei residents reportedly met regularly to wish the Chairman a long life, to ask for his directives in the morning, to report to him in the evening, and to sing "The East is Red" and "Sailing the Seas Depends on the Helmsman." In early February Wugong was praised as first among Hebei villages in setting up "Mao Zedong thought study classes."[23]

Wugong as a Revolutionary Model

In mid-March 1968 revolutionary committees were set up in Raoyang's 16 communes. In May Wugong established a village revolutionary committee, uniting "the old, the middle-aged and the young" under Geng's chairmanship. There were no posts for the rebels of early 1967. Leaders prodded villagers to condemn yet again the bitterness of the prerevolutionary past and praise the sweetness of the present. More than 1,000 adults were organized in study groups that memorized and recited writings by Mao.

The revolutionary committee included the pre–Cultural Revolution leaders except Geng's wife Xu Shukuan, who "retired," plus the young who had recently protected Geng. The Boss and his east- and west-village allies, the Geng, Qiao, Yang, and Zhang lineages, were in charge. The west-end Xus were in limbo. The southern Li families residing in the village center remained marginalized.

By fall 1968 the village party branch was restored by prearranged ballot of its 110 members. Zhang Duan again was party secretary, with Geng's daughter Huijuan a deputy. Zhang, paralyzed by the politics of chaos, never recovered the full power of his title. Three additional deputy secretaries were soon added. Brains Zhang Chaoke, who had kept economic work going during the turmoil, remained in charge of production. Red Successor Yang Tong was made deputy secretary in charge of administration. Macho Li Shouzheng was the deputy secretary for public security. This trio — Zhang, Yang, and Li — joining administrator Qiao Liguang and Chief Huijuan, again united the east and west villages.

By the end of 1968 Wugong leaders pushed the virtues of a free supply system, a goal of the revolutionary 1958 Leap. Teams were urged to distribute more regardless of work. At one meeting all villagers were asked to identify themselves by name and declare "yea" or "nay" to expanding free supply. No one dared say "nay."[24] The accountant believed that Wugong went furthest in the county in egalitarian distribution. Labor intensity dissipated.

In early 1968 Chen Boda and Lin Biao set up an experimental site to restrict household plots and markets in Evergreen Commune in suburban Beijing.[25] Authorities in Hengshui prefecture, who began collectivizing household plots in 1964, with Wugong a pacesetter, four years later moved to eliminate all remaining plots. Model units were told to take the lead, with activists surrendering their own plots first. Henceforth, "household plots" would be collectively cultivated in common fields. Households lost control over these crops and the right to market what was produced. Villagers dared not oppose agreement by acclamation to pull up capitalist sprouts as an expression of loyalty to Chairman Mao. When the campaign was over, only 190 of the prefecture's almost 20,000 production teams retained household-cultivated plots.

State pressure to "learn from Dazhai," Mao's model village, promoted amalgamation into larger units, reducing the number of teams nationwide by almost 20 percent.[26] Sullen families in many communities moved to village accounting. But Wugong, which had long maintained unusually large teams, resisted. Prosperous team 3 adamantly rejected further income pooling.

In 1968 a measure of order returned to the countryside. But life did not seem to improve. Some Hebei villagers fled stagnant collectives for the less populous northeast. At times entire neighborhoods pulled up stakes, eventually registering the land they opened and tilled, sometimes collectively, sometimes as families.

Raoyang was home to one anticollective anomaly. Less than a mile from Wugong near Caozhuang village, a particularly well cultivated field was tilled by a family that had never joined a collective. Having lost both sons during the resistance war, it had the protection of the army. This family alone pursued household production in the county in the 1970s.

The more revolution advanced, the more villagers started work later, returned earlier, slackened pace, ignored calls to hurry, and sought easy tasks. They would be paid the same anyway. More and more, the state seemed parasitic. Officials, compelled to drive people to work hard, felt themselves vital to the system. Revolutionary dynamics splintered society from the state, "us" from "them." Revolutionary officials made absolutes of food and clothing. For tillers, that meant growing grain and cotton, the staples of subsistence. When Geng directed Wugong's three teams to plant more cotton, the power centers in the east and west resisted. Li Wer, the head of team three, virtually illiterate, seldom speaking, proving himself by action not words, not a party member, knew that growing more low priced cotton would impoverish his team.

In 1968 the Raoyang county leadership sent three cotton specialists to Wugong from Shanxi province to testify to the wonders of close planting. Geng then ordered compliance with close planting norms that had ruined crops during the Leap.

Wheat and cotton accounted for 2,007 of the 3,643 mu that Wugong planted in 1968. By 1971 these agricultural fundamentals had risen to 75 percent of all agricultural output. Lucrative economic crops like peanuts and fruit were further cut. Fundamentalist imperatives also required that each locale feed itself. Growing grain on unsuitable soil brought impoverishment and increased the economic gap between regions. The wealth-expanding benefits of specialization and exchange were lost.

Survival dictated that villagers skirt irrational rules. Agents came to purchase Wugong rope. Wugong villagers went out to buy the ginger they preferred. In indebted villages where pay was exclusively in kind, villagers received no cash for collective labor. Urbanites sent to rural Hebei were shocked at the misery, emaciated bodies, and patched, tattered clothes. Villagers would sell almost anything to earn a pittance. The outsiders were startled by how little money was asked by cash-starved villagers.

Market substitutes came to life. Villagers traveled illegally to find spare parts and supplies, to make repairs, and to purchase needed goods and services that a market had once provided. Corruption increased, and a second economy surged. Intended to enhance morality and devalue markets, revolution unintentionally fostered the opposite.

Boss Geng as Polemicist

Boss Geng tried to accommodate both revolution and production. Between May and October 1968, five major articles with the Geng byline appeared in prominent venues. The essays were penned by writers sent by Monarch Liu Zihou or North China party head Li Xuefeng. Drafts were reworked, often by writers under the direction of revolutionary theorist Chen Boda, editor of *Red Flag*. Geng later told us that "the only truths in those essays were the anecdotes. Since I am not even smart enough to describe what is true, I am obviously incapable of inventing lies," he lamented. That is, others lied.

Still, Geng had to approve the articles. He welcomed the publicity. The articles presented the Wugong narrative worked out in mid-1967 to show the village in constant struggle against President Liu Shaoqi and former Hebei party secretary Lin Tie, Liu's agent in Hebei.

On May 19, 1968, for the second anniversary of Mao's May 16 circular launching the Cultural Revolution, *People's Daily* featured Geng's "Firmly Remember Chairman Mao's Teaching and Tenaciously Grasp Class Struggle."[27]

Geng found a basic lesson in Mao's directive: "Forgetting class struggle means forgetting revolution, forgetting political power, forgetting the dictatorship of the proletariat. This is the greatest disloyalty to Chairman Mao." Lashing out at both the fallen President Liu and deposed Hebei party secretary Lin Tie, the article described capitalist roaders as representatives of landlords, rich peasants, reactionaries, bad elements, and rightists.

Since 1943 Wugong had followed Mao's path. As a result, "for the past 25 years we have experienced a serious nonstop struggle between the two classes, the two roads, and the two lines. China's Khrushchev [President Liu] and his agent in Hebei [Lin Tie] tried everything under the sun to restore capitalism in Wugong." The article praised the first two years of the Cultural Revolution, ignoring the attacks on Geng for being Lin's client.

In line with Mao's March 1, 1968, instruction against anarchy and in favor of discipline, a line reestablishing many fallen officials and Premier Zhou's state networks, Geng also took as his enemies people "who spread anarchism, destroy labor discipline, and destroy production." In spring and summer Geng attended numerous rallies and meetings in Shijiazhuang. On March 30 he spoke to the Hebei revolutionary committee on Mao's latest directive on revolutionary committees.[28] On June 5 he attended a gathering of 100,000 people to celebrate the formation of the Sichuan provincial revolutionary committee.[29] On July 24 he participated in a forum of rural labor models devoted to Mao's instructions on the revolution in education.[30]

A second article with Geng's byline appeared in *People's Daily* on August 5, 1968.[31] "Resolutely Eliminate the Poison of the Bourgeois Headquarters" celebrated the second anniversary of Mao's big character poster "Bombard the Headquarters." The article was second in prominence to one by the Shanghai Workers' Revolutionary Rebel Headquarters. Shanghai, led by ideologist Zhang Chunqiao, an ally of Mao's wife Jiang Qing, was a national leader in continuing the Cultural Revolution.

Geng's essay echoed the line that the ongoing revolution against the bourgeois headquarters was a struggle for state power waged by the new revolutionary committees. It warned that the bourgeois headquarters was "using all sorts of tricks and secret plots to attack the proletarian headquarters led by Chairman Mao with the help of Vice Chairman Lin, and the newly born revolutionary committees."

On August 28 in Guangzhou, a Lin Biao stronghold, *China News* featured a long article by Geng that celebrated the tenth anniversary of the commune frenzy. Ignoring Wugong's own Leap tragedies, the killer grain requisition, Geng's encounter with malnutrition, and his 1960 protest letter to the state center, Geng proclaimed that the masses warmly supported Mao's Leap. Geng insisted that President Liu and his Hebei agent had tried to keep Wugong from the Leap to communism in 1958.[32]

Blaming the "three hard years" caused by the Leap on natural disasters and

Soviet sabotage, Geng attacked the post-Leap reforms that stimulated food production. Because Wugong staunchly resisted President Liu Shaoqi's "three freedoms and one guarantee" reform and stuck to the big collective, Geng averred, it achieved rapid advances in production.

Ignoring the manifest discontent in team 3, Geng insisted that Wugong's success reflected the superiority of the large collective. "The greater the number of people, the more power" (ren duo, liliang da). Larger units facilitated larger collective labor projects, a favorite theme of revolutionary ideologues. Geng promised increased grain sales to the state. He pledged that Wugong would further embody the fundamentals of communism: no private income or investment, all sharing equally from collective production, and a priority on securing such basic needs as food (grain) and clothing (cotton).

Most villagers, however, now realized that the revolution left field workers with only the commodity equivalent of pennies a day, with virtually none of the cash necessary to purchase the means to mourn, marry, or celebrate. Villagers consequently looked for any way to earn some cash. In almost every village, including Wugong, a handful of young men found ways to flee the collective and earn money.

Villagers noted that, within the revolutionary system, only connections got people what they needed. Gifts and bribes greased the socialist economy. The powerless railed at the corruption surrounding state allocation of everything from rations to fertilizer; they cursed a system that forced supplicants to grovel and bribe officials:

Fine wine, fine food, get any plot of land you choose.
Don't wine, don't dine, end up in a ditch.

Villagers could compare the state's low purchase price for grain with the high black-market prices. Tillers had happy memories of pigs slaughtered for the New Year and extended families gathering for a customary celebration, parts of Chinese culture that revolutionaries attacked. Yet Geng would have Wugong rise as a model of revolution. Its neighbors groused that connections might permit the model to prosper, but not others. In the commune, favored Wugong village was becoming "them."

As in the Leap, sacred practices were maligned as feudal. Raoyang leaders would boost agricultural production by removing graves from the fields. The policy was not popular. In some villages, resisters threatened to kill anyone who dug up the graves of their lineage. In others, graves were forcibly leveled, coffins dug up, and bones moved to new burial sites. Sometimes the coffins were used for fuel in local industry, never in people's homes. Some people stole coffins. High-quality wood went into furniture sold in Zoucun and Yincun. Villagers said that on rainy days the furniture emitted the smell of death.

In the national model village of Dazhai, Chen Yonggui ordered the leveling of the graves in 1967. When "rich peasant" Jia Bingheng died, Chen initiated a new burial practice. The deceased was carried on a board and placed in a hole, thus dispensing with coffins. Dazhai also sought to sever the links of lineage by imposing random burial.[33] It profaned the sacred. Such antilineage policies were resisted in Raoyang.

Educated Youth and the Rise of Geng Huijuan

On September 6, 1968, Geng Changsuo's byline again appeared in *People's Daily*. He hailed Mao's call for millions of urban youth to go to the countryside to settle as field workers.[34] Just prior to the publication of this article, on August 25, Geng had attended an "emergency" meeting of the Standing Committee of the Hebei revolutionary committee to discuss Mao's latest instruction on the role of the working class in the "proletarian revolution in education" and revolutionary ideologist Yao Wenyuan's article, "The Working-Class Must Exercise Leadership in Everything."[35] The "educated-youth" program neutralized critically minded urban red guards by exiling them to the countryside and reducing pressure to provide costly state-sector jobs for youth. Geng's article condemned young people who "study in order to become officials" or "go to the countryside only to become officials." Such people might be in the villages, but their hearts "were still in the city." Geng pledged that Wugong was open to honest and sincere educated youngsters who sought to transform their bourgeois ways by doing field work. Hailing a "great opportunity for revolutionary educated people," he proclaimed: "We warmly welcome educated people who are taking the path of integrating with workers and peasants . . . to build a new socialist countryside."

Actually, Wugong never accepted a sent-down youth. The village only received "returning youth" (fanxiang qingnian) born and raised in Wugong. Villages could not refuse such returnees. Li Man returned from Tianjin in 1968 after graduating from junior high. She worked for years in the fields before becoming an elementary school teacher and marrying in the village. Some returnees cursed the poverty and turned to petty theft. Most villagers thought strangers a burden. Doggerel mocked the urbanites.

> Green youth, useless in the fields;
> They earn the same work points and get the same grain as we;
> Stealing chickens, imitating dogs,
> Boys and girls hang around together.

Only a small number of the 20 million or so sent down from the cities in the 1960s were integrated. Living as isolates, regarded as politically suspect and economic burdens, separated from villagers by education, speech, and expectations, many went hungry or were abused, at times, sexually. Hundreds of thousands fled back to cities. But many more had no way out of rural exile.

Li Guijie from Tianjin farmed in a Raoyang village for eight years, study-ing English at night. Rejecting the sexual advances of the local party secre-tary, Guijie was the last youth allowed to return to the city. But lacking reg-istration cards and food coupons, returnees survived on their parents' dole, at times becoming black marketeers, pimps, or prostitutes. Cynicism ran deep.[36]

Five days after Geng's article, *People's Daily* ran a piece by daughter Huijuan entitled "Resolutely Take the Road of Integrating with Workers and Peas-ants."[37] It described her as an "intellectual youth" who had voluntarily re-turned to the village. While Geng Changsuo derided educated youth seeking to become officials, skeptics thought his words a perfect description of Chief Huijuan. He had worked to get her out of the village and start her on an urban career. His patrons rewarded Huijuan. She was appointed to the county revo-lutionary committee in September 1969. Unlike real urban exiles trapped in the countryside, she was on the rise.

In her *People's Daily* article Huijuan presented herself as a paragon of revolutionary virtue. She touted her many efforts to promote Mao Zedong thought, press class struggle, and expose Liu Shaoqi's crimes. Her narrative was one of successfully integrating with rural people. The issue, yet again, was shit. One day she and an east-end friend found livestock shit on the road. Huijuan moved it to the west end for use as fertilizer. Her friend objected, "Team 3 produces the most grain, but they never invite those of us from team 1 over to eat." Huijuan responded that Mao emphasized the collective good. Her friend apologized. "All I saw was the world of our team 1. I failed to see the whole collective and the entire revolution!" A careful reader might deduce the actual tensions in the village.

Huijuan had long been engaged to her former high school classmate Zhang Ping, son of Zhang He, a former vice magistrate of the Raoyang government toppled by rebels in 1967. A well-liked, barely literate former guerrilla leader, Zhang He always produced a small notebook at meetings and scribbled away. Younger, better educated Raoyang officials would snatch the notebook and roar with laughter at the "notes," little more than the name of the meeting followed by a series of loops.

Jobless, Zhang He was still under a political cloud in the late 1960s.[38] Many families broke engagements to keep heirs from inheriting the pariah caste of a bad-status father. Some brides, left at the alter and hence doubly tarnished as divorced and politically dirtied, unlikely ever to find a mate, and knowing that life for a single woman in the countryside was intolerable, com-mitted suicide. But Geng Changsuo would not block this marriage. He did not draw a line separating himself from Zhang He as called for by class-struggle logic.

When Zhang Ping visited Wugong in December 1968, the couple decided to marry that very night. There would be no ceremony for Zhang's family to attend. With his politically active parents almost never at home, he had been raised by aunts, as Huijuan had been reared by her elder sister Xueren. Huijuan invited aspiring writer Shi Guiying. When Huijuan told her mother that she and Zhang would marry that night, Xu Shukuan, who also never enjoyed a wedding ceremony, said, "If you two agree, that's enough."

Geng Changsuo, away at a meeting, was not informed. Huijuan imagined someone asking him, "How come you're not at your daughter's wedding?" She told us that she relished her father having to reply, "What? I didn't know she was marrying." Present or not, Geng's support for the groom was crucial. The next day Zhang Ping left for a job that Geng had already secured for him in a state petroleum refinery in Tianjin.

In response to Mao's directive on education, Wugong, now a model of Mao's line on education, sent 13 virtually illiterate "poor and lower-middle peasant" elders to run the commune junior high school, which reopened in early fall 1968, to see that students identified with the interests of workers, peasants, and soldiers. Teachers were demoralized. Most students found no reason to care about learning. Class time went to talks about the bad old days and to criticizing the soft life of youngsters today.

Children of tillers had to grow food on the school playground to learn the hardships of rural life. Teachers too had to engage in field work, usually for half a day each week, but sometimes for three full days consecutively. Exhausted teachers tried to prepare classes at night for the few who studied and to teach, when possible.

The bond between caring students and dedicated teachers remained warm and respectful. Such students hated policies that deprived them of an education and savaged their teachers. Most learned that schooling was useless. It was a conclusion underlined by income distribution and reward patterns: more education, even mastery of technological skills, brought villagers no reward or advancement. Chief Huijuan's *People's Daily* article proclaimed that her father was overjoyed when she announced her decision *not* to apply for college admission! Higher education was suspect. While elementary, junior high, and high schools reopened, many colleges remained closed.

In late 1968 the state slashed resources for education. The old 12-year program (six-three-three) was reduced to eight years, with four years of elementary school, two years of junior high, and two of senior high. Raoyang attempted to set up a "self-reliant" county school system. This meant that villages, no matter how impoverished, had to supply and pay teachers out of their own meager resources. In October all the junior and senior high school students who would have graduated in 1966, 1967, and 1968 if the schools had been open were issued diplomas and sent back to their home villages. Some barely educated youths were made teachers, receiving work points from their villages. The state would cease to pay their salaries. Then in December, in accord with a central policy emulating a model in Jiaxiang county in Shandong province, officials ordered the vast majority of the teachers in 205 county elementary and secondary schools back to their home villages. The rural education system was eviscerated. Discipline was taken as counterrevolution. Illiteracy soared, especially among females.

In 1969, with Russian studies delegitimized because the Soviet Union had abandoned revolution, the Ministry of Education instructed high schools to teach English. It was a harbinger of reform. But where were the teachers? There were few trained English teachers in the countryside. In most cases, Russian-language teachers received crash courses in English and were put in rural classrooms. But students had learned to identify English as the language of imperialism. Few were willing to learn English. A handful had parents who could teach them at home. While the rest of East Asia advanced into an age of computerized high technology, China's educational system hurtled backward.

From National Day to the Ninth Party Congress

Geng Changsuo kept rising. He attended National Day festivities in Beijing. Outfitted with a set of false teeth, on October 1, 1968, he stood with state power holders on the rostrum in Tiananmen Square.[39] A photo of a smiling Geng and the Wugong leadership holding aloft red flags and huge portraits of Mao even appeared in a newspaper in Hong Kong.[40]

In mid-October an article with Geng's byline appeared in *Red Flag,* the party's theoretical journal edited by revolutionary Chen Boda.[41] "Always Follow Chairman Mao in Making Revolution" elaborated a history of Wugong informed by public security specialist Kang Sheng's spring 1967 secret denunciation of President Liu Shaoqi. Ever since 1943, when "four households of poor peasants" in Wugong had responded to Mao's call to "get organized," the village had been marching in "large strides on the road of collectivization." Wugong never wavered in its loyalty to Mao. But for 25 years President Liu, Lin Tie, and their henchmen had tried "to block our path and sabotage our work." No other village leader could claim such unbroken loyalty to revolution.

Geng wrote that enemies of socialism had tried to silence him in early 1967. But he "rose up to rebel," producing "one big character poster after another to condemn the crimes of China's Khrushchev [President Liu] and his agent in Hebei [Lin Tie] in sabotaging collectivization." Geng said he had always supported class struggle and opposed household plots, household quotas, and markets. The "movement to fight self-interest" was so successful in Wugong that "those who had formerly misappropriated public property now stood in front of Chairman Mao's portrait and made their confessions."

Wugong had been commemorating the 1943 founding of the coop every ten years. But with the village's socialist path linked to Mao's "Get Organized!" a celebration was staged to honor "the 25th anniversary of Mao's article and the coop." Party secretary Zhang Duan the Ox asked Geng Xiufeng, the initiator of the original coop, to speak. Twenty students from the Tianjin College of Music were then visiting. They worked with Geng Huijuan and articulate Li Zhongxin to put together song-and-dance routines. The head of the Tianjin group prepared an opera for the gala.

"Three Struggles with Liu Fang" was a hit. "Liu" evoked the fallen President Liu Shaoqi. "Fang" was the name of the state official who came in 1953 to "slash" the big coop. Geng Xiufeng wrote the script. Roles went to village cultural activists. The music was performed both by the Tianjin students and local artists. It was fun, a scarce commodity. The production won acclaim in neighboring villages in late 1968.

On December 5 Geng Changsuo was selected as a Hengshui prefectural representative to the Ninth Party Congress in Beijing. A proven "party builder," Geng won "unanimous approval." He also represented Hebei. Photos of the congress show Geng sporting a new hearing aid and dark-rimmed glasses.

The April 1969 Congress was publicly dominated by Lin Biao. A new party constitution listed him as vice chairman and "Comrade Mao Zedong's closest comrade-in-arms and successor." While Geng had been voicing Lin's line, behind the scenes Premier Zhou Enlai, with Mao's support, was making a comeback.[42] Hebei Monarch Liu Zihou's powerful patron, Politburo member Li Xiannian, whose son was believed to be married to Monarch Liu's daughter (it was not true) warned Liu to distance himself from Lin Biao and his ally, revolutionary theorist Chen Boda. But no one told Geng Changsuo.

9 ❀ WAR

COMMUNISM

In March 1969 Chinese and Soviet forces fought along the Ussuri River.[1] Preparations for war further militarized Chinese society. Between 1969 and 1971 China increased military spending at the fastest rate since the end of the Korean War.[2] In February 1969 a new leap in agriculture and industry was announced.[3] Each small region was to become self-reliant so it could regerminate true communism if China was attacked. The center ordered localities to "grow grain everywhere." Military representation at the April 1969 Ninth Party Congress soared from 19 to 45 percent. More Politburo seats were filled by the military.[4] The economy and society were militarized in ways reminiscent of the Leap. It was war communism. Militarization, class struggle, forced labor, and grain-first self-reliance pervaded the countryside.

The Economics of War Communism

Making the economy self-reliant to survive war brought more toil and little reward. In 1969 Brains Zhang Chaoke, representing Wugong at a meeting in the Hengshui prefecture model village of Kuixingzhuang, was told that former president Liu had suppressed Mao's call a decade earlier to raise pigs in order self-reliantly to increase meat supplies and fertilizer. Each village should raise one pig for every person or, better, one pig for every mu of village land. Mao's slogan was "each pig is a small fertilizer factory."

Premier Zhou promoted household pig rearing that used family food scraps, kept pigs away from contagious disease, and guaranteed close care. Revolutionaries countered that raising pigs at home fostered profit mindedness, since a fat hog or two could sell for more cash than a household earned in a year of collective field labor. Raising hens to sell eggs was likewise anathema. These revolutionary policies impoverished households.

Brains Zhang could not see how to step up pig production without household pig raising. So Wugong retained collective sties that required full-time workers, additional space, structures and feed costs, and increased loss due to contagious disease. Zhang kept touring advanced pig-breeding units. Wugong looked active but took no action.

Efforts to increase grain and cotton output centered on water, but throughout North China the water table plummeted. Water from old wells was often too salty. Shifting sandy soil rendered old well tubes useless. New and deeper wells were costly and required technical support from the state. Hengshui prefecture had been sending water specialists to Raoyang since 1966. In late 1968 the prefecture dispatched 30 technicians to Wugong for three months with deep-drilling equipment. The water table had dropped so far that the new wells had to be sunk more than 300 meters, using iron sidings.

Prefectural specialists drilled more wells in 1970. To be self-reliant, Raoyang began purchasing drilling rigs and training ten drilling teams. State policy to "grow grain everywhere" led to grabbing water everywhere. No attention was paid to the 1964 geological survey that called for a minimum of drilling, to preserve aquifers that fed surface water. The mass campaign recklessly mined water and augured future disaster.

In 1968 Hengshui drillers billed Wugong 5,000 yuan for wages and more than 11,000 yuan for materials and equipment. But each well was quietly subsidized by up to 5,000 yuan. Wugong also received an interest-free loan to pay for everything. Repayment would come later from higher yields and increased sales to the state. The technicians demonstrated how to combine the new deep, sweet water with shallower, old, salty water to render the salt content benign. By ensuring that Wugong stayed a model, the prefecture guaranteed links to higher leaders, while poorer villages had no access to state-monopolized resources.

The goal was to irrigate the North China plain. In 1950 just 16 percent of Hebei's farmland was irrigated. By 1965 that had doubled. In the early 1970s the pace both of tube well drilling and hydropower development accelerated. In 1970 *People's Daily* praised Hebei's success, crediting the class and two-line struggles and learning from Dazhai. The article boasted that since 1966 Hebei had drilled 160,000 wells, 2.5 times more than in the prior 17 years.[5]

A new power station, funded in spring 1969 with 60,000 yuan from the state center, linked Raoyang to a source in Hengshui capable of delivering 35,000 volts. Fueled by war communism priorities, Raoyang drilled 650 new motor-driven wells. It claimed it met the provincial target: one mu of farm land per capita was irrigated by well water. The powered wells required canals and ditches to carry water to the fields and drain the land during summer floods. Crews led by activists and including numerous black elements "supervised by the masses" worked with mostly hand tools. In 1970 more than 4,000 irrigation ditches were built in Raoyang, moving more than one million square meters of earth.

The water campaign also involved massive dike repairs. In mid-summer

1969 Raoyang was congratulated for strengthening a thousand-meter stretch of the ancient dike running along the northern shore of the Hutuo River that was threatened by heavy July rains.[6] In the fall, it initiated a "once every half century" repair of a 29-kilometer portion of the southern dike, completing the project in 1970. Villages were under constant pressure to provide corvee labor.

The Health of the Revolution

Beginning in late 1968, and especially in the spring and summer of 1969, dispersing health care providers became part of the war communism agenda. Mao, it was said, had decreed on June 26, 1965, "In medical and health work, stress the rural areas." Seventy percent of villages in China trained primitive paramedics called barefoot doctors and inaugurated cooperative health care clinics.

Wugong commune had a prefecturally funded clinic in Wugong village. It already had ten real doctors. During the rural health drive it abolished its registration fee. The commune promised to subsidize 80 percent of charges at the ten mostly new village health stations.

But some villagers figured that it made no sense to set aside as much as 13,000 yuan a year, almost 20 yuan per household, a major chunk of annual income, to support village health care. The previous system, featuring a 40 percent subsidy plus special appropriations to help the needy, had cost much less. Besides, the really weighty expense for surgery and hospitalization still far exceeded the capabilities of rural clinics or paramedics. Free comprehensive health care only served state-sector workers and officials and their families. The state provided no medical support for villagers. Without redistribution, rural self-reliance placed impossible burdens on each poor village.

In 1969 Wugong built a small pharmacy and a home to hold a physician. But costs could not be met. The annual health station fee soon jumped from .50 to one yuan per person. After a few months, most brigades, with lower incomes and no state subsidy, could not cover costs. The claim of free health care was a sham. The new clinics and health stations lacked medicine, equipment, and skilled practitioners. The state, preaching local self-reliance, did not provide resources. Families, of course, appreciated having a paramedic to set a child's broken bone. But it was the old system established in 1949, including inoculations reaching even the poorest hinterlands and water purification efforts, that kept increasing life expectancy.

Wugong's privileged commune clinic commanded unique resources. It provided lying-in services for four communes. Director Zhang Xuequ was an honest, retired soldier who knew nothing about medicine. He was a nephew of a Hebei party leader, Zhang Shuguang. Sent to the Wugong clinic during the rural health campaign was Doctor Wang Keqi, former chief of the radiology department of the Number 2 Hospital in Shijiazhuang. Under the banner of ending urban monopolies, central places that could serve more people were starved of resources, and hard-to-reach locales with good political ties were rewarded. In general, city and countryside both lost, except for a handful of privileged models.

Ordinary rural health units like the Raoyang county hospital decayed. Completed in the mid-1950s, part of the life-enhancing construction following the founding of the People's Republic, it barely survived on the meager budget of a poor county. Crowded and overworked, it became shabbier and ever less hygienic. Patients who were largely immobile were told to defecate on the floors of their rooms, after which the site was swept up but not sanitized. There was no disinfectant to scrub the floor.

In accord with Mao's directive, urban doctors and medical school graduates were sent to the countryside, the medical front of war communism. Surgeons were without instruments, electricity, medicine, supplies, or backup. Dentists went to rural communities with no equipment. Former centrally located specialists offered basic or emergency care in a few isolated communities. They also trained paramedics. Most doctors adapted. Uncertain whether exile was permanent, divided from families, subjected to criticism as "bourgeois specialists," and unable to apply their skills, some physicians committed suicide.

In summer 1968 Hebei Monarch Liu made an inspection tour. Before he entered a county clinic, patients were confined to their rooms and ordered not to utter a word. Guards fanned out so that no one could interfere with the appearance of revolutionary success.

The socialist elite seldom used rural clinics. The military, with first access to medical goods, staffed the top hospital in Shijiazhuang. The hospital that served the 38th Army in Baoding was famed for surgery. State officials were rushed to such hospitals in emergency military vehicles. Yet even elite military hospitals felt a strain when staff moved to the countryside. All lost. Villagers experienced a two-tier system. "They," the elite, had topflight military hospitals. "We" had ignorant barefoot doctors.

Li Who Is Thankful to the Army

Wugong's leaders dramatized their commitment to Mao's health agenda. In 1969 nine-year-old Li Zhixin fell ill. Her belly swelled. Her father was dead, and her mother had remarried into Zoucun village. Zhixin and her two brothers, in accord with Confucian ethics, remained in the village of the deceased father's lineage and were raised by their paternal grandparents.

In May 1969 Li Zhixin was sped to an urban center, the Number 2 Hospital in Shijiazhuang. She had constrictive pericarditis. But Mao's order to make medicine serve the people, and the concurrent attack on specialists and intellectuals, had led to the dispersal of doctors, leaving incompetents in charge. Surgeon Ma was away doing manual labor. The other surgeon was a "black academic authority." His filth could not be allowed to pollute a pure red. The hospital sent Li home untreated.

By early 1971 little Li's condition was critical. To show that Lin Biao's army served the people, an army medical team visited Wugong. The favor thrilled villagers whose only other recourse was the miserable rural clinics. The traveling army medics told Li's guardians she was curable. She was rushed back to Shijiazhuang. Patriotic villagers saw Lin Biao's army as theirs, just as they learned to see former president Liu Shaoqi's Soviet-style state as alien.

Boss Geng went to the hospital to see what he could do. He was told that surgeon Ma, back from the countryside, felt a need to consult specialists in Beijing. Geng understood this to mean that the surgeon worried that if the red girl died, he would be held responsible. Assuring the surgeon that he knew that the girl was likely to die, Geng guaranteed the staff that no one could be held responsible.

The operation succeeded. Little Li went home after convalescing. A reporter wrote up the tale. Saving Li's life was described as the "greatest, greatest success" of the Cultural Revolution. The official story was that bourgeois intellectuals failed in 1969 but doctors with faith in Chairman Mao operated and saved the girl.

Li pledged to join the army, changing her name to Li Xiejun, Li Who is Thankful to the Army. She actually became an herbal medicine pharmacist. Part of its Maoist legend, Thankful Li married into Geng's team 1 and bore a daughter. A brother became the soldier.

Order Number 1

In February 1969 Chief Huijuan, Boss Geng's political daughter, helped set up poor and lower-middle peasant Mao Zedong thought teams in each of Raoyang's 16 communes. On average each commune had 750 team members. In early September the county revolutionary committee, now chaired by former county party secretary Li Chunyu, brought one thousand activists to the county seat for a conference on the "living study and living application of Mao Zedong thought," a Lin Biao slogan. Later in the month one hundred Raoyang model youth, a "vanguard collective," went to Hengshui for a prefectural "living study, living application" congress. In September Huijuan was appointed one of five deputy chairs of the Raoyang revolutionary committee, the county's highest-ranked woman.[7]

Her work on the county committee focused on the militia. The military again sent her to Beijing. Each of China's more than 2,000 counties sent a representative. The state acted as if there were no budget constraints on military projects. For almost two weeks Huijuan attended meetings and lived in

Zhongnanhai, an enclosed area of lakes and gardens adjoining the old imperial palace that housed Mao and other top leaders. On October 1, National Day, she stood with honored guests in Tiananmen Square looking up at Chairman Mao, Premier Zhou, and Lin Biao, who gazed over a million celebrants. Loyalty to Mao's thought, as propagated from Lin Biao's military and into Wugong through its militia, won exciting rewards.

On October 17, as Soviet leaders weighed an attack on China, Lin Biao issued Order Number 1 detailing emergency measures to deter or resist "sudden attacks from the enemy."[8] He then moved to "protect" veteran military and political leaders who were his rivals, sending several of the marshals as well as top party leaders into internal exile in Hebei. Marshal Nie Rongzhen was sent to Handan in southern Hebei; Foreign Minister Chen Yi went to Shijiazhuang, the Hebei capital. A tortured and weakened Deng Zihui, who had long fought for rural reforms, was dispatched to China's southwest, where he died.

Restored Raoyang county chief Li Chunyu distributed rifles to village militias to defend the nation. Invaders were not the only militia target. In mid-December a campaign was waged to stamp out "illegal capitalist buying and selling." County chief Li organized thousands of zealots, led by militia and Mao thought propaganda activists, to comb the countryside to ferret out trade and household enterprises. All 16 regional periodic markets and many local cooperative enterprises were investigated. More than 50 roadblocks went up throughout the county to catch peddlers. Wounded commerce was further crippled.

In late December Li Chunyu called a five-day emergency meeting of nearly one thousand leaders at the county, commune, and village levels. The gathering listened to a dramatic tape-recorded report distributed by the Hebei revolutionary committee describing Chinese martyrdom along the Soviet border. The group also viewed a film of Soviet aggression on sacred Chinese soil. The assembled leaders then observed militia field exercises.

Accused of taking the Soviet road, former President Liu, after years of degrading treatment, died on November 12, 1969, and was secretly cremated. Hebei set about exorcizing his memory. In Xibaipo, a mountain village on the upper reaches of the Hutuo River in west Hebei, an exhibition hall honoring Liu's contributions to the 1947 land reform was closed. It was worse for Ningxiang, his home county in Hunan. It was pilloried for the sins of its most prominent son. The leaders of Wugong had much at stake in distancing themselves from losers like Lin Tie, Geng's patron for more than 20 years, who was branded as Liu Shaoqi's agent in Hebei.

The war scare heightened political anxieties. In Tianjin in 1969 many workers were given a week to move to Baotou in Inner Mongolia just as the province was exploding with vigilantism against Mongols that would send the official Cultural Revolution per capita death toll there far higher than that of any other province. Tianjin workers were told that the small family had to be sacrificed so the big family, the nation, could survive. Trains heading out of northern cities were jammed. Additional cars were added. Those who refused to abandon family were coerced. Some committed suicide.

The threat of war added impetus to Mao's 1964 third-front program that had already moved, at great expense, some heavy and military industries from border and coastal areas to mountains in the southwest. In addition to the strategy of a big third front (da san xian), Hebei participated in a strategy of a small third front (xiao san xian), preparing for Soviet invasion by relocating industry to mountain areas within the province.[9] Hengshui prefecture leaders, with no mountains to retreat to, built a steel mill in Handan at the southern tip of Hebei. The complex was connected by road to the War Preparedness Highway intended to speed national leaders through Hebei to safety in the Taihang Mountains.

Liu Zihou had Hebei provincial government files moved to a storage facility in Zanhuang county in the Taihang Mountains, 80 miles southwest of Wugong. Cave shelters said to be capable of withstanding nuclear attack were prepared for the Hebei elite, including Boss Geng. A three-month supply of food, fuel, and medical supplies was readied.

With war looming, Beijing's remaining urban schools moved to the countryside. Cherished books, manuscripts, and art owned by the exiles, some centuries old, were confiscated. Most were pulped, that is, turned into "useful" paper. Everything was for war.

Revolutionary theorist Chen Boda went to Tianjin to help transfer Hebei University to Baoding, a hotbed of revolution. The university took over the site of the former provincial government. Families stayed in Tianjin, preferring family separation to descending from centrally endowed Tianjin to marginalized Baoding.

No Raoyang plant was relocated to a mountain hinterland. There were only four significant factories in the county — cotton seed oil, cotton textiles, ball bearings, and dyeing. All were subsidized money losers.[10] None was valuable enough to move elsewhere to save from invaders.

The Four Goods

As part of the war scare, in late 1969 Wugong militia youth were drawn into a "four-good" movement promoted by Lin Biao's network. Baoding was the urban exemplar and Wang Guofan's Zunhua county, a favorite of Mao's, the rural model of this army-led campaign to heighten revolutionary consciousness and promote loyal successors. Militia youth throughout Raoyang were urged to prepare for war and give their all in corveé labor. At the provincial level, the 38th Army trained and promoted militia stalwarts as revolutionary heirs. *Hebei Daily* presented militia heroes as revolutionary successors. The

Hebei provincial publishing house issued the collected articles as a book, *Stories of the Revolutionary Struggles of the Hebei Militia.*[11]

In late 1969 detailed orders came through the military chain of command that ran from the Hengshui Military Commission to the Raoyang armed-forces department. As one village leader put it, "The military talks to the military." Village militias were ordered "to emulate the People's Liberation Army" by finding young people who excelled in four goods: good in political thought (meaning Mao Zedong thought as explicated by Lin Biao), good in work style (meaning emulating the soldier Lei Feng who was said to have sacrificed his life to serve the people), good in production (meaning enthusiasm for manual labor), and good in military training.

The army was heralded for winning the revolution and making the nation independent, and then preserving that independence by standing up to the United States in Korea and Vietnam, India at the border with Tibet, and now the Soviets to the north. Village men were eager to serve in the military. Village leaders recommended only a few. Military service increased prospects for party membership and a job on a state payroll with cash income, free health care, early retirement, and pensions. Right after the lunar New Year in 1970, the recruits received a community send-off. Villagers believed the soldiers would soon see action.

Demobilized soldiers made army life sound lively. There were more activities in the military and more young people to interact with. Returnees maintained ties with veterans and martyr families, assuring that the village helped them during holidays and in times of need. Veterans took patriotic pride in explaining the news to other villagers. Wugong veterans, many of them party members, met in Li Dazhai's home on the first, 11th, and 21st of each lunar month, that is, every other gathering of the periodic market in neighboring Zoucun. Veterans were a base for Lin Biao's revolutionary politics.

Li Guoqiang, the head of the Raoyang armed-forces department, visited Wugong in late 1969 to help set up a four-good platoon and make it the county model. He worked with militia commander Li Shouzheng and political adviser Zhang Duan. One hundred and eight four-good members were chosen from the 300-plus militia on criteria that included the study of Lin Biao's little red book of Mao quotations. The honored platoon was organized in three teams of 36 members each, 12 women and 24 men. Members met every ten days. As the war scare intensified, meetings occurred nightly.

Delayed two years because of Cultural Revolution chaos, on April 24, 1970, the military took credit for China's first space satellite. Nothing was made of the role of scientists and engineers. The launch thrilled patriots who recalled when China could not even manufacture a bicycle.

The patriotic message was popular in the North China countryside. The north seemed like China's heartbeat. So many key individual and village models were from the north. In northern households whose members had fought to establish the new nation, soldiers were heroes. The dead were martyrs. During the Korean War, when Geng had loyally condemned alleged American germ warfare, Wugong donated money for the war.

Geng saw revolutionary economics as a contribution to national survival. Wugong may have lost money when it eliminated peanut processing and marketing in the early 1950s, but a patriot's first duty was to grow food and defeat the American-led embargo. In the 1960s when the Soviet Union cut off aid, patriots needed to provide as much grain and cotton as possible, even if the state's price was low. For China to stand up, a strong, well-provisioned state nurtured through self-reliance and "growing grain everywhere" was a priority. Revolution meant independence. The four-good militia campaign embodied Chinese patriotism.

At the start of a meeting, platoon members stood at attention, little red book clutched in the right hand. Waving the book, they shouted, "A long life to Chairman Mao!" and "Good health to Vice Chairman Lin!" Members displayed martial skills. In a skit, they killed Soviet revisionists or drove American imperialists out of Vietnam. Team 2's Li Zhanguo was adept at acrobatic bayoneting. He had the physique of a body builder. Liu Shaoqi was ridiculed and Chairman Mao and Lin Biao praised.

Villagers competed to memorize the works of Mao. More than one hundred militia members memorized the little red book. Even 69-year-old Boss Geng tried to put time each day into memory work on his rare visits to the village. People also tried to memorize two funeral orations to martyrs and Mao's retelling of a traditional fable, known collectively as the three constantly read articles. Articulate Li Zhongxin, whose interaction with the Beijing Experimental Theater Troupe made him a dramatic reciter, also studied works of Marx, Lenin, and Stalin, including the *Communist Manifesto, State and Revolution,* and a collection on armed struggle. Li won many Mao memorization contests.

Wugong's outstanding four-good platoon members joined prefectural assemblies held by the Hengshui military and won praise as revolutionary successors. The key quote of Mao's came from a November 17, 1957, talk in Moscow: "The world is yours as well as ours, but in the last analysis, it is yours. You young people, full of vigor and vitality, are in the bloom of life, like the sun at eight or nine in the morning. Our hope is placed in you. . . . The world belongs to you. China's future belongs to you." Leaders would then repeat that youth "are like the sun at eight in the morning" and add, "We hope you will continue to rise." It was exhilarating to be Mao's and Lin's chosen successors.

Wugong promoted its outstanding militia loyalists. Xu Ming, the son of 1930s revolutionary hero Xu Dun, was put in charge of village security. Geng's grandson, Zhang Mandun, who married Macho Li Shouzheng's younger sister, toured the commune with a Mao thought propaganda team in 1969. In 1970 administrator Qiao Liguang and Zhang the Ox introduced Mandun into the Communist Party. Geng's grandson was heir to the political throne. Another rising militia star was Yang Bingzhang, a cousin of Red Successor Yang Tong. A system of blood ties and personal loyalty was labeled revolution.

Villagers with good class labels and political and military ties won state payroll plums. Zhang Duan's eldest son, Heng, in 1969 began an army career stationed in Beijing, while his wife was given a position in the commune office. Han Jichuang, son-in-law of public security specialist Zhang Zhensheng, had been stationed at the Beijing Aviation Institute, a place loyal to Lin Biao. In 1968 Han, a lieutenant, was transferred to a state factory in Beijing.

Village army veterans trained the four-good platoon. Early each day the 108 members, sometimes carrying weapons, jogged through the village. They enjoyed shooting practice with live ammunition, something denied the regular militia. The four-good campaign reinforced militarism, nativism, leader worship, and anti-intellectualism. Elders were glad that an era when the young seemed out of control was over. They identified with Mao, anti-intellectualism, and the patriotic army. The growing number of elders celebrated their longevity in an annual feast for males over 70. Longevity proved the value of socialism. Expecting little more materially out of life, the elders approved ascetic leveling and disciplined living. They enjoyed the military spectacles and liked seeing the idle energies of youth channeled. The four-good campaign was popular.

Spies in Raoyang

Key party, government, and educational institutes were sent out of Beijing in response to Order Number 1. In spring 1970 the International Relations Institute (Guoji guanxi xueyuan), part of the Central Investigation Department under the Central Committee, went to Raoyang. Classified as officials transferred to lower levels (xiafang ganbu), the institute's top leader established good relations with county chief Li Chunyu. The institute set itself up in the Raoyang junior high and carried on instructional programs. Except for one woman who taught French and married a villager, most remained immersed in their own organization, studying Mao's works and struggling against political targets.

Raoyang had long been receiving urban students. In January 1969, just before clashes with Soviet troops, the county set up an office to process sent-down youth.[12] By the early 1970s Raoyang had taken more than 500 junior high and high school graduates from Tianjin schools. Many feared the transfers were permanent. Only a small percentage of villages was asked to accept the students. Most villagers felt too poor to feed unproductive urban youth.

Six hundred college graduates were also sent to Raoyang, most to teach in village schools.

Cao Shijun, a teacher at the International Relations Institute who had once helped run Chinese intelligence in France, was so angry at being subjected to internal exile and manual labor that he went on a hunger strike. His complaint reached Premier Zhou's office. Many intellectuals and officials viewed the premier as a national ombudsman who could intervene on behalf of victims of injustice. Zhou chaired the Central Case Examination Group, an intraparty organ that investigated and punished scores of high-level officials who fell under suspicion.[13] Zhou's office wired Raoyang, ordering that teacher Cao be protected and not forced to do hard labor. The institute taught English, French, German, Japanese, and Spanish to prospective foreign intelligence operatives. When Cao refused to teach, he was permitted to read Arabic and French.

Stories about Premier Zhou led some townspeople to think of him as Bao Gong, China's legendary Lord of Justice, the last best hope for fair play. One prisoner from Beijing in the Raoyang jail had been accused of spying. The county authorities kept checking to see whether the accused should be executed. Raoyang did not want to protect a traitor. Beijing ordered a delay until evidence confirmed the accusation. The gossip was that the premier had intervened to save an innocent's life.

Many among the institute's faculty and accompanying family members were relieved to be safe in the countryside. Beijing had been hell, an ordeal of meetings, charges, mistreatment, confessions, and imprisonment. Raoyang seemed tranquil. Still, urbanites were shocked by the poverty. There was little fine grain, no rice at all for the palates of southerners. The filth and backwardness were numbing. There was no electricity, no running water, and few paved roads. Town streets were full of animal droppings. Pigs roamed freely. However, the students found it a lark to light candles at night. Those on urban salaries felt rich in the cash-starved countryside. Villagers tried to earn money by selling them pork, chickens, and vegetables.

Raoyang youngsters mocked the strangers who could not comprehend local argot. They asked if the newcomers were "si haizi," meaning a private child or bastard, and then roared when the outsiders answered "yes." Bastard was the favorite term of address for city youth when adults were not listening. For their part, the Beijing sojourners captured Raoyang life in a jingle:

> They use dogs to slaughter hogs;
> Brake bicycles with their feet;
> Men wear pot covers for hats;
> Women don't use belts to hold up their pants.

That is, the slaughterhouse kept dogs that pulled pigs by ear and tail en route to slaughter. Home-built bicycles had no brakes. To stop, a rider pressed a foot against the front wheel. Straw hats resembled pot covers. And rural women rolled up and tucked in their pants at the waist rather than use a belt.

The Raoyang authorities felt they were walking on eggs with so many connected and controversial people in town. The father of the Russian-born teacher, Yao Xiaoyue, was in jail in Beijing. She and her husband were assigned to manual labor in Raoyang. Her father had worked as Moscow director of Russian broadcasts to China in the 1950s and took charge of China's broadcasts to the Soviet Union in the 1960s. Because he had Russian friends, he was arrested as a Soviet spy.

The case led Premier Zhou to assign a jeep and driver to Raoyang public security. The only county vehicles were an ambulance (regularly commandeered by Li Chunyu) and a jeep assigned to Boss Geng on his elevation to vice chair of the Hebei revolutionary committee (a vehicle he turned over to the county government). Yao Xiaoyue's mail was monitored, and any suspicious material was sped to Shijiazhuang. But Yao's father was never heard from again. Not until 1975 was Yao, then a teacher in Raoyang, notified that her father had died in jail. He had been tortured to death. Not even his ashes were returned, only a diary of his final days.

Exile in bleak Raoyang was too much for some. Teacher Dong Lili, assigned to work in a local factory, went mad. So did Huang Xiyuan from Beijing Normal University.

A few bridged the cultural gap. Pan Weilo, the dean of English at the International Relations Institute, loved the *erhu,* a two-stringed bowed instrument. He played with the local propaganda team. Those with artistic talent who could show locals how to play Jiang Qing's model operas were warmly welcomed. Villagers delighted in almost anything that lent color to lives made drab by the revolution's assaults on popular culture. Decades later, youth of the day remembered the words of revolutionary songs with nostalgia.

Serving Time

Counterrevolutionaries were moved out of Beijing. Political prisoners were dispersed. Hundreds went to prisons in Hengshui prefecture. More than 60 arrived at the Raoyang Public Security Guard House (kanshousuo) in October 1969, including arts student Zhang Langlang, a poet whose father was arrested by the Nationalists in the 1930s for his cartoons and who later helped run the fine arts academy in Yan'an, Mao's guerrilla-era headquarters, and Zhou Qiyue, whose mother had played the lead in the first Yan'an production of the revolutionary opera "The White-Haired Girl." The jail, once a landlord home, had been turned into a prison by the Japanese invaders.

Arriving at night, prisoners were surprised to see no lights. In Beijing, cell lights were never off. Much of Raoyang, lacking electricity, used kerosene lanterns. Most prisoners lacked *kangs,* bedding down on tick-infested straw mats. On day 2 the warden assembled the prisoners. They did not even understand his opening command until a Raoyang-born convict explained in the nationally taught pronunciation that he had ordered them to squat. Raoyang had few stools or chairs.

Local inmates treated the transferees well, remembering ancient lore about victims of court intrigue sent into exile, only later to be pardoned and rise, taking with them those who had been kind during exile. Locals asked only for state payroll jobs for their sons.

Food was skimpy, tasteless, and lacking in nutritional value. There were two meals a day of millet porridge that seemed all liquid and no grain, plus a bit of vegetable. Prisoners scavenged for insects to supplement diets. A prisoner from Shandong ate a cricket. His stomach swelled; soon he was dead. Within a few months, seeing each other's skin hanging on protruding bones, prisoners made analogies to Auschwitz.[14]

Poet Zhang Langlang was accused of spying for the French. He and a fellow student had befriended French students at Beijing University. In June 1966 they went out in rowboats on the lake at the summer palace. The police watched them. When Zhang's fellow student handed over a newspaper, that was the proof of "spying" needed to jail both Chinese for a decade.

When inmates were marched to Raoyang Hospital to see a doctor, youngsters ran after the shackled prisoners shouting, as if aliens had landed, "The prisoners from Beijing, the prisoners from Beijing!" Townspeople stared. What the prisoners saw was a miserably poor county town where many still lived in houses made of mud bricks.

Prisoners slept 25 to a room in two big rooms. There were some smaller cells for six. A women's facility was in the rear. Guards were armed with submachine guns. Inmates made willow baskets and hemp dusters for cleaning bicycle wheels. Two hundred dusters per day were worth ten work points. Prisoners were not actually paid for their work, but those fulfilling quotas received more food. The products were sold by public security.

The scarcity of water was particularly trying. Prisoners carrying in water from a well were treated as bearers of treasure. Each got only two cups a day, and theft of water was commonplace. One hated prisoner, a former party official, stole the water from his cell mate Guo Hai, a former medical student, and then accused Guo of stealing his water. Guards grabbed Guo and fastened a pole so that his shackled hands protruded straight out. The hands were then beaten blue with a belt buckle, swelling to double their size. Guo could no longer use his hands. He went mad.

In winter, prisoners huddled around a clay stove that radiated little heat. The starving and brutalized political prisoners froze. There was an underground room where they were taken for beatings. County officials told us it was necessary to treat enemies of the people cruelly. State-promoted adages included "All movements have excesses," "Don't press a frozen snake to your breast," and "It's right to beat a rabid dog that's drowning." The maxims meant "no mercy."

Inmates informed on each other, sometimes falsely, to gain favors. Inmates were told that the authorities knew everything: if inmate A did something wrong and inmate B knew and did not tell, both would be punished. When a prisoner went to the toilet, a minder recorded how much paper was used for wiping.

Arbitrary brutality was mixed with stringent adherence to rules. A prisoner in his twenties named Zhang Xuewen suffered a complete breakdown, talking endless drivel. One day a guard heard him curse Jiang Qing. Before Zhang's swift execution, all prisoners who heard him speak of Mao's wife were forced to attest to it in writing, proof the guilty deserved to die. The freezing winter night before Zhang was killed, he was taken out in thin clothes and shackled, hands forced painfully high behind his back. He was left outside moaning in agony for all to hear what happens to enemies of the revolution.

Fung Guo Chiang, an Indonesia-born former guerrilla fighter from Malaya, was kicked in the face, groin, and skull by guards when he attempted to explain that Zhang was mad and should not be killed for insane mutterings. Fearing that he too was being killed, Fung screamed. A prison official who heard stopped the terror. Fung concluded that not all guards were sadists, not all officials murderers.

Compared to Beijing, the Raoyang prison was lax on thought reform. It did not closely monitor reading materials; it did not compel groups to sing hymns of praise to Mao. In Beijing political prisoners were tested on their knowledge of Marxism-Leninism and Mao Zedong thought. Prisoners in Raoyang, by contrast, could sing almost any song. Poet Zhang Langlang, who had received taped Beatles songs from French student Marianne Bastid, introduced them to the other inmates. Russian, Indonesian, and Scottish favorites also alternated with Beijing opera and contemporary Chinese songs.

Some Raoyang youngsters returning from Beijing to avoid dispatch to distant borders were in prison mostly for theft. They told the Beijing prisoners that virtually everyone in Raoyang stole from the collective. As a substitute for real cooking oil, they said, people extracted the oil from waste corn seeds. Money was so scarce that anyone who had cash seemingly could buy anything or anyone. They said that in the old days, when the Hutuo River overflowed, it had enriched the saline or alkaline soil. After 1963, with no more floods and insufficient fertilizer, crop stagnation reinforced entrenched poverty. Locals told the political prisoners from Beijing that villagers kept trying to get around the crippled market system to buy or sell what people wanted. County officials were seen as eating sumptuously while hypocritically preaching revolutionary austerity.

Meat was served to prisoners four times a year, on Labor Day, National Day, the solar New Year, and the lunar New Year. But some racked bodies could no longer digest meat. Such people ate eggs. But with misery entrenched and vengeful vigilantism pervasive, it was not just prisoners who suffered.

Hit One, Oppose Three

In mid-January 1970 Li Chunyu's revolutionary committee announced ambitious targets for the new year: 450,000 mu for grain, 30,000 mu for cotton, and 20,000 mu for oil-bearing plants. Grain targets were 300 catties per mu, with 60 catties per mu for cotton and 200 for oil-bearing crops. The new motorized wells and irrigation canals, it was claimed, along with the recent flood-control, pig-raising, and land-leveling drives, justified high targets. Raoyang should be able to "contribute" 240,000 catties to the state. Shirking was unpatriotic. After all, *Hebei Daily* claimed, even old Geng Changsuo, a delegate to the Ninth Party Congress, still worked in the fields.[15]

To make sure villagers focused on agricultural fundamentals, in January the county joined with the military to sponsor a campaign to smash the fragile market activities that kept springing back to life. It punished trade, denounced as speculation and profiteering. A sweep was led by nearly 4,000 county militia, supported by another 4,000 militants, including students, commune and brigade officials, and Mao thought propaganda team activists. Violence again exploded.

A "hit one, oppose three" campaign spread across North China in February 1970 after the lunar New Year, attacking counterrevolutionaries and class enemies. Investigators again combed the countryside looking for theft and so-called speculation. Those who confessed and exposed others were to be treated leniently, while those deemed guilty of serious crimes were to be dealt with as counterrevolutionaries.

Militia and Mao thought propaganda team activists in Raoyang pressured villagers to expose bad eggs. Some village leaders came up with fresh struggle objects. In late March 1970 in Shaojiacun, northwest of Raoyang town, a new target, Wang Enhua, was beaten to death in a gruesome surge of the hit-one campaign.

Wugong merely rounded up the usual targets of institutionalized cruelty— Li Maoxiu (the patriotic son of a landlord), Daoist Li Jinzhua, sex offender Xu Jichuan, provider Li Peishen, and a few others. Dragged to party headquarters, terrorized and vilified, they again "bowed before the masses," acknowledged their antisocialist crimes, and promised once more to reform. Boss Geng's political machine emerged unscathed.

Executions were public spectacles. Typically, once a death sentence was announced, the condemned had to sign a confession. If the condemned refused, the larynx was severed or injections into the throat were administered, making it impossible to proclaim innocence or defiance.

The trip to the execution ground was a public ritual. After the removal of handcuffs, the arms were bound behind the back by rope, with a loop tied around the neck. A placard with the condemned person's name crossed out in red ink was then hung over the shoulders. The condemned was paraded around on an army truck with head lowered, a position of contrition maintained by a sharp knife in the back. The prisoner was driven to the banks of the Hutuo, brought to a recently dug hole, and shot. Crowds were selected to witness revolutionary justice. After the execution, officials demanded that the family of the deceased pay 47 cents for each bullet used. Embarrassed local people dismissed that practice as something picked up from the immoral Soviet Union.

Execution supposedly required sentencing by the provincial court and approval by the supreme court. During the war scare, however, death sentences could be handed down by prefectural courts with final approval at the provincial level. Prison officials understood it as a campaign to execute 3 percent of prisoners. To fill quotas, they selected prisoners who had previously been sentenced to life imprisonment or death with a two-year stay of execution, or killed any prisoner who had incurred their wrath.

In 1970, Zhang Langlang was sent back to Beijing, trussed up, and placed in a preexecution cell. But he was not executed. He returned to Raoyang prison in June 1971 to find that the prison now had electricity. Many had been sent off to Beijing to be executed. Zhang was one of very few to return alive.

One Raoyang execution followed a crime of passion. Zhou Liang, a native of Xuzhangbao village and a graduate of the Foreign Trade University in Beijing, had worked in the northeast and traveled abroad. Married to a Raoyang woman in his youth, he lived apart from his wife and two daughters for 15 years. Alone in Dalian, he fell in love. But his wife in Raoyang, with the backing of local officials, rejected his divorce appeal. Finally, after unsuccessfully pursuing the case in court for ten years, Zhou returned to Raoyang and murdered his wife.

Prior to sentencing, he poured out his heart in a memoir and a series of paintings. Thousands went to witness the execution. Bound and gagged, Zhou was displayed on the back of a truck. When guards removed his handcuffs to tie his hands before the execution, Zhou is said to have twisted his head to smile one last time at his beloved, who had been arrested but not prosecuted after implicating her lover.

Executions carried out by public security organs stimulated mass vigilantism, prompting a wave of suicides. Hengshui prefecture officials reported that more than 1,000 people died in the hit-one campaign, including executions, suicides, and tortures. That, they told us, made Hengshui, compared with hundreds of other prefectures, very low in deaths. Credible estimates of Cultural Revolution deaths range from 300,000 to ten million, but those who count only urban victims clearly underestimate the toll.[16]

The campaigns did uncover some real problems. Starting in late 1968 the county sent in specialists to scour the books of Yanggezhuang village. Grain yields in 1968 of 81 catties per mu were no higher than before the establishment of the People's Republic, when there were far fewer mouths to feed and much income from sideline work and off-farm employment.

Yanggezhuang's tough leaders grew greedier and nastier. Party secretary Bai Zhongxi and his associates pilfered grain and cotton, sold electric motors on the black market for personal profit, and embezzled village funds. They intimidated and beat villagers. But no one dared report them. As a hero of the revolutionary war, militia chief Bai fancied that he had saved villagers from the Japanese and thus had earned the right to take what he wanted.

A county team dispatched to the commune in 1969 to prepare for the reestablishment of party organs heard about the Yanggezhuang leaders. The team used the hit-one campaign to investigate Yanggezhuang "social scum" who had taken advantage of and personally profited from recent disorders, as the campaign's language put it. The county work team of about a dozen ousted Bai in March 1970.

Four Yanggezhuang leaders were sentenced. One received a prison term of three years (eventually suspended), one of 15 years, one of 18. Bai got the stiffest penalty, 20 years in prison in Baoding. He and his supporters believed they were victims of a factional vendetta, penalized for his total commitment to war communism, scapegoats to legitimate a 1969–70 policy turn toward order and production and away from revolutionary fundamentals. The Bai faction's jailing further split the village. Lineages and neighborhoods vilified each other so that over the next quarter century leaders rose and fell rapidly, permitting little united action.

Communalist strife also split Xipu, the Wang Guofan Paupers' Coop favored by Mao. The hit-one campaign there permitted Wang, now a member of the Hebei revolutionary committee, to persecute Du lineage adversaries who had toppled him in the vigilante phase of the Cultural Revolution. He imprisoned his opponents in a new jail, a capacious fortresslike structure complete with moat, wall, and drawbridge. Brutal attacks injured Du Kui. No doctor was summoned. In 1971 Du died. Yet, patrons continued to lionize Wang as a socialist hero.

Old Grudges

Since April 1968 there had been numerous efforts to "purify the class ranks" (qingli jieji duiwu), that is, to identify and purge those who had "wormed" their way into positions of authority. During a July 1969 countywide rectification (zheng dang), all Wugong party members were investigated and asked to provide evidence about the circumstances of their membership.

The purification campaign allowed old grievances to resurface. Frustrated in their attempts to dislodge Boss Geng's political machine, discontented villagers, especially west-enders, tried to use the class struggle campaigns to counterattack. Older villagers recalled that Geng's east-end coop had been labeled a "rich-peasant" organization in late 1947 when the initiator of the coop, Geng Xiufeng, was classified as a rich peasant. Those damning designations were reversed in early 1948. Still, as in 1967, Boss Geng was again linked by a few in the west end Xu lineage to landlord elements and exploiters.

By spring 1969, while a powerful Geng Changsuo was politically untouchable, that was not true of his irascible kinsman, Geng Xiufeng, retired and living at home. In March, as Chinese and Soviet forces battled, a special office was set up in Raoyang to investigate local officials. Xiufeng soon heard rumors that questions were being raised about his background. In spring 1970 Wugong party secretary Zhang Duan, a west-ender, summoned Xiufeng to commune headquarters. West-ender Zhang Zhensheng, in charge of commune security, and Hu Jibao, the head of the commune armed-forces department, joined the meeting. They questioned Xiufeng about the Wugong party branch founded by landlord Li Huaqi in mid-1938.

Xiufeng said he knew only what Zhang Zhensheng himself had told him years earlier: Li Huaqi, a prominent member of the southern Li lineage, had set up the first party branch at the behest of a relative, county party secretary Chen Mingshan. Within months, however, at the urging of the district party authorities, a branch centering on such poor peasants as Xu Yizhou, Xu Chuan, and Li Wenkao was established. Soon after, the Li Huaqi branch dissolved.

When Zhang asked Xiufeng if he had been a member of the Li Huaqi branch, Xiufeng smelled a rat. Zhang informed Xiufeng that a member of the branch had incriminated him. "It's all right to admit it," the enforcer said, "After all, it was a Communist Party branch! If you were a member, you should just say so."[17] Xiufeng insisted that he had joined the party in 1946, eight years after the Li Huaqi branch had disbanded.

Xiufeng believed that the charges came from Xu Chuan (the brother of revolutionary martyr Xu Dun), Xu Yue (the son of Xu Dun), and other west-enders who had attacked Geng Changsuo's political machine in 1967. Veteran west-end party members of the Xu lineage, including pioneer Xu Yizhou, who had fallen out with Boss Geng in 1953, felt slighted. They were also bitter, Geng Xiufeng believed, because Geng Changsuo had survived the bombardments of January 1967. Having led the brief and unsuccessful rope-making revolt in summer 1967, Xu Chuan and Xu Yue were also concerned that team 3 riches were channeled unfairly to the rest of the village. Given their unimpeachable "poor-peasant" class status, the west-end Xus now sought "to purify the class ranks."

The Wugong party had only recently investigated the case. Why, Xiufeng wondered, were questions about his party membership being raised yet again?

In July 1969, Li Fengxiang, who had sponsored Xiufeng's party membership, had sent a letter explaining Xiufeng's political history. But Fengxiang had been a rich peasant, the nephew of landlord Li Huaqi, while the Xus were from the poorest of the poor.

A few days after Xiufeng's interrogation, a big character poster signed "An Old Party Member" charged: "Geng Xiufeng is a fake party member!" "Geng Xiufeng is a Nationalist Party member with links to Li Huaqi!" Geng Xiufeng was sure it was the work of Xu Chuan. For Xu, Geng concluded, "The only thing that mattered was one's class origin."

Zhang Duan ordered Xiufeng to criticize himself, but he refused. His opponents mocked his "good deeds." His habit of volunteering his time to do minor road repairs was called a "slick strategy" (gaoji shouwan), and the money he contributed monthly to the collective medical program was called an attempt to "buy people's hearts" (shoumai ren xin). Geng retaliated with a poster of his own.[18] Dated June 10, 1970, and peppered with Mao quotations, it portrayed the "old party member" (Xu Chuan) as an unreliable "subjectivist" who neglected the call of the Ninth Party Congress to "unite to achieve greater victories." Had not *Hebei Daily* recently published an article praising party unity in Wugong?[19]

Taking the offensive, Xiufeng branded the attack on him an assault on Geng Changsuo. The stakes were high. If Xiufeng really was a landlord manipulating Boss Geng, then political power had never been in the hands of the poor. Changsuo had "protected" a landlord element. Lineage, neighborhood, and patronage splits and ambitions were concealed in the language of class struggle.

Xiufeng gave his poster to village headquarters, showing he would not be intimidated. The leaders then opted to defuse the matter. The poster was never displayed, and the dispute seemed to dissipate.

People had a lot at stake in figuring out which way the political winds were blowing. It was confusing. Attempts were made to rebuild the party and end vigilantism. Yet war scares and the imperatives of war communism infused politics. The military seemed omnipotent. Villagers could not see that Mao's anointed successor, Lin Biao, was losing favor.[20] Premier Zhou and reform moved toward the center of the political stage.

Geng Xiufeng (left) meets in 1963 with the members of the original Wugong coop of four households formed in 1943. Geng Changsuo is in the center. Rao-yang county archive.

Raoyang county secretary Li Chunyu presents award to Geng Changsuo, 1963. Provincial party secretary Lin Tie (right), dressed in fur, looks on. Raoyang county archive.

Geng Changsuo's wife, Xu Shukuan (right), lectures orphan Li Mengjie and Shi Guiying (left), 1963. Raoyang county archive.

The 1972 campaign in Wugong to criticize Defense Minister Lin Biao, who was said to have died in a plane crash while attempting to escape to the Soviet Union. Raoyang county archive.

Preparing Wugong collective grain for delivery to the state, circa 1973. Raoyang county archive.

Revolutionaries from Laos visit Wugong, September 1975, and are greeted by Geng Changsuo (right), administrator Qiao Liguang (center right with head wrap), and party secretary Yang Tong (center left with head wrap). Raoyang county archive.

Wugong militia leader Li Shouzheng,
circa 1975. Raoyang county archive.

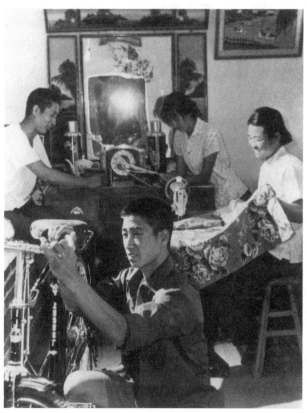

Wugong newlyweds and parents inspect wedding gifts,
1978. Raoyang county archive.

Geng Changsuo's extended family mourns his passing in Raoyang ceremony, November 1985. Raoyang county archive.

Geng Xiufeng attends Geng Changsuo's funeral in Raoyang, November 1985. Raoyang county archive.

Cang Tong, The Hengshui prefectural official who investigated
Wugong during the controversial four-cleanups campaign in
1964 and 1965. Photographed by the authors, 1995.

Dazhai village leader and Vice Premier Chen Yonggui (second from right) meet
with the leaders of Hengshui prefecture's three model villages, Nanwangzhuang,
Houtun, and Wugong (right). Raoyang county archive.

Wugong's ritual scapegoat, landlord son Li Maoxiu (right) and his wife, Fan Shufang. Photographed by the authors, 1980.

Geng Changsuo's grandson and political heir, Zhang Mandun. Photographed by the authors, 1978.

Wugong collective corn being distributed to households. Photographed by the authors, 1980.

Village pathway in Wugong's team 3. Autumn corn dries on the roofs, and corn-stalks are piled outside homes for use as fuel. Photographed by the authors, 1980.

Wugong youths who helped the authors administer a household survey of team 3. Photographed by the authors, 1978.

Schoolgirl in Wugong sporting customary hairstyle and colorful new-style clothing. Photographed by the authors, 1978.

Local martial arts champion from Raoyang performing in Wugong. Photographed by the authors, 1978.

Vice Premier Chen Yonggui (right) and Mark Selden during a meeting with the authors in the Great Hall of the People in Beijing, 1978. Photo courtesy of Chen Yonggui.

A Wugong family tills its own contract plot following decollectivization. Photographed by the authors, 1983.

The newly constructed Roman Catholic Church in the market village of Zoucun. Photographed by the authors, 1995.

Villagers gathered in the market place enjoy a good laugh. Photographed by the authors, 1980.

Old-timer rolling his own cigarette with local tobacco in the Zoucun market. Photographed by the authors, 1980.

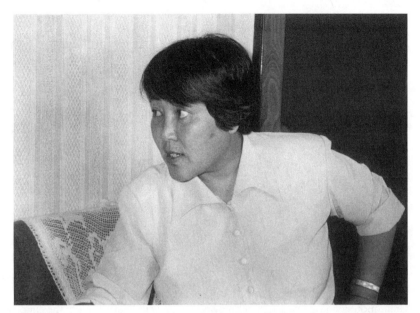

Geng Changsuo's political daughter, Geng Huijuan. Photographed by the authors, 1980.

Geng Changsuo's urban granddaughter Han Peng visiting grandmother Xu Shukuan's grave in Wugong, 1990. Photo courtesy of Han Peng.

Grandmother and granddaughter enjoying the Zoucun market. Note the child's colorful clothing and Buddhist makeup. Photographed by the authors, 1980.

Villagers in Zoucun acting on the state's decision in 1980 to allow grain to be sold in market villages at market prices for the first time since 1953. Photographed by the authors, 1980.

Wugong youngsters shooting pool. Photographed by the authors, 1984.

Wugong grandmother with bound feet pulls off corn kernels with her bare hands in a team threshing ground. Photographed by the authors, 1980.

Young Wugong leader Li Zhongxin
presides at a village wedding.
Photographed by the authors, 1978.

Itinerant dentist displays extracted teeth at
the Zoucun market. Photographed by the
authors, 1980.

Wugong children playing by a haystack. Photographed by the authors, 1980.

American cameraman Bestor Cram filming village drummers for the documentary film *The Mao Years*. Photographed by the authors, 1992.

10 ❦ SPROUTS OF REFORM

Revolutionary theorist Chen Boda was in trouble. Short and a bit rotund, Chen had a thick Fujian accent that often required a translator in Hebei, where his call to support rebels to the hilt was seen as an invitation to execute counterrevolutionaries. On August 23, 1970, Mao sharply criticized Chen.[1] Among other things, Mao questioned the agricultural briefings Chen submitted while a member of North China Bureau head Li Xuefeng's core group. Mao's attack also implicated Chen's ally, the chairman's "closest comrade-in-arms," successor Lin Biao.[2]

Reverberations were felt throughout Hebei. Former foreign minister Chen Yi ended his exile in Shijiazhuang on October 21 and returned to Beijing. Mao's attack provided an opening for economic reform.

The North China Agricultural Conference

Chairman Mao had Premier Zhou take the lead in restoring the party, improving relations with the United States, opening to the world economy, and modernizing. The organs responsible for agriculture had been wiped out at the start of the Cultural Revolution. By 1970, with Zhou in charge, the Ministry of Agriculture and its provincial and county organs were reestablished. Large numbers of administrators were called back from internal exile and labor camps.

Since 1969, when Zhou convened a national conference on agricultural mechanization, questions about the household sector, production incentives, the market, and mechanization had been on the table. Chen Boda and other revolutionaries opposed both sideline expansion and mechanization.[3] Mechanization, they said, would contribute to disguised unemployment. It would not help rice-growing or poor mountainous regions. It would especially divert attention from the heightening of socialist consciousness through class struggle, thereby opening the way for capitalistic preoccupations.[4]

Agriculture was a battleground. A three-point consensus emerged in favor of a conservative modernization agenda: reestablish work points as a basis for remuneration (an lao fenpei), maintain household plots, and end leveling moves toward brigade accounting (that is, block attempts to move to a bigger accounting unit). These policies to strengthen production incentives became the basis for a reinterpretation of the Dazhai model.[5]

Conservative modernizers did not challenge collective predominance. They did promote a green revolution in agriculture involving greater attention to seeds, fertilizers, electrification, and mechanization, all slighted by revolutionaries. In the early 1970s China developed new high-yielding varieties of grain. Collective sidelines and rural industry were said to stimulate rather than detract from agriculture.

On June 25, 1970, Premier Zhou convened a meeting in Beijing to prepare for a North China Conference in August in Xiyang county, the home of Mao's nationwide village model, Dazhai, heretofore an inspiration for the class struggle, self-reliance line. The State Council directed Hengshui prefecture to select delegates for the conference who specialized in production, that is, not ideology or politics.

The eight prefectural delegates were led by four officials: government chief Han Peipu, a deputy party secretary, the head of the administrative office, and an agricultural specialist. Raoyang sent the vice chairman of the county revolutionary committee, Pu Shaoli. Hengshui's most famous villages, Mao-blessed Nanwangzhuang, Wugong, and Kuixingzhuang, each had a delegate. Wugong sent production specialist Zhang Chaoke.

Zhang bussed to Hengshui, where the prefectural group assembled at the official guest house. It was built like the socialist system, in strict hierarchical order. The perquisites of power were secret. Crowded rooms without toilets or other amenities were on the ground floor. More commodious accommodations with better appointed rooms and toilets were above, hidden from those below. Whenever Geng was there, he stayed in a first-floor room because he had trouble climbing stairs. He appeared to reject privilege.

The Hengshui delegation rode three hours by van to Shijiazhuang, the provincial capital. All the delegates had been to Wugong and were known to Zhang. Shijiazhuang's more elegant guest house was organized like the one in Hengshui. Almost one hundred Hebei representatives were led by Ding Tingxian, head of the provincial bureau of agriculture. Zhang mocked Ding for his mincing, pigeon-toed walk.

The Hebei delegates piled into a dozen vans for a five-hour drive west into the Taihang mountains to Xiyang. Zhang shared a room in the Xiyang guest house with the Nanwangzhuang and Kuixingzhuang delegates. In Xiyang, too, the same architectural principles held. An auditorium was nested in a walled compound that held a hostel, convenient for meetings. The high walls and armed guards separated official doings from the eyes and ears of the public, encapsulating the state-society gap and mirroring the ruling hierarchy.

Similar principles applied in official housing. Raoyang county officials, at the level of revolutionary committee chair Li Chunyu, vice chairs, and Standing Committee members, lived in a walled and guarded enclosure. The compound was divided into three parts separated by walls, with county chair Li living in an inner courtyard with a tree-shaded back garden. Rent was a nominal one yuan per month. The houses for the vice chairs had a kitchen, a living room, and two bedrooms. They were built in a single line with a separate outhouse and private garden. Standing Committee members lived two families to a building and shared an outhouse among five or six households within a courtyard. It was in no way luxury, but it was far above village amenities.

At the provincial level, Monarch Liu lived in a compound behind revolutionary committee headquarters in Shijiazhuang. The two-story building was set apart from the houses of the other top leaders. Liu had two cars, one a Red Flag limousine for special functions, a writing secretary, and a personal servant-cum-bodyguard, as well as a cook, janitor, driver, and large official staff.

The North China Agricultural Conference opened in the Xiyang county auditorium on August 25, 1970. Qian Zhenying presided. An engineer, the American-born daughter of a Cornell University graduate, she was minister of water conservancy and electric power.[6] Eleven hundred delegates from 14 provinces and municipalities attended. Dazhai's Chen Yonggui and Premier Zhou were still at Lushan, where Chairman Mao was criticizing revolutionary theorist Chen Boda. Chen Yonggui later told us that his draft statement was altered by Chen Boda allies.

Delegates visited exhibition halls and communes to study production. Xiyang county had combined soil improvement, land leveling, and irrigation to obtain higher output. Then delegates went to Dazhai village. Wugong's Brains Zhang had not visited in almost four years. He was impressed by the fully mechanized irrigation. The gossip was that army engineers had set up the sophisticated irrigation system. In 1967 the army used heavy equipment to build drains, dams, culverts, and a large reservoir after the 1963 deluge proved that back-breaking efforts by villagers alone could not prevent floods. But Dazhai's revolutionary secret of success, the visitors were told by young Guo Fenglian, who took over during Chen Yonggui's absence, was class struggle, ignoring hardship, and uniting the masses. That, she said, permitted Dazhai to accomplish what might seem impossible.

Talk of miracle models never persuaded Wugong's neighbors. Villagers painted "emulate Wugong" on Zoucun walls, but they had seen their market shrivel, their court disappear, and their clinic and school move to Wugong. Even a county granary, which had been in Zoucun since at least 1748, had recently been relocated to Wugong. Zoucun villagers did not appreciate being told that they lagged behind model Wugong. They felt that they had achieved wonders, given the odds against them.

Already in the early 1950s, technical and financial support enabled Wugong to strike sweet water. Zoucun, even at 100 meters and great expense, came up dry. Villagers were proud of their success in filling in, leveling, and enriching wretched soil when little value was returned and when, its leaders emphasized, Zoucun did it *on its own*. Likewise, in Yanggezhuang, where good old boy Bai had just been sacked, villagers mocked Wugong. They found that Wugong's success was premised on access to government largesse that made water and all else available only to the favorite of the state. Visits to models did not automatically inspire.

After six weeks in Xiyang, a special train took the delegates to Beijing. Brains Zhang found the soft mattress at the Friendship Hotel comfortable compared to his cement kang bed at home. The delegates reassembled in the auditorium in the walled compound of the Friendship Hotel to hear Chen Yonggui, just back from Lushan, where the Central Committee had approved Premier Zhou's new economic policies. The delegates then broke into small groups by province and prefecture for four days of discussion. Such national leaders as Politburo member Li Xiannian (the patron of Hebei Monarch Liu) and Ji Dengkui (an alternate Politburo member) attended. Mao did not. The delegates reassured each other that Mao would have come if not for more pressing matters.

The Hengshui prefectural group concluded that pig manure, combined with more irrigation, would enrich fields and, supplemented by a small but increasing supply of chemical fertilizer, permit new seeds to ripen faster, thus making possible intercropping, double cropping, and triple cropping. The delegates stayed in Beijing for three more weeks. On National Day, Brains Zhang gazed upon Mao at Tiananmen Square. Like Chief Geng Huijuan, Zhang recalled it as "the happiest moment of my life."

A few days later, at ten in the evening, the delegates assembled in the Great Hall of the People to hear Premier Zhou. Foreign policy was on his mind. He had been to Egypt, joining mourners at Nasser's funeral. Zhou began by discussing the rise of Sadat, who would soon break with the Soviet Union. The premier then turned his attention to Cambodia where, he said, the Soviet Union was trying to get China bogged down fighting the United States, thus leaving China's north more vulnerable to Soviet attack. Zhang saw that foreign affairs were in flux and would have a large impact on China's future. He decided to begin reading the classified *Reference Materials* (Cankao ziliao) containing translations of the foreign press kept under lock and key in village headquarters.

Finally, near midnight, Zhou turned to Dazhai. As Zhang recalled it, the premier stressed three abstract points: politics in command, self reliance and hard work, loving the collective and being patriotic.[7] But politics no longer meant class struggle. The key lay in uniting to overcome poverty. Zhou called for more corvée labor, great stress on hog production, constructing high- and stable-yield fields, selling more grain to the state, and increased local invest-ment in modernizing and mechanizing agriculture. Villagers were to get rich by tightening their belts for a while, investing more, and working harder. The line evoked vague memories of the Leap. But this time, Zhou stressed, the state would invest in such suitable technology as fertilizer and irrigation and would not tolerate the squandering of precious resources.

The North China Conference increased investment in water conservancy and chemical fertilizer production.[8] There would be more support from spe-cialists and increased imports and availability of agricultural machinery and pesticides. Collectives were encouraged to diversify by investing in such side-lines as animal husbandry and small industries, with profits plowed back into agriculture.[9] Zhou's nocturnal speech set a modernizing direction while hew-ing to the collective.

The morning after Zhou spoke, the Hengshui delegates agreed that the goal of the conference was to boost agriculture through modernization and mechanization. Class struggle was interpreted as a matter of leadership atti-tude. Dazhai had claimed to create work enthusiasm by having leaders work in the fields hundreds of days a year. If leaders did not shirk, villagers would work hard. The conferences in Xiyang and Beijing legitimated a conservative mod-ernization agenda.[10]

Oil and Water

Many Dazhai claims were unbelievable. The Dazhai campaign required local officials to work in the fields 300 days a year. But that was impossible given meet-ings, administration, preparation, reading documents, conferences, travel, and drafting reports.[11] The claim that Dazhai prospered by self-reliance was also unpersuasive. The Ministry of Construction provided free explosives to level the mountain so that Dazhai could construct new fields. Army transport pro-vided free services. However hard others applied themselves, their villages could not reap similar rewards from the state.

Deeply alienated from collective work, villagers (especially young males) sought to tap external connections to get out of the village and into cash-earning jobs. For money, people worked harder. Zhou sidestepped that and other politically charged issues. Local leaders still had to fear that meaningful incentives might be damned as capitalism. The risk was all the higher, since the conference initiative was so clearly Zhou's. Perhaps the premier enjoyed Chairman Mao's support, but Mao neither attended the conference nor pub-licly endorsed its recommendations. What was to prevent another onslaught on officials branded as "capitalist roaders"?

A hidden issue was capital. Where would the money come from to buy more fertilizer, seeds, insecticides, irrigation, and machinery? As in the Leap, the poor were exhorted to create capital. That meant deferring better diets and new houses. Collective units were directed to invest more in soil improvement, irrigation, machinery, and equipment. In the early 1970s, China's rate of accumulation for investment rose to the highest level since the Leap, averaging more than thirty percent for the period 1970–78.[12] From 1970 to 1978, rural industry, in step with foreign trade, grew at 25 percent annually, spurring an industrial revolution in the countryside. However, with markets suppressed and incomes low, much investment lost money or was wasteful.[13] Many villagers felt too poor further to exploit themselves, seeing no gain for their families from more collective work and investment.

Early in October delegates went home. Back in Hengshui, Han Peipu reported for more than two hours. Each county was directed to go all out for agriculture and draw up three- to five-year plans to show it could achieve higher yields. Brains Zhang told a Wugong village meeting that success would be measured by increases in grain yield. The secret to success lay in expanded hog breeding to produce fertilizer that would enrich the soil. Zhang also promised to find improved seeds.

Later in October, a 12-day Raoyang meeting disseminated the results of the conference. It was six of modernizer Premier Zhou and half a dozen of Chen Boda, a combination of oil and water, economic modernization and political revolution. County chief Li Chunyu pressed grassroots leaders to join the "new mass movement" to learn from Dazhai and "cross the Yellow River" in grain output by 1971, that is, get the substantially higher grain yields already achieved in lush southern rice-growing regions. He exhorted all to combat "rightist deviations" through a new "Great Leap Forward in agriculture." Villagers ridiculed yet another movement, commenting that, under socialism, meaningless campaigns replaced satisfying rites.

With no succor from the center, localism intensified. Nostalgia for ancient times surged. People kept alive the words of the local poet Mao Chang whose works were said to have been burned by the tyrannical first emperor of the Qin dynasty. The chaos of the Three Kingdoms era gave birth to local martial arts traditions whose lore and lure persisted. Raoyang veterans linked local heroism in the anti-Japanese resistance to memorable deeds of the past. History infused contemporary meaning.

Following revolutionaries in Beijing, Hebei Monarch Liu Zihou resisted stressing economic crops and collective sidelines and industries as ways to earn income for reinvestment in agriculture. It was, he said, "capitalism in the guise of collectivism." To focus on profits and enterprise accounting smelled like "attempts to pursue capitalism with money as the key link."[14] Provincial leaders like Liu, county heads like Li, and village leaders like Geng would not risk committing capitalism.

Ideological dictates contradicted the reform message of the North China Agricultural Conference. The September issue of the party theoretical journal, still controlled by Chen Boda, contained an article credited to Geng Changsuo urging villagers to learn "dialectics" in order to apply the principle of "one divides into two." Engaging in the "living study and living application of the philosophical thought of Chairman Mao" taught one how to "defend the motherland" and grasp "class struggle." Former president Liu was pilloried as a "renegade, hidden traitor, and scab." Wugong's team 3 was criticized for refusing to "close plant" (mizhi) its grain seeds. Counterrevolutionary elements, Geng contended, never stopped trying to "restore capitalism."[15] Given the political atmosphere, even the few steps of the North China Conference toward economic rationalism were anathema to revolutionaries.

After the conference, *People's Daily* ran an article attributed to the Wugong party branch on revolutionizing thought by applying Mao's philosophy "in a living way."[16] This was how to combat self-interest, emulate the "Dazhai spirit," defeat class enemies, and supply ever more grain to the state. It blamed, "failures in recent years" on "inadequate attention to consciousness."

Resistance to modernization and reform seemed like an ethical imperative to the Raoyang leadership. This lesson was embodied in the experience of Wang Ruijin, a son of a village policeman, who had graduated from the teacher training school in Raoyang and had been making propaganda for Wugong since 1953. After a short stint as a teacher, Wang made a career in the county party, rising to head both its administrative office and its youth league. He was the sharpest pen among veteran county leaders. He ascribed all that was good politically to Mao, the party, and the collective economy. They served the poor. Wang could rise because of them. From beyond China's sacred soil came evil — imperialism, exploitation, and polarization — caused by money and capitalism. Wang embraced socialism, understood as statist initiatives that guaranteed the basics of life to all. That was superior to the misery of village China before the revolution and was purportedly still the sad destiny of compatriots exploited in Hong Kong and oppressed on Taiwan.

Geng Changsuo's ties to top Hebei revolutionaries were reinforced by a late October 1970 visit by North China party boss Li Xuefeng. Li, an alternate Politburo member and chair of the Hebei revolutionary committee, was the highest-ranking official ever to set foot in Wugong. Accompanied by Hebei's top woman rural leader, Lu Yulan, Li toured Raoyang. Li and his retinue arrived in Wugong in two late-model Chinese cars. Villagers remembered Li as tall, wearing sun glasses and surrounded by aides and bodyguards. Mocking the mighty, villagers quipped that Li feared assassination. Li had a meal at Geng's home, proclaiming his oneness with poor peasants.

Geng called on Wang Kai, a Zoucun chef who once sold delicacies at the now dead market. Locals boasted that Li Xuefeng was so impressed with the pork sausages that he invited Chef Wang to his home to instruct his own cook. Wang Kai, locals joked, turned out to be a doer, not a teacher; he failed to pass on his skills.

On the first night of the visit an aide to Li complained about village dogs.

With strangers around, the dogs, trained to curb rising theft, yowled out a cacophony of warnings. The next morning, before action on an order to kill the offending curs, owners raced to the butcher and sold the animals for meat. Li's sojourn was cheered and jeered for bringing abundant, low-priced dog meat. After his visit, dignitaries poured into Wugong. The county spread the slogan "The flower of Wugong blooms all over Raoyang."

Odysseys

Li Xuefeng's visit to Raoyang, like Brains Zhang's trip to the North China Conference, was official travel. Officials went in delegations. Transportation, lodging, meals, and internal travel documents were provided. The traveler was told where to go and what to do every step of the way. Unofficial travel was discouraged. Villagers had to be available for collective labor assignments every day. Travelers were supposed to have official letters of introduction to purchase train tickets or rent a hotel room. Unofficial travel required cash, which revolutionary policies squeezed out.

Nonetheless, in fall 1970, independent-minded Geng Xiufeng decided to see China and its history and culture for himself. He was retired, in good health, and had saved the precious money. Bitter about the Xu lineage allegations that he once had links to landlord Li Huaqi, he wanted to get away. Assuming that village party secretary Zhang Duan would not approve, Xiufeng wrote his own letter of introduction and got the village accountant, a kinsman, to stamp it with the brigade seal. Xiufeng then took off on a 100-day odyssey to historical sites and Mao shrines. Fearing that his village-level document would be rejected at train stations and hotels, he was surprised to get a through ticket to Nanjing without even presenting the letter.[17] When he failed to find accommodations, he slept in train stations, bus depots, or public bathrooms.

In the Shandong provincial capital of Jinan a former Wugong commune resident took Geng to the Temple of Three Women (San nü si) and other famous sites. While he was exhilarated by the freedom of physical mobility, much that Xiufeng saw disturbed him. The water level at the famous Baotu Hot Spring outside Jinan was low. Locals said that drilling had lowered the water table. Wugong's pains clearly were not merely those of one village.

Approaching the southern metropolis of Nanjing by train, Xiufeng looked forward to seeing the Yangzi River Bridge, touted recently as a revolutionary engineering feat. Armed guards were visible as the train approached the bridge. Passengers were then ordered to shut the windows and, in the name of national security, refrain from looking.

In Nanjing, Xiufeng found northerners and southerners to be different. People with strange accents assigned him a room in the Worker and Peasant Hotel and told him to take a shower. "Because it is so hot in the south," Xiufeng noted, "people like to be clean and take frequent showers. . . . But I didn't even know how to take a shower!" In the water-rich south, villagers washed with a bucket of water before going home from the fields. In the north, a popular adage had it that males washed only three times: at birth, marriage, and death. Xiufeng observed and then imitated the others in showering.

Xiufeng was impressed by the Sun Zhongshan (Sun Yat-sen) Mausoleum and was "eager to pay respects" to Sun's remains. In school he had bowed to a picture of Sun, father of the 1911 republican revolution that ended divine monarchy in China. But Sun's body was not on view. A bystander claimed, falsely, that the defeated Nationalists had taken Sun's remains to Taiwan.

Xiufeng went downriver to Shanghai. Military security again was tight. Passengers were ordered off the deck when the steamer passed under the Yangzi River Bridge. Shanghai seemed too crowded, the buildings too tall, the roads crooked. Xiufeng blamed semicolonialism. With no one to direct him to the site of the First Congress of the Communist Party, he wandered for three days around Nanjing Road and the old International Settlement.

Finding it impossible to sail directly from Shanghai to Guangzhou, Xiufeng went to Wenzhou on the Zhejiang coast. Xiufeng and other passengers vomited below deck in rough seas. In Wenzhou, he discovered people acting on their own. The socialist system did not function there as it did in Hebei. Local lore held that anything could be bought in Wenzhou, even women. There was not even a reception office in Wenzhou where Geng could present his letter and request a hotel assignment. Adopting local methods of circumventing the system, Xiufeng found a hotel by himself.

With no ship service between Wenzhou and Guangzhou due to Taiwan's naval patrols, Xiufeng changed course and bussed west across southern Zhejiang and northern Jiangxi to Shaoshan in Hunan, Mao's birthplace. As the crowded bus wound through the mountains, Xiufeng was shocked by the backwardness and misery. "Everyone says the south is rich in water, mountains, and intellectuals," he wrote, but "this area is even more backward than Hebei." Mountain villages had no electricity, no machinery, and no modern irrigation. The crops were dried out and spindly. At a stop he bought a pear, took one disappointing bite, and threw the rest away.

The contrast between a controlled Shaoshan and an open Wenzhou was sharp. While the other pilgrims waited docilely at Shaoshan station for a bus to Mao's childhood home, Xiufeng, fresh from a Wenzhou experience, walked the three miles or so on his own. But entrance was denied until a guide arrived with a group. The guide lectured nonstop, leaving no time for questions.

Xiufeng then went by train to Guangzhou. When a fellow traveler pointed to the cassava growing along the tracks, Xiufeng recalled that these starchy southern roots had fed hungry northerners after the 1963 flood. In Guangzhou (the most enjoyable stop on his odyssey) locals mesmerized him with stories about arrogant Japanese businessmen. Premier Zhou, they bragged, had once kept Japanese from renting all the rooms of the best hotel, which would have left guests from other countries at the Export Commodities Fair with substandard accommodations. Gossip about Japanese evil did not pervade only North China.

Mao's Peasant Movement Training Institute was to have been a highlight of the trip. But, as with Mao's birthplace, it offered a dull, tightly organized collective tour for youth wearing red-guard armbands. More enjoyable was a stop at the Mausoleum of the Seventy-two Martyrs (Huang hua gang), immortalizing heroes killed in a republican uprising against the Manchu monarchy. Standing before the tomb, Xiufeng "read the names of the martyrs silently and with great respect."

Xiufeng then caught a train to Changsha, stopping at the Teacher Training School where Mao had studied and taught. A Wugong friend convinced Xiufeng to skip a tour of the Peasant Movement Institute that Mao directed in Wuhan in 1927 in favor of a visit to Xiangfan in northwestern Hubei, where the friend worked at the Danjiang Reservoir, a third-front effort to supply electricity to central China. Xiufeng was amazed to find a major project in so remote an area. Fellow passengers said a new railroad would go into Sichuan. Xiufeng also heard that, as part of preparation for war with the Soviet Union, the Changchun Number 2 Motor Vehicle Factory in the northeast was being relocated in distant mountains. Xiufeng's host spoke candidly, reporting that a poorly constructed bridge had recently been washed away in a flood, killing one person. The project engineer committed suicide.

Xiufeng next headed north toward Xi'an, stopping at Nanyang in southern Henan to visit a temple honoring Zhuge Liang, the third-century strategist immortalized in one of Xiufeng's favorite novels, *Romance of the Three Kingdoms*. He turned back, however, on learning that the historic temple had been converted into a "class education" exhibition hall.

The following day, in Luoyang, Xiufeng toured the Longmen Buddhist Caves. Most of all, he wanted to visit the 20,000 worker factory complex that produced the East is Red brand of tractor. But, fearing that his beat-up letter of introduction would not win him entry, he climbed a hill and merely peered from afar.

En route north, Xiufeng was startled to see bare hills. A passenger said that the trees had been cut and burned when "communist winds" had swept through during the Leap. From Xi'an, Xiufeng went by bus to Yan'an, Mao's guerrilla headquarters. Xiufeng was again taken aback by the stark poverty visible on the two-day bus trip. The earth was yellow, dry, and barren. He was told that the government did plant trees, but, with firewood scarce, villagers kept cutting them down.

Xiufeng was thrilled to visit Mao's Yan'an cave residences, the hall where the Seventh Party Congress was held, and sites where Mao spoke with the foreign sympathizers Norman Bethune and Anna Louise Strong. He noted the spot where "Chairman Mao asked his son, Mao Anying, to go to the countryside and learn from the peasants."

With winter approaching, Xiufeng headed home, shivering as his rickety bus poked through rugged northern hills. Back in Wugong, he learned that, when he left, retired party elders of the Xu lineage charged that he had run off to Tianjin to contact Li Zhi, a member of the wartime party branch organized by landlord Li Huaqi, now labeled a secret Nationalist Party branch. Ordered by party secretary Zhang Duan to report to the village office, Xiufeng acknowledged that his trip broke party rules. But he had not gone to Tianjin. Zhang ordered Xiufeng to write a self-criticism. A few days later, Zhang Hu, from the Raoyang military management committee, interrogated Xiufeng. Again Xiufeng detailed his odyssey, summarized his party history, and rejected the charge of affiliation with landlord Li Huaqi's party branch. Forced again to write his political history, Xiufeng wondered if the harassment would ever end.

Pigs, Cash, and Sidelines

Striving in autumn 1970 to carry out Premier Zhou's reforms while not alienating Hebei Monarch Liu, Wugong pondered policy on pigs. The state wanted more pigs, so as to provide manure for crops and pork for villagers and to end a shortage of meat in cities.[18] Natural fertilizer was to transform farmland into Dazhai-type high-productivity fields. The droppings of one hog when mixed with stalks and mud and then fermented could transform four mu. Wugong set out to boost pig raising. By late November *People's Daily* reported that the model unit had 1,100 head, or 1.8 per household.[19]

Specialized teams bred and cared for piglets and sold them to households at 10 to 20 percent below market price. Households would raise the pigs for home consumption and sale to the state. Small pigsties in household courtyards symbolized the reformist turn. The collective would pay work points for the manure with a small bonus for quality. Household, collective, and state would all benefit from more meat, income, and fertilizer. The reformist key to success was strengthening the household's money-earning capacity.

Teams 1 and 2, however, declared that rewarding households for pig raising was capitalistic. Only team 3, targeted by Geng Changsuo for failing to "close plant" and still upset about having to share so much of its pace-setting output with the rest of the village, committed itself unreservedly to pigs.

Forty-year-old team leader Li Wer, whose family owned but one mu of land in the old days, had lost all three younger brothers to illness and his only sister to hunger in the 1930s and 1940s. In 1970 Li ordered large pigpens for team 3 to rationalize pig raising, to collect more fertilizer, to have more pork to eat, and to earn cash from meat sales to the state. The team bred the piglets. But the secret ingredient was household pig raising.

Every team 3 household happily looked forward to slaughtering a hog at the New Year. The hogs weighed more than 140 catties. It felt a little like the honeymoon of the early 1950s when each household butchered a pig and welcomed home members of the extended family. Economy and culture comingled. Pork that could not be eaten at New Year was salted and savored over the next two months, or sold to the state for cash to put toward weddings, funerals, New Year celebrations, gifts, furniture, or better-brand consumer items.

But when team 3 continued raising questions about inflated crop projections as a form of hidden state taxation that left villagers "eating air" (chi kong), Boss Geng again publicly criticized the west end. He urged high estimates. If team 3 thought it might be the first to harvest more than 1,000 catties per mu, Geng insisted, why not claim the target, even if a subsequent shortfall meant giving the state more and keeping less.[20]

No matter what Geng said, all could see that reform helped Wugong's neighbor, Yanggezhuang, to inch out of stagnant poverty. Led by returned student agronomists, it enriched soil, dug deep wells (with Wugong's help), and leveled and transformed the fields. Most important, villagers grew suitable economic crops, not just grain. Life improved for 500 poor households for the first time since the early 1950s, when the village had been wounded by nationalization of the grain market and forced to substitute grain for profitable peanuts.

Some poor Raoyang villagers experimented with collective industries. Beginning in early 1971, Zhangcun opened five enterprises, one earning it national attention. Taking advantage of the technical skills of urban sent-down youth and underemployed labor, it manufactured pocket warmers for soldiers serving in frigid border areas. The village purchased metal cigarette boxes, drilled holes in them, and installed spring-loaded charcoal sticks made from local willow trees. One two-inch stick could provide warmth for four hours. In addition to the 120 workers in the factory, women at home sewed small bags to hold the warmers. Hundreds of thousands soon sold annually, providing cash income. Another factory produced thermometers. A third turned out handcrafted wooden chess sets, primarily for export. Three hundred people in a single village had found industrial employment.

No longer did "taking grain as the key link," a phrase that was authoritatively Chairman Mao's, mean that collective sidelines were disreputable. Premier Zhou urged rural units to promote sidelines and industry and use the earnings to mechanize and modernize agriculture, acquire new seeds, and raise incomes. Hebei, Hengshui, and Raoyang, with Geng Changsuo in multiple leading positions, mainly promoted irrigation and agricultural mechanization, while resisting reform initiatives — incentives, diversification, household production, and marketing activities.

Hengshui threw more resources into the unecological search for water.

Producing its own inefficient equipment, the prefecture raced ahead in well drilling, frequently, as in the past, slighting scientific knowledge and cost. Hengshui, which in 1968 drilled fewer than 2,000 wells a year, would drill 48,000 between 1970 and 1975. It planned to increase its irrigated area from 2.8 million mu in 1970 to nearly 4.7 million mu by 1975, just over half of the nine million mu of arable land. The cost of inputs was so high that increased production brought little income gain. The revolutionary state got more grain, but "rich state, poor people" was the popular plaint.

In 1970 Raoyang county drilled another 650 mechanized wells. County officials boasted of an irrigated mu of land for each of its 240,000 people. To make way for more than 4,000 irrigation ditches, corvée laborers in 1970 moved nearly 1.5 million square meters of earth.

Wugong's Boss Geng stood with those who resisted reform and promoted collective labor. In January 1971, he published yet another essay on studying Mao's philosophical ideas "in a living way."[21] Leaders who went in for speculation and smaller farming units were neglecting the "public interest" in favor of "bourgeois self-interest," Geng averred. He warned against caving in to "majority opinion." "Any opinion that agrees with the implementation of Chairman Mao's revolutionary line is the correct one." Leaders should worry about capitalist pigs behind household gates, not about how many villagers support a policy.

Party Resurgence

Following the restoration of the Raoyang party organization in fall 1969, the political power of the military faded. In September, Li Chunyu, the pre–Cultural Revolution party secretary, replaced military leader Li Guoqiang as chair of the county revolutionary committee. Heading a "party nucleus" within the revolutionary committee, Li presided over the formation of party committees in all sixteen Raoyang communes in the latter half of 1970. On November 22, 1970, the county party nucleus summoned 60 party members to a four-day meeting to form a new county party committee.

On December 22, 1970, Premier Zhou convened another North China Conference and renewed criticism of revolutionary theorist Chen Boda.[22] The conference contributed to party building and to a weakening of the power network of Lin Biao's military, advancing the reformist goals of the North China Agricultural Conference and further opening international relations.

In January 1971 a People's Representative Congress met in Raoyang to approve a new 29-member county party committee. The former head of the county military, Li Guoqiang, lost all his remaining positions. Then a Raoyang Party Congress convened for the first time in four years.[23] Seventy-year-old Boss Geng, Geng Huijuan, and Wugong secretary Zhang Duan were among the 455 delegates chosen from 8,622 party members in the county.

Resolutions praised both the "living study and application" of Mao's thought, a Lin Biao slogan, and the "learn from Dazhai" movement, that is, the program emanating from Zhou Enlai's North China Agricultural Conference. The congress named Li Chunyu county party secretary.

On March 7, 1971, the Hengshui prefectural government hosted a "learn from Dazhai" conference in Wugong. More than 90 delegates heard people from model Wugong, Kuixingzhuang, and Nanwangzhuang describe how they learned from Dazhai — Premier Zhou's modernizing Dazhai.

From February 6 to March 24, 1971, Hebei held a 47-day rectification meeting to attack the fallen Chen Boda. During that meeting, Chen's ally, Li Xuefeng, was replaced as chairman of the Hebei revolutionary committee by Liu Zihou. In May 1971 a Hebei Party Congress was convened, with Liu presiding as party secretary.[24] Grassroots party rebuilding followed. All Raoyang brigades reactivated their youth league organizations in spring 1971. By mid-summer, 94 percent of village party branches had been restored.

Dear Chairman Mao

Geng Xiufeng wrote Raoyang county party secretary Li Chunyu a protest letter, copying prefectural and provincial authorities. He criticized Li's failure to implement North China Agricultural Conference policies. He also faulted Li for exaggerating forecasts of grain yields and then, when far less grain was harvested, refusing to lower the figures. Instead, Li had summoned commune secretaries and forced them to accept a share of the burden of state deliveries by reporting the inflated numbers as their own. Villages were left short of grain despite normal harvests.

Also, Xiufeng asked, why did Li exclusively stress the "four-big" jobs of irrigation, pig raising, soil improvement, and tree planting when the North China Conference found that the best way to boost rural incomes was to encourage village-level sidelines?[25] Xiufeng criticized Li for making Gengkou a "key point" when it had virtually no sidelines and, therefore, no capacity to earn money for reinvestment. The market village of Zoucun, by contrast, had 12 sidelines. It reinvested earnings in the four bigs and did not need state handouts. Fearing that village-level sidelines "would lead to capitalism," Li had bled successful collective sidelines rather than let them reinvest earnings. The county had forced the Wugong commune brick factory to provide a "loan" of 50,000 yuan. Experience taught that the money would never be seen again.

Receiving no response, Xiufeng wrote to Mao. The July 21, 1971, letter blamed county authorities for grain shortages and hunger.[26] Xiufeng told Mao that villagers dragged their feet because excessive requisitions left a pittance as pay for collective work. He quoted Zoucun villagers who said, "We get three catties a day to eat at the river project, but we're lucky to get 1.5 catties in the brigade. So we can't work so hard."

Raoyang villagers mocked the collective regime: "The gong sounds 'Go to work.' But work is empty time. Meetings are for shouting slogans. And food? Only gruel." The focus on collective production ignored needed services. There had been no restaurant in Wugong since commerce was nationalized in the mid-1950s. In 1970 a state-run restaurant opened in the village center. But service was abysmal. The state demanded "serve the people," but revolution gutted services. The cavernous building stood dark and empty.

Xiufeng reported that some families could not live on grain allocations. Survival forced them to get the cash to buy 200 to 300 catties a year at the black-market price of .20 yuan per catty. He quoted a Zoucun villager: "Even if you have the cash, grain can't be sold in our own market, so you have to waste a lot of time going to find it in other villages." Xiufeng wrote Mao that 60 to 70 percent of Zoucun villagers complained of grain shortages.

The county seized too much after the fall harvest and then resold a small fraction to tide villagers over the spring dearth. Zoucun, whose 1969 grain quota was 40,000 catties, was forced to turn over 110,000 catties that year. The state sold back a bit more than 10,000. In 1970 Zoucun delivered 170,000 catties and received only 3,000 in return. Zoucun leaders rejected the paltry amount. While Raoyang was celebrated as the prefecture's top grain-delivering county, "the masses in the poor villages, especially those old poor peasants who have gone out begging," Xiufeng quoted a grass roots official saying, "have lots of criticisms of the cadres. Isn't this the result of requisitioning too much grain?" Rich state, poor people.

Geng Xiufeng told Mao that the county party committee had praised poor Yanggezhuang for handing over 80,000 catties in 1970, far above its quota. In spring 1971 Xiufeng found the resulting grain shortage was so acute that villagers gathered wild grasses to survive. The county sold 45,000 catties of grain back only after villagers had turned to famine food and the black market. "If harvests are poor and we go hungry," villagers said, "there's nothing much we can say. But if the harvests are good and we are still hungry, when will life ever get better?" Villages that had a surplus but no storage facility were not allowed to divide the bounty among households. The state took it.

Chinese are supposed to be "one family," Xiufeng wrote, but "when it's time to requisition grain — a time when life itself is at stake — we aren't one family any more." Villagers saw two families: "higher-ups" and people "down below." When it is time to requisition grain, "there is no more talk about 'serve the people,' 'caring for the lives of the people,' 'storing grain in households,' and 'the masses as the true heroes.'" Instead, two phrases prevail: "Resolutely complete the task. Don't make any mistakes."

Whenever villages were slow to turn over grain, Raoyang county secretary Li called an emergency meeting of commune party secretaries. "There is serious class struggle on the issue of grain requisitions," he always began. "Don't you want to prepare for war? Don't you want to continue as commune secretaries?" Then Li produced an official who confessed to having lowered production figures. Eventually all committed to overfulfilling quotas. Locals mocked, "Oil comes out of the ground only when you apply pressure."

Finally, Xiufeng complained to Mao that anticommercial, grain-first policies hurt the local economy. Wugong commune had once harvested three million catties of peanuts, an important commercial crop. But in 1970 the harvest was but 100,000 catties.

Xiufeng ended his letter by proposing a binding "contract" for at least three years. The county should not change it, even if output rose. Surplus grain should be stored in homes. Consumption ought to rise with good harvests. Villagers needed "commercial networks" that offered reasonably priced grain instead of high-priced black markets. Finally, communes and villages alike ought to set up more sidelines and encourage light industrial production.

County secretary Li was furious that Xiufeng had written to Mao. Geng Changsuo, away in Shijiazhuang, sent his daughter, Huijuan, to ease Li's rift with Xiufeng. Both trusted Huijuan. Xiufeng affectionately referred to her as Xiao Bang, "the young standout." Since January 1971 Li had worked with Huijuan as the only woman on the county party committee's Standing Committee.[27] She invited Li Chunyu to a special meeting of the Wugong village party branch to try to end the feud.

In early August, Wugong party secretary Zhang Duan informed Xiufeng that the party would consider his "problem" resolved if he would make a self-criticism in front of the village party branch. Xiufeng refused. He would only summarize his differences with Li Chunyu since the 1963 book controversy. Soon thereafter Zhang Duan announced, "After repeated investigations, and with the testimony of Zhang Yuzhou, the party secretary in those days, it is clear that Comrade Geng Xiufeng is a true party member and not a phony one."[28] But the decade-long battle between Geng Xiufeng and Li Chunyu persisted.

County Industry

County party secretary Li continued to curb village-level sidelines, but, given North China Conference policies, he promoted state investment in county-run factories. In October 1970, the county committed to building a chemical fertilizer plant and a cotton-spinning mill. A smaller shop that produced wire screening and employed 17 workers was up and running by the end of the year.

Then, in March 1971, a factory making canvas products and another producing ball bearings were launched, each requiring more than one million yuan in investment. The ball bearing plant was projected to generate annual profits of more than 13 million yuan. That fall, three more projects were announced: a mill to produce uniforms, clothing, and blanket covers, a factory to make stretch fabrics, and a farm-machine repair plant. More then 600,000 yuan were invested. Triggered by a campaign rather than by market demand, profits proved elusive.

Change was in the air. On July 16, when *People's Daily* announced that Henry Kissinger had concluded a secret visit to China and that President Nixon had accepted an invitation to visit in spring 1972, Li Chunyu summoned more than 200 county party leaders for a week of political study. Held spellbound by lectures on China's new global strategy, the assembled were told to study Chairman Mao's instructions on international relations and to read Mao's December 1970 talks with American journalist Edgar Snow.

In October work began on a vastly expanded Raoyang bus station, promising direct service to Beijing, Tianjin, Baoding, Shijiazhuang, Hengshui, and smaller regional towns. The county party also set up a group to study commercial relations between the county town and lower-level marketing centers, designating Guanting in the north and Wugong in the south as experimental sites. There were many sprouts of reform.

Remodeling Dazhai

From August 16 to September 15, 1971, Premier Zhou's State Council convened a Beijing conference on agricultural mechanization. Hua Guofeng chaired it, calling for 70 percent mechanization of agriculture by 1980.[29] Hua, a fast-rising helicopter, had worked in Shaoshan, Mao's birthplace, and attracted the attention of leaders in Beijing.[30] Associating himself with the policies of the North China Conference, Hua hailed a "new Great Leap" in which collective sideline profits provided the capital to modernize China, turning it into "a prosperous and strong socialist country."[31] Wang Guofan's Zunhua county, a favorite of Mao's, was made Hebei's mechanization model. On August 23 Dazhai leader Chen Yonggui, who now worked at the state center with Hua Guofeng and Politburo member Li Xiannian visited Zunhua.

Geng Changsuo, attending a September 1971 Hebei conference to learn from Dazhai and accelerate mechanization, heard Liu Zihou tout agricultural mechanization. Wugong, which was a pioneer in this realm in the 1950s, again invested heavily.[32] In the late 1960s, Wugong owned only two 12-horsepower diesel engines, bought in 1955. In 1970 the village bought the first of three 55-horsepower tractors acquired in the next five years. More machines were used to power irrigation. Wugong also mechanized flour milling. Women no longer had to push heavy stone rollers.

Wugong was a pacesetter in Liu Zihou's drive to use diesel engines to overcome the unreliability of the electric power system for irrigation and make agriculture self-reliant in case of war. To get the equipment, Boss Geng pulled strings, overriding objections about cost from Brains Zhang and Administrator Qiao. The commander of the Xingtai Military District provided inside information about ways to acquire diesel generators. Geng Changsuo asked Geng Xiufeng to look up Chen Zhe, the party secretary of Baoding prefecture, to press Wugong's case.[33] The province approved Wugong's purchase of 15 generators in distant Tangshan. Wugong went from four diesel engines and electric motors with 44 horse power in 1969 to 43 diesel engines with 464 horsepower and 53 electric motors with 259 horsepower in 1972.

Production costs soared. With the state holding farm-gate prices low, investment in machinery and equipment was rarely profitable. Higher officials pressured local units to use costly inputs. Agricultural performance was judged on grain yields, not on efficiency or profitability or standards of living.

Wugong grain yields rose from 708 catties per mu in 1969 to 1,108 in 1972. Per capita distributed income rose much more slowly, from 115 yuan in 1969 to 130 in 1972, with just 28 yuan paid in cash. Wugong's cotton yields skyrocketed form 1968 to 1970 to average 134 catties per mu compared with 81 over the three preceding years. But in 1971 and 1972 yields plummeted to just 99 catties.

Winds from opposing directions blew throughout 1971. Baoding still promoted "a new upsurge in the mass movement for the living study and living application of Mao Zedong thought," the Chen Boda–Lin Biao line. While in Baoding lobbying for generators, Geng Xiufeng had noted that the prefectural headquarters was guarded by an armed unit with several artillery pieces positioned inside the compound.[34] Told of continuing vigilantism and vengeance in Baoding, Raoyang people blamed peculiarities of Baoding, not revolution.

Revolution checked reform. The Raoyang Party Congress held in January had called for a new surge in the "living study and application" of Mao thought and emphasized "politics in command" and "class education." The military-linked "four-goods" movement designated 51 model villages, including Wugong. To "combat revisionism" and continue the "hit one, oppose three" campaign, more than 400 county officials fanned out to investigate more than 40 villages. In late 1971, Raoyang insisted that the top priority was "combating the bourgeois education line." County schools set up supervisory committees of poor and lower-middle peasants to monitor the revolutionary struggle.

In 1971 a Raoyang May Seventh University opened, inspired by Mao's May Seventh Directive that had set up propaganda schools cum labor reform camps several years earlier. Actually, it was the old high school with a new name. The school offered a regular track and a vocational one that provided training for barefoot doctors, agricultural mechanics, rural electricians, veterinarians, agricultural technicians, and surveyors. The largest concentration was in teacher training. Converting Russian-language teachers into English teachers was a high priority.

Still, education lagged. A rural "lost generation" viewed campaigns with jaundiced eyes. Youth whose education ended with the Leap or the Cultural

Revolution were keenly aware of the gap between the material plenty that modernization promised and the actual stagnation of rural life. They mocked their hopes for better times as crazy utopianism. They joked about new campaigns magically building better houses and furnishing them with television sets and washing machines. To them, reform had not sprouted.

The Fall of Lin Biao

After revolutionary theorist Chen Boda's fall, his ally, North China and Hebei party boss Li Xuefeng, was also arrested. Boss Geng, who had worked with Li on the Hebei revolutionary committee, joined in Li's denunciation. Geng ridiculed Li, who had recently dined at his house, explaining that Li's phony love of the poor masked a real love of privilege.

Mao reorganized military power in the capital region. A powerful prop of Lin Biao in North China, military commander and Politburo member Zheng Weishan, whose troops controlled the capital, was relieved of command. In September 1971 Lin Biao disappeared. Official sources said he died in a plane crash while fleeing to the Soviet Union after a failed coup.

The 38th Army was suspected of being the main military prop Lin Biao had cultivated in Hebei. Since 1967 it had been stationed in Baoding, the "southern gate of Beijing."[35] Lin Biao's son had described the 38th as a force "that can be manipulated." But an investigation of the Lin family plot exonerated the 38th Army leadership.

Following Lin's death, military unit 438 overcame armed groups in Baoding loyal to him. Still, networks of people tied to revolutionary politics dominated Hebei's Bureau of Agriculture, the provincial party newspaper, and many other institutions. There was no reform breakthrough in Monarch Liu Zihou's Hebei.

Tall, dark, and with an expansive paunch, Monarch Liu visited Raoyang in 1970 and again in 1971. He expressed shock at the rock-hard white soil of miserably poor Yanggezhuang. Locals, as always, snickered about officials who were ignorant of obvious realities. Militia youth joshed about the portly governor's shaved head, styled to imbue him with a military aura. With the decline of Chen Boda in fall 1970, Monarch Liu had been required to write a self-criticism, on which Mao noted, "It is easy to board a pirate ship, but very hard to get off." Protected by Politburo member Li Xiannian, his patron, Liu escaped ignominy.

Xie Xuegong, the revolutionary leader of Tianjin, also still rode high. His ties to power, like those of the Hebei military commander Ma Hui, were not through Lin Biao's Fourth Field Army. He too was not implicated in Lin's conspiracy against Chairman Mao and Premier Zhou. Geng maintained close ties to Monarch Liu and to officials in the former Hebei capital, Tianjin. Whether on Lin Tie or Li Xuefeng or Liu Zihou, Geng relied on patrons.

Increasingly Dazhai's Chen Yonggui, now ensconced in Beijing, was helpful to Geng.

In November 1971 the Central Committee ordered a halt to the "four-good movement."[36] Lin Biao's system of tapping loyalists for promotion from among militia youth like Chief Geng Huijuan ended. Raoyang held its last four-good conference in June 1971. Its plan to study outstanding four-good units in neighboring counties was scrapped when Lin Biao fell.

If Lin Biao, Mao's "closest comrade-in-arms," was a traitor, villagers asked, who could be trusted? The party called study meetings, excluding only those with bad class labels. The documents circulated to discredit Lin described Mao as an emperor with the nickname B-52, the American bomber used in Vietnam. The plotters denounced agricultural collectives. Never before had villagers heard so strong a critique of Mao and revolution.[37]

Raoyang officials faced a dilemma. At Nanshan commune, east of Wugong, Xu Laige, a tiny elderly woman with bound feet, paraded in broad daylight carrying a lantern and cursing the darkness brought by bad officials. She called Lin Biao the opposite of just and upright and described Jiang Qing as a fox spirit, a term long applied to the courtesan Yang Guifei, said to have ill served a Tang emperor and the Chinese people. County secretary Li Chunyu chose to err on the side of caution. Rather than praise Xu for seeing through the fallen Lin Biao, he sentenced her to death for having cast aspersions on Jiang Qing. Before Xu, white haired and toothless, was shot, some observers fell to their knees. She remained brave to the end.

What could one believe? Words had no meaning. Only personal ties seemed to matter. The Raoyang contingent in the 69th Army, which had been transferred from Baoding to Datong in Shanxi province, was shocked by denunciations of a Lin Biao conspiracy. It had passionately identified the revolution with the military, and the army with the person of Lin Biao. Politics seemed unfathomable, meaningless.

In October 1971, Raoyang party secretary Li Chunyu, addressing a gathering of villagers and commune officials in Wugong, denounced Lin Biao as a "bourgeois careerist and traitor." Geng Xiufeng understood this to mean "criticize whomever we are asked to criticize." Li Yunman, a mechanic, explained state-village relations: "If they say it's good, we say it's good. If they say it's bad, then we say it's bad." Politics was a ritual of survival, not a ceremony of conviction.

In late 1971 prisoners in Shijiazhuang noticed the disappearance from the press of the names of Lin Biao and other top generals. Before new prisoners arrived with the official story, the old prisoners speculated that China's military chiefs had left Beijing to prepare an invasion of Taiwan. Prisoners who cleaned latrines in official quarters looked for strips of the classified *Reference News* used as toilet paper. This is how they learned of Henry Kissinger's visit to

China. Such writings were cleaned and circulated. One fragment reporting on new ties with America cheered political prisoners, who saw it a sign of better times.

In 1972 the Raoyang prison warden read inmates a notice from Premier Zhou stating that beating prisoners was illegal and that tortured prisoners could sue their tormenters. Poet Zhang Langlang, who had been repeatedly brutalized, then told the warden he planned to sue. The warden said he would accept the document but under no circumstances would he forward it to higher authorities. Suddenly Zhang understood the meaning of the term independent kindgom, a phrase used to describe the arbitrary cruelty of unaccountable leaders.

The fall of Lin ended praise for chaos. Village anarchy could be curbed. School discipline had been shattered when teenage males ran wild. They barged into the teachers' dormitory looking for victims to beat. During class students ignored or denounced teachers. The blackboards were full of vituperation against powerless educators. Now, it was said, all of that had to change. But for Raoyang's lost generation, it seemed too late. Deprived of schooling, they were stuck in low-paying collective work.

Wugong reimposed order on young males who bullied teachers. Administrator Qiao Liguang went into the junior high and walloped his disorderly son. Macho Li Shouzheng made an example of his eldest boy, who was finishing elementary school. Knowing that Keqin did no school work, ignored teachers, and promoted fighting, Macho Li stormed into the school, pulled Keqing by the ear, and smashed him into obedience.

In summer 1972 Wugong's senior high held its first graduation. A 1972 senior high graduate, however, received fewer years of schooling than a 1966 junior high graduate; moreover, with more time spent on politics and manual labor, with the curriculum watered down, and with no incentive to pass college entrance exams (abolished in 1966), literacy and skill levels fell. The rural lost generation kept growing.

Still, the countryside benefited from reforms. In January 1972, shortly before Nixon's China visit, Mao and Zhou approved the import of American ammonia-urea fertilizer plants to spur China's green revolution. The fruits of the North China Agricultural Conference and China's new international relations included more and better fertilizer and above-quota purchase of cereals at premium prices.

Serving Power

Wugong continued to rise. In spring 1972 Geng Huijuan became deputy party secretary of Nanshan commune, east of Wugong, another step up. In early 1973, at the age of 27, she was promoted to party secretary and chair of the Nanshan revolutionary committee. Her daughter, Zhang Yan, born in 1971, was reared in Wugong by Huijuan's elder sister, Caretaker Xueren, who had earlier raised Geng Changsuo's younger children.

One Raoyang woman cashed in on Huijuan's fame. She visited neighboring counties, passing as Huijuan. She was invited to lecture, feted, and richly rewarded but eventually was arrested and imprisoned for embezzlement. Her local accent seemed proof enough to strangers that she was Huijuan.

Liu Zihou made Wugong village a regional model of the new economic policies. While just yesterday Geng Changsuo had exemplified the Chen Boda–Li Xuefeng fundamentalist line, Raoyang leaders now advanced the slogan "Externally learn from Dazhai; internally learn from Wugong."

On January 15, 1972, *People's Daily* published a long article under Geng's name identifying him as chair of the Wugong village revolutionary committee, not the deputy chair of the provincial committee, a post he had held for five years.[38] Geng's experience was recast to legitimate the reform agenda of the North China Agricultural Conference. While reiterating that "with Chairman Mao's revolutionary line one has everything," Geng distinguished Mao's true line from that of "sham Marxists," meaning both former president Liu Shaoqi (the Cultural Revolution target) and Lin Biao (the Cultural Revolution avatar). Geng averred that he had always put the interests of the majority first, completely reversing the thrust of the article he published a year earlier in which he expressed skepticism about leaders who blindly followed the majority. In the new myth, Geng had always listened to the majority. Therefore he had opposed getting involved in marketing peanuts in 1951, favored a big coop in 1952, and opposed the 1953 slashing of the big coop.

Geng now recalled that during the Leap he refused to report grossly false numbers. "If it's one, say one; if it's two, say two," he iterated. Geng took back his mid-1970 criticism of the west end for complaining about the constant pressure to make high estimates of future grain harvests. He even criticized a militia go-getter swept up by "ultraleftist" and "anarchist" currents who had "raised questions about me during the Cultural Revolution." Villagers, Geng declared, were angry about such disruptions. Prospects for modernization, even reform, sprouted even in Wugong.

Geng wrote that output and income had been hurt by the singular focus on subsistence crops by sham Marxists. Correct policy would avoid both dogmatic "leftist" errors and capitalist-style errors because "the 'left' won't do and the right won't do." The correct policy was to combine grain with overall development. That was why, Geng explained, Wugong had recently explained its collective orchard and its raising of hogs. If that was not quite what Wugong had actually done, with Chen Boda and Li Xuefeng in prison and Lin Biao dead, Geng would certainly implement such reforms now.

Geng acknowledged error in spring 1970, when mass water campaigns were stressed, for a wasteful irrigation of fields that were not properly sprout-

ing when the problem was cold weather, not a lack of water. C
should have relied not on his own subjective ideas but on pra
That was the way forward, Mao's way, not that of a pri
sobriquet for fallen revolutionary theorist Chen Boda) who
the truth in advance of experience. Villagers should focus
results.

The article used Geng's words and name to legitimate a
tion. Still, Hebei monarch Liu merely prioritized technology and diversinca-
tion of collective activity, a step toward modernization that went hand in hand
with a continued crackdown on the market.

The new Wugong myth illustrated that whether "a priori idealists" or
"capitalist roaders" won, rewards went to those whose words and ties were
best connected to the needs and networks of victors. Deft Geng, with allies
throughout Hebei and beyond, embraced winners. Nevertheless, policy had
shifted; reform was in the air.

11 ❀ STALEMATE

In 1972 modernizers called for economic diversification, rural industrialization, and trade. Collective rural industries increased, but
many lost money. State-imposed low farm-gate prices and grain and
cotton delivery quotas kept villagers toiling for a pittance. In March
1972 the hopes of modernizers were frustrated when Mao found
that the principal danger came from the right, that is, reformers. The
conflict between reform and revolution stalemated.

Exercising Caution

Following Lin Biao's fall, life improved for millions. Many were
released from prison or internal exile. Boss Geng's scribe Ji Suozhu,
tortured in 1966 and 1967, became deputy head of the Raoyang
Bureau of Education and Culture. Lu Guang, Wugong's fallen 1950s
adviser, managed a steel plant in Handan. In June 1972 Raoyang
rehabilitated commune-level leaders overthrown during the Cultural
Revolution. Of the 183 top commune officials denounced during the
stench, 179 were officially cleared. Of the 394 Hebei commune party
secretaries and vice secretaries who had been attacked, all but ten
were "liberated." The rehabilitated were reassigned to state jobs.

Liu Zihou's Hebei apparatus, however, reinstated few victims.
Former Hebei party secretary Lin Tie and his closest associates remained in limbo. Village leaders who openly opted for reform were
vulnerable to attack.[1]

Jiang Qing's group used culture to promote revolution. In 1972
Hebei's Chengde Prefectural Drama Troupe, with links to Jiang's
allies, filmed a new color version of the movie *Qingsong Peak* (Qingsong ling). The heroine was a young village woman, an ever-vigilant
Jiang Qing–like red successor.[2] One of only four feature films released in China in 1973, it praised self-sufficiency and war communism. Legitimated by a need for grain for the army, the movie incited
class struggle against those who went into the mountains looking for
timber and medicinal herbs to sell.

In one Raoyang village forced to plant grain on ill-suited land, the
harvest hardly exceeded the seeding. Villagers literally went through
the motions. On a strip in Dacaozhuang village, to Wugong's south,

tillers walked up and down furrows only pretending to seed. With the revolutionary line increasingly seen as a line, more and more villagers focused on meeting family needs.

A locale that went far in circumventing revolutionary policies in order to generate wealth through petty production and peddling was Wenzhou in the south. As Geng Xiufeng had seen on his odyssey, Wenzhou, which pioneered household contracts in 1956, was astir with household-centered economic activities.[3] Stories of such forays into the market spread.

Geng Changsuo was wary of expanding profitable sideline enterprises, even collective ones. Income generated in collective sidelines barely inched up from an average of 19 percent in the period 1966–70 to 23 percent in the period 1971–75, only half of what sidelines had earned in the early 1960s.

Yet Geng's revolutionary writ did not deter team 3. Led by Li Wer, the west end bought a 55-horsepower tractor. In addition to plowing, the tractor hauled goods and equipment for sidelines and industry. Because revolution had long starved commercial transport, anything that could move could turn a profit. The west end bought another tractor the following year and yet another two years later. Tractors were the only transport vehicles that villages could legally purchase. Team 3 explored income-earning off-farm opportunities but blocked household enterprise.

Production gains in Wugong resulted from improved irrigation and expanded double cropping. Grain yields, led by wheat, increased from an average of 722 catties per mu in the period 1966–70 to 1,175 catties per mu in the period 1971–75. Grain sales to the state more than tripled. Wheat sales nearly quadrupled. The model proved its value to the state.

Only Wugong among Raoyang's 197 collectives produced more than 1,000 catties of grain per mu in 1972. Two villages produced more than 800 catties; an additional 37 villages had "crossed the Yellow River," that is, achieved a high southern standard by reaping at least 500 catties, and another 77 had reached 400 catties. The rest lagged.

While most stagnated, Wugong incomes rose. Average annual per capita distributed income rose from 103 to 144 yuan between 1966 to 1970 and 1971 to 1975. Cash income also doubled, from 23 to 47 yuan, still only a few pennies a day. Production gains mainly led to more deliveries to the state at artificially low prices.

Hebei leaders slighted calls from modernizers in Beijing to stop bending with the wind.[4] Another campaign to learn from the national village model, Dazhai, became the rural political focus.

Chasing Dazhai

Wugong tried to heed the campaign's class struggle and mobilizational directives, while also promoting technological modernization through mechanization, well drilling, and pig raising. It became the Hengshui prefecture model in emulating Dazhai. Wugong was not, however, selected as the Hebei provincial model, an honor awarded to the cotton-growing village of Hehengcheng in Cheng'an county, south of the provincial capital.

During a cold spell in November 1972, Yang Tong, a rising party leader from the west end, joined a prefectural group touring Dazhai. It was crowded with soldiers and sailors. Visitors were run through in a couple of hours. Yang was impressed that Dazhai people worked hard and cared about the nation. But by probing, he learned that Dazhai did not have very good food. And its slogans and claims about spirit motivating people were mumbo jumbo.

Wugong tried to implement the Dazhai pay system. Once a year, villagers publicly evaluated their own worth, putting a premium on civic contributions, with everyone then publicly assessing each self-evaluation. But cultural norms taught good people to be humble, kept poor and uneducated people silent, and left most believing that only smooth talkers would brag to win more money. A pay system premised on speaking in public was humiliating.

After a single trial Wugong fixed work points at ten per day for most men and six to eight for women. Then each small work team considered whether circumstances merited particular adjustments. Wugong also rejected a reformist bonus scheme to induce harder work.

Confucian cultural norms legitimated higher income for older men. As a consequence, vigorous young men and women, even those with technical training and expertise, earned no more than frail illiterates in their seventies. Schooling had no payoff. In 1972 most members of the International Relations Institutes left Raoyang for Jixian county. Six of the institute's graduates remained as teachers. However, continuing anti-intellectualism wasted their talents.

Wugong's leaders tried to provide each household with at least ten yuan a year in cash for necessities beyond distribution in kind. Army and martyr households were assured of incomes 10 percent above the average. Villagers received a minimum of grain, cotton, cooking oil, vegetables, and firewood. Higher paying jobs went to households with less labor power or more expenses. The elderly, particularly males, were given workfare. One 80-year-old man sat at Wugong's main intersection supposedly watching so no harm came to the nearby trees. The system guaranteed subsistence minimums, but villagers craved money.

With a shriveled service sector and huge transaction costs, even modern investments could be wasteful. Spare parts for pumps were stored in Wuyi county, 25 miles from Wugong. To avoid hauling its modern machinery there by cart, Wugong trained a local welder to try to fix machines. Villages were proud of local compensations for state socialist inefficiencies. Nevertheless, costly new machines were inoperative much of the time.

Wugong leaders tried to raise cotton output by introducing incentives to rid the fields of boll worms. The quarter-inch pests had to be picked by hand. It was defined as women's work. The toil was tedious and low paying. Piece rates in the form of work points were offered. One woman field worker then quickly earned 550 work points by seizing 11,000 worms. Yet yields hardly changed. Workers merely grabbed the most available pests, ignoring the impact on plants. The market-disregarding system turned misdirected incentives into empty gestures. New incentives were legitimated as Mao's socialist task rates, replacing President Liu's capitalist task rates.

Cotton yields per mu in Wugong village stagnated between 1966 and 1975, while cotton acreage increased. Deliveries thus rose from an average of 61,000 catties between 1966 and 1970 to 90,000 catties between 1971 and 1975. But with cotton prices artificially low, overworked and underpaid villagers subsidized the state economy. Labor went unrewarded. Slacking off particularly pervaded the cotton fields.

Despite a leveling pay system, the cash gap between households could be immense. A household of seven with only one full-time laborer ended the year with no cash. The collective gave it ten yuan for the New Year. Another household of four, all of whom worked, earned 1,000 yuan. A widowed woman with low work points and young children had no cash, while a family with few young or old dependents, with someone on the state payroll, or with many able-bodied male workers involved in sidelines or the second economy, was far better off. Some of the largest intravillage income differences were cyclical, with fortunes waxing and waning with the family life cycle. Best off were those with access to the state payroll, who received cash incomes as well as pensions and free hospital care. Gender and political ties structured significant disparities.[5]

Hebei dragged its feet on the 1970 North China Agricultural Conference agenda. But it could not ignore it. On March 5, 1973, provincial authorities convened a large conference in Hehengcheng village to promote the Dazhai line. Three weeks later Raoyang county officials chose Wugong as the site for a five-day follow-up gathering to learn from Hehengcheng and Wugong. With good access to water and state resources, Hehengcheng increased fertilizer use fivefold in the early 1970s. Monarch Liu Zihou and Paupers' Coop leader Wang Guofan advised the 1,078 delegates in Hehengcheng to focus on the fundamentals, grain and cotton, making industry serve agriculture, with leaders partaking in strenuous collective labor. Monarch Liu ousted agricultural officials who promoted household and market-oriented reforms.

The state fostered a crude scientific agriculture. In 1963, when modernization was emphasized, Raoyang had established a Wugong insect control station serving 197 villages. In 1970, with modernization again a watchword, the county assigned a young technician from Tangshan to Wugong. She and three others were paid by the county to combat insect pests. They experimented with nonchemical insecticides.

In 1973 Wugong closely inspected cotton aphid eggs on corn and cotton plants. Led by former guerrilla Zhou Yuanjiu in round-the-clock observation, the group saw that cotton interplanted with corn virtually escaped injury because most eggs fell on the corn and only 5 percent survived to damage the cotton. Researchers from Qinghua University in Beijing wrote up the data in *Entomology Sinica.*

Despite Wugong's winning "four-without" awards in 1973, 1974, and 1975 for eliminating insect pests and rats that ate grain, the problem festered. Revolutionaries presented Zhou's discovery as a mobilizational success. They praised the achievements of Mao-inspired common folk. The impression was that a self-sufficient Wugong could handle its own problems. Nothing was said about the state supplying it with sulphate-based insecticide to combat wheat rust. The state touted self-reliance while denying less favored villages the scarce insecticide.

In response to the 1970 North China Agricultural Conference call for all-around development, Wugong encouraged innovations in collective orchards, animal husbandry, sidelines, and fish. In spring 1971, at the suggestion of county officials, Li Wer committed team 3 to aquaculture, turning a ditch into a fish pond. (Previously it had served as a pool for naked boys on hot August days.) West-end leaders promised that by the 30th anniversary of Wugong's 1943 coop, November 1973, villagers would feast on fresh fish. Fish were trucked in from the south. Wealth came from the south, politics from the north. The fish seemed tiny. Water kept escaping through the porous, sandy soil.[6] The costly boondoggle was abandoned.

Despite economic loss, aquaculture was a political success. *Hebei Literature,* run by provincial culture czar Tian Jian and others close to Jiang Qing's group, praised the fish venture as class education. Seventy-year-old Xu Zhuang, a detractor of the east end's Geng Changsuo and Geng Xiufeng, won media attention. Xu described fish raising as good class struggle. "Little red soldiers" won an education in class struggle by listening to Xu. Actually, high blood pressure and other maladies rendered Xu unfit for hard toil.[7] So he sat by the pond to prevent theft, a manifestation of rural alienation from the revolutionary system.

Wugong experimented with rice, long missing from the nonmarket. The Hutuo River region and other swatches in the north had once been famed for rice. In 1971 production specialist Zhang Chaoke went to Hengshui seeking rice seeds. The rice venture failed everywhere but in team 3's area. Its 1972 rice yield of 537 catties per mu compared with 166 catties for team 1 and 158 for team 2. Still, Wugong had prudently kept rice cultivation to 34 mu in yet another money-losing experiment in self-reliance.

Wugong masked the losses of its collective rope factory. It also barred wage incentives in collective pigsties. Opponents of reform hailed those who cared for nursing pigs or protected collective property at the rope workshop. Actu-

ally, a family was willing to stay with an ailing hog it owned, while a sick collective porker would be left to die.

Rural Industry: Green, Yellow, or Red Light?

Touting self-reliance, Hebei leaders began to back the production of diesel engines, pumps, tube wells, pipes, and fertilizer.[8] They encouraged self-reliance regardless of costs. In line with third-front policies, in 1973 Hengshui built an iron-and-steel plant in Handan, which already boasted two steel mills. The factory lost money every year.

In 1974 many counties in Hengshui built long-planned chemical fertilizer factories. The 4.5-million-yuan Raoyang plant, which opened in 1975, was its largest and costliest. The province provided two-thirds of the funds. Local officials boasted that the plant was designed by a Raoyang high school chemistry teacher and a Wugong-born fertilizer factory technician. In fact, the province provided blueprints and a Tianjin University chemical engineer from Raoyang supervised construction. The engineer had returned to Raoyang when his wife and children were barred from joining him in Tianjin.

In January 1972 China began importing fertilizer plants from the United States.[9] When Nixon visited in February, Raoyang officials gathered daily to listen to the radio coverage. Foreign trade rose as a consequence of reform openness, and Raoyang began importing fertilizer from Japan. Villagers coveted the large white nylon urea sacks, dying them dark blue and making them into pants. But officials took most. Villagers rhythmically ridiculed:

> Officials, officials, nylon trousers, one pair each.
> In front, made in Japan. In back, urea.

Although Raoyang opened an office to stimulate collective sidelines and industrial activity, there were only 5,000-plus workers in township and village industrial enterprises by the mid-1970s. Gross industrial output was just 11 million yuan. In the ball bearing plant, at the final stage of a process meant to produce a precision product, a young woman held the steel balls up to the sun, squinted, and applied a file to remove the most obvious imperfections.

Despite enormous waste, Wugong was part of some 20 percent of rural China, principally suburban and model villages, in which material conditions improved. For the first time since the 1963 flood, personal savings began to grow, reaching a village total of 30,000 yuan by 1972 and 80,000 in 1976. Savings had been 100,000 yuan in 1963. Recovery from revolutionary economic irrationality was slow.

In 1972 the state inaugurated three tiers of grain prices. The key reform was a higher price for a second tier of above-quota sales and a third tier of negotiated prices beyond that. Wugong responded in 1973 by planting 450 more mu in wheat. While state-blessed Wugong could take advantage of new

programs, most villages had no cash reserves, access to credit, united leadership, expertise, or connections. In 1970 Wugong's machinery and equipment were valued at 2.9 million yuan, after stagnating at around one million yuan in the 1960s. The value increased to 6.4 million in 1972 and 10.9 million in 1974. Wugong led the prefecture in mechanization.

Team 3 leader Li Wer, who had taken the initiative on tractors, pigs, rice, and fish, set the village pace in money earning, mechanization, and market expansion. In 1972 he sent buyers to Baoding and Shijiazhuang for diesel engines to keep water pumps going when state power failed. Li also expanded the west end's profitable paper string factory, the product used to wrap the tops of cigarette packs and liquor bottles. The team dispatched 30-year-old Zhang Xu to the northeast, where his veterinarian father had worked in the 1940s. He was soon so busy selling he seldom returned home. The commune's credit coop opened a credit line of 200,000 yuan. In sum, farm-gate prices closer to market value combined with travel that circumvented economic irrationality to promote cash earnings.

Income in team 1 lagged one-third behind that in team 3, with politically wounded team 2 equally far behind team 1. The east end rejected the marketing of even collective products. In 1974 the politically stigmatized village center, looking for a way to expand wealth, invested 24,000 yuan in machines to spin yarn for a Shijiazhuang textile factory. To boost team 2, party secretary Zhang Duan had moved his registration to the village center in 1972. Villagers joked that what team 2 really needed was someone like Xu Shukuan, Boss Geng's wife. The Tigress had the vital juices (qi) of a man. If the old team 2 leaders ordered villagers who were eating to jump, it was said, not only would they not jump, they would not even miss a bite of food. But Xu, with her sharp tongue, villagers chuckled, would shape up team 2 in no time. Misogyny aside, the village center at last began to rise, seizing opportunities to diversify.

Xu Shukuan also cared about her own extended family. She weighed in on the future ownership of the family's residence in favor of her oldest daughter, Xueren, who had virtually raised the younger children. Husband Geng wanted the younger son, who lived in Raoyang town, to inherit the property. That was proper. Xu disagreed. The daughters sided with her. The tiff went on for a couple of years. Finally Geng conceded, and Xueren became the heir. Xu Shukuan and justice prevailed over patriarchy.

Several dozen young women toiled in new village workshops. Females constituted the core of the textile and apparel work force. Yet no facilities served pregnant or menstruating women. Incomes rose, but, because of a lack of social protections, there was a Dickensian quality to the new industries. The air was unbreathable, the noise was deafening, and safety measures were nonexistent. Still, off-farm jobs cut the number locked into undervalued collective agriculture. After two years of watching life improve in the west end, revolutionary

team 1 began seeking subcontract work from mills. Small factories provided the most rapidly growing rural income source. While state factories in Raoyang town were costly boondoggles, village factories, using inexpensive second-hand machinery and abundant cheap labor, generated jobs and income.

Rebuilding the Party

A party-building drive surged. By spring 1972 party branch organizations were functioning in every Raoyang village. A thousand new members were enrolled. The youth league, women's association, police, and courts were restored. In June 1972 the prefecture ordered Raoyang to erase all memories of the fallen Lin Biao. Within a month, officials reported the confiscation and destruction of 589 portraits of Lin, 1,289 pages of his writings, 9,876 books that discussed his life, and 1,780 badges that featured his facial profile!

One casualty of the drive was Zhao Enpu, a military man who had served as vice secretary of the county armed-forces department in the early 1960s and as a deputy secretary of the Raoyang revolutionary committee from 1968. Zhao was fired in July 1972.[10] In late summer, huge rallies criticized Lin Biao. Activists were urged to study "Chairman Mao's letter to Comrade Jiang Qing" that commented negatively on Lin. In November Wugong was designated a model site for the anti–Lin Biao campaign.

In Dongsong village, west of Wugong, secretary Wei Cunhou was ousted from the party in late 1974. In mid-1968 his claim that there were 111 Nationalist Party spies in the village had led to an orgy of torture. A leading village official had committed suicide. County authorities acknowledged that in Chengguan commune during the 1970 "hit one, oppose three" campaign, Dong Wenguang, now posthumously praised as an "outstanding" party official, had committed suicide under torture.

Wugong was cited as a model of party organization. A plenary meeting of the county party was held in Wugong in late June 1972. At a follow-up plenum in Wugong in March 1973, Geng was chosen to represent the county at the Tenth Party Congress scheduled for Beijing in August 1973.

With promotion of revolutionary women emphasized, Geng Huijuan rose rapidly. In March 1972 she was put in charge of the county's birth control program. A year later Raoyang proclaimed a two-child limit for each family. Huijuan pledged to reduce the birth rate to 15.9 per thousand by 1975. Raoyang was a key point in a Hebei birth control drive. In autumn 1973 Huijuan was promoted to deputy director of the provincial health bureau in the provincial capital, Shijiazhuang. Such stunning upward mobility was dubbed "rising like a helicopter." Huijuan's superior, Han Qimin, had befriended Geng Changsuo while hiding in Wugong from the Japanese 30 years earlier. Huijuan's provincial-level health job, she told us, was one for which she had no training.

Another rising local woman was Song Xingru, Raoyang's "other" national labor model. Though overshadowed by Boss Geng for many years, Song long presided over Chang'an village, a model unit in Liuchu commune in the middle of the Hutuo flood plain east of Wugong. At the 1963 celebration of the Wugong coop, she had spoken honestly. As Lin Biao's forces had promoted the militia, so now Jiang Qing's forces promoted women. In June 1973 Song was the leading Raoyang delegate to a women's congress in Hengshui prefecture. A few months later *Hebei Daily* featured her in an article on the leadership capabilities of women.[11] By early 1974 Song's village was named a pacesetter in a movement to criticize Lin Biao and Confucius, an effort pushed by Jiang Qing revolutionaries to discredit modernizers associated with Premier Zhou. By the end of 1974 she was a delegate to the Fourth National People's Congress in Beijing.

Modernizers were also mobilizing. Deng Xiaoping, a top Cultural Revolution victim, was rehabilitated in 1973. He took charge of modernizing reforms for Premier Zhou, who was smitten by cancer. But after December 17 when Mao branded the fallen Lin Biao an ultrarightist, reformers were again forced into self-criticism as Mao called for another attack on all things "capitalist."

Quota management was again denounced. Geng Changsuo's byline appeared on an article in *People's Daily* contending that ever-larger collectives, following Mao, sticking to agriculture, and emphasizing spiritual change would conquer drought and expand production.[12] Silent on recent money-earning village initiatives, it applauded Mao's call to foster selflessness and cut capitalist tails, that is, to nip the burgeoning informal economy in the bud.

Corruption and Crime

Lin Biao was denounced for bribing people with gifts, food, travel, and cash, but cynicism deepened. Villagers cursed being left behind. Those locked into low incomes could see the gap between themselves and the few who enjoyed the perquisites of power: cars, banquets, travel, resorts, scarce foreign commodities, quality medical care, and preferred consumer goods.

Because much collective labor was a waste and the campaign to cut capitalist tails kept living standards down, the logic of household improvement required economic "crime." With many market and household activities banned, the second economy intertwined with criminality. Wugong's Yang Bingzhang, who was appointed party secretary of team 3 in 1974, hid in the fields at night and caught a peanut thief from team 2. Yang fined the thief 15 days of work points. According to Yang, as soon as he took office, friends approached him for loans of team funds to splurge at the New Year and for better paying sideline jobs.[13]

Precautions against theft intensified. Strong locks secured front gates. More families obtained watchdogs. Slogans painted near the threshing grounds warned "Beware of thieves." In Raoyang town, more steel bars, barbed wire, and broken glass were put up to protect valuables. Neighboring villages blamed Wugong for an upsurge of theft. Fairly or not, people in poverty-stricken Yuanzi muttered that Wugong villagers stole Yuanzi's fruits and vegetables. Wugong's ties to higher-ups made it immune to investigation.

Villagers fixated on local pains and pleasures. In Raoyang there was a wave of arrests for gambling in the early 1970s. In 1973 four leaders of a Daoist-oriented sect from Tianjin were jailed in Hengshui, where more than 1,000 prisoners engaged in labor reform. A few women were incarcerated for crimes related to marital infidelity, including revenge murder. One was imprisoned along with her lover after her husband committed suicide. The lovers, found guilty of causing an unbearable loss of face for the husband, were sentenced to five years of labor reform. Infidelity to soldiers was treated harshly. But officials who raped young urban women who had been sent to the countryside were rarely punished.

In a few villages where young males were too poor to marry, gangs raped women who were engaged to be married. Accounts of rape varied. Educated youth in the Raoyang countryside gossiped that most rape took place in regions with numerous troops.

Aware that people assumed the worst about officials, leaders tried to establish their incorruptibility. When someone told Macho Li Shouzheng that his wife had caused a field to flood, he raced to redress the wrong. On seeing the water, he grabbed his wife and smashed her across the backside. An onlooker then told him his wife was not the one who had flooded the field. Macho Li stared, turned, and walked away.

In this atmosphere of state-induced alienation, cynicism, fear, and violence, villagers drew closer to those they could trust. Urban gangs, lineages, and secret societies grew as foci of ultimate loyalty. Scarcity, rationing, and privileged access compelled people to cultivate the powerful. When Wugong's Li Mandui wanted a Flying Pigeon bicycle, China's top brand, he saved the necessary 160 yuan. But lacking the required ration coupons, he struck a deal with a friend in Raoyang with connections. Bonds of loyalty delivered valued goods.

In June 1974 poet Zhang Langlang, having languished in the Raoyang jail for five years, was transferred to a prison in the Hebei capital. Compared to Raoyang, it was heaven. Food was more plentiful and better. Working in auto repair, Zhang found issues of *Reference News* left by party officials. He reacquainted himself with the world. An office map showed prison labor exports to Vietnam and countries in Africa. Shijiazhuang paid prisoners less than a yuan per month. But earnings could be turned into occasional sweets, salt, and eggs, none of which was available in Raoyang.

Reformers tried to expand the use of law. The Hebei provincial court, abolished in 1966, was restored. In 1974 the county appointed 49-year-old

Zhang Hu, a public security officer with a junior high education and no legal training, as a judge. He was the only legal officer for a ten-commune area. The court in Zoucun, just east of Wugong, had closed in 1953. For more than two decades plaintiffs in divorces, inheritances, and injury disputes could seek redress only at the county seat. But courts there had closed when the Cultural Revolution erupted. Consequently, local party secretaries or their aides meted out rough justice. With only one judicial official for more than 200,000 people, the party and militia retained ultimate power.

In January 1974 a campaign was launched to stop children of officials from receiving special privileges "through the back door." It called for emulation of the son of an army man who renounced his father's effort to bring him back from the countryside. The popular perception, however, was that there were two kinds of rural youth, noble princes and princesses, whose well-connected parents would get them up and into the palace of power with "proletarian" credentials, and ordinary youngsters, who were abandoned to a lifetime of poverty. Geng Huijuan was privileged. Her husband Zhang Ping, trained as a mathematics teacher, left his job in an oil refinery to join her in Shihjiazhuang in 1974, with a job arranged in the Hebei cultural bureau.

Wugong was hailed for resisting corruption. A village workshop that made rubber items sent out a salesman. A potential buyer argued that the product was of low quality and therefore, in return for a premium price for a low-grade item, some under-the-table sweetening with peanuts and Hengshui's white lightning whiskey was necessary. This was how the informal economy worked. But Wugong refused, reported the incident, and lost the sale. The salesman was lauded for exposing a capitalist roader.[14]

Boss Geng was praised for rebuffing a wartime comrade who wanted her son recalled from a wretched area of Shaanxi province. Geng told her, "In fighting Japan, we feared neither hardship nor death. Surely conditions today in Shaanxi are far better than in the old days." Gossipers recalled that six of Geng's seven children, and most of their spouses and adult children, had secured state payroll jobs, many of them in the city. Official claims of fairness rang hollow.

Rural dwellers ridiculed stories that hid the chasm between the privileged and the marginalized. The system forced self-protective petty corruption on ordinary folk. They bridled at being told that their defensive arrangements, personal ties, small deals, little gifts, trading of favors, and reliance on connections were corrupt. A drowning person should not be blamed for grabbing a life preserver or for detesting those who, while sailing on a yacht, boast that they alone never get dirty. County folk especially despised one physician, the wife of a top Raoyang county official, who was notorious as a "backdoor specialist." She offered her services to the connected and never had time for villagers, who suffered half-trained paramedics.

The Dazhai Edge

The Hebei press touted the honesty of Wugong leaders, but neighbors muttered that the village received extra fertilizer. They also grumbled about Wugong's special access to loans, seeds, tractors, water drilling, and student labor from the county during the busy farm seasons. In theory, prefectural guidelines allocated fertilizer on humane criteria: some was set aside to help disaster areas, Muslim minorities, and the poorest places with the worst soil; the rest was divided based on arable land. But in practice much was reserved for advanced units. Locals believed Wugong was the leading seller of cotton and wheat to the state because it got almost half of Raoyang fertilizer.

Wugong people saw it differently. Realizing how much more went to Dazhai, continuing to engage in heavy manual labor, living without the blessings of urban modernity, remembering how many gave their lives for the cause, resenting the way outsiders took credit for the achievements of villagers, and ridiculing the ignorance of officials and the inappropriateness of purported help, Wugong villagers and leaders did not ascribe gains to state assistance. Villagers in model units believed their hard work and patriotic loyalty were the keys to success.

Boss Geng's grandson Zhang Mandun and Macho Li Shouzheng visited Dazhai in 1974. Neither saw anything to copy. The hilly terrain was so different. Besides, Li considered Wugong superior. He carried home two ears of corn to prove that Wugong corn was better.

Technical specialists dispatched to Dazhai in 1970 from the Academy of Agrculture developed "short-stalk, wind-resistant high-yield hybrid strains" to replace the village's long-stalk corn, which was easily blown down.[15] The Academy of Science posted Gu Pingyuan in Dazhai to work on the fermentation of hog fodder. Gu eventually produced a ferment for hog fodder attuned to Dazhai's particularities that fattened hogs at twice the national rate. Packaging this success for agroscience as the fruit of self-reliant labor, the product was called "Dazhai new ferment."[16] In 1971 the academy's Institute of Atmospheric Physics produced a "semiconductor lightning counter" to help Dazhai's county distinguish between "hail clouds and rain clouds." It gave local farmers a more accurate early warning tool.[17]

Positions for Dazhai students were reserved at Qinghua University, the nation's top science university. In summer 1970 the 36-year-old village bookkeeper entered its Department of Water Conservancy. He was the first Dazhai resident to attend college.[18]

Bulldozers went in to level the fields. A fertilizer factory built in the county seat turned out precisely the nutrients Dazhai's soil needed. Dazhai benefited from "the construction of the Xiyang County nitrogen fertilizer plant that fixed atmospheric nitrogen with coal, and the phosphate plant that followed." These plants "made it possible for Dazhai and the whole county to break through to world-class yields of corn."[19] The county built a tractor factory, producing ten-horsepower crawler tractors suited to Dazhai's hilly conditions.[20]

In 1973 a technical team from the Ministry of Agriculture spent 40 days in Dazhai setting up cable cars to move dirt and rock to speed the leveling of fields. In sum, once Dazhai became the national agricultural model in 1964, scarce state inputs made it uniquely successful in hogs, grain production, water control, agricultural mechanization, and everything else that was on the stage agenda. The unprivileged were told to get rich by copying "self-reliant" Dazhai.

Cutting Capitalist Tails

In 1974 Hebei embarked on yet another campaign to cut capitalist tails. Not even collective enterprises were safe. A village south of Raoyang town, which earned a little money in a collective sideline manufacturing transformer switches, was forced to stop and grow more grain.[21] The campaign also targeted the quietly expanding household sector and rural industry. A new rug factory in Wugong's poor neighbor, Gengkou, had made good use of under-employed labor. It was forced to close. Villages with the poorest land that most needed cash to buy food were hardest hit. With soybeans, chickens, eggs, goat milk, fresh vegetables, and peanuts among the targets, some regions again confronted malnutrition.

Wugong lost its local source of hemp, which had been processed in Shen-xian county before being made into rope in Wugong. At greatly increased cost for the already subsidized product, trucks had to haul hemp from Shandong province.[22] Even in Wugong, the area's most collectivized village, noncollective income declined. An exception was a west-end beekeeper whose honey was sold by the collective.

Party secretary Zhang Duan criticized Li Wer's prospering team 3 for stressing sidelines.[23] Zhang demanded that team 3 focus instead on grain. This seemed nonsense to Li Wer, whose mother, a strikingly handsome, bound-foot woman, had just returned to care for her great-grandchildren and raise a pig, two geese, and four hens in the household courtyard. The 73-year-old had lived in Beijing with her grandson, party secretary of a hat factory, for ten years. Gaining access in the capital to scarce medicines, she filled the requests of relatives and friends whose needs could not be met by the inadequately stocked collective pharmacy.

Her son, Li Wer, accepted Zhang's criticism and promised to change. Back in team 3, however, Li supported collective sidelines. How else could villagers improve their diet and earn money to boost living standards and reinvest? The west end continued to be the richest part of the village. More and more people acted like Li Wer, saying what the party wanted to hear but doing what villagers knew would improve life. At night, after collective labor, hidden by courtyard walls, money-earning work expanded.

More villagers were charged with economic crimes. Some locals fled to the northeast to castrate pigs or to Inner Mongolia to trade horses as generations had prior to the revolution. Village youth sought any alternative to being locked in stagnant agricultural collectives. Illegal firecracker sales were the number 1 source of cash in Raoyang, pig castration, a local specialty, number 2. And Raoyang was more loyal to revolution than most of village China.

History Revised — Again

In May 1973 the Hebei authorities approved a 30th-anniversary celebration of the original Wugong coop. The scale, however, would be much smaller than of previous celebrations. There would be no exhibition hall, and news coverage would be limited. Geng Xiufeng noted that with dubious models "popping up like bamboo shoots in the spring rain," Wugong seemed less distinctive.[24]

The Hebei Bureau of Literature and Art, which had just resumed publication of *Hebei Literature and Art,* was headed by culture czar Tian Jian, who set the line for the Wugong celebration. After Hebei monarch Liu Zihou obtained Tian's release from a labor reform camp in 1972, Tian promoted Jiang Qing's cultural policies. Writers from Hengshui came to Wugong in early 1973 to explore the possibility of a book. But with stalemate at the state center between reform and revolution, the story line was not obvious.

Wugong's old friend, writer-official Wang Lin, still influential in Tianjin literary circles, suggested recycling *The First Flower,* the book he had edited for the 20th anniversary in 1963. Wang had ties to Jiang Qing going back to the resistance-war era. His task was to portray Geng Changsuo as a hero who, inspired by Mao, led a community of pure revolutionaries. This line was exemplified in Jiang Qing's model operas. Once the Tianjin People's Press committed itself to the book, Wang accompanied writers to Wugong in early 1973. Whereas the 1963 book introduced Wugong in terms of former Hebei party secretary Lin Tie's vision of mechanized Soviet-style collectives that brought material plenty to impoverished people, the 1973 volume had to explain how Mao's 1943 speech "Get Organized!" set the village on the path of ever larger socialist collectives through a continuing struggle between the two classes and the two lines.

Geng insisted on the removal of every word written about him in the 1963 volume by an author who later was denounced in the Cultural Revolution. The writing team wanted to tell how villagers protected Geng from misguided red guards. That was vetoed. Instead, Geng was represented as a miniature Mao, beyond reproach.

In the 1963 volume Geng Xiufeng, who told us that he first heard about

the village general store, got the idea for the coop from a 1940
on Soviet collectives. In the 1973 edition, Xiufeng was inspired by
ader, Chairman Mao. With the book's emphasis on the village's
ng Changsuo, the original controversial ten-page chapter on an
ial Xiufeng was cut to four. County secretary Li Chunyu wanted it
ltogether.

Positive references to the Soviet Union were excised. No longer was Geng
Changsuo inspired by how "the Soviet Union took the path of collectivization." Negative references to the United States were removed. With heroes
made 100 percent positive, Lu Molin responded to Xiufeng's 1944 suggestion
that Geng Changsuo take charge of the initial four-family coop by saying,
"Great! Changsuo is the most suitable one." In the earlier version, Lu said, "I
don't think he'll do it."

An account of giving charity during the 1960s Leap dearth to children
from another village who lacked even a penny for a hard roll was deleted. In
fundamentalist fantasy, rural poverty vanished. Models had to be model perfect. The diaries of aspiring writer Shi Guiying and pepperpot Li Huiying,
already heavily contrived for the 1963 edition, were purged of selfish desire
and complex motive. Worthy people acted selflessly.

Yet the revised book also incorporated modernization themes. Wugong
promoted agricultural science and mechanization. A new picture showed people with a microscope. The chapter "The New Army on the Agricultural
Front" was retitled "The New Army for Scientific Farming." A photo of Geng
was added with a backdrop of mechanized agriculture. Leap-era loyalty was
recast to show adherence to Geng Changsuo's admonition against exaggeration and for "seeking truth from facts."

The book omitted Zhang Duan's Leap-era attack on mourning, a campaign
pressed by the now imprisoned revolutionary theorist Chen Boda. Losers
became nonpersons. All over China, library card files eliminated Chen's name
and his books.

The writing team wanted to describe Boss Geng's visits to Dazhai and how
Wugong learned from Dazhai. But with revolutionaries and reformers stalemated on what aspects of Dazhai to feature, the section was scrapped. The
book's omissions and contradictions mirrored China's political tensions. People in Jiang Qing's fundamentalist camp did not like the compromised narrative. The 1973 book was limited to a run of 16,000 copies.

Local Realities

The party was losing the power to impose its heroes and villains. While the
media presented an omnipotent state, villagers in fact lived by getting around
state restrictions. The local became the real.

Thirty-seven-year-old veteran Ji Tiebang of Nanshan village was a leader in unearthing local culture and history. The only son of an Eighth Route Army veteran, he returned home in August 1972 from a New China News Agency job in Beijing to care for his dying mother. Ji had become intrigued by local lore while researching the history of Raoyang earthquakes. After a fellow soldier had ridiculed him for hailing from "uncivilized" Raoyang, Ji set out to discover a proud history.

He found that Raoyang had been much larger two millennia earlier in the Han dynasty, when it specialized in pig castration and watermelon cultivation. He was thrilled when Han artifacts were unearthed in Zoucun in 1974. Ji took pride in local scholars who had succeeded in the civil service exams. He collected ancient Raoyang poetry. He learned that the dried-up river beds of today had once watered lush lands, abutting beautiful pavilions that attracted visits by emperors. Ancient glories commingled with recent pride in contributions to the resistance war. Raoyang fireworks were used by Ming dynasty emperors and were among the gifts presented to a delegation from Burma led by U Nu just before the Cultural Revolution. Raoyang had won a 1948 visit by a land-reform team that included Kang Keqing, the wife of Red Army leader Zhu De. While the party told Ji to show how socialism served the people, what intrigued him was the richness of the culture.

Ji and other cultural buffs thrilled to Raoyang achievements in martial arts and stage craft. Though the media were silent, locals were immensely proud of Wang Runlan of Liuchu village, who served in the Nationalists' 34th Army. He was a member of the Chinese Olympic team sent to Berlin in 1936.[25] A martial arts specialist and patriot, Wang believed that physical fitness was critical in defense against foreign aggressors. Another legendary martial artist, Wang Shaoxian of Beihan village, graduated from the Hebei Martial Arts Academy in Tianjin in the 1930s before pursuing a career in police work.[26]

With masters like Wang Shaoxian as advisers, martial arts and other sports made a comeback in Raoyang in the early 1970s, brightening a drab world. Song Fengge took first in three track-and-field events at a prefectural high school competition in early 1972, and for three consecutive years beginning in 1972 the boys' and girls' high school volleyball teams came in first in prefectural games. A county sports committee was set up in early 1973. In September Wang Shaoxian's daughter placed first in a prefectural martial arts competition, and in 1974 the Raoyang team won first place.

Elders delighted in listening to old-timers talk about Raoyang's glory days as a center of theater art. Storytellers remembered the legendary Chang Xiangting, whose ancestors had migrated from Shanxi province in the Ming dynasty. After settling in Yanggezhuang, the Changs struck it rich and relocated just outside Raoyang town. Prosperous landlords whose living quarters consisted of one hundred rooms in the late Qing, the Changs loved opera. From 1888 to 1917 Chang Xiangting ran the Chongqing Theater Training Program from the family compound. Chang's troupe traveled to Beijing,

Tianjin, and Shanghai to perform Beijing opera and the beloved local theater form, Hebei *bangzi*.[27]

The most renowned local actor was Tian Zhenqing, known as the Seventh Golden One. Local legend has it that one night in 1924 when Tian was performing Beijing opera in Shanghai, a secret agent arrived in hot pursuit of a young revolutionary. Tian and his friends saved the patriot by plastering his face with stage makeup and hiding him in a group of extras. The young rebel was Lin Tie. In the early 1950s Hebei first party secretary Lin reciprocated by arranging a 30 yuan per month stipend for the old master.[28]

In the early 1970s local historians also kept alive the memory of locals who had established a name elsewhere. Sun Minqin, a native of Dongwan'ai village, earned a coveted *xiucai* degree in the final years of the Qing dynasty. After teaching Chinese medicine at Beijing Normal University in the 1920s, Sun became a respected teacher and practitioner of Chinese medicine in Inner Mongolia.[29] Pride in Chinese culture and respect for those who promoted it clashed with the revolution's war on the popular as feudal.

Thirtieth Anniversary of What?

In spring 1973 Raoyang secretary Li Chunyu, learning he was to be transferred to Hengshui, requested a delay so he could help organize Wugong's 30th-anniversary gala. This led to another incident in Li's decade-long clash with Wugong's Geng Xiufeng, who rapped Li's plans for the anniversary.

Xiufeng claimed that Li's exhibition was riddled with errors. The depiction of revolutionary class struggle was untrue. Xiufeng told a Li aide that back in 1935 it was rich peasant Li Yingzhou, not landlord Li Jianting, who was involved in a violent confrontation over a stolen chicken. "The goal of an exhibition is to educate people," Xiufeng complained, "but if no one believes it, whom are you educating?" Villagers knew the facts. The aide countered, "A landlord is a more outstanding example of evil, so the emphasis should be placed there. Secretary Li instructed us to act according to Comrade Jiang Qing's principle of emphasizing 'things that stand out' [tuchu]. You credit one outstanding person for the good things, and you blame one evil person for the bad things. This is how typical cases become distinctive."[30] The exhibit went unchanged.

Xiufeng was indignant to find a huge photo of Li Chunyu giving instructions to underlings. To the right of the photo, a chart provided inflated county production figures. Xiufeng understood it as hewing to Jiang Qing's instructions to stress "things that stand out." Mao got the credit at the center, Li Chunyu at the county, and Geng Changsuo at the village. In a letter to an old friend Xiufeng worried, "Throughout the ages, the idea about heroes making history was held by all reactionaries who sought to keep the people ignorant.

Their motive was to foster blind worship and unconditional obedience. concluded that the exhibition promoted only "ignorance and schemes."

Li Chunyu saw to it that Xiufeng was not invited to the celebr Higher-level friends and Boss Geng confided to Xiufeng that the coun thorities had branded him a troublemaker tied to arsonists, secret sc members, and rapists. On the celebration day, November 29, Xiufeng was denied entry by a security guard. But when a Wugong contingent arrived, accompanied by cymbals and gongs, Xiufeng merged with them. The group was greeted by a huge portrait of Mao and the dazzling sight of Boss Geng, daughter Huijuan, and Zhang Duan draped in red bunting on stage beside the secretary of the prefectural party committee. Xiufeng found the speeches hollow. The ceremony failed to clarify what was special about Wugong. But he was delighted that county secretary Li Chunyu was not there. His successor, Wang Yumin, presided.

Press coverage was sparse. *Hengshui Daily* published Boss Geng's speech. *Hebei Daily* praised Wugong's public spirit of contributing unselfishly to the nation. *People's Daily* noted the selflessness of the Wugong collective and the resolve of the people to combat "the tide of bourgeois thinking."[33] Stalemate did not permit much of a story.

Revolutionary Education

Changes in education reflected Jiang Qing's notion of class struggle to heighten communist consciousness. In September 1973 the Hebei party committee launched a campaign to criticize the "Lin Biao counterrevolutionary clique," but Lin's policies were not targeted. In model Hehengcheng a seventh-grade teacher was condemned for seeking to reduce manual labor so students could prepare for the high school entrance exam. Revolutionaries decreed that children work longer hours in the fields.[34]

On December 4, 1973, Wugong commune hosted a week-long conference on the "revolution in education" sponsored by the political department of the prefectural revolutionary committee. Delegates toured the elementary school and observed evening political classes.

In early 1974 the Hebei Bureau of Education sent instructions to revolutionize consciousness based on the case of an English-language teacher in rural Henan who criticized the poor performance of student Zhang Yuqin, who then drowned herself. The teacher's "bourgeois dictatorial attitude" was labeled lethal. Oppressed students and oppressive teachers were locked in a "class struggle" to the death. The principal and several teachers were fired; some were jailed. In Wugong, the campaign targeted a math teacher thought to be too strict. Virtually all the trouble-making students in the commune school were from Wugong village. Some parents even joined in beating teachers, leaving one at death's door. Serious students tended to come from the poorest villages.

School authorities were told to teach the case of Zhang Tiesheng. He was lionized by a Jiang Qing ally after turning in a blank exam on July 19, 1973. He contended it was counterrevolutionary to test for knowledge he lacked because he gave his all to revolution. Zhang was not only enrolled in the Chaoyang Agricultural College but also elevated to college party secretary.[35] Wugong teachers found that the more they taught the Zhang story, the worse school conditions became. Students refused to study or take exams. Big character posters covered the walls. Teachers were accused of acting like lords and criticized for stressing book knowledge and slighting revolutionary virtue.

In one Hebei agricultural college, teachers were forced to take exams on subjects they did not teach. It was a case of life copying art. The 1975 film *Spring Sprouts* (Chun miao), an orgy of intellectual bashing, pitted a militant, Jiang Qing-like paramedic against arrogant and antisocialist teachers and administrators.[36] The paramedic is forced into retreat until the Cultural Revolution saves her. To humiliate teachers, they are examined on topics on which they have no expertise.

Some Wugong students with less than red class backgrounds again became targets of political bullies. Their parents then kept them home. The few with well-educated relatives were taught at home. Teachers did what they could for the few who applied themselves. When classes resumed in Wugong after a month of turmoil, teachers and administrators substituted a superpatriotic tale, "The Red Army Did Not Fear the Long March," for the Zhang story. Patriotism was the last refuge.

Wugong teachers did not dare to keep order, correct student errors, or give exams. Students bullied teachers and played hooky. Enrollment fell. Wugong wasted the graduates sent from colleges in Beijing, Tianjin, Shanghai, Wuhan, and Baoding who could have taught.

In 1972, English replaced Russian as the foreign language for high school students. But in 1974, instead of the alphabet, students learned a ditty attributed to Zhang Yuqin, the student from Henan province who committed suicide:

I am Chinese. Why study English?
Even without ABC, I am still a revolutionary.

Two students confronted Cheng Tiejun at his home on the school grounds, demanding that he stop teaching English. One of them was a grandson of Boss Geng. With anti-intellectualism ascendant, English classes were canceled.

In 1972 a special performing arts program to promote revolution began in Raoyang's youth "cultural palace." The training, as in days of old, was rigorous, even brutal. Errors earned beatings. Some older teachers were seen as sadistic torturers. Performers who survived the ordeal went on to opera careers, a few winning fame throughout Hebei. The program accepted 20 to 30 high school students each year. In theory, admission was based on proven performance. But no one dared reject a Wugong applicant. The village, with barely 1 percent of the county's population, took a third of the plums. Two of the seven staff members were from Wugong; one was Geng's daughter Jin-xiang. She was given the title of bookkeeper but, with little to do, she mainly stayed at home, collecting a state salary.

In the early 1970s, as universities began to reopen, places were reserved for the politically pure, dubbed children of workers, peasants, and soldiers. With Mao rejecting Premier Zhou's effort to permit some high school graduates to proceed direct to college based on test scores, and with tests condemned as bourgeois, priority was given to those who claimed to be red. The "worker-peasant-soldier" students were overwhelmingly drawn from official families.[37] Yang Yuexin, daughter of Wugong's rising red successor Yang Tong, became a worker-peasant-soldier student at Tianjin's prestigious Nankai University, meaning that admission was based on recommendation, not examination re-sults. A local ditty expressed rage at the unfairness.

> From the county party committee, one can enter a good university.
> From the commune courtyard, one can get into a college.
> Village secretaries, they take what's left.
> As for the mass of commune members, see the whites of their eyes!

Yang Yuexin, who became a good student at a top university, was more than a beneficiary of connections. But children of rural illiterates, whose homes had no books, generally were deprived of educational opportunities, reversing the pre-1966 gains that had begun to close the gap between edu-cated urbanites and villagers. The children of illiterates would be left ill pre-pared for life in a technical-scientific world that needed people who under-stood instructional manuals, signs, notices, receipts, labels, warnings, and handbooks and who were schooled in modern technology.

A New Party Secretary

In late 1973 Zhang Duan, Wugong party secretary since 1959, was felled by desperate head pain. Geng Changsuo accompanied him to a hospital in Tian-jin. In 1974 he fell into a coma. Permanently incapacitated, his family cared for him in the neatest, brightest house we found in the village.

To replace Zhang, Boss Geng tapped Qiao Liguang. Administrator Qiao had loyally served Geng for a quarter century. Not a take-charge person, the east ender proved ill suited to the electric atmosphere of political campaigns. The next choice was west ender Yang Tong. Relations between Geng and his critics in the west-end Xu lineage were strained. Selecting Yang strengthened bonds with west-village allies in the Zhang and Yang lineages.

:r Yang Tong was born in 1931, his father, a veterinarian, mi-
:un county northeast of Beijing. Yang Tong's mother, whose
l not at first write when we asked him to do so, raised him, a
er, and two younger sisters under the protection of his grandun-
ed one of the village's first mutual aid teams. When Japanese
l in 1942, 11-year-old Yang Tong, a third grader, fled. Between
3, he taught evening literacy classes. Catching Boss Geng's eye,
he rose in the youth league to head its propaganda and education section.
During the Leap, he administered the communal mess hall when it was a soup
kitchen to the hungry. At a time when most leaders were suspected of caring
only for kin and allies, Yang Tong won praise for fairness. He joined the party
on July 1, 1961. His father was one of 20 million people sent back from cities
in the 1962 dearth. Educated, affable, and flexible, in 1965, at the age of 34,
he was put on the village party branch committee.

Yang Tong lacked the earthy touch of Zhang Duan and Li Shouzheng.
Their toughness won admiration, sometimes tinged with fear. Not one to get
carried away with enthusiasms, or to squat and gossip with old timers, Yang
nurtured a vision that the village would one day bridge the gap separating city
and countryside. That meant irrigated, mechanized agriculture, rural industry,
and access to radios, bicycles, sewing machines, and other consumer goods
that eased and brightened life. Following his apppointment as party secretary,
his team 3 purchased the village's first television set, placing it in team headquarters for public viewing.

When Yang Tong became party secretary, Geng's neighbor Li Shouzheng
began to work full time on the village party committee. Li was replaced as
party secretary of team 1 by his brother-in-law, heir Zhang Mandun, Geng's
grandson. Family connections, political alliances, and patronage networks
were the real capillaries of power despite propaganda on selflessness and class
struggle.

The United Family

For the Geng family, New Year 1974 was the last the four generations would enjoy together in good health. To the 30-plus family members who crowded into
Xu Shukuan's home for the festivities, the joy contrasted with her wretched
youth when her family disintegrated. Having married with empty hands, she
left behind a secure family. Her seven children, all party members, came home
along with spouses, children, and even grandchildren.

Eldest daughter Xueren had three sons. The eldest, Zhang Mandun, was
Boss Geng's political heir. Xueren's second son, who was in the army, came
home to seek a bride. A third was a driver on the state payroll in Shijiazhuang.
The only daughter had married into the model village of Nanwangzhuang.
After her marriage, Xueren's daughter continued to live in wealthier Wugong

and bore two daughters. Caretaker Xueren cooked for everyone. Her husband, a good-natured retired soldier, helped out.

Xu Shukuan's eldest son, Geng Delu, a demobilized soldier, worked at the commune power station. He was joined by his wife from Baoding, who enjoyed the city's higher living standard and whose children received an urban education. Their eldest son, a party member and high school graduate, would become a banker. Four daughters, aged nine, eight, six, and four, also came. One would marry the party secretary of Yincun village, another would obtain a job in the procurator's office in Beijing. The other two would be added to the Raoyang county payroll.

Old Xu's second daughter, Sujuan, who had been a publicized tractor driver during collectivization, came with three children from Tianjin, where she worked in a watch factory. Her husband, about to be demobilized from the army, would join the organization bureau of Tianjin University, a small cog in the military machine overseeing revolution in higher education. Their two sons would become engineers, their daughter a nurse at a Tianjin hospital. Geng loved to spoil their oldest son, sharing the best foods reserved for the patriarch and denied to females.

Xu's political daughter, Huijuan, returned with her husband from her provincial-level health ministry job in Shijiazhuang. Their son would enter the army.

Geng Duo, the fourth daughter, came from a Beijing sewing machine factory. Her husband, Han Defu, was a cameraman at a Beijing film studio. Both had been brutalized during the Cultural Revolution, and Duo had served time in prison. Their daughter, Han Peng, would study English seriously as a college student and benefit from reform and openness.

Geng Jinxiang, the youngest of Xu's daughters, taught in Wugong's junior high. Her husband worked on the Raoyang party committee staff and would eventually serve as secretary to the county head. Their firstborn, a boy, would become a doctor.

Xu's youngest son, soldier Zhuanluo, came from Datong, Shanxi, with a new wife. After demobilization he would work in the Raoyang procurator's office. With children and spouses in jobs on state payrolls either in the military or in administrative or industrial jobs in Raoyang, Baoding, Shijiazhuang, Tianjin, and Beijing, the upwardly mobile household network of Boss Geng mirrored the privileged state hierarchy.

Villagers joked that Wugong's nationally famous model of agricultural labor had seven children but not one who labored in agriculture. Still, Geng kept helping the village. He lived simply and asked little for himself. He did not steal food during the dearth. As corruption intensified, his reputation for honesty and simple living grew. Now in his 70s, in the busy harvest season he still tried to do a bit of manual labor. But if Geng was seen as relatively clean, Wugong was not. Neighbors gossiped that the 1973–74 move of the commune supply and marketing coop into the village gave Wugong "back-door" access to scarce meat and other goods.

Xu Shukuan was felled by a stroke in late 1974. She was driven to the ill-equipped county hospital and then, for a longer convalescence, to Shijia-zhuang. Xu returned home permanently bedridden. She had frugally saved to cover the 1,000-yuan medical bill. Villagers were excluded from national health care coverage. A distant relative came to administer acupuncture daily, but Xu remained on the kang for her final years.

The loss of his wife seemed to weaken 74-year-old Geng. His jeep driver, married to the daughter of a key Raoyang party family, was increasingly called on to help Geng get medical care. The driver was a devastating ping-pong player. Other underemployed county functionaries in the ever larger state apparatus passed time by squatting and competing fiercely and loudly in Chinese chess. Geng's hair turned white. He went deaf. He got a hearing aid, but it did not help much. Brains Zhang Chaoke and Geng's grandson, heir Zhang Mandun, communicated for others by shouting into Geng's less bad ear. Geng chose, however, not to hear the rumble that augured an earthquake of reform.

Historical Confusions

In late 1973 news spread through the Hebei party apparatus loyal to deposed party secretary Lin Tie that better times might be in the offing. Premier Zhou had been protecting the ousted Lin. In 1973 Lin was sent to a hospital in Beijing. It was a sign of political rehabilitation. In December 1974, Mao elevated the rehabilitated party general secretary Deng Xiaoping to vice premier.[38] Deng then ran the State Council and the government for the ailing premier. Mao also elevated Deng to chief of staff in the Military Advisory Commission and to Politburo membership.[39] Deng, with military backing, rehabilitated victims of Cultural Revolution vigilantism and pressed reform in education, technology, agriculture, and foreign trade.

Wugong's original patron, Lin Tie, participated in the 1974 National Day celebrations in Beijing and, for the first time since his 1966 fall, was given low-level assignments. Zhang Kerang, who had run Lin's bureau of agriculture in the 1950s, was also rehabilitated after seven years in a labor camp. In June 1974, on the way to a job in Xingtai prefecture, Zhang visited Wugong and Mao-blessed Nanwangzhuang, whose leader, Wang Yukun, still struck Zhang as incapable of bringing people together. In contrast, Geng Changsuo seemed truthful when he described the depredations of the Cultural Revolution. Zhang Kerang saw that irrigation, enterprises, electricity, soil improvement, mechanization, growth, and house building had improved life in Wugong. But villagers also felt locked out of the material blessings of a modern world that could provide television sets, indoor plumbing, cameras, baby strollers, and colorful, comfortable clothing.

Zhang Kerang told Geng Changsuo, Geng Xiufeng, and ⟨
that he had visited 24 counties since rehabilitation. "I could ⟨
ties and it wouldn't do any good," he complained, because "t
good news." He asked for frankness. Xiufeng did not disapp⟨
higher-ups who insisted that villagers plant crops that wer
local conditions. Xiufeng urged Zhang to look at Dacaozhuaɪ
south. Forced to plant corn on inappropriate land, the collec
catties per mu but got a harvest of only 40 catties per mu. Xiufeng estimated
that peanuts grown there would produce a whopping 300 to 400 catties
per mu.[40]

In 1974 Premier Zhou sent Wang Guanglin to Hebei to advance the reformist interpretation of the Dazhai model. Wang too was recently rehabilitated. Nearly 80, he had served on the party's land committee in Yan'an during
guerrilla days and risen to become vice minister of agriculture and president of
Beijing Agricultural College before falling in the Cultural Revolution. He was
Premier Zhou's troubleshooter for agricultural policy.

In February, a week-long Hebei conference on learning from Dazhai held
in Handan and Hehengcheng village redirected a revolutionary campaign
directed at Lin Biao and Confucius into an effort to promote agricultural science, economic crops, and sideline enterprises.[41] Conference leaders quoted
Premier Zhou: "Who says Hebei has no Dazhai? Hehengcheng is Hebei's
Dazhai." In Hengshui prefecture, Raoyang was reconfirmed as a Dazhai
county model and Wugong as a village model. But the content of the Dazhai
model remained contested.

In November a Hengshui conference called to promote criticism of Confucius also hailed production achievements in Kuixingzhuang, a village famed
for pig raising.[42] Revolutionaries opposed the reformist pig policy. They promoted an attack on Confucian culture, widely understood as an attack on
reform or on Premier Zhou. The stalemate between reform and revolution at
the center and in the provincial capitals paralyzed local leaders and villagers.

12 ❖ TREMORS

Jiang Qing and her revolutionary associates virtually monopolized the media, while modernizers rallied around Vice Premier Deng Xiaoping. China faced a high stakes succession crisis. While Geng Changsuo and Wugong won accolades in the revolutionary press, the tremors of intraparty conflict reached Raoyang.

Empowering an Empress

Throughout 1973 and 1974 the center touted gender equality and criticized Confucius. On January 31, 1974, after receiving a document prepared under Jiang Qing's aegis, Boss Geng joined 20,000 in the Hebei capital to denounce the dead Lin Biao and the long-dead Confucius. Whatever villagers may have made of this combination, they were again told to destroy old customs, culture, ideas, and habits. Hengshui prefecture's well drilling was described as overcoming Confucian fatalism.

The campaign to criticize Lin Biao and Confucius indirectly targeted Premier Zhou, Vice Premier Deng, and other reformers.[1] Raoyang highlighted the experience of Kongdian, where most villagers were named Kong, the surname of Confucius. The new Jiang Qing–type village party secretary, Kong Xianghuan, after criticizing her father and grandfather, was promoted to vice secretary of the commune party committee. Changing her name to Kong Pikong, or the Kong who criticizes Confucius, she became one of 15 activists cited in Raoyang.[2]

During the campaign, policies favorable to women received backing both from reformers and from revolutionaries.[3] Premier Zhou reactivated the national women's association abolished in 1966. It promoted family planning and facilitated full-time work for women in nurseries, sewing centers, and canteens. The Hebei association, restored in 1973, advocated fairer wages for women and stressed birth control.

Jiang Qing's movement searched for young female loyalists. It praised grooms who married into brides' villages rather than insisting that brides marry into grooms' villages, where they were marginalized. Jiang sought a model that combined revolutionary culture with empowered women, thus legitimating her own rise. Tianjin leader Xie Xuegong issued a call to find a village experience for Jiang Qing to popularize.

General Wu Dai, who served concurrently as vice political commissar of the Beijing Military District and second secretary of the Tianjin party committee, suggested Xiaojinzhuang in Baodi county, 45 miles north of Tianjin and 53 miles southeast of Beijing. This village of fewer than 600 came to Wu's notice in the early 1970s when it registered significant production gains and set up a political night school as part of the Dazhai movement.[4] On an October 1972 visit, Wu confirmed that village night school programs involved not only agricultural science but also literacy classes and cultural activities. In fact, Baodi county, famous for itinerant barbers who brought songs home, had a lively tradition of local opera. Old-style opera troupes were disbanded during the Cultural Revolution, but locals, including Xiaojinzhuang villagers, enjoyed singing the Jiang Qing model operas. Wu suggested to Tianjin first secretary Xie Xuegong and Tianjin cultural leader Wang Mantian (she was Chairman Mao's cousin) that Xiaojinzhunag would be music to Jiang Qing's ears.

On June 11, 1974, *Tianjin Daily* began promoting Xiaojinzhuang, citing it as a pacesetter in criticizing Lin Biao and Confucius. Eleven days later Jiang Qing arrived and told villagers, "Chairman Mao sends you his regards." She was pleased that the village welcomed grooms into brides' families. Calling Xiaojinzhuang "my spot," Jiang emphasized the need to promote young females to positions of power and to expose sexist practices. When she left, party secretary Wang Zuoshan hung a huge picture entitled "Comrade Jiang Qing" at the entrance to the village.

Jiang's ally, Minister of Culture Yu Huiyong, sent Hebei cultural affairs head Tian Jian to Xiaojinzhuang with researcher Jiang Zilong to generate publicity.[5] Tian wrote poems extolling the village, and Jiang trumpeted its supposedly anti-Confucian orientation. Jiang Qing returned to Xiaojinzhuang in September 1974 with Philippines first lady Imelda Marcos.

Work units were told to promote young female activists. Wugong chose Wang Pengju. She became the lone woman on the party committee, replacing the long-serving Qiao Wenzhi. But Wang did not represent women. Self-organization and self-representation by women was counterrevolutionary.

Wang was family. When Boss Geng's grandson Hongtao returned from the army late in 1974, his mother, Xueren, suggested a match to Wang Pengju. Boss Geng thus had a grandson's wife to prove that revolution empowers women. Villagers mocked the campaign to include a female on party committees. "Like a stepmother, it does nothing for you," people snickered. Patriarchy still ruled, and mothers-in-law dominated daughters-in-law. A popular Raoyang adage held that, after years of walking, even a road becomes a river and a daughter-in-law becomes a mother-in-law. Until that time, young brides were subservient.

The Zoucun party was unusual in using the campaign to help daughters-in-law whose mothers-in-law treated them like slaves. In most activist villages the party just rounded up the usual suspects to demonstrate class struggle.

Males feigned incomprehension. A veteran Wugong leader commented that if eliminating the bride price was opposing Confucius, then his austere marriage decades earlier proved Wugong did not need an anti-Confucian campaign. Campaign documents were rolled to make homemade cigarettes. But villages with political aspirations had to act. Demonstrating loyalty, Wugong announced an end to discriminatory practices. Women no longer had to do all the cooking. Whoever got home first would cook. Household chores would be rationally shared.

It was empty talk. Collective disincentives left so much idle time that women could almost always be home to cook. A few, however, used the campaign to legitimate cooking breakfast before going to sleep and serving the rolls cold in the morning instead of getting up before dawn to prepare fresh hot rolls, a tedious process that involved feeding straw to a grill fire. Mothers still tried to turn over the burdensome chores of washing clothes by hand to daughters and daughters-in-law.

The English-language textbooks the province distributed to the Wugong junior high exemplified gender stereotyping that transcended socialism versus capitalism.[6]

> My brother studies hard. Liu Ying studies for the revolution.
> I wash for the PLA. Xiaoling washes for the PLA uncles.
> Tom is a little boy. He is eleven. He lives in New York.
> His father works in a factory. His mother washes for capitalists.

Laundry was treated as women's work. China manufactured no washing machines. Women did the clothes in the cold of winter using frigid water and cake soap made from pig organs. Village China had almost no running water.

One of the few men in Wugong who took on a real share of household work was party secretary Yang Tong, who fed the pigs and drew water. He told us he feared that his wife might otherwise speak up and discredit him. Few men had such fears.

The village women's association used the anti-Confucian campaign to demand higher wages for cotton work. Two hundred and twenty women shared the painstaking toil. Backed by the state, which pressed for more cotton but would not raise purchasing prices, the women won. Pay went from 6.5 to 8.5 work points per day. Young women treasured the higher pay. Many elderly women, however, sensitive to male resentment, rejected the higher work points to preserve family harmony.

Men resented the wage boost. It gave high pay for low-value work. Few villages raised women's wages. Males held that women received what weaker workers deserved. The change was meaningless, they claimed, since value earned ultimately went to a united household. Blaming Jiang Qing for vacuous nonsense, many found tough patriarchal values ever more worthy. Hard-drinking builder Li Lu's plaint was typical. What should be rewarded, he declared, was real work, heavy work, men's work. By nature women were patient and had the nimble fingers for picking cotton or transplanting rice, work that merited low pay. The women's association shared the prejudice of rewarding physical strength.

The consensus was that it was wrong to foster immorality by undermining respect for parents and elders who gave life and nurtured. Yet if Mao insisted on a campaign (and Jiang Qing appeared to speak for Mao), then it had to be done. Despite the call for greater gender equity, women were hurt by a revolutionary cutting of "capitalist tails" that included crafts passed on through the generations that won women status and wealth. Embroidery, a specialty of Hebei women, was denounced as bourgeois. The wealth-expanding informal economy was once again wounded. Young women were deskilled and restricted to collective field work.

The poorest in Wugong were elderly women who had married into the village and were widowed. Eight widows, none with male children to support them, lived alone in the west end. Not one owned a single significant consumer item. They could not even afford tea leaves to add to boiling water served to guests. Their plight was invisible. Women cooked and served but did not eat with male guests. Instead, they ate alone in the kitchen or waited for leftovers. Women's blood was seen as thin as water, hence useless. Young men, not women, were invited to donate their thick, rich blood and were then treated as heroes for contributions that could restore the strength of soldiers on the battlefield.

Nonetheless, exogamy was weakening. The young met in school and at work and chose to marry. Increasingly, parents wanted daughters to marry within their home villages so as to help elderly parents. Such wives could look to kin and friends for support. Revolutionary Baoding prefecture became a model for intravillage marriage. More and more, marriages joined friends and neighbors.[7] A new adage asserted, "A good woman does not leave the village. A good man does not bring in an outsider." Village women's leader Wang Pengju as well as the two sons of builder Li Lu even married within what were once incest-taboo neighborhoods. In the 1950s and 1960s one-fourth of team 3 brides were born in Wugong. In the 1970s the figure shot up to 43 percent (see table 12.1). In villages where members lost historic marriage ties to models, people gossiped about the birth of freaks. Models seemed ever more inbred, socially isolated and culturally alienated from "us."

The anti-Confucian campaign was silent on violence against women. Any wife who challenged her husband in public risked a beating. In addition to such abuse, rape by unaccountable male power holders seemed pandemic. It was popularly believed that in 1974 and 1975 the six men running the Raoyang

Table 12.1   Birthplace of Wugong village, team 3 married women, 1978

Year of marriage	Born in Wugong		Born outside Wugong	
	No.	%	No.	%
Prior to 1949	13	22	47	78
1950–1959	7	27	19	73
1960–1969	17	25	50	75
1970–1978	21	43	28	57

Source: Data from the authors' 1978 household survey.

textile factory, which employed about 80 workers, raped more than half the young women in the work force.

The campaign's imbrication in power conflicts at the center and the impossibility of self-organization by women at the local level blocked real change. The women's association did not question the view that it was fine to reward old men but unfair to raise the wages of old women, seen as weak, ill, and spoilers of grandchildren.

Poetry Wars

Jiang Qing and her allies urged people, especially women, to study theory and engage in cultural activities that embodied a communist ethos. A poem attributed to former women's leader Qiao Wenzhi described as "nonsense" the claim of those who, noticing the growing gap between the blessed of the state and the forgotten of society, decried such places as Wugong that touted the priority of state and collective interests and thus fostered "a rich state and poor people."

Some elderly women in the west village, styled the Red Old Ladies, responded to Jiang Qing's call by celebrating the big collective and leveling distribution. Most had suffered miserable marriages in the 1930s and early 1940s. Widows now, they said life was better than before. Asked what revolutionary change had most improved things, one smiled at the innocence of the question, got nods from the other widows, and explained, "He's dead." These activist widows had nicknames like "the bell" and "busybody." Most villagers did not appreciate the way they pried into family affairs. These watchdogs of mores were popularly scapegoated for the detested policies they monitored, further inflaming antifemale passions.

A group of younger women from the east end started studying communist theory. Heirs of red families, women's leader Wang Pengju and the other members of the Eight Red Sisters preened as red princesses. Gender posturing was offensive.

Several recently rehabilitated filmmakers visited Wugong. Drama coach Yi Xi, who last visited in 1965, taught songs and dances from the model operas promoted by Jiang Qing. Military ballets were highlighted. Villagers loved action and color. They went in droves to Zoucun during the 1975 lunar New Year, paying 15 cents a ticket to see the model opera *Red Lantern*. Many brought home colorful opera posters for bedroom wall decorations. But, compelled to hear the same few works over and over, village wags chortled:

How nice the model operas.
800 million watch with bellies full.
Turn on the radio, hear them everywhere.
Adults and children can shout the words together.

Li Wenying, the village director of propaganda, perhaps the sort of woman the Jiang Qing group was eager to recruit, was chosen to attend Hebei's annual conference on cultural affairs. On September 17, 1974, she went to Langfang, midway between Beijing and Tianjin. It was an adventure for the 23 year old, her first extended trip. The topic set by the conference chair, culture czar Tian Jian, was "How to mobilize the masses to study creatively Chairman Mao's talks at the Yan'an Forum" of 1942. Then, without warning, the 100-plus participants were whisked by bus to Xiaojinzhuang.

Some delegates raised questions. Why had there been no party directives about Xiaojinzhuang? What was its relationship to the Dazhai model? How was it possible to move across administrative boundaries to visit the realm of Tianjin? Something was going on.

Xiaojinzhuang was said to have revolutionized its culture and popularized communist consciousness. Villagers supposedly had transformed the cultural superstructure with ten new creations. Jiang Qing cited Xiaojinzhuang as a "national pacesetter" for studying Leninist theory in its political night school. A propaganda writing group known as "the two schools," referring to two of China's premier universities, Peking and Tsinghua, described Xiaojinzhuang as a "model of ideological revolution."[8] Everyone in Xiaojinzhuang, promoters claimed, wrote revolutionary poetry. Villagers attacked commerce, decried selfish concerns about earning work points, inveighed against petty producers, and denounced worshippers of Marshal Zhao, the god of wealth. Before long, untold resources, including military and civilian labor from Tianjin and Hebei, flowed to Xiaojinzhuang.

Wugong's Li Wenying noted that the village of 101 households, just south of a river, enjoyed excellent irrigation. The militia chief, a dark fellow in his 30s, greeted the travelers. He apologized that the party secretary was busy. The militia chief then led a tour.

Li Wenying lacked confidence in her local dialect, feeling it a mark of cultural inferiority. Little had changed since the 1940s when villagers feared that the more cultured tones of two Red Army women hiding in Wugong would give them away. Speech still marked status from rural periphery up to metropolitan centers. Wenying worried that she might not comprehend a more cultured Tianjin accent.

Xiaojinzhuang's guide spoke about Jiang Qing's June visit. She had come in a fleet of cars with an entourage of 40 or so, including Tianjin's leader Xie Xuegong. Wearing a straw hat, she had lectured on Confucian evils, contrasting them with the virtues of legalism that highlighted state administration and strong sanctions. She contended that both of China's two ancient women emperors were legalists, praising their use of punishment and discipline to maintain order.

Jiang Qing and her party toured the village, stopping to read poems on walls. Villagers dutifully recited their poems. Jiang promised to get the poetry published. In fact, most of it was written by one of Jiang Qing's favorites in Xiaojinzhuang, party vice secretary Wang Du. When a woman activist said her name was Zhou, reminiscent of the Duke of Zhou (the revered disciple of Confucius) and Zhou Enlai (the implicit political target of the anti-Confucian campaign), Jiang suggested she change her name to Zhou Kezhou, or Zhou who smashes Zhou.

Villagers listened to Minister of Culture Yu Huiyong sing and watched Liu Qingtang dance. Opera star Hao Liang sang "Thank You, Mom." The 66th Army, stationed outside Tianjin, sent a chorus to perform. A polite Jiang Qing left a good impression on some.

The Xiaojinzhuang guide reported that Jiang Qing had directed them to learn model operas and study theoretical works. She arranged for Hao Liang, the male lead of the opera *Red Lantern,* to give guidance on integrating revolutionary culture into daily life. Li Wenying tried to figure out what she would say when she got back to Wugong. She worried that if she got it wrong, party elders would curse her.

Dozens of freshmen from Nankai University in Tianjin, including Yang Yuexin, the daughter of Wugong party secretary Yang Tong, also toured Xiaojinzhuang. Like Li Wenying, painfully conscious of how Tianjin people made fun of the Raoyang accent, Yuexin worked hard to speak standard Mandarin. Like Wenying, she found Wugong to be more praiseworthy than Xiaojinzhuang, especially with regard to results achieved by hard collective toil.

On October 3, 1974, 14 members of the Wugong party committee listened to Li Wenying's ten-minute report on Xiaojinzhuang. Questions followed. How did it organize culture so as not to interfere with work? Given learning from Dazhai, how could there still be time to copy Xiaojinzhuang? No directive insisted on emulating Xiaojinzhuang. Still, Wugong would not ignore Mao's wife or the Hebei culture czar. Wugong introduced breaks in the workday for politicized operatic arias by a male and female worker in the fruit orchard. They sang well, whatever the words. Political night school classes were also added.

Wugong village and Raoyang county sent a group to see the Xiaojinzhuang exhibit at the Museum of History in Beijing. They were thrilled to run into the Dazhai leader, now Vice Premier Chen Yonggui, at the exhibit.

Hebei Literature and Art published more Wugong poems. One poem ascribed to the Eight Old Ladies went,

> This old lady of 68, on the way to pick cotton,
> Ran into dung in the west end.
> I picked it up with my hands not to gain praise
> But to add food to the crop and grain to the state.

Villagers danced to a tune with Mao as the sun and the people as the adoring sunflower. Wugong women calling themselves sisters wrote,

> Big Sister wrote to Chairman Mao.
> Second Sister wrote to the Communist Party.
> Third Sister said the motherland was good.
> Fourth Sister wrote that communes are powerful.
> Fifth Sister was too young to write.
> She painted a sunflower.
> It looked up to the sun.

Given the state's unappetizing cultural interventions, local culture became more beloved. The "Eight Ancient Wonders of Raoyang," described in an old poem, survived in the memories of older folks and others alienated by empty propaganda:

> Spring comes early in Liubanzhai.
> In Yingqu the yellow and red autumn leaves linger.
> In the north, springs ever flow.
> In summer, the Hutuo River boasts floating lilies.
> And gravestones are so transparent that one can almost see through them.
> In Guocun and Xicun, you can see a garden float in the air.
> The iron drum in Caodi sounds without being beaten.
> From the Raoyang town wall you can see five willows and a peach.

Each line evoked a delight in a different part of the county. Liubanzhai village was famed for a small hill whose grass was first to turn green in spring. That knoll, however, was leveled in the 1960s. The trees of Yingqu, with their lush fall foliage lasting beyond all others, had likewise long since been felled. By the 1970s not one of the eight wonders remained. Success was measured not by local beauty but by Raoyang being featured in a May 23, 1975, article in *Hebei Daily* as a pacesetter in the Jiang Qing drive to get rural children to sing revolutionary songs.

In 1974 the Jiang Qing group moved the North China Agricultural College to Zhuoxian in northern Baoding prefecture better to advance revolutionary policies on agriculture and intellectuals. As in Shanghai, their stronghold, Jiang and her supporters promoted Baoding as a model of a strong militia committed to class struggle. In opposition, Monarch Liu Zihou strove to keep the Hebei militia in the grip of the party and himself. While Xiaojinzhuang sang and Wugong wrote poetry, ruling groups vied for control of weapons.

Revolutionary Baoding sent out teams to carry through an "all-around dictatorship over the bourgeoisie in all spheres of the superstructure." While Monarch Liu tried to control Baoding, Jiang Qing and her supporters regularly visited the city to woo the 38th Army and the local party. But having almost been burned by suspected ties to Lin Biao's alleged plot against Mao, the 38th rejected Jiang's suit and pledged loyalty to senior military officials in Beijing.

Against Money

Geng Changsuo supported revolution, exhorting villagers to spurn money-earning activities. "What do people live for?" he asked in the *People's Daily* in early June 1975.[9] While exploiters seek wealth so they can eat, drink, and dress well, "We communists live to make revolution" by allowing the state to invest for all. Ethical people put their cash in the bank for state use. Bad people use cash for feudal, black-market, selfish, illegal, and capitalist purposes, thus supporting the expanding informal economy. State investment provided Wugong with electric lights, mechanized flour milling, and stable high levels of grain distribution, and it would soon provide new homes for all. It would assure ever-higher levels of common prosperity, Geng claimed.

In May 1975 an article by Wugong's Eight Red Sisters, the sort of women's group favored by Jiang Qing, appeared in *People's Daily*. It urged villagers to read excerpts from Lenin's *State and Revolution* to learn about the dangers of a small peasant mentality that could restore capitalism and lose the gains of revolution.[10] But the notion that their own worldview or money-making acts were evil was never palatable to villagers.

The Eight Red Sisters were joined by Ten Sisters from the west end who found that ideological transformation explained the village's march toward communism. Wugong would have abandoned the path of common prosperity in 1947 had Geng not stopped coop member Li Huiting from turning new wealth into household land, a step toward pitting the landed rich against the landless poor. In the early 1960s, when reforms were initiated to end the Leap famine, Geng instead prioritized the basic needs of all. Had he failed, had President Liu succeeded in invigorating the market, the countryside would have become polarized again. Everyone should study how to cut capitalist tails because Mao's revolutionary thought had identified new forces—bourgeois right, commodity production, monetary exchange, and distribution according to labor—that would, if not reversed, restore the horrors of old.

The elderly were most fearful of a return to the bad old days and fc in placing faith in Mao. But people needed money. The political line c persuade. If the state said money was dirty, then villagers would h Officially reported savings were only a fraction of money squirreled Weddings, funerals, and new homes cost money. So did New Year feasts, and desired goods that were scarce or unavailable. A large black market grew in furniture. One family with three daughters gradually filled a room with the furniture the daughters would eventually take with them as dowries. Yet routes to cash through the market were risky.

During the 1975 campaign to uproot capitalist sprouts, Jiang Qing's model Xiaojinzhuang opted to dispense with money. It would not recognize money (bu ren qian).[11] Actually, money was so precious that every treasured cent was remembered. Wugong villagers meticulously recorded all economic interactions, from work points to earnings for fodder and fertilizer. The numbers spelled out, as Confucian culture required, the division of family propery and the obligations of each son to parents at the time of household division. With revolution making scarcer the money that was essential for an ethical life, villagers focused even more intently on money.

The drive to cut capitalist tails even hurt Wugong, whose collective sidelines had grown rapidly since the North China Agricultural Conference. Team 3 was forced, temporarily, to close its profitable paper string factory. Families that raised chickens and sold them on the black market had to stop in 1974 and 1975.

Although the remnant Zoucun periodic market still met every five days, it had shrunk to a shadow of its pre-1957 size. In late 1975 Raoyang implemented an additional antimarket policy initiated by Jiang Qing's allies. Scheduling all markets to occur on the same day, county authorities struck a blow at traveling sellers whose livelihood followed the cycle of periodic markets on consecutive days. This also inconvenienced consumers. Efficiencies built over millennia vanished.

The second economy continued to expand with the use of ration coupons as a money equivalent. Nevertheless, by 1975 the 80 percent who lived outside cities had only about 20 percent of the nation's cash, and much of that was held by suburban dwellers. The rural poor had virtually no money to turn into productive investments, auspicious marriages, moral burials, joyous holidays, or the building of homes. As a result, violence exploded within families, and villagers even beat local officials.

With markets closed, villagers sought out lenient or corrupt officials to turn a blind eye or act as intermediaries. In October 1975 alone Raoyang authorities reported 17 major criminal cases that involved money making, including the hiring of private labor, official graft, speculation, and drug dealing.

Revolution canceled out the real gains of modernizing reforms. Despite better seeds, more water, more fertilizer, and more farm machinery that increased total output, incomes seldom rose. In Wugong, however, per capita distributed collective income rose from 120 yuan in 1970 to 156 yuan by 1975, with the share paid in cash doubling from 31 yuan to a still modest 67 yuan. Most neighboring villages stagnated or declined.

The marginalizing impact was heaviest in regions with the worst economic geography.[12] In certain hill areas of Sichuan province, households that carried out triple cropping and grain growing on ill-suited soil were reduced to child selling. Some of the children showed up in Raoyang, 2,000 miles away. By the mid-1970s, Sichuan brides were in many Raoyang villages. They were reputed to be diligent, skilled workers. The bride price was less than half that for a local bride.

Not all the marriages were real. Some Sichuan women were sold into prostitution. In Xiaodi commune just west of Wugong, truckers knew where to stop to have food cooked by the "husband" and sex provided by the "wife." The county regarded Xiaodi, an important market center in the mid-18th century, as a disaster, and sent in a special work team in November 1975 to deal with "unending problems." The work team's solution was to set up a "class education" exhibition hall. Villagers were told to learn from Wugong.

Water Flees

Well drilling accelerated in the 1970s. The number of Raoyang wells soared from 1,685 in 1970 to 5,860 in 1975. In mid-summer 1975, determined to win merit in the Dazhai campaign, Raoyang committed to still more drilling: 2,000 new wells in 1976 were intended to boost average grain yields to 740 catties per mu throughout the county. However, with Deng Xiaoping insisting on applying science to the economy, a Hengshui prefectural survey of the long-term impact of years of campaign-style drilling disclosed a pending disaster. Raoyang had just 149 deep wells in 1970 but 3,107 in 1975. Wugong was drilling to depths of 200, 300, even 500 meters, where two decades earlier 30 to 50 meters were sufficient. Not only was such drilling inordinately expensive, but with unecological mining, water fled from precious aquifers.

In 1975 one deep well brought a delight to Wugong. The water was warm and pure. No chemical slime developed on the sides of the well. It was a perfect site for young women to attend to their long hair. They lovingly washed their youthful tresses in that soft water, relaxed, and chatted.

In 1975 Raoyang called for economic accounting to conserve water in response to Vice Premier Deng's call for economic rationality. Villagers were told to stop treating water as a limitless, free good, to calculate the cost of irrigation, and to prevent waste. But revolutionaries mistrusted economic calculation. Agriculture continued to waste enormous quantities of water. In the collective, no one felt responsible for consequences. Much water soaked into soft irrigation ditches, never even reaching crops. Leaders got villagers to line irrigation ditches with a thin film of a sticky clay to reduce seepage. Still, water fled. Raising water prices to encourage conservation was politically taboo, since revolutionaries treated concern about price as a deadly capitalist disease. The water crisis was a political crisis.

The Locomotive

On June 23, 1975, Chen Yonggui, the Dazhai leader, now a vice premier and Politburo member, came to Wugong for seven hours. He was the highest official ever to visit. It was exhilarating for villagers to see someone who had risen so high honor their own 75-year-old Boss Geng. Chen pushed the Dazhai campaign, saying, "A fast-moving train depends on a fast-moving locomotive to haul it. Who is the locomotive?" Chen's answer was leaders and pacesetters.

A public exchange between Geng and Chen was framed by the metaphor about locomotives as the leading force of history. Geng asked Chen, the locomotive leading China's countryside forward, for advice. "No," Chen answered. "You are the locomotive, and I am still the caboose. You instruct me." Geng, 19 years Chen's senior, responded, "No. We have switched places. You are now the locomotive."

Chen was accompanied by the top former villager in the Hebei party, provincial vice secretary Lu Yulan, and her associates from Shijiazhuang. Hengshui and Raoyang leaders joined in to network with these national and provincial leaders. Present at the deliberations and the picture taking were village party secretary Yang Tong, Macho Li Shouzheng, former women's leader Qiao Wenzhi, administrator Qiao Liguang, articulate Li Zhongxin, and Geng's grandson, team 1 leader, heir Zhang Mandun. Most soon had a picture of Chen hanging on a bedroom wall. Boss Geng chose one of himself holding back while others pushed him forward to shake the hand of the vice premier.

Geng wanted to talk about railroads. In the early 1970s he had heard that the center planned to build China's third north-south line, this one linking Beijing and Kowloon (Jiulong) in Hong Kong, the Jingjiu line. Some said that helicopter Hua Guofeng was behind it; others speculated that it was Monarch Liu Zihou's Politburo patron, Li Xiannian. In 1972 and 1973 Geng had met with Li Xiannian to learn more about the project.

In 1975 the state began field surveys for the rail line. Rumors had it that the railroad, at nearly 40 billion yuan China's costliest, was slated to pass just east of Raoyang en route to Hengshui. Fierce lobbying by provinces, counties, even localities focused on winning the line to one's own region. With a train scheduled every eight minutes, it would become the nation's busiest line. Geng dreamed of winning the route for Raoyang. The visit by Chen Yonggui was an opportunity to garner high-level support for a project of immense potential benefit to the local community.

Geng promised Chen that, by emulating Dazhai, Wugong would surpass 2,000 catties of grain per mu by 1980, almost doubling already high yields in just five years. Chen promised to return in 1980. Then, in return for his support of Chen's policies, and for years of loyalty to party purposes, Geng asked Chen's help in moving the Jingjiu railroad west into Raoyang. Geng reminded Chen that Wugong was part of an old base area that had sacrificed blood and treasure in defending against Japan, that its young men joined the Red Army in large numbers and were martyred in the civil war, and that, after liberation, they had again sacrificed to promote socialist common prosperity. Yet the region's transportation was as backward as ever. Indeed, Raoyang had lost its river lifeline to Tianjin as a result of the damming of the Hutuo. Chen was asked to use his good offices to get national leaders Li Xiannian and Hua Guofeng to consider the advantages of a routing through Raoyang instead of Xianxian to the east. Chen told Geng he would try.

Following Chen's visit, Hebei sent officials to judge whether Wugong was suitable for foreign visitors to witness the success of the Dazhai model. They concluded that Wugong was too remote. Instead Hebei fostered Zhoujiazhuang, a cotton-growing model just off a paved highway close to the provincial capital with ties to military leader Lu Zhengcao going back to the 1930s.

Still, increasing numbers, including foreigners, visited Wugong. In August a ten-person delegation from Tanzania heard a briefing and viewed militia drills. In September 1975 eight visitors came from the People's Liberation Army of Laos. The soldiers had been wounded in combat and were receiving medical attention at the Norman Bethune Hospital in Shijiazhuang. In early November seven athletes from Taiwan "temporarily residing in the United States" arrived to meet with Geng and observe exercises by the militia. The athletes were to participate in the third national games. In early October 1976 delegations arrived from Rwanda and the overseas Chinese community in Japan; in late October four visitors came from Mexico to study irrigation systems.

Domestic visitors far outnumbered foreign guests. Hebei Agricultural College in Baoding sent groups in 1975 and 1976 to learn how to build socialist agriculture. Ten young propaganda officials from as far away as Yunnan were taken to Wugong by the acting head of the new Department of Party History of Nankai University in Tianjin. The Department of Modern Chinese History had been renamed and given a new mission. The former chair, Wei Hongyun, a leading historian of the revolution in North China, had been sentenced to forced labor in the Baoding countryside, which was full of labor camps.

The propaganda officials were to learn about revolution. They visited Wang Yukun's Mao-blessed Nanwangzhuang and then settled in Wugong, living with families and talking to Geng Changsuo. But they mainly learned from the pilloried Geng Xiufeng how Wugong had pioneered the socialist road.

With reform stymied, there was a surfeit of surplus labor. The old Southern

Li lineage temple in the village center, long the headquarters for the party, was torn down to make way for new houses. The party moved into new offices in the northeast, between Geng's east village and the official reception area. Before 1975 was out, Raoyang won approval to construct a Wugong exhibition hall to celebrate Geng Changsuo. The county put up the money and sent artists to paint portraits of the continuous class struggles of the revolutionary poor. It was the Jiang Qing line on art and culture.

The Wugong builders were led by heavy-drinking Li Lu. Designing the huge structure was a delight for 47-year-old Li, whose family had begged in the 1930s and whose home had been burned down by the Japanese in the early 1940s. Life was better now. His brother worked for the county agricultural department. His own household, with three children, seemed secure. His married daughter had recently given birth to a boy and a girl. Both his sons were engaged to neighbors. And now he was designing a building far grander than any ever attempted before in Wugong. The exhibition hall, built of large, light-colored bricks, was to rise just northeast of the village center near commune headquarters.

Storm over Dazhai

While Deng Xiaoping promoted science, modernization, and rewards for labor to drive economic performance and improve life, Jiang Qing focused on uprooting capitalist remnants, fostering communist consciousness, and intensifying class struggle. While Deng looked to agricultural science, Jiang argued that new energies created by communist ideals born of class struggle and income leveling would boost agriculture and build socialism.

In early July 1975 a conference on professional work in agriculture met in Shijiazhuang, the capital of grain-deficient Hebei. Shijiazhuang was a preferred place to hold Beijing-run conferences, both because it was so much cheaper than the national capital and because it was so loyal that anything said there would be kept secret. Politburo member Wang Hongwen, whom Mao helicoptered in 1973 to the number 3 position in the party in the wake of Lin Biao's demise, represented the Jiang Qing group in Shijiazhuang. She sent a letter asserting that class struggle, not food, should be kept to the fore.[13]

In Beijing, Vice Premier Deng needled promoters of Jiang Qing's Xiaojinzhuang model. Bidding to end educational chaos and promote scientific, technical, and economically oriented education, Deng mocked the claim of improved grain output through class struggle. That village, he said, was fattened by special inputs from its political friends. But this was true for all models, whatever the policy line.

In mid-September and October 1975, the Deng and Jiang forces clashed in a follow-up to the 1970 North China Agricultural Conference in which 3,700 delegates assembled in Dazhai's Xiyang county for a National Conference to

Learn from Dazhai. They met in Xiyang's newly built tractor factory. Raoyang secretary Wang Yumin, who consulted with Wugong leaders both before and after, pledged that Raoyang would achieve an average output of 600 catties per mu in 1976. Vice Premier Deng, Hua Guofeng, and Jiang Qing each addressed the meeting.[14] Chen Yonggui set the tone in his keynote address: "The conference will sum up . . . experience . . . particularly since the North China Agricultural Conference of 1970. It will discuss . . . accelerating the construction of Dazhai style counties . . . and discuss how to fulfill farm mechanization in the main by 1980."[15]

Jiang Qing, arguing for larger collectives, urged communist leveling and implored people not to compete for money. After five days, conference leaders equivocated on her agenda. Hua Guofeng opined that "important policies that deal with the system of ownership must be handled with caution." His call to "realize agricultural mechanization as soon as possible and carry out scientific farming" defined the immediate priorities.[16] Pushed by Vice Premier Deng, with support from Hua, now head of public security and an alternate Politburo member, the modernization agenda prevailed.

As in 1970, the delegates next moved to Beijing, where state officials doubled their numbers. Jiang Qing's presentation condemned as capitalistic those rural sidelines that did not directly support agriculture. She called for a return to the commune ideal, with emphasis on leveling and class struggle. Yet Mao, no foe of class struggle, dismissed her comments as "farting" and said they should not be published. With Premier Zhou, who had delivered the final report at the 1970 conference, dying of cancer, Hua Guofeng gave the concluding report on October 15 to 7,000 people in the Great Hall of the People. The conference declared that to achieve China's developmental goals by the year 2000, agriculture had to be rapidly modernized with Dazhai-type counties showing the way.[17] As Chen Yonggui recalled it three years later, the conference was tense: "We were not in a position to denounce [Jiang Qing and her allies]. There were struggles. We had to be careful in our tactics and methods. That does not mean we feared them. . . . Hua Guofeng's report was approved by Chairman Mao. His markings are on the report. We could not just stand up to her and say that was nonsense. So we fell silent. It was best to use tactics. She was trying to use her opposition to the conference in Dazhai to get publicity for herself, to paint herself in bright colors. We did nothing to help her get that publicity. . . . So we did resist. But our resistance was based on tactics. In other words, she was still in the process of being exposed."

When Raoyang secretary Wang Yumin returned home, officials gathered for six days to study conference documents, with emphasis on Deng Xiaoping's address. The new campaign focused on building Dazhai-style counties. In late fall 1975 Hua Guofeng claimed that "since 1970 more thn 300 counties have excelled in learning from Dazhai."[18] Two categories of success were established: Dazhai-style counties and counties learning from Dazhai. Success

was calculated on how well a county approximated three politi economic criteria. The political criteria pivoted on having a loy group dominated by poor and lower-middle peasants who coml ist activities and participated in manual labor. The economic crit construction, mechanization, and science, expanding the colle raise the income of poorer units, and all-around development to raise sai... the state and living standards.[19] Many administrators felt that criteria of class struggle clashed with calls for production breakthroughs.

The Hebei authorities met from October 28 to 30 to decide how to build more Dazhai-style counties and achieve agricultural mechanization. Hebei vice party secretary Lu Yulan reported to 11,000 delegates in Shijiazhuang about the national conference. The provincial meeting was followed on November 10 and 11 with prefectural meetings and the dispatch of 650 officials to organize local work teams.[20] A telephone conference on December 4 instructed county party committees to build Dazhai-style counties. At each level, the top political leader was told to make the latest Dazhai campaign the top priority.

The Wugong party committee took the political criteria to mean that leaders had to prove they were the servants, not the masters, of the people. Leaders vowed to go to work earlier, toil harder, and seek out the most dangerous and dirtiest jobs. Cynicism would be countered by heroism. Li Shouzheng and Yang Bingzhang volunteered to go down by rope into a crumbling well. Their repairs upset the structure. Colleagues yanked them out just before the walls collapsed.

Higher officials urged Wugong to promote the latest Dazhai campaign in other villages. But it was virtually impossible to counter skepticism about mass campaigns that offered villagers no material support. Worse yet, Wugong's wealth was popularly resented in neighboring villages that received none of the benefits lavished on models. The leader could not lead.

Raoyang was not a Dazhai county but declared it would reach that goal by 1977. The county sent officials to reorganize the poorest communes. But no funds or jobs were set aside for the chronically poor. Poor communities continued to stagnate. Revolutionaries evinced a political will but offered no economic way to end poverty. The constrained modernization agenda eschewed a turn toward the market and the household sector.

Hebei announced that 25 of its 149 counties met the criteria for Dazhai-style counties in 1975. The claims were based on self-reports. Raoyang declared it had collectivized all vegetable plots and concentrated all burial land so as to maximize cultivated land and demonstrate revolutionary bona fides. Actually, consolidating cemeteries and ignoring lineage, as in Dazhai, provoked anger. Graves remained scattered across the fields.

Much about Dazhai and the campaign was incomprehensible. The province put aside no money or personnel to check on self-serving claims of success. Many were fraudulent. Gains in standards of living were limited by the system, by caution, and by revolutionary politics. Media preoccupation with learning from Dazhai obscured the plight of rural people. With resources focused on political campaigns, the state provided no direct funding to aid the poorest localities facing high hurdles to development.

Widespread frustration about seemingly endless "learn from Dazhai" campaigns was captured in two letters written by Wugong's Geng Xiufeng. The first was to village administrator Qiao Liguang on National Day, October 1, 1975. Xiufeng, having visited Dazhai several times, puzzled over the continuing gap between Wugong and mountainous Dazhai. Despite inferior natural conditions, Dazhai had increased agricultural production tenfold in a 20-year span, while Wugong had improved five- to sixfold in 30 years. How, Xiufeng wondered, could Dazhai deliver four times as much grain to the state?[21]

Xiufeng pursued the matter in a January 15, 1976, letter to the Hebei vice party secretary who had accompanied Chen Yonggui on his recent visit to Wugong. Xiufeng argued that there was no way for counties to learn from Dazhai if the state would not allow villagers to take initiatives on economic matters. "There is serious conflict between the national plan and local methods." He cited Nanshan village, northwest of Wugong. "Originally, it was a rich village, . . . but these days it relies on grain subsidies from the state. So my relatives sometimes ask me for cash and grain. Last year's harvest was not as good as the year before, but the state grain requisition is the same."[22]

Desperate people in Nanshan eventually took matters into their own hands. Instead of planting the required sorghum and wheat, low-yield crops unsuited to local conditions, villagers "secretly planted 40 mu of peanuts." Despite criticism, the following year they planted 140 mu of the cash crop and intended to expand peanut production even more in the future. To meet the state grain quota, villagers exchanged expensive peanuts for cheaper grain on the burgeoning black market. Xiufeng's relative told him, "You don't need to help us any more because we have found a way: plant more peanuts!" Xiufeng asked the provincial deputy secretary to imagine what might be possible within one year "in the province and in the whole country" if villagers were allowed to make their own economic decisions. Mocking revolutionary rhetoric, Xiufeng charged that those who blocked the money-making informal economy were Mao's true enemies in the "two-line struggle."

Beyond poverty, life in Raoyang was pervaded by brutally unaccountable power. In Luhan village in northern Raoyang, the commune militia seized village head Bai Gao for not meeting targets for deliveries to the state. Hoisting him to the ceiling with his hands tied behind his back, they beat him for . . . He was not cut down until after nightfall. Bai dragged himself home . . . self from the courtyard gate. Officials then dug up Bai's court-. . . buried grain to prove that the deceased was guilty of corrup-. . . buried grain, they seized the little corn the family had. Vil-. . . aid the devastated widow and children.

Political prisoners in the Hebei capital, Shijiazhuang, discussed how China was doing. They got information from drivers, released prisoners barred from returning home, and new prisoners. They heard that some Chinese walked across shallow parts of the Tumen River into North Korea and then made their way to Soviet Russia. From there some took a train to Western Europe, where they no longer had to fear being forced back to China. While North Korea was worse off, even a maligned Russia seemed better off than revolutionary China.

Death of a Premier

On January 8, 1976, Zhou Enlai died of cancer. Vice Premier Deng Xiaoping gave the memorial speech. Three days later Wugong commune leaders met in the yard that held its mechanized vehicles. Drizzle fell all day. Each commune village sent a wreath and a representative. Isolated in a bare, walled-in compound, two dozen people sobbed. Posters were banned, public mourning deterred. The commune party secretary offered cliches about turning sorrow into strength.

Premier Zhou had never entered the Wugong mythos. Not even party secretary Yang Tong's daughter, Yuexin, studying at Nankai University, Zhou's alma mater, would remember Zhou's death. No villager we interviewed recalled his death, though he had been a key mover in the 1970 North China Agricultural Conference and in the promotion of the Dazhai model.

In Raoyang one unit actively commemorated Zhou's passing, the petroleum exploration team that had been in the county for five years. Inside its compound, close to the high school, technicians constructed a memorial site, played mourning music, and spoke of the premier's contributions to the nation in a courtyard filled with poems and posters. The ceremony, organized by these mostly Beijing-educated outsiders, attracted local teachers and intellectuals.

A succession struggle of earthquake proportions was well under way. Even before Zhou's death, signs of renewed political conflict reached Raoyang. In late fall 1975 a speech by Mao circulating at the highest levels indicated that he had withdrawn support for Vice Premier Deng's modernizing agenda.[23] Hebei officials noted that at the very end of 1975, Dazhai's prominence in *People's Daily* suddenly was overshadowed by Jiang Qing's Xiaojinzhuang, which was headlined on December 25, 1975. Following Zhou's death, Mao bypassed Deng to appoint helicopter Hua Guofeng as premier.[24] Some Hebei officials were unnerved when Xiaojinzhuang received more press than Dazhai. Anxious, they buried themselves in such local affairs as opening a paved highway between Raoyang and Hengshui.

Officials from revolutionary Baoding prefecture denounced interpretations of Dazhai that stressed production and income, as Premier Zhou and Deng Xiaoping had, rather than class struggle and ideology. Revolutionaries targeted reformers, dubbed capitalist roaders, as struggle objects. Monarch Liu

Zihou, under attack from Jiang Qing allies, wrote another self-criticism.[25] Officials throughout Hebei grew more fearful of association with a loser.

Escalating Tensions

In January 1976 Hebei officials approved the return to Wugong of Professor Zuo Zhiyuan of the Department of Party History at Nankai University. As a graduate student in 1958, he had gathered material on Leap-era Wugong. He now sought to write a book. Zuo found that the village was still poor. Clothing was drab and of low quality. When it rained, dirt lanes turned into bogs, imprisoning people in their homes. Rats were a pestilence. There was no sewage, no hot water, no running water, no toilet seats, no toilet paper, no refrigeration.

Yet the small trees Zuo had seen planted in the late 1950s had been harvested, the timber used for houses, coffins, and furniture. New seedlings had turned into tall trees that provided windbreaks and beauty. Three-quarters of the village had moved into newer and larger abodes built with fired bricks. That cold January, however, villagers shivered outdoors under temporary sheds built in response to an area-wide earthquake alert. Remembering the aftershocks from the 1966 quake, villagers respected earthquake warnings.

Zuo proposed a book featuring revolutionary Geng Changsuo leading class struggle to smash capitalist obstacles that impeded an advance toward communism. He talked with Geng, party secretary Yang Tong, and administrator Qiao Liguang. They liked the concept. History would begin with the desperate conditions that gave rise to a 1943 four-family semisocialist coop and end with the ongoing effort to create new socialist things, stressing how today's agenda sprang from the Cultural Revolution. Zuo was invited to return with worker-peasant-soldier students after the lunar New Year.

On February 19, 1976, *People's Daily* hailed Wugong as a model of socialist society. The piece appeared in an irregular column on "newly produced things," which after December 20, 1975, replaced space headed "In agriculture, learn from Dazhai." The article celebrated Li Keqi, a 73-year-old representative of the "poor and lower-middle peasants" for his work on the school committee. Li saw to it that students labored in field and factory. He taught about the hard struggles of elders. Mindful of the anti-intellectual ditty about schooling, "First year, still a native; second year, a foreigner; third year, don't recognize one's own parents," conservative elders hoped to protect children from the alienating influence of "stinking intellectuals."

Another celebrated Wugong creation was a two-room clinic in the west village staffed by paramedics, one room for women, one for general illness. The small clinic had been well received in 1973, its first year. But by 1976 the staff had turned over, costs were up, and villagers mistrusted the amateur medics. Some villagers preferred traditional village practitioners. They liked to think healers were the scions of special families, that medicine was an art fathers passed to sons. Elders preferred to be seen at home by their inherited practitioner. Some villagers preferred the modern doctors at the commune clinic. But the war on "stinking intellectuals" had halted the expansion of regular medical schooling in favor of crash courses for village paramedics, "barefoot doctors."[26]

Party secretary Yang Tong invited deputy village head Li Chengzhang to take over the clinic. Li, son of the 1940s village chief Li Zihou, was heir to the medical practice of his father that was closed in 1956 during collectivization. In the tense political climate of 1976, Li declined an overture to compete with new socialist things.[27]

People's Daily praised Wugong's 127 "advanced theoretical workers" for stamping out enemies of socialism. The youngsters memorized tracts on the theory of the dictatorship of the proletariat. To foster proletarian consciousness, the Eight Red Sisters, led by women's association leader Wang Pengju, criticized Macho Li Shouzheng, her brother-in-law, for grasping money and abandoning Mao's line. Li had insisted that classes on politics should not interfere with speedily bringing in the harvest.

The Jiang Qing group used Mao's backing for class struggle in education to discredit Deng Xiaoping, who had been trying to modernize education to serve economic growth. *People's Daily,* led by Shanghai ideologue Yao Wenyuan, a key figure in Jiang's camp, featured Xiaojinzhuang in a front-page article on February 26. The article used the name of the party secretary to attack China's "innerparty unrepentant capitalist roader," the code name for Deng, for trying to enhance technical and scientific education. The next day Raoyang people were assembled to listen to a "radio broadcast rally" that criticized a "reversal of correct verdicts." Again, the target was reformer Deng Xiaoping, who had been labeled a leading enemy of socialism at the outset of the Cultural Revolution. Beginning on March 27, a three-day party meeting was held in Raoyang to denounce Deng and oppose rightism, that is, promoters of economic and educational reform.

Professor Zuo, accompanied by 11 Nankai students, returned to Wugong at the end of February. They stayed in the village's east end. Zuo moved in with Geng Xiufeng, who loved to describe Wugong's early socialist history. Hearing that in 1967 Boss Geng Changsuo's daughter had prodded her parents to struggle against capitalism, some students left for Shijiazhuang to interview Huijuan. In March two representatives from a Beijing publishing house came to assess Zuo's project, agreeing to publish a book presenting Wugong as a model of revolutionary class struggle. The unofficial village scrapbook contained an unusually large number of clippings from 1976 showing support for fundamentalism.

Fame had its rewards. Factory recruiters came. The head of the team 1 irrigation group, 46-year-old Wei Shuwei, found a job for his son in a Raoyang ɔkie factory. The son received 32 yuan a month in cash, a small bonanza in ɪe countryside where most income was paid in kind. The money, however, was paid to the village government. For bringing in cash, the laborer received work point distribution that was 10 percent above the village norm. He also enjoyed such free perquisites given to urban workers as haircuts, baths, and movies. With so many underemployed people locked into low-value collective agriculture, villagers appreciated off-farm employment. Work that produced cash income, not the emulation of Dazhai or Xiaojinzhuang, offered a path out of poverty. Increasing off-farm work made the number of villagers holding temporary or contract jobs in the towns far higher than official statistics suggested, while keeping urban overhead low by shifting to villagers the burden for feeding, servicing, and educating their families.

As the first week of April drew to a close, the Nankai University researchers traveled to Nanwangzhuang, Wang Yukun's Mao-blessed village. Wugong families then celebrated the Qingming holiday by visiting the cemetery and ritually cleaning the grave mounds. Before families visited burial mounds, garlanded them with leaves, and respectfully marked each mound with a stone, a patriotic procession was held. The party tried hard to transform Qingming from a time to remember ancestors into an occasion for honoring revolutionary heroes. Each year the politically active in Wugong joined army families in a march to the shaded cemetery, paid homage at the mounds of revolutionary martyrs, and listened to epic tales of the fallen soldiers who gave their lives to resist Japanese invaders. Alienated from the party and from economic irrationality, villagers still felt the military was the people's army.

Qingming in Beijing produced an outpouring of grief for Zhou Enlai. In the week leading up to Qingming, the monument to the heroes of the revolution in Tiananmen Square was covered with wreaths, poems, and messages honoring the late premier. On April 4, Qingming day, an estimated two million people visited the square. Many added their own sentiments, viewed the wreaths and statements of others, and listened to speeches. Numerous poems and broadsides denounced Jiang Qing and her revolutionary allies, some in allegorical fashion, others with startling directness.[28] Zhang Guangping, who had returned to his village in Raoyang from service in the 69th Army, was so excited by the news that he bicycled to Beijing.

A Politburo meeting blamed provocateurs, particularly Vice Premier Deng, for the events in Tiananmen Square. With Mao's approval, the square was cleared of wreaths and writings. On the evening of April 5, following clashes between demonstrators and the police, protesters were ordered to leave the area. At 9:35 P.M. the square was flooded with light. Militia, public security forces, and Beijing garrison troops moved in and beat those who remained with batons, arresting hundreds. The Politburo branded the peaceful protest a "counterrevolutionary riot."[29]

Deng was stripped of all his positions (but not party membership). Hua

Guofeng was promoted to vice chairman of the party, and thus positioned to succeed Mao. A hunt began for people who had been in the capital. Visitors had to account for every hour. In Tianjin, Nankai University students were ordered to report anyone who had gone to Beijing. Raoyang authorities demanded the names of recent visitors to Beijing in an effort to seize anyone who might be disseminating poems that honored Zhou Enlai or cast doubt on revolutionary initiatives. Throughout Hebei, security forces detained and interrogated people. Some were imprisoned.[30]

Raoyang's Zhou Guangping reached Beijing by bicycle three days after the crackdown. He was detained. One of his interrogators was a Raoyang native, so Zhou was saved. After telephoning Raoyang to determine that Zhou was a veteran and not a "reactionary," security forces released him. One person from Raoyang had indeed returned with poems exposing the wounds and scars inflicted on the Chinese people. No one turned him in.

Wugong sought to avoid trouble. Saying "I don't understand," party secretary Yang Tong invited the Nankai University visitors to explain events. The intellectuals lectured at the night school on the "counterrevolutionary incident." Then villagers painted slogans in huge red characters denouncing Deng Xiaoping. A raucous villagewide meeting branded him China's unrepentant capitalist roader.

The militia was instructed to ferret out class enemies. The cruel ritual called class struggle was repeated. Women's leader Wang Pengju was especially active. Harmless black element Li Peishen was targeted. Militia members claimed to have spied him removing earth from the roots of seedlings. Li was accused of sabotaging socialism. Villagers were summoned to the fields to learn of the evil ways of class enemies. Knowing that claims of innocence were proof of counterrevolutionary obstinacy, Li confessed and vowed to remold himself.

The party again targeted the old village center. The house of a team 2 leader was found to have a courtyard slightly larger than permitted. Another team 2 leader purportedly obtained timber from trees in the collective orchard for his house. The two reformist leaders of team 2's recent economic rise were ousted.

Li Xiantao, the youth league chief from the village center who had led young men to the Hai River project in 1975, was found guilty of squandering 100 yuan of public funds. He had bought laborers coverlets to keep dirt off pillows, handkerchiefs to tie around brows to keep sweat out of eyes, and gloves to protect hands pushing loaded wheelbarrows up steep river banks. Items like these had long been given for such toil. Now it was said that Li's spending made for the sort of separate stratum that led to capitalist restoration in the Soviet Union. Revolutionary China would nip it in the bud. Li had to criticize himself first before a meeting of party members and then before all collective members, that is, in the absence of all black-label people who were excluded from political rituals.[31]

But Li Xiantao's career was not in jeopardy. The local party was skilled at

ry theater. Unlike black elements, party loyalists who confessed
ded. In June, with the wheat harvested, the new leaders of team 2
azhai to show that they worshipped at an orthodox shrine.

s Xu Shukuan fell into a coma in May. A commune vehicle rushed
ndomitable companion to the hospital. She lost the power of speech
ld not stand. She would live out her remaining years at home nursed
by her elder daughter, Xueren. Lu Molin, one of the four original members of
the 1943 Geng coop, died in 1976 at the age of 91. In summer 1976, Zhu De,
who had headed the resistance-era red armies, died at 89. The old guard was
rapidly passing. The chairman was fading. Maneuvering was under way all
over China.

On June 17 *People's Daily* quoted Xiaojinzhuang villagers who said that
Deng Xiaoping's reversal of verdicts on Cultural Revolution political targets
was like the behavior of a landlord who returned in 1947 with an armed band
and killed 32 villagers. Revolutionaries seemed to be calling for a new round
of deadly class struggle. But in June Mao ignored Xiaojinzhuang and again
embraced Dazhai's Chen Yonggui. Premier Hua, the helicopter who had access to Mao, now dying of Lou Gehrig's disease, likewise promoted Dazhai.
Lower levels responded. Wugong's team 3 party secretary promptly visited
Dazhai. Hebei intensified the Dazhai county campaign, announcing the success of 22 such counties and one prefecture, Shijiazhuang.[32] In July Vice
Premier Chen Yonggui, Dazhai's leader, visited Houtun, the top Dazhai vil-
lage model in Hengshui prefecture. Chen had recently clashed with Jiang
Qing in Beijing.[33] Chen gathered Wugong's Geng Changsuo, Mao-blessed
Nanwangzhuang's Wang Yukun, and other rural allies.

On July 17 *People's Daily* carried an essay ascribed to Xiaojinzhuang that
sought to maintain the focus on Deng Xiaoping's "crimes." It protested Deng's
criticism of their night school and his attempt to overturn the Cultural Revolution's thrust in education. Smashing Deng and his allies was the top priority:
"The main target of the revolution is the capitalist class inside the party."

· An article attributed to Geng that appeared two days later in *People's Daily*
agreed. Wugong was said to have called more than 30 meetings to criticize
Deng and held more than 80 cultural events at which more than seven hundred poems and skits attacked Deng's crimes. Geng denounced Deng as an
enemy of the poor peasants, as an ally of those who had slashed Wugong's big
coop in 1953, and an opponent of distribution to the needy in the famine of
the early 1960s. Using the jargon of the moment, Deng was likened to the
traitor Song Jiang in the novel *Water Margin* and to the followers of Khrushchev, said to have destroyed socialism in the Soviet Union after even Hitler
had failed to. Revolutionaries had to squash people who refused to abolish
money, wipe out commodities, destroy markets, or get rid of bourgeois intellectuals. Unless such survivals were ripped out, capitalism would be restored
and ghastly evils would return. "The capitalist roaders in the party," Geng's

article claimed, "really are fiercer and more dangerous than the landlord capitalists."

In this tense political atmosphere, more data were gathered for the book on revolutionary Wugong. Geng Xiufeng went to Shijiazhuang hoping to see former Hebei secretary Lin Tie. Modernizer Lin had been freed when Deng Xiaoping was first rehabilitated. But Hebei Monarch Liu denied Lin a high post, and, with Deng's latest fall, Lin Tie was again in limbo. Xiufeng was surprised that Lin received him immediately and displayed great interest in Wugong. Lin agreed to stop off in Wugong the following month when traveling by car to Renqiu, northeast of Wugong, to inspect oil fields.

In August 1976, accompanied by his personal physician, a service provided to elderly leaders, Lin Tie returned to Wugong for the first time in 13 years. He stayed in the hostel and met with Geng Changsuo, Geng Xiufeng, and Professor Zuo. Lin told Zuo that in order not to alienate villagers, Mao had said little about promoting socialist agriculture during the war against Japan and the civil war. Therefore, prior to 1949, top leaders were cool to making the semisocialist Geng coop a major model. Lin was circumspect in answering questions about the big 20th-anniversary celebration in 1963 when he had supported a policy line stressing production, mechanization, and modernization that had been approved by President Liu Shaoqi. Although dead, Liu was still damned as China's biggest capitalist roader. With the purported number 2 capitalist roader, Deng Xiaoping, under attack, who knew what political earthquakes lay ahead.

Before summer ended, Professor Zuo returned to Tianjin to craft a book showing Wugong as an exemplar of Cultural Revolution virtue. Even as Zuo wrote, however, the political ground was shifting as tremors turned into earthquakes.

13 ❀ EARTHQUAKES

From summer 1976 to fall 1978 earthquakes shook the highest levels of power and began to reverberate throughout society. First, however, nature erupted.

Tangshan

An earthquake measuring 7.8 on the Richter scale devastated the Hebei coal-mining center, Tangshan, 175 miles northeast of Wugong, on July 28, 1976. More than a quarter of a million people died. In Tianjin 40,000 perished, in Beijing a few thousand. The disaster cascaded across rural Hebei.[1]

Guo Baofan worked at the insect-control station in Wugong. Her parents were in Tangshan. Local authorities rejected her request to go home. When a letter arrived from her parents saying they had lost everything, Guo was relieved. At least they were alive. Li Peishen, recently scapegoated in the cotton fields, had family in Tianjin, where more than 10 percent of the structures collapsed. His brother-in-law was killed. Black element Li knew better than to ask permission to join mourning relatives.

The daughter and mother-in-law of Wang Fengyue, director of the Raoyang hospital, were in Tangshan. Dr. Wang and nine other physicians sped to the stricken city with a Raoyang team. No trace of her kin was found. The head of the Hebei Women's Association, Meng Zhongyun, who had twice inspected Wugong, rushed to Tangshan. Her husband had been crushed to death. Knocked from their beds that sweltering summer night, some virtually naked teenage girls dug out trapped people and became the talk of the survivors.

Young males committed gang rapes. Some of those who looted jewelry from dead bodies were beaten to death by outraged citizens. Taking food and water, however, was seen by survivors as necessary. The state sent in 100,000 soldiers, including units of the 38th Army in Baoding. The army had a different view of necessity. It imprisoned hundreds who were desperately scavenging at local granaries. Locals remember the help provided by military doctors. The needy received inoculations. To prevent a spread of disease, bodies were plowed under. Truck and car fleets from all over Hebei carried steamed bread and other staples. Nearly 4,000 Raoyang residents donated 5,000 articles of clothing, 1,260 ration coupons, 12,000 catties of cooked food, and 529 yuan in cash. Families in Shijiazhuang and Hengshui adopted orphaned children.

In Raoyang 275 houses collapsed, 29 people were injured, three died. Ten Raoyang natives working or traveling in the Tangshan area were killed. Fearful of aftershocks, officials ordered Raoyang residents out of their homes and offices. Many lived in makeshift quarters for a year. Tent cities sprang up at the high school and outside all government offices. Most villagers built housing of cornstalks and plastic. In Zhangcun, children playing with matches set a tent ablaze, burning two to death.

"Self-reliant" China spurned foreign aid. Rumor had it that allies of Jiang Qing insisted that revolution came before relief. Hua Guofeng was the top official to go to Tangshan.[2]

"Our Great Leader Is Dead"

On August 17, 1976, *People's Daily* printed an article with the byline of Wu-gong's Li Who Is Thankful to the Army claiming that only socialism saved people. It told how Mao's thought and his army had saved young Li when bourgeois doctors would not. Li expressed determination to defend the Cultural Revolution and Chairman Mao's revolutionary line, and to fight unrepentant innerparty capitalist roader, Deng Xiaoping.

Jiang Qing's model Xiaojinzhuang attacked Deng, claiming that villagers survived the quake because they ate out of "one big pot." People were told that in 1962 after natural disasters (the Great Leap famine) Deng had tried to destroy the collective, extinguish class struggle, and promote household contracts for farming and animal husbandry. But revolutionary Xiaojinzhuang saw that reform would hurt the poor. Better to spurn relief, join with class allies, and forget family.

Jiang Qing went to Xiaojinzhuang on August 28. Pictures showed her helping villagers rebuild. Stories spread that she had brought her own food, drink, toilet seat, and chamber pot. Hinting at the ongoing succession struggle, she gave no gifts lest her adversaries use that against her. She described her opponents as male chauvinists.[3] The next day Xiaojinzhuang was headlined in *People's Daily*. The article attacked Deng's stress on modernization and condemned small-scale agricultural contracting.

In early September Jiang Qing went to the national model village, Dazhai. She told Guo Fenglian, the young woman who had succeeded Chen Yonggui as party secretary, that communism was related to matriarchy. Under communism there could still be an empress.[4] Jiang complained about the Dazhai pigsty, fretting that even collective hog raising, a 1970 North China Agricultural Conference reform priority, meant straying from grain-first fundamentals. On learning that a seriously ill Mao had taken a life-threatening turn, she rushed to Beijing on September 5.[5]

On the morning of September 9 at Nankai University in Tianjin, student party members were assembled and told that Chairman Mao was dead. They returned to their rooms crying uncontrollably. They did not tell their classmates why. Students guessed.

At noon on September 9, Wugong's public-address system announced a special bulletin at 4 P.M. By 1 P.M. Raoyang denizens with shortwave radios had heard the news on Radio Moscow. Finally, official word came: "Our great leader Chairman Mao is dead." Wugong leaders stared and cried. No one spoke. Throughout the village work stopped. People froze in place. Years later all remembered what they were doing on hearing the news. Men sobbed, women wailed. The old cried loudest. Some shook wildly. To most villagers, Mao was the revolution, the one whose strategies won power and saved villagers from invaders, landlords, usurers, and broken families, from all the plagues of old, from civil war, uprooting, and famine. Villagers never blamed Mao for their troubles.

Hundreds of wreaths were made. Half a dozen memorial events followed. Boss Geng tried to give a eulogy. Instead he cried. From all speakers, tears flowed more freely than words.

Villagers wore white cotton blossoms above their hearts. At memorial services, people stood mute, dazed, and confused. Quiet sobbing grew into loud wailing. As elders recalled it, even the babies seemed to be grieving. "Without Mao, what will happen?" "The heavens have collapsed." Although weather reports preclude it, old timers distinctly recall that the heavens opened and let loose nature's tears.

Raoyang observed seven days of mourning. The county town opened 11 mourning halls, and a site was set up in each village. In the first two days virtually every adult in the county paid respects. All units sent traditional white mourning wreaths. A solemn throng of county leaders gathered at the high school on September 18 to listen to a broadcast of the memorial ceremony in Beijing. Boss Geng then attended a memorial rally in the provincial capital. Provincial notables, model villages, and model policies were represented.[6] Mao's way seemed eternal. But political earthquakes were coming.

Relief

In late September Wugong sent a team of 30 led by Li Xiantao to help rebuild Tangshan. It was Li's opportunity to reestablish himself after ritualistic criticism for spending on workers at the Hai River project. Party secretary Yang Tong told the young men that under socialism Chinese were one big family. Tangshan's difficulties were Wugong's. Team members should finish tasks early and then do extra good deeds. The 30 climbed into three wagons, each pulled by a tractor. Official opposition to commerce had denied villagers trucks, and Raoyang lacked a through train. The tractors chugged east 50 miles to a rail line. After a night on a station platform, the team and hundreds more went by special train to Tangshan, whose tracks had been mangled by the earthquake. From the drop-off, it was a two-hour hike to a work site where tents awaited. The Wugong team helped with the harvest and repaired waterworks.

Outsiders were kept away from local people. Most never met a Tangshan person. There was a three-hour midday break. When it rained, work halted. During free time, outdoor movies were shown. But the only Cultural Revolution–era films were the often-screened model operas and Jiang Qing's revolutionary melodramas; the best old movies were banned. Li never went. But everyone enjoyed visits by song troupes. Boss Geng and county secretary Wang Yumin visited to praise Li and his team.

Li trekked into Tangshan, where he saw that no house stood. Survivors lived in the streets under makeshift cover. The government prioritized rebuilding state structures — hospitals, post offices, and banks. Li helped families rebuild homes.

In early October a rumor spread that Jiang Qing and her allies in the military would march on Beijing from Baoding in a southern pincer to link up with a northern one from Liaoning. Units of the 38th Army headquartered in Baoding were said to have left Tangshan to join in. But they remained loyal to the senior generals backing helicopter Hua Guofeng. On October 6, Jiang Qing and her closest allies were seized and denounced as a "Gang of Four."

Raoyang held rallies on October 22 and 23. The next day, an ugly case that had long been festering was settled. Song Dongyue, a county official who had committed suicide in 1970, was cleared of all charges. A Shijiazhuang rally of 500,000 on October 25 celebrated the fall of the "Jiang Qing counterrevolutionary clique." Isolated fighting erupted in Baoding, whose remnant revolutionaries were disarmed on November 16. Fear of mass vigilantism receded. Prisons and labor camps released inmates, allowing millions to try to resume normal lives.

An International Relations Institute member still in Raoyang asked to return to Beijing. To succeed, she had to divorce her villager husband. Some institute members claimed that this teacher of French had brought the trouble on herself. Since she was of mixed blood, with a French mother, of course she had married a peasant, seen by some as a virtually uncivilized race apart from urbanites.

Xiaojinzhuang denounced Jiang Qing as a capitalist roader who hated Chairman Mao.[7] Too late. The model fell when its backers fell. By contrast, Wugong's patrons seemed strengthened. Monarch Liu Zihou's patron Li Xiannian was closely associated with Premier Hua Guofeng and Dazhai's Chen Yonggui. Wugong pasted up posters of Hua, drawn to resemble Mao, next to pictures of Mao. Hua's portrait had his name printed under it to facilitate recognition. Wugong seemed tied to victors.

After a month of hard work, the Wugong relief team was feted in Raoyang by the county secretary. A village meeting honored the returnees. Hebei designated the team a model and praised its leaders for helping the stricken. Li Xiantao was made secretary of team 2.

In December villagers viewed a film of Mao's funeral. Geng's ally from the Paupers' Coop, Wang Guofan, was a pallbearer. The film legitimated Hua as successor. Wugong seemed immune to earthquake damage.

The New Dazhai Campaign

Hua Guofeng convened another national Dazhai conference in December. The Raoyang delegation included Wugong's relief team leader Li Xiantao. Hua excoriated an evil Gang of Four and promised to restore stability and to further agricultural mechanization.[8] It was acknowledged that the poor in Sichuan province had been devastated by cutting capitalist tails and planting grain everywhere. A ten-year era of chaos was said to be ending.

The conference cited Liu Zihou and Hebei as Dazhai models. The conference message brought back by Li Xiantao was to develop sideline and industrial enterprises, understood as post-1970 modernization successes that had been threatened by a 1974–76 revolutionary counterattack. Income from Wugong collective enterprises reached 43 percent of total income in the period 1976–78. Party secretaries were told to invest in agricultural mechanization, farmland construction, and rural industrialization. Hebei dispatched one-third of all provincial-level officials to the grassroots to raise poorer units, criticize capitalist sprouts and household contracts, and turn one-third of all locations into Dazhai-type counties. Already 400 counties across the nation had been designated as Dazhai counties.

In spring 1977 Hebei directives stated that Dazhai counties exemplified 14 characteristics: skill in criticizing the Gang of Four, strong leadership, the ability to focus on "key" points of development, officials who worked in the fields, the fostering of "socialist labor competition," the ability to implement policy, effective irrigation policies (at least 80 percent irrigation of cultivated land or an irrigated mu of land per capita), successful fertilizer policies, achievements in transforming the quality of the soil, an experimental field, a stable high-yield field, an effective tree-planting program, small-scale sidelines, and mechanization. Raoyang was designated a Dazhai-style county in 1977, as it was said to be relatively productive while stressing collective income and curbing the household sector.

Because Wugong and other densely populated villages had more people than mu of farmland, they could not meet the Dazhai criteria of an irrigated mu of land per person. An alternative standard was proposed: grain yields of

550 to 600 catties per mu, cotton yields of 60 to 80 catties per mu, and peanut yields of 250 to 450 catties per mu. However, 19 of the Hebei counties dubbed "Dazhai-style county" produced less than 500 catties of grain per mu, six less than 400. When criteria were lowered, political success rates soared. Rural living standards did not. In fact, while Hebei investigators uncovered pervasive prevarication, official claims permitted Premier Hua to announce great gains from the Dazhai campaign. The problem was endemic. With the fate of leaders on the line, performance claims soared.

Conservative Hebei leaders demanded that income equalization be achieved by enlarging the distribution unit. However, villages resisted revolutionary leveling. From spring 1977 to spring 1978 the number of villages serving as income-distribution units increased by only 394, for a total of fewer than 6,000 of Hebei's 50,097 villages. Raoyang prodded Wugong to go to villagewide distribution. But as before, the east and west ends had no desire to share with the center. The status quo remained.

Liu Zihou's call to increase cotton production by investing more in fertilizer and insecticides was unpopular, given low state cotton prices. Production gains impoverished. Wugong, however, tried to deliver. It kept women in the fields even during rainstorms. When the Hebei Women's Association complained, plastic raincoats were provided for the dragooned field workers. Tillers resented working for virtually nothing and dragged their heels. Wugong's cotton output plummeted from 1976 to 1979.

Villages and villagers made side deals, hoping to earn money. Wugong delivered sorghum to the Hengshui White Lightning distillery for 40,000 catties of scarce chemical fertilizer. Gengkou tried to make more profitable a rug factory that revolutionaries had earlier closed. It contracted with Hengshui prefecture to export a product whose quality was improved by hiring skilled craftswomen as instructors and by putting village women weavers on a quota system. In 1977 average worker incomes were more than 70 yuan a month, more than four times the pay for collective agriculture.

Revolutionary pressures eased. During the 1977 lunar New Year, villages that had hidden cherished drums brought them back to beat a welcome to a new beginning. The state exonerated the April 5, 1976, demonstrators who had honored Premier Zhou in Tiananmen Square. A Tianjin merchant family and a Shanxi landlord family that had found succor in Wugong for 20 years returned to Tianjin. Collective weddings ended. Marriage was again a family affair. For the first year since the 1958 Leap, no corvée labor was dispatched to distant places. Making its first appearance in more than a decade, the Raoyang drama troupe again performed Hebei opera, to the special delight of the elderly. Martial arts flourished.

The new administration of Hua Guofeng, bidding for popular support, made a wider variety of consumer goods available. Wugong, as the most prosperous as well as the most favored village in Raoyang, enjoyed access to goods available to few others. Under the influence of the modernization agenda of the 1970s, consumer purchases in the model village increased at a brisk pace. Between 1970 and 1978 team 3 households added 126 radios to the existing 21. There had been no watches in the west end before 1970. By 1978 the 232 households owned 77. The first bicycle, a Japanese-made Fuji, was obtained in 1944 by a member of the party underground. China manufactured no bicycles at that time. In the next 15 years, only eight more bicycles were purchased. Forty-seven were bought in the 1960s, and 120 more from 1970 to 1978. Of team 3's 100 sewing machines, three were purchased in the 1950s, 12 in the 1960s, and 85 between 1970 and 1978. There was never enough Hengshui White Lightning, which sold for 2.86 yuan a bottle.

A factory in Shijiazhuang sent Wugong a free television set to test. It projected a large image onto a big screen. Product trials were pretexts for gift-giving that fostered ties of reciprocity. Set up in the new party headquarters, the set broke almost immediately. In 1978 team 3 purchased a 24-inch black-and-white model to replace a 12-inch set placed in team headquarters for villagers to enjoy indoors in winter, outdoors in summer.

Still, reforms were limited. The Wugong party committee discussed quota management, reminiscent of the precollectivization 1950s and the post-Leap reform response to famine. Fearful that quotas meant abandoning Dazhai, leaders stuck with relatively equal per capita distribution.

Helicopter Hua in Beijing argued that with the end of class struggle, Dazhai's policies would prove their worth. Declaring his allegiance to Mao's words and deeds, Hua would embrace the big collective, curbing the household sector and the market. By importing new technology and other resources, he held, state commanded modernization would pay off; collective agricultural production and rural wealth would leap forward.

New Reform Openings

Reformers wanted more. They sought to contract agricultural production to households, broaden markets, and end leveling distribution that slighted labor contributions. They advocated price reforms to spur underpaid farmers and investment in light industry so that desired consumer goods would become widely available.[9]

Hebei officials scapegoated the Gang of Four while continuing to resist reform. Monarch Liu Zihou attributed Hebei's problems to Jiang Qing's allies, said to have defied Liu from their Baoding bastion. The Raoyang party attacked a villager from Hefang as a "Gang of Four element" for accusing former county party secretary Li Chunyu of covering up a murder. Wugong dismissed the 1975 charges against Li Xiantao for unauthorized expenditures on the Hai River project as a case of "Gang of Four interference." Boss Geng claimed he had resisted Jiang Qing's effort to treat all villagers as latent capitalists, enemies of revolution.[10]

Raoyang assigned Zou Liji, the 21-year-old son of the county director of cultural affairs, to Wugong. As a youngster he had visited Wugong when it was a model of Lin Biao's four-good movement. Beginning in 1977 he traveled with Geng to keep him on message.

Reformers touted Geng's meetings with the deceased Premier Zhou, whose aura legitimated modernization.[11] Conservatives cited Geng's insistence that the big collective won common prosperity.[12] *People's Daily,* controlled by reformers, celebrated Wugong on June 10, 1977, for economic accounting that produced higher incomes. The August issue of *Red Flag,* run by opponents of reform, had Geng argue in conservative terms.

Wugong and Hebei hailed frugality as efficiency. The accountant, Boss Geng said, bought office pens at his own expense. Wugong cut pesticide costs, reduced spending on tool repair, and began calculating the cost of running its 72 deep wells. The price of irrigating a mu of land varied from a high of .63 yuan to a low of .20 for a well that was run by a conscientious woman. In 1977 Wugong claimed to have cut average irrigation costs by .33 yuan per mu and the production cost of a catty of grain from .064 yuan in 1965 to .024.

Actually, Wugong leaders distrusted efficiency. It seemed unsocialist to calculate time and money rather than serve the nation and revolution. While Geng parroted the reform slogan "practice is the criterion for testing truth," he defended the collective, insisting it protected the vulnerable poor. In late 1978 county officials estimated that 35,917 people in Raoyang, nearly one in six, including the blind, the deaf, the mute, destitute households, five-guarantee households, veterans, martyr households, and those wounded in action, required public assistance of 400,000 yuan. Geng opted to "do only what accords with the words of Chairman Mao." He stood with Hua Guofeng, Chen Yonggui, and the collective way. The 77-year-old Geng, despite incipient deafness, was a delegate to the Eleventh Party Congress in August 1977. With reformer Deng Xiaoping restored to the Politburo Standing Committee, Hua's power was threatened.[13]

Hua promoted an ambitious ten-year plan at the Fifth National People's Congress in February and March 1978. Raoyang's "other" national labor model, Song Xingru, represented the county. Hua urged a new "Great Leap." The Hebei government echoed his line.

In Tianjin, party secretary Xie Xuegong lost his position along with others linked to the Jiang Qing group. Xie was demoted to party vice secretary of Shaanxi province.[14] Seeking neither revenge nor justice, Deng Xiaoping tried to remove opponents of reform from key positions.

Aware that villagers were alienated by leaders who lived high, reformers sought to reduce burdens on the poor. Wugong reprimand articulate Li Zhongxin for gluttony. He was ordered to enjoy less and work more. Geng intoned in Mao-like phrases, "The masses are the water and the officials are fish. A fish that leaves the water cannot live."[15] As with youth leader Li Xiantao's earlier demotion, the penalty was a ritual to display mettle. Villagers mocked the proletarian gilding of coddled princes and heirs.

Reformers and modernizers insisted that villagers enjoy the fruits of their labor. Wugong removed obstacles to house building. Li Zhongxin immediately began erecting an abode for his family of four.

With the center's blessing, Raoyang established a foreign trade office. Throughout Raoyang, including 22 villages without a single collective enterprise, locals seized market opportunities. The county's foreign trade would soar from a puny 130,000 yuan in 1978 to 56 million yuan by 1983. Representatives of the foreign trade office in Hengshui prefecture, which sold peanuts to Japan, sesame seeds to Southeast Asia, and willow baskets to the United States, acted as agent for the Gengkou rug factory in 1977, finding buyers in Hong Kong, Japan, the United States, Italy, Malaysia, and Australia. Reforms in conservative Hebei brought gains.

Science, Education, and the Economic Reform Agenda

By 1978, modernizers associated with Deng Xiaoping criticized the fetish of manual labor, insisting that science be taken as a major productive force and that the contributions of knowledge to growth be recognized. Wugong purchased journals on agricultural science for discussion at youth league meetings. Experienced farmers gathered to pass on knowledge. The junior high added vocational classes on agricultural machinery, agricultural technology, and forestry.[16] People with technical skills rose, and Bugs Zhou Yuanjiu was belatedly rewarded for his 1973 cotton aphid research.[17] The incentive system no longer denigrated knowledge.

Two village women were enrolled in college. Yang Yuexin, the daughter of party secretary Yang Tong, was at Nankai University, en route to a medical research career in Beijing studying the impact of infant nutrition on adult health. Li Kuiying, whose father worked at the county trade bureau, studied medicine at Tangshan Mines Medical College. In addition, Li Genyu, a 1975 graduate of Nankai University, taught at Hebei Normal College. Three students passed the fiercely competitive 1978 college entrance exams. All had been tutored at home; all were male. Li Jinying, the son of high school math teacher Li Zonggui, entered Qinghua University, China's leading science school. These successes hinted at what the Raoyang countryside had lost in a revolution that crippled education.

In April, county authorities selected Wugong junior high as one of three prefectural key point junior high schools eligible for special funding. Economic resources continued to be channeled politically. Geng's loyalty still earned rewards.

Wugong tried to be loyal to reformers in Beijing while tied to adversaries of reform in Hebei. In spring 1978 Geng criticized himself for not having implemented a reward system promoted by the North China Agricultural Conference to encourage pig and fertilizer production.[18] Li Lai, a recent graduate of the provincial forestry school, was picked to make the money-losing village fruit orchard a productive asset.[19] But with the fruit purchased in advance by the state at a set price, there was little incentive to assure quality. In April accountant Geng Lianmin went to a provincewide meeting about the role of statistics in economic development. It was the first such gathering he had attended in 25 years.

The center decided that improving living standards required controlling population. Family planning had been urged since the early 1970s. Wugong had significantly reduced fertility rates. Officials ordered rigorous restrictions under the slogan "later, longer periods between births and fewer" children. The county target for 1979 was 2,800 new births, or twelve per 1,000 people. Macho Li Shouzheng took charge. We asked Li, the father of four sons, about his credibility with parents who found it immoral to have only daughters, who could not continue the patrilineal family. He replied, "It's not a problem. It's a contradiction. And Chairman Mao said the world is made of contradictions."

County officials were told to implement policies denounced only yesterday as fostering polarization, capitalistic greed, and a return to old insecurities. They were directed to promote household incentives and implement quota systems with bonuses for oustanding work. Instead of ever-larger collectives, more-autonomous small teams were fostered. Instead of restricting the household economy, families could use pig fodder to boost income. Household plots were returned to families and expanded. Yanggezhuang decollectivized vegetable growing, although about 30 percent of households, those short of labor, preferred collectivized vegetable plots. Some poorer households began to rise.

Hebei monarch Liu resisted reversing negative verdicts on long persecuted scientists, intellectuals, and others. Reformers sought to return such people to useful work, even to elevate them to power to enliven the economy. Liu responded that righting wrongs would demoralize security forces, leading to a rise in crime.[20] Liu, accompanied by Ma Hui, the top military official in Hebei whose work involved planning the new railroad, visited Wugong on April 27 following an inspection tour of earthquake-ravaged Tangshan. Geng backed Liu's policies and kept lobbying for the Jingjiu railroad to go through Raoyang.

Boss Geng as Lobbyist

Geng pulled strings in Shijiazhuang and Beijing to bring the railroad into Raoyang. Since the reformist center declared that its decision would be scientific, Raoyang presented technical data to the State Planning Commission and to the State Council.

Nanjing native Zhang Jiabo, a graduate of Hydroelectric Power College in Beijing, was among those sent to Raoyang in the Cultural Revolution. Posted to the county water-conservancy bureau, the engineer taught himself tunnel and bridge architecture, geology, materials testing, and related construction skills. He helped prepare a technical case for routing the line through Raoyang, even though it would add two miles to the track. In six trips to Beijing, each time armed to the teeth with sacks of the best local peanuts, sesame oil, bone sculpture, glass flowers, and garments, Zhang argued that the Raoyang route would save money, material, and labor. He marshaled geological and construction data to demonstrate that the Hutuo River crossing farther east would be more costly and more vulnerable to flood damage. Soon Zhang was made head of the Raoyang construction bureau.

The Raoyang route required constructing China's longest two-way continuous railroad bridge, 2.6 miles, as well as two other bridges totaling 2.2 miles. Large sections of the track would rest on pillars 15 feet above ground, designed to withstand the once in a century major flood anticipated for the region. Throughout the late 1970s Geng continued appealing to Chen Yonggui and Liu Zihou to use their ties to Premier Hua and Li Xiannian. Geng used his prestige to try to win over key officials in the Department of Water Conservation and the Ministry of Agriculture.

Lobbying was intense elsewhere, too. Xingguo county in Jiangxi province, the heart of the Red Army's base area in the 1930s, had produced 54 generals who were still active in the 1980s. They drafted a letter to the railroad bureau and followed it up with a full court press demanding that the line include Xingguo and an express stop be located there in recognition of the county's revolutionary role. They won.

Bad Timing

In May 1978 Nankai Professor Zuo Zhiyuan returned to Wugong with a book manuscript, *The Battles of the Wugong People*. The propaganda departments in Shijiazhuang, Hengshui, and Raoyang had already drastically altered it. The book criticized the fallen Lin Biao's four-good campaign and skipped over the fundamentalist onslaught of mid-1976, when Wugong was drawn to Jiang Qing's Xiaojinzhuang policies. A long chapter on the achievements of the Cultural Revolution had been cut back. With reformers branding the Cultural Revolution a catastrophe and Hua Guofeng defending a mild version of it, a vague 22-page chapter covering 1966 to 1976 presented Wugong as a model of Dazhai virtues, a big collective combining class struggle and high productivity to defeat the capitalist lines of both Liu Shaoqi and Lin Biao. Not a word was said about how, in 1976, the writing team advised villagers to denounce Deng Xiaoping and to oppose the April 5 movement in Tiananmen Square that commemorated Premier Zhou.

Starting after dinner and running close to midnight for five successive evenings, Zuo read the manuscript. Individuals took responsibility for facts relating to themselves. Xu Yizhou, the early resistance leader from the west end who broke with Boss Geng in 1953, was ill. The parts of the manuscript that referred to him were read at his home.

Geng Xiufeng was not consulted. Four months earlier he had fired off a letter to Premier Hua to complain about matters not mentioned by Zuo. Grain-requisition quotas were still far too high, and the policy of "taking grain as the key link" was misguided, Xiufeng wrote. Officials "lied" about grain production, foolish experiments to grow rice on dry land had failed, inter-cropping beans with wheat (an effective measure decried by revolutionaries) was not permitted because it might decrease grain output, and cash crops like peanuts were not allowed to be planted on sandy land that was unsuited to the required grain. While Zuo portrayed leaders as heroes, Xiufeng found, "the people were slaves." Leaders, appointed according to "nepotistic" norms, tried to please superiors, believing that in socialist politics it was better to err "to the left than to the right."[21]

After Zuo left Wuogong to hand his manuscript to the publisher, Vice Premier Chen Yonggui summoned Geng Changsuo to Shijiazhuang to discuss hosting another team gathering materials for a book. We arrived ten days later.

American Visitors

Since reformers wanted to send Chinese abroad to study subjects central to modernization, they reasoned that China would have to welcome foreign researchers to China. Our long-standing application was then approved.

On May 12 Geng met with Chen Yonggui, party vice chairman Li Xian-nian, and forestry specialist Yao Fuheng, the head of Houtun, a top Dazhai model village in Hebei. Spying Geng, Chen Yonggui shouted out a ditty that played on a meaning of the word *geng,* loyal: "Old Geng, Old Geng, ever loyal, ever loyal." But near-deaf Geng heard not a word. The group decided to send us to Wang Yukun's Mao-blessed Nanwangzhuang and to Houtun as well as to Wugong, three models. Wugong would feature economically suc-cessful team 3 and hide the village center. Southern Li families in team 2 gossiped about the charade. To keep us focused on revolutionary achieve-ments, we were kept not only from all black elements and adversaries of Boss Geng but also from Geng Xiufeng, who might mention high requisitions, production lies, irrational planting, and nepotism.

Since we had asked to go to a typical village, we would be told nothing about Professor Zuo's book or about earlier writings on model Wugong. Since we wanted to know about local history, cultural aficionado Ji Tiebang briefed county party officials on 1,500 years of local history, recounted as socialism defeating feudalism. Since we wanted to know about health care, charts were prepared and mounted at the commune hospital to display socialist success. Seeing only the best, and ignorant of historically rooted lineage and political conflicts, we could learn how a harmonious village built socialism.

Americans had to be handled carefully. They were from a capitalist country. Bourgeois intellectuals might lack goodwill toward the party. Still, since the visitors were interested in improved Sino-American relations, they could be treated as new Edgar Snows. But all conversations had to be reported to leaders. Official minders would constantly be at the side of the foreigners, even in the barber shop. Villagers were warned to say nothing about the Leap famine or Cultural Revolution violence.

There were smaller cultural barriers to overcome. Bugs Zhou Yuanjiu was warned not to eat garlic and onions because foreigners could not stand the smell. "We were afraid to get too close for fear you would smell our breath, and afraid to be too far away because you might not catch what we said." As else-where, speaking loudly to foreigners was assumed to improve comprehension.

Our visit was taken as proof that Wugong's virtue was at long last recognized on high. To Geng, helping Li Xiannian and Chen Yonggui improved chances they would in return reroute the railroad through Raoyang.

Public security officers fanned out to see that nothing untoward took place. When a granny from poor Yanggezhuang walked south a mile and a half to show her grandson what foreigners looked like, public security officials subjected her to four hours of interrogation. People heard. They were meant to. During our stay county officials also lashed out behind the scenes at an unruly student named Pu Quanyou who resided in nearby Xiaodi commune. Pu and others had recently beaten up a village school teacher. County officials were adamant that students had to show "greater respect for teachers." Not a word was said to us about anti-intellectual vigilantism.

Village history was a Maoist parable. From the semisocialist coop in 1943, Wugong acted on Mao's policy of getting organized. The big coop in 1953 and collectivization in 1956 won great successes. The Leap brought further economic gains. No corrupt or flawed leaders were found during the four cleanups or the Cultural Revolution. Wugong was united, revolutionary, and spotless. Village leaders had never heard of Jiang Qing's Xiaojinzhuang. They had resisted the 1976 anti–Deng Xiaoping campaign. When we witnessed officials shooing away popsicle sellers from team 3's burgeoning sideline economy, we were told these were outsiders, capitalist roaders.

We were introduced to the Li Mengjie–Shi Guiying marriage as the revolution incarnate. In June 1978 Li returned to Raoyang after 18 years in the army. In 1967 Li had married aspiring writer Shi. A daughter was born in 1972, a son in 1974. The Raoyang organization department put Li in charge of militia work in Xiaodi commune, just west of Wugong. For the first time, Mengjie and Guiying saw each other frequently. The veteran did not like what he saw. Guiying worked at the Raoyang cultural bureau. Writing was her passion. She devoted every free moment to a novel.

Mengjie declared himself a liberated male who permitted his wife to work outside the home. But at home, he told Guiying, she would devote herself to serving him. Inside, Guiying would be his wife and the mother of his children. There was to be no writing, no painting, and no singing. Mengjie backed up his views with explosive violence. To escape his beatings, Guiying devoted herself to work at the office and to family at home. After Mengjie fell asleep, however, Guiying fearfully worked on her novel for a couple of hours. It was a painful and degrading life.

Staying in households, we saw the wife rise early to get a fire going and cook us holiday foods. Worrying that we were a burden, we asked to move into the village hostel. Actually, the food we ate, festival dishes, came from the state. Our host families were also enjoying delicacies. They bargained with officials over food, turning the Americans into possessors of gargantuan appetites so the families could save good food for other occasions. We were fitted into a patron-client system of gifts and exchanges.

In June 1978 Chen Yonggui, a chain smoker who lit each new cigarette with the butt of the old one, met with us in the Great Hall of the People in Beijing to review rural politics and policies. What Chen did not say was that he and his ally, Hua Guofeng, were fighting for their political lives as Deng Xiaoping reached the pinnacle of Chinese politics.

Resistance and Reform

In 1978, Hua Guofeng pushed high production targets, reminiscent of the early Leap. Monarch Liu Zihou denigrated reform as "rightism." To many, Hebei's capital, Shijiazhuang (Shi Family Village), still seemed worthy of its Cultural Revolution nickname, Zuojiazhuang (Left Family Village). Wugong responded, setting goals for 1980 of 1,500 catties of grain per mu and 150 of ginned cotton, promising 2,000 catties of grain per mu and 200 catties of cotton by 1985.[22]

National leaders Li Xiannian, Hua Guofeng, and Chen Yonggui continued to promote a Dazhai model of mobilizing collective labor for farmland construction and agricultural fundamentals (grain and cotton), slighting the new economic policies pressed by Deng Xiaoping and reform-minded associates that stressed money incentives, markets, diversification, and household efforts. In July 1978, after a National Conference on Capital Construction in Agriculture, Monarch Liu backed his patron Li Xiannian's approach, blaming difficulties on the "disruption and destruction of Lin Biao and the Gang of Four."[23] Household- and market-oriented reforms were enemies. Village party leaders in Zhengding, a model Dazhai county north of the Hebei capital, stormed into a high school, beat up teachers, stole their stored grain, and let the educators know that they were still "stinking intellectuals."[24]

But Deng Xiaoping was gaining power. On April 5, 1978 Beijing approved rehabilitation of 450,000 people branded as "rightists" in 1957 and 1958 and 300,000 more denounced from 1959 to 1964.[25] Hebei posthumously rehabilitated batches of officials persecuted to death in 1968. Since a black label attached itself to wives and descendants through the male line, those who had died in prison in Raoyang had their names cleared. Older survivors received pensions.

On August 21, all Hebei units down to the commune were ordered to assign the top or number 2 leader to trade and financial work.[26] Shriveled markets like Zoucun sprang to life. The illegal became legal. Villagers who had risked turning to the market had been way ahead of the state.

Wugong villagers assembled to discuss economic incentives and quota management. They saw poor Yanggezhuang moving up that way. The Geng leadership conceded to pressures from above and below to restore rewards for effort during the upcoming fall harvest.[27] The collective system, however, remained intact. Hebei and Wugong resisted the earthquake of reform.

Under pressure from reformers in Beijing, the Hebei provincial party committee declared in early October that former first secretary Lin Tie and his supporters, including reform pioneer Hu Kaiming, had been groundlessly labeled "absolutely unrepentant capitalist roaders" a decade earlier and should be exonerated and treated as comrades.[28] Yet Monarch Liu would not restore cleared victims to power.

Rooting out perpetrators of inhumanity was hampered by the unreformed political system. On October 22, 1978, the Hengshui prefecture party committee acknowledged abuse by a party secretary in Wuqiang county, southeast of Raoyang. In January 1977, another vice secretary had been sentenced to seven years for embezzlement and rape. But the culprit soon secured release on a medical pretext. In January 1978, before committing suicide, he murdered the parents who had reported him and shot three other relatives of the young woman he had raped. The deputy secretary who had released his crony was now punished, but with a mere two years of probation.[29] The party protected its own.

Yet, from beneath the rubble of the political earthquake, truths surfaced. Raoyang county officials acknowledged that water was increasingly scarce. Many hastily constructed wells ceased to function after just a few years. Raoyang slowed its drilling from an average of 1,415 wells per year in the 1973–75 peak period to 916 in the 1976–80 period. Technological and environmental factors began to enter the developmental calculus.

In another act of facing up to painful truth, Mao pallbearer Wang Guofan, the leader of Hebei's Paupers' Coop, was ousted in October, charged with corruption and waste and with persecuting to death in 1971 his village adversary, Du Kui. Again, no criminal penalty was imposed. The party declared that, given Wang's contributions to socialism, it was enough to make him a nonofficial. By contrast, the smallest theft of public property by an ordinary villager could be grounds for execution.

Geng Changsuo still backed the big collective assuring subsistence for all. He would hold Wugong back from seeking profit and entering the market. He stressed putting a solid economic floor under the vulnerable. Yet Geng also favored modernization policies of more pay for more work, utilizing the achievements of agroscience and technology, and economic diversification.

On November 2, 1978, *People's Daily* published a front-page article about Wugong. Geng, acknowledging miserable Yanggezhuang's sudden tripling of grain yields, stated that Wugong had returned to the "labor quota management system" of the precollectivization past. That cut the time and cost of irrigation. "Ever more material incentives" were needed. Still, Geng and his patrons at the provincial, prefectural, and county levels remained committed to the collective and were leery of reforms.

Our second visit to the village preceded the 35th anniversary of the 1943 Wugong coop. The celebration began on November 30, 1978. It promoted Hua Guofeng's policy of emulating Dazhai. Regional military officials from Hengshui and Raoyang and such notable Hebei leaders as forestry specialist Yao Fuheng of Houtun, Wang Yukun of Mao-blessed Nanwangzhuang, and Song Xingru of nearby Chang'an village were among the 3,000 attending. A movie was shown, a county arts troupe entertained, Wugong children performed in colorful costumes, and villagers had time off from work. But the new county party secretary, Yang Zhiyong, a former Wugong commune party secretary, was the highest-ranking speaker. News coverage was limited to the prefectural daily.[30]

Geng's theme was "only socialism can save China." Guests hailed the Dazhai model, spelled out at the 1970 North China Agricultural Conference, ignoring the fact that Wugong's grain yields had stagnated since 1974 and that cotton yields had fallen sharply. In contrast, Wugong's neighbors moved ahead rapidly by boosting sidelines and entering the market. The poorest villages were most enthusiastic about the reforms.

In December 1978, an antireform *Hengshui Daily* editorial celebrated Geng's conservative stance.[31] The "renegade and traitor" President Liu Shaoqi was blamed for Wugong's problems of the 1940s and 1950s. Jiang Qing's Gang of Four had falsely attacked Geng in 1972 for using capitalist methods to increase productivity. Patrons in Hengshui and Shijiazhuang used Wugong to legitimate their collective Dazhai model, the policy line of Chen Yonggui, Hua Guofeng, and Politburo patron Li Xiannian, then in conflict with the reform program of Deng Xiaoping and the market-oriented thrust from below.

As 1978 ended, Deng jettisoned the Dazhai model. It was a political disaster for both Chen Yonggui, who refused to join in or to accept the criticism of his model village, and for Premier Hua Guofeng, Chen's ally whose power was closely linked to the Dazhai model. Chen was isolated in Beijing under house arrest, never to return to Dazhai. Hebei monarch Liu Zihou also resisted Deng's reform agenda. When asked to criticize Hua's approach, Liu stood with Hua against Deng.[32] Wugong's patrons were losing power.

In December the party ratified the new agenda. Grain procurement prices were increased by 20 percent, with a 50 percent bonus for above-quota sales. Subsidies on fertilizer and insecticides for poor regions were also increased. The recently reestablished Agricultural Bank lowered interest rates to stimulate projects in poor regions. In the years 1978–84 agricultural subsidies rose from 5.5 to 30.5 billion yuan, reaching 20 percent of state revenues and contributing to a one-third increase in grain production. Adjustments in the price structure turned cotton from a crop that lost producers an average of 22.6 yuan on every mu tilled in 1976 into one that could produce an average profit per mu of more than 50 yuan.[33] Cotton production surged. China's output surpassed world-leading American production in six years, providing the raw material for a boom in the cotton clothing industry centered in rural factories. Apparel exports earned foreign exchange.

From 1978 to 1984 rural living standards rose substantially as China's agricultural production soared at the highest rates since recovery from the Great Leap Forward in the early 1960s. Rationing was phased out. Wugong's neighbor, Zoucun, a historic market center, burst with energy. By contrast, in conservative Wugong, builder Li Lu erected a state-owned general store. This white elephant was a cavernous monument to a bygone era.

Wugong's Dilemmas

When revisiting Wugong in late November 1978 we carried Professor Zuo's tome, framed as progress through class struggle. *The Battles of the Wugong People* had gone to press in June, before Deng Xiaoping dropped Dazhai.[34] As for the book, a party official vaguely "remembered" that some educated youngsters visited in 1975. Maybe, he conjectured, they wrote up the data and never told anyone. Truth remained a scarce commodity in Wugong. We sought out Zuo in Tianjin, aspiring writer Shi Guiying in Hengshui, four-cleanups investigator Cang Tong in Raoyang, Geng Huijuan and Hebei agriculture official Zhang Kerang in Shijiazhuang, the family of former Hebei party secretary Lin Tie, the Beijing actors who once lived in Wugong, the secretaries assigned to aid Geng, former Raoyang prisoners, and many others outside Wugong.

Wugong leaders feared burial by the reformist earthquake. They removed from the village office scrapbooks that contained clippings celebrating the new

socialist things of 1975 and 1976, and Wugong's 1976 participat
on the new paramount leader, Deng Xiaoping. Wugong created
while relying on old networks. Geng's daughter, Huijuan, head
zation bureau of the Hebei youth league in Shijiazhuang, and
Chaoke served as party secretary of Wugong commune.[35]

In the village, tremors began to be felt. Li Xiantao, who had led the
gong relief team to the Tangshan earthquake site and was imposed as leader of
team 2, was removed by the village center. The Southern Li took initiatives
and began to surge ahead.

Rehabilitations were ordered throughout the county. A memorial meeting
was held in late December for Dong Wenguang, a county official "persecuted
to death" in the 1970 "hit one, oppose three" campaign led by former county
secretary Li Chunyu. In Wangtun and Dasongjiazhuang villages in Dongliu-
man commune, 32 residents who had been denounced as Nationalist Party
operatives in 1968 were exonerated. Their files were burned. The poorest
received a bit of compensation for ten years of persecution.

Greater earthquakes were coming. On December 24, 1978, a commem-
orative gathering was held in Beijing for former defense minister Peng De-
huai, who had criticized Mao's famine-inducing Leap policies in July 1959.
Lin Tie, who fell when Beijing mayor Peng Zhen was sacked at the start of the
Cultural Revolution, attended the memorial service.[36] On January 17, 1979,
Peng Zhen was rehabilitated. The Peng Zhen / Lin Tie network was reviving.

Monarch Liu Zihou's Hebei network resisted reform policies and personnel changes. Wugong maintained its ties to the Liu camp. But Geng Changsuo
also reached out to a rehabilitated Lin Tie, Wugong's original patron. Despite
the reformist earthquake, political patronage was still vital. Revolution or
reform, Geng and his allies knew how to network within the entrenched
political system.

14 ❀ REFORM

Reform, contested and delayed in Hebei and in Wugong, promised wealth, normalcy, and ethical meaning. But the debris of the past and decisions among the national, provincial, and local leaderships, made any path ahead excruciatingly painful.

Reform and Its Enemies

While Hebei resisted reform, ever more villagers sought money-earning work beyond the reach of the collective in construction, peddling, crafts, and transport. In 1978 a fireworks factory opened in Raoyang's Dongcaolu village, famous for pyrotechnics since the Ming dynasty. Demand soared. Fireworks were sought for marriages, funerals, New Year celebrations, and opening of enterprises. The Cultural Revolution had ended legal manufacture of the explosives.[1] Still, Raoyang officials dragged their heels on reform.

On December 26, 1978, Raoyang leaders set aside only one day for commune party secretaries to discuss the Deng Xiaoping agenda. Not until February 1979 did county officials, pressured by the center, convene a three-week conference on distribution, sidelines, and other reform policies. Political campaigns were to be superseded by modernization. Officials were to "respect and protect" the decision-making rights of small production teams, to base remuneration on labor, to allow "labor contracts for groups" (bao chan dao zu), and to facilitate family sidelines (jiating fuye). The county leadership acknowledged that 27 villages were unusually poor, with collective annual incomes less than 60 yuan per capita. The sinews of the collective structure remained intact.

In February Monarch Liu was summoned to a provincial work conference to admit his errors. Since deposing Lin Tie as Hebei party secretary in 1966, Liu had purged loyalists of modernizer Lin, sending them to labor camps, prisons, torture, and death. Liu had promoted campaigns that spread vigilante violence and obstructed reform efforts. Liu apologized and announced "the rehabilitation of Lin Tie and other comrades." Liu, however, still ruled Hebei.

A county telephone conference in mid-March 1979 passed along

Beijing directives on creating a peaceful environment, checking revolutionary turmoil, and implementing the new economic policies. Commune-level officials were ordered to foster village conciliation by eliminating mistaken and negative class labels. Within days more than 1,200 cases had been reviewed and settled in Raoyang. All but six people had damning labels removed. Many descendants of landlords and rich peasants lost the black class designations of a prior generation.

While Raoyang officials, recalling that reformers invariably became political targets, remained cautious, villagers seized new economic opportunities. As early as autumn 1978, poorer Wugong commune villages reintroduced material incentives and bonuses in everything from hoeing weeds to harvesting. Throughout the prefecture others sowed less grain and grew more peanuts and other valuable oil-bearing crops.[2] The rug factory in nearby Gengkou brought in a technician from Jiangsu province to instruct loom workers on quality so more could be earned in exports.[3] The scuttlebutt was that modern skills abounded in southern ports.

Monarch Liu, however, protected officials who destroyed watermelons grown on household-managed collective plots in Zhengding county, north of the Hebei capital. Revolutionaries saw counterrevolution growing on those vines. The local party chief insisted that households could not, without official permission, turn land meant for cotton, a communist fundamental guaranteeing clothing for all, to economic crops, taken to mean wealth only for some. Reformers retorted that revolutionaries kept villagers impoverished.

Reformers did not challenge the system of arbitrary power. Tian Wanzhen, party secretary of Yincun commune in northeast Raoyang, kept a vicious dog. Many people with business at the commune office were bitten. In 1979 a harassed villager killed the cur. The local militia captured the culprit, hung him from a tree, lashed him, and assigned him to two days of labor without pay. The victim appealed to the county court to no avail. On his return, Tian had the poor soul strung up and beaten again. Infuriated, the villager appealed to the prefectural court. On returning, defeated, secretary Tian had the victim hung and savaged yet again. This target of cruelty appealed step by step all the way to Beijing. Each time, he was spurned by higher levels and whipped again in Raoyang. He then committed suicide by hanging. *People's Daily* sent an investigator. The internal report, showing it was better to be a dog in a party secretary's family than a man in a peasant family, led to a hearing. The penalty involved a horizontal job transfer. An innerparty directive ordered an end to beating people. But the new rule had little effect, since the party would not punish its own criminals.

Monarch Liu continued to back the journal *Hebei Culture,* which contended that socialist China did not have the problems that reformers insisted on addressing. The Hebei cultural apparatus, still controlled by Tian Jian, a Jiang Qing favorite, regarded criticism of the Cultural Revolution as treason.

Mao's revolutionary road was China's way; reform was the path of anti-Chinese foreigners, Tito and Khrushchev, leaders whom Mao had denounced. But reformers worked to prove they were the real patriots, initiating policies that would make China rich and powerful and improve the livelihood of the people. When the party center insisted on action against conservative culture czar Tian Jian and his followers, Monarch Liu had to convene meetings to criticize local handling of the watermelon and vicious-dog incidents.

Revolutionary icons were smashed. Writer Wang Lixin wrote about the rise and fall of Wang Guofan, Mao's favorite from Xipu village. Branding Wang Guofan a murderer, the investigators concluded that total power for local tyrants led to brutality against villagers and the rise of people like Wang's corrupt son. The writer called on the party to release its stranglehold on the throats of villagers.

The poorest villages in Wugong commune began to taste the fruits of reform. Yanggezhuang, for the first time in a quarter century, sent buyers to the northeast to purchase timber for furniture making and house building. But when party leaders from the ten villages in the commune discussed whether to decollectivize vegetable plots, only two opted to do so. Seven followed Wugong village in rejecting even a small opening toward a household economy. Boss Geng accepted the reform line of "ever more material incentives" only for the collective sector. Wugong agricultural yields stagnated. Wugong leaders feared that reversing revolutionary socialism would unleash immoral and destructive forces. Geng's rejectionism was conveyed in two spring 1979 articles bearing his name: "Only Socialism Can Save China" and "Do Things According to the Theory of Dialectics."[4]

The Hebei leadership tried to limit reform. It announced in April that household plots could be collectively or individually managed. In other words, collective management was fine. Collectivized household vegetable plots in Hengshui, Cangzhou, and Baoding prefectures remained. Hebei governor Liu Zihou visited Wugong on June 9. He was greeted by Geng Changsuo and Song Xingru, who led Raoyang's other model village. Both backed Liu. But his influence was waning. It would be Liu's final visit.

With the Hebei party trying to conserve the collective, Zoucun villagers working in the market were compelled to reimburse the collective 1.5 to 2 yuan per day for labor missed, well above what the collective paid its most productive workers. Nonetheless, growing numbers of villagers bought out of the collective. Several Zoucun residents earned more than 1,000 yuan buying and selling, compared with collective annual incomes of 120 to 130 yuan. Market-oriented Zoucun rapidly overtook revolutionary Wugong to become the commune's most prosperous village.

As seen from Zoucun, "they" (Wugong villagers) prospered in the Mao era because of connections, while all that benefited "us" (ordinary folk) had

been denounced. Seen from impoverished villages like Zoucun and Yangge-zhuang, socialism was a polarizing system. While socialism locked up villagers in the countryside and kept them from moving freely to better jobs, with reform a trickle turned into a flood of villagers fleeing the collective. Like freed serfs, they styled themselves *ziliu ren,* people who belonged to themselves, not to the lords of the manor. Two cooks at the long-stagnant Zoucun market went far south to Guangzhou, where wages were much higher. Many more took to peddling or found construction jobs closer to home. Some villagers hung portraits of the rich, verdant south in their homes.

On December 26, Liu Zihou was ousted. With ties to patron and party elder Li Xiannian, Liu was transferred to Beijing in January 1980 as deputy director of the State Planning Commission. Liu's network continued to exercise great influence. His former subordinates were entrenched.[5] Reform continued to face formidable foes.

At the end of 1979, Xu Shukuan, Geng's wife of more than five decades and a staunch believer in the collective, passed away. More than 3,000 people, including leaders from Hengshui, Raoyang, and the commune, attended her funeral. The wailing was deafening, the procession to the cemetery a grand moment. Party secretary Yang Tong eulogized her.

Right after the New Year, Wugong's articulate Li Zhongxin took charge of building a water tower. No more would villagers shoulder pole water at dawn and dusk. No more would women squat at outdoor pumps in every kind of weather to wash clothes. Running water for cooking was a delight. Watches, previously denounced by revolutionaries as feudal, proof that one did not engage in manual labor, became popular. All three teams bought 22-inch color Hitachi television sets. But taxes made the sets more expensive than a new house.

Pictures at an Exhibition

In 1980 a county exhibition hall honoring 80-year-old Geng Changsuo opened in Wugong. Upon entering, visitors faced a huge portrait of Mao. At opposite ends of the hall two traditional paintings of large cedars framed the exhibit. The exhibit showed Geng joining the party in 1944, with the original coop members, with the oil press built for the land-pooling group using materials taken from his own home, receiving awards from the state, and visiting the Soviet Union in 1952. The narrative pitted revolutionaries against landlord brutes. Geng's lieutenants were introduced, but there was nothing on leaders who had crossed Geng: pioneer Xu Yizhou (the old militia leader), Wei Lianyu (the deputy coop leader prior to his fall in 1952), and former party secretary Xu Chuan (who had attacked Geng during the Cultural Revolution). Coop founder and whistle-blower Geng Xiufeng went unmentioned.

One corner of the exhibit featured internationalism, including photos of us. A diorama illuminated by push-button lights delineated factories and square fields. A wall mural imagined a modern future; surveying a blueprint of a new Wugong were a student and worker (both women) along with a white-shirted official, a farmer with a hoe, and a tractor driver, all youthful. Airplanes sprayed vast rectangular fields. Giant tractors harvested wheat by combine while sprinklers irrigated fields. Villagers lived in four- and five-story apartment buildings. Towering over all was the leader, Geng Changsuo. But all across China, the cult of personality, the big collective, and class struggle were losing out. By fall 1980, the exhibit was closed. The hall was converted to industrial use.

The Cultural Revolution–era Wugong narrative no longer impressed power holders. After the rehabilitation of former president Liu, who had been persecuted to death in the Cultural Revolution, Geng asked that we not write that he had criticized Liu, the only time Geng ever asked that we not tell the truth. What we should say, he suggested, was that Mao was fooled by Chen Boda, Kang Sheng, Lin Biao, and Jiang Qing. Still, Geng suspected that President Liu had led the 1953 attack on the Wugong big coop. If Liu's errors really were small, Geng averred, the record should be set right. Geng, who worked hard at knitting ties to leaders, was upset not to be invited to President Liu's posthumous rehabilitation ceremony.

Geng worried about villagers bowled over by modernization. While sharing the popular joy at running water, he shook his head at the vision of multistory apartments. Geng was not against the modern. He sought a railroad for the community and had long pushed mechanization. He had nothing against material comforts. He brought back a phonograph and a camera from the Soviet Union and welcomed television. Since his wife died, he even indulged himself. Seniors customarily relaxed stern moral prescriptions. Geng lit up a cheap cigarette and jibed at reformist claims that smoking was harmful. He noted in self-mocking Maoist jargon that it would not do for a patriot to quit smoking. Given the high state tax on cigarettes, a patriot should put his tax contribution to the state before self. Joking aside, Geng was upset by reform.

In June 1980 Professor Zuo told us he wished he could delete the slanders against President Liu contained in his recent book. He would also cut the material on the "new creations" of the Cultural Revolution. It should have been obvious that illiterates could not run schools. It made no sense that Dazhai, or any single model, could be uniformly copied in as diverse a land as China. Furthermore, his book had not looked at cost factors. A health system had to be assessed in terms of costs and actual services. Perhaps the old system of special appropriations for rural families with sudden health bills really was more sensible. Professor Zuo's 1980 remarks, like his 1978 book, hewed to the line. The political system made it difficult to speak independently.

Drought

Drought in 1980 and 1981, with Hengshui prefecture the epicenter, was the most severe since the 1943 famine. Some villagers fled illegally to cities. Many scavenged and begged for food. Between August 1979 and June 1980 no rain fell. Of the 6,400 lakes and ponds, 5,200 dried up; the water table fell on average another 30 to 50 meters. Of the 36,000 wells, 3,800 went bone dry, while 14,000 more soon held less than half their former water. The drought, which continued into 1982, cost Hebei $1.4 billion, including $860 million in crop losses.[6] The greatest damage was in the province's southeast, scorched by a hot southern wind. Raoyang, located in northwest Hengshui, was not among the hardest hit. Still, summer and fall harvests dropped, and it was declared a "disaster" area. In 65 of the worst-hit villages in the prefecture, people stripped trees of leaves for food.

In December 1980 the World Health Organization reported "the worst drought in 37 years in Hebei province," detailing malnutrition among Hengshui children.[7] It also found an efficient government relief effort. In 1980, 14 million people in Hebei received government rations. The authorities rushed 18.6 million yuan in aid to the prefecture, including a 10.5 million yuan relief fund and 50,000 tons of grain. In March 1981, the People's Republic for the first time requested international assistance through the United Nations disaster relief coordinator.

China sought 1,600,000 tons of grain, 10,000 tons of cooking oil, 2,000 tons of powdered milk, 4,400,000 padded coats, 1,500,000 padded quilts, 20,000 tons of seed, antibiotics, and 200,000 tons of chemical fertilizer. The aid, which arrived after the disaster had passed, was far less than the $1 billion worth requested or the $700 million United Nations estimate of needs. Twenty-one countries and five intergovernmental agencies pledged $25 million. UNICEF provided vitamins, Canada, Argentina, and the United States wheat, and Japan and the European Community powdered milk.[8]

The drought lowered Hebei's 1981 grain output by more than 5.1 billion catties from the 1979 level to just 30.4 billion catties.[9] With state aid of 400 grams of grain a day (1,400 calories), few starved. International investigators were shown the worst places, reverse Potemkin villages. In contrast to the revolutionary era, when statistics were Brobdingnagian, reformers proffered Lilliputian numbers to qualify for free goods from international donors. The reform state also seemed interested in displaying how international openness helped the most disadvantaged. Hengshui took a United Nations loan at 1 percent interest through the International Fund for Agricultural Development. Officials told the World Bank that China could best use the money not for well-drilling equipment—which China could produce, if at far lower quality—but for chemical fertilizers that would save on the high cost of commercial credits for importing fertilizer.

North China water crisis was brought on by revolutionary drilling
ns that treated water as a limitless and free good. The number of
vells had zoomed from 100,000 to more than 2.3 million between
nd 1979. Short-term gains augured a long-term crisis. Wugong re-
no international aid, but it was given 370,000 yuan from the center to
construct a national standard power station, the only one in its prefecture. It
was up and running in seven months. With power-driven irrigation, Wugong
harvested a credible 1980 crop and a record yield in 1981. Revolution or
reform, Wugong benefited from its networks.

Zoucun's Rebirth

The Zoucun periodic market came alive. Before reform several hundred buyers met a few sellers of vegetables, cooked meats, and such handicrafts as straw
mats and baskets. Our presence at the moribund event nearly created a riot in
spring 1978. But 4,000 people gathered every five days by 1980. Twice that
number arrived during New Year.[10] Beginning in 1980 above-quota grain was
legally sold for the first time since 1953. Villagers also bought furniture,
books, equipment, and consumer specialties. Snake oil touters promised to
cure all. Life was enhanced by bolts of colorful cloth, lounge chairs for the
elderly, ice cream, and spots to meet friends, family, and one's betrothed.
Hawkers, squatting before painted open tents, displayed rat poisons and
traps. Raoyang was infested. Pitchmen piled up rat carcasses. Some dropped
live rats into crushing steel traps. Onlookers nodded approvingly as the rats
writhed. Not far away, at the top of East Street, goats and pigs were on sale.

By 1983 eight to ten thousand people crowded Zoucun on market day.
Before the New Year, the throng exceeded 50,000. Scores of small outdoor
food stalls and tented tea houses thrived on the edge of the market. A dusty
sales lot held two hundred to three hundred braying livestock. Squatting
elderly men peddled homemade whips, harnesses, and leads.

Vegetable purveyors on North Street mixed with craftsmen offering funeral accessories. The senses were suffused by tantalizing smells, sounds, and
sights. Colorfully clothed girls giggled and darted off at the sight of ambling
boys.

South Street featured cooked and uncooked meats. In household courtyards just off South and East Streets, villagers dressed up for color photo-
graphs in front of painted backdrops, some suggesting exotic southern locales.
An advertising photo showed a fat baby boy naked from the waist down.
South Street was also home to massage specialists, bone manipulators, and
dentists displaying mountains of teeth.

West Street featured a woodworking shop, coffins, wooden farm tools, and
wagons, as well as old and new furniture. Antique chests that once graced the
homes of local elites were on sale. A large section displayed cloth, including

synthetic fabrics, and numerous stalls with machine-made clothes, primarily for women. Seamstresses, many from distant cities, took orders for custom-made clothes.

By 1980 the Bank of Agriculture for the first time provided loans to enterprising villagers. Five Bank of Agriculture branches opened in Raoyang in four historic market centers, Yincun, Liuchu, Chengguan, and Guanting, and in one politically favored village, Wugong. Dwarfing all other structures, the bank helped revitalize the village.

In June 1980, 50 miles northwest of Raoyang, North China's largest medicinal market, which had been closed since the Cultural Revolution, re-opened in Anguo county. Healing herbs earned enormous sums in both the national and international markets.

Yet opposition to reform among elders was strong amont military families in anti-Japanese base areas. In addition to fears of losing their privileged position, such patriotic families felt that reform brought chaos, crime, and alien ways. Alarmed elders claimed vindication when Raoyang reported a 50 percent increase in crime during the second half of 1979.

Hundreds of Raoyang county military families were disadvantaged by the loss of a son's or husband's labor. In line with national policy, the county guaranteed army-dependent families a living standard equal to the local average. Still, military families fell behind. Young soldiers could not build a cash nest egg to win a proper bride. Soon, retired local officials stopped receiving their monthly pensions on a regular basis. Rural patriots experienced a jarring transvaluation of values, a reversal in which the "good," the martyrs of socialism and military families, and the "evil," the practitioners of wheeling and dealing in the market, no longer received their just deserts.

Rehabilitation

Reformers sought to heal old wounds and motivate people. Raoyang investigated more than 2,000 cases involving black class labels. Of 622 pre–Cultural Revolution era cases reviewed, 564 were cleared. In the 1,600 cases involving the Cultural Revolution era, investigations led to the "rehabilitation" (ping-fan) of 1,114 people. Back salary cash awards for those wrongly accused totaled 35,594 yuan. At less than 35 yuan on average, it was a pittance. Yet apology, reparations, and restoration set an important tone. Political labels or "hats" were removed from 1,236 of the 1,241 "bad elements" whose cases also were reviewed, and an additional 4,491 sons and daughters of people once classified as "landlords" or "rich peasants" were removed from those pariah castes. Of 93 people said to have been tortured during the Cultural Revolution, including some who attempted or committed suicide, 77 were cleared.

The county party was supposed to identify those responsible for persecutions and to penalize beneficiaries of vigilante political campaigns. Fifty-two younger officials, most of them commune-level "helicopters," were demoted. One hundred and eighty were found to have committed "major mistakes" during the Cultural Revolution: 20 county and commune officials, 69 village cadres, and 91 ordinary commune members. County investigators found that 23 people had tortured others, destroyed property, or looted goods. Twenty-one then lost their jobs. Two remained under review. To some, the investigations seemed like justice. Others saw them as a cover-up, scapegoating a few to protect the well connected.

In Wugong, aspiring writer Shi Guiying's father, who had told the truth about the catastrophic Leap, was rehabilitated. The forced labor corps of "black elements," including Li Peishen, Li Jinzhua, Xu Jichang, and Li Heiyan, was disbanded. Reform promised normalcy.

At the age of 53, "landlord" Li Maoxiu, his back badly misshapen by prolonged physical abuse, was notified that he was now an ordinary villager. Li shaved his hair to the scalp, as local elders historically did. When he spoke, his long slender hands kept moving. Maoxiu and his son, Wei, tinkered with machinery. Inspired by a newspaper story, Maoxiu produced an aluminum-iron alloy with a resistance capacity of 1,100 degrees centigrade. Cutting the tops off two 20-gallon oil drums to make a smelter, he began producing high-resistance metal plates. Small contracts were won with factories in Tianjin, the competitive advantage being widely accessible cheap materials. Li's open-air "factory" was squeezed between team 3's now legal popsicle sideline and the old donkey stable. The village west end was astir with small, collective, and semiprivate market-oriented enterprises, and its households surged still further ahead of the rest of the village.

Not so Li Maoxiu. His metal plates were declared substandard. His operation closed. Some speculated that state inspectors were defending inefficient state-owned enterprises. Others thought that local officials had had second thoughts about a former "landlord," whatever the rhetoric of rehabilitation. Local wisdom held that the political system had not fundamentally changed. An entrenched group still took care of its own. Officials seemed self-servers blocking the rise of villagers, not just of Maoxiu.

Boss Geng maintained ties to power. An award ceremony on December 28, 1979, in Beijing's Great Hall of the People honored the 79 year old and Raoyang's other model, Song Xingru, among 340 model workers nation-wide.[11] Geng was presented as a deserving survivor of a heroic generation. The national women's association honored Song with a major award in late 1979 and featured her in the English edition of its monthly periodical.[12]

The Wugong mythos could be reinvented. A 1980 exhibition in the national historical museum in Beijing identified only two peasants for 1940s contributions, Li Shunda and Geng Changsuo. Reform narratives stressed that Li's Shanxi village, Xigou, had survived the famine of 1943 and prospered by doing sideline work. Wugong also had risen in the late 1940s based on a sideline economy featuring rope and peanut oil. But during the collective era, its mythos passed over the role of the market in villagers' salvation in the 1943 famine.

In summer 1980 Geng's Beijing granddaughter visited. Han Peng, a political activist at college, was drawn to reform and openness. But many villagers mocked reformers like party secretary Hu Yaobang, who was nicknamed Hu Naobang, the Hu who roils the country. Han Peng visited a grandaunt in Yanggezhuang. The aunt had cataracts and was virtually blind. The house was shabby, her clothes were old, and she had almost no possessions. To Peng, the old lady's poverty seemed an indictment of revolution.

Although some grumbled, villagers grabbed reform opportunities. Improved transport and market opening won cash, brought in goods that had long disappeared, and made the economy far more efficient, despite corruption. Geng family members now dove into the market. Han Peng's uncle purchased a motorbike to transport goods. Households tended more chickens and raised more pigs. Food and clothing improved. New truck drivers, however, could get licenses faster with bribes than with driving lessons. Accidents became ubiquitous. The innocent victims of China's economic rise would be legion.

Boss Geng reached out again to his former patron, modernizer Lin Tie, who was a Hebei delegate to the National People's Congress in February 1979. Lin then revisited Geng's home, arriving by car with his wife and his physician. Wugong erased from its political narrative ties to the fallen North China party head, Li Xuefeng, and boasts of Cultural Revolution achievements.

Nevertheless, Geng and the Wugong party remained leery of thoroughgoing reform, as did Hebei and Hengshui authorities. Provincial officials emphasized the threat of imperialism and maintained warm ties with North Korea. The threat to Pyongyang, the press kept reporting, was from South Korea, Japan, and the United States. Military vigilance was necessary. Hebei highlighted national security, warning of spies from Taiwan. Such talk legitimated the entrenched dictatorial system as patriotism and put a damper on openness.

Contracts

Well after many other provinces had decollectivized, distributing land for household cultivation and auctioning collective property, the Hebei party resisted. In spring 1980, 60 percent of Hebei teams merely utilized long-term work point incentive schemes to energize collectives. Just 3 percent opted for *da baogan*, a contracting of major tasks to the household that eliminated collective work points and collective organization of labor. On May 4, 1981, the Agricultural Work Department of the Hebei party issued guidelines on "agricultural responsibility systems," still insisting that "the collective economy is our nation's firm basis for carrying out agricultural modernization."[13]

The state center then removed two foot-dragging Hebei governors. A visit to Hebei in August 1981 by reformer Hu Yaobang, who replaced Hua Guofeng as party chairman, showed that the center meant business.[14] Only then did Hebei villagers begin to divide land use rights, with each person receiving an average of 1.9 mu, just under one-third of an acre. Typically, a household received one to two acres in the form of eight to 12 scattered parcels. The land was leased, with the village government retaining ownership and a claim to a share of the harvest. Large rectangular fields, the pride of collectivizers, disappeared.

By spring 1982, following the appointment of a Deng Xiaoping ally as Hebei party secretary, 60 percent of villages implemented da baogan, that is, the distribution of collective fields and the leasing of land to households. The following spring the number reached 96 percent. In response to price incentives, average annual net grain marketing then rose from 40 million metric tons during 1976 to 1978 to 77 million metric tons in the years 1982–84.[15] This time rising grain output translated into cash incomes.

After the 1982 fall harvest Hengshui prefecture, pressured from above, ordered village leaders to adopt the household contract system or lose office. When Houtun village, the Dazhai pacesetter, resisted, its leader, Trees Yao Fuheng, was fired. Houtun's prior success had rested on collectivized trees and shrubs. A special team now was set up to manage trees, much like a local government providing a public service. By January 1983 collective animals and tools were contracted to households. By March the fields were redistributed, and the village considered how to divide up the trees.

Worst-off villages dropped collectives first. In Wugong commune, three of the four poorest villages, Dongsongjiazhuang, Nanguanzhuang, and Yuanzi, with 1979 per capita collective incomes of just 70, 74, and 80 yuan, respectively, decollectivized in spring 1981. The only commune village resisting household farming in spring 1982 was Wugong.

In Raoyang, by mid-1980, 98 percent of tillers were experimenting with a quota responsibility system. The county was praised by the provincial daily as a leader in this limited reform.[18] Only about 10 percent of the county's 197 villages initiated da baogan, household contracting. The county was ordered by higher levels to summon commune and village party leaders in August 1981 to speed up decollectivization. By spring 1982 household contracting reached 90 percent.

In 1981 in drought-stricken Wugong commune, per capita incomes plummeted to 37 yuan in Nanguanzhuang and 41 in Yuanzi. But after the 1982 fall harvest, ten of the 11 villages with prior per capita incomes below 70 yuan soared to average incomes of 220 yuan. In a single year, two villages surpassed favored Wugong. Many villages in that first year of shifting to the household economy saw their per capita incomes triple, quadruple, or more (see table 14.1).

Table 14.1   Per capita income of villages in Wugong commune (in yuan)

	1981 Per capita distributed collective income	1982 Per capita total income (includes household income)
Wugong	257	279
Zoucun	100	250
Nanguanzhuang	37	283
Dongsongjiazhuang	76	285
Yanggezhuang	65	250
Wangqiao	60	258
Songqiao	57	240
Gaoqiao	86	242
Yuanzi	41	220
Gengkou	104	228

Stories spread about the newly rich. In Raoyang county 40 households were said to have net incomes of 5,000 yuan in 1982, 30 more exceeded 8,000 yuan, and 25 were classified as 10,000-yuan households, the state-touted yardstick for rural "millionaires." Reform allowed the commune's chronically poor villages to reach revolutionary Wugong's income level in only two years.

Insecurities

Elders used to the collective worried about crime and their own welfare. County propaganda focused on Li Guoluan of Matun village in Jingtang commune, who beat a neighbor to death. Local authorities then staged a grisly execution of Li.[17] In March 1982 the county acknowledged that 34 Raoyang villages had serious security problems. Ignoring the rising crime of the late Mao era, conservatives contended that reform brought disorder.

In spring and summer 1982 Raoyang county leaders organized meetings on public safety and crime. Special crime-fighting units were set up, and a call went out to crack down on illegal acts. The county secretary criticized wasting public funds for gluttonous eating and drinking sprees, using "backdoor" political influence to place sons and daughters in lucrative jobs, and spending public funds to build private homes. The warnings had no teeth. In June 1982 a county tax office was set up to combat tax evasion, but it had little impact.

Zhang Shuguang, a county native about to assume the post of Hebei governor, returned to Raoyang in early February 1982 and convened an "old cadres" conference to reassure old-timers. Within days Raoyang orderd that retired officials be given annual physical examinations. Forums were organized so that elder revolutionaries could be heard. A major concern was that the county might renege on monthly pay packets. In an effort to win the support of old revolutionaries, the county ordered that retired officials should be visited during the lunar New Year, helped out with household chores, and presented with New Year gifts.

Conservatives scapegoated cultural openness, said to erode bedrock Chinese values. Nativistic warnings about "spiritual pollution" touched a responsive chord. In early September, top county officials met to study speeches by conservative spokesmen Hu Qiaomu, Deng Lichun, and Hu Sheng at the recent Twelfth Party Congress. To combat a "bourgeois liberalization" said to be infecting China, county leaders suddenly discoverd Confucian ethics. Female party members were praised for exemplary filial conduct (xiao). Zhang Xiangling of Tunli village was cited as an inspirational model.[18] Her example led a young woman in Shandong province to move to Raoyang to become Zhang's "adopted daughter." Together they would respect the elderly and combat the alien and polluting.[19]

The April 1982 Hebei people's congress still emphasized "upholding socialist collectivization." If the bourgeois way of life was not defeated by class struggle, then pornography and juvenile delinquency would spread. Individual interests had to be subordinated to state interests. Families should not be permitted to build homes or burial mounds without permission. Hengshui delegates denounced household responsibility systems for dispersing land, undermining management and rendering large machines useless. Conservatives warned that stressing economic results and cost accounting detracted from a survivalist priority of amassing collective labor and funds to drill more wells. The province continued large-scale corvée labor to repair the works built to control the Hai River system.

Wugong Reforms

Wugong's collective sideline economy lost subsidized ties to state factories. Gross collective sideline income plunged from 420,000 yuan in 1979 to 127,000 in 1982, with collective sidelines accounting for only 14 percent of collective income, the lowest level in 21 years. When sweetheart contracts to state-owned enterprises in Shijiazhuang lapsed, the yarn spinning factories in each of the three teams closed. By 1982 all three team-level pig collectives converted to household sties. With collective sidelines in disarray, villagers sought noncollective income. They saw neighbors doing better that way.

Beginning in fall 1981 Wugong leaders visited pacesetting reform villages. But Wugong did not rush to reform. Only in October 1982, pressured from above, did Wugong discuss reform in both the sideline and agricultural sectors. Initially, all three teams resisted decollectivization. Geng Xiufeng begged Boss Geng not to give up on the possibilities of the collective ideal. But a beleaguered 82-year-old Geng Changsuo could no longer block reforms.

Collective sidelines, including rope making, were shut down. After the fall harvest, teams 1 and 2 adopted da baogan. Team 3 held out. Village party secretary Yang Tong, a west-ender, told us of "troublemakers" among the party veterans in his team 3 who seemed to delight in disrupting Geng Chang-suo's plans. Seniors in the Xu lineage who had long attacked Geng and re-sented team 1's domination of the village party organization once controlled by the Xus wanted to demonstrate team 3's superior revolutionary credentials. But by spring 1983, team 3 also agreed to decollectivize.

Reform provided each person with 1.4 mu of land, approximately one acre per household, and carried a responsibility to fulfill crop quotas. Three-year contracts fixed grain deliveries to the state. At first only 7 percent of the land was reserved for unrestricted use. The party determined the crop to be grown on all other land. But labor and markets were freed.[20] At home courtyards were turned into profitable vegetable or medicinal herb gardens.

In spring 1983, all across southern Hebei small family groups, including young children and elders, energetically worked strips of land, but many now found time to work on other sideline activities. The earth still lay parched. Clouds of fine dust swirled. It had not rained or snowed all winter. The serpentine Hutuo River was like a desert of smooth white sand.

In Shijiazhuang, Raoyang, and Wugong, officials now praised reform and criticized Soviet-style collective farming. "We did not meet the needs of the people during collectivization and the Great Leap Forward in the 1950s." Yesterday's touters of revolution insisted that villagers had always lacked en-thusiasm for collective work, because labor was poorly managed and there was staggering waste and inefficiency. Collectives may have facilitated recovery from war and chaos in the 1950s, but "in the past, filling your belly [chi bao] seemed enough; now people insist on eating well [chi hao] and more." For years pork had been in short supply. Now Hebei exported it to Poland, and Chinese still ate more meat. Indeed, during 1978 to 1984, as reform gained momentum, agricultural productivity soared and consumption of meat, fish, and eggs as well as grain rose sharply.[21] Dramatically improved quality went along with quantity and variety. Now "people are going after money," a pro-vincial leader said approvingly in 1983. Some folk rose by investing in small-scale private sideline enterprises. A provincial official echoed paramount leader Deng Xiaoping: "There is no way to move ahead unless some rich people take the lead." Dynamic enterprise capable of market competition would propel China, not collective labor.

The small and flexible rose. Revolutionary China had produced giant trac-tors of 75 horsepower and more. In 1983, 15 Wugong households bought, at 3,800 yuan each, small 12-horsepower walking tractors. Households obtained

21 small threshers, 13 diesel engines, and 300 sprayers. With the land distributed to households, Stalinist gigantomania ebbed.

Reform made superfluous the command economy apparatus. Within a year of decollectivization, Wugong cut the number of paid officials from 46 to 15. Remaining officials received low fixed salaries, in most cases 20 yuan per year, which forced them to engage in household production. The return to the household economy made credible the jest that socialism had been a long and painful transition from capitalism to capitalism. What actually returned were some of the dynamic efficiencies of rural China, for many centuries a world leader in both agricultural production and rural industry.[22]

In winter 1982–83 Wugong auctioned three-year rights to most collective enterprises. The still powerful village government was owner, leaser, and arbiter. In 1983, in addition to land contracts signed by the 741 households, 55 contracts were signed for specialized tasks, with a limit of one contract per household. By the end of 1983, 365 households, more than half of the village, had entered into special village and team contracts.

The Wugong fruit orchard was divided into three parts, with 12 people responsible for each. In competitive bidding, the lease price rose from the prior year's gross income of 16,000 yuan to 26,100. More than 150 people bid. In addition to producing fruit, the new manager could farm the three mu of land within it, growing medicinal herbs, sunflowers, beans, peanuts, yams, melons, and vegetables. The winner turned the money-losing orchard into a bonanza, building underground storage and saving prized fruit for sale during the high-priced winter season. Beijing residents would no longer be limited to turnips and cabbages in winter. Reform brought income surges and greater autonomy for those with the skills and energy to seize the new opportunities. Both producers and consumers benefited from market resurgence.

The village's bicycle-repair shop, welding shop, electricity system, water tower, restaurant, rope-making shop, candle shop, carpentry, tailoring, and grain processing were all leased out. Team 3's large plastic bag factory employed 40 workers, 20 of them members of contracting families, while 20 others were low-paid hired laborers eager to earn hard cash. Incomes rose. So did economic differentiation, outraging villagers accustomed to a leveling notion of equity.

Wugong's three deep pump wells, penetrating 300 to 550 meters, were contracted to two villagers. They irrigated fields at fixed fees. Meters measured electricity consumption. Between March and July 1983 no electricity was available on Mondays and Thursdays. Brownouts were nothing new, but with household income dependent on electric power, families squawked.

Wugong's 55-mu experimental plot, the village's best land, was contracted out. Villagers specialized. Ten guaranteed to cultivate specified strains of wheat and corn to provide high-quality seeds for villagers. The village provided fertilizer and insecticide and plowed the experimental fields. Contracting households retained the surplus above the quota. With economic crops no longer treated as counterrevolutionary, team 3 contracted hundreds of square meters of good land for mushroom cultivation. Wherever possible, families shifted to economic crops and out of the grain and cotton crops that the state had long imposed. With specialization and a division of labor, wealth grew.

Still, village-level political power remained formidable. Many services continued to be run as "unified management" (tongyi guanli). Administrators controlled large machinery. Most plowing, sowing, irrigation, threshing, and fertilizer supply were at first done by the village and performed by salaried workers. Land improvement, including leveling fields and drilling wells, and the purchase and supply of insecticide and fertilizer, also remained official functions. Most Hebei villages maintained only three such functions. Wugong kept 12. Yet the power of local officials ebbed. The 19 militia members were cut to two part-time guards. As in the past, households did their own crop-watching. Wugong had begun to reform.

Population Control

Reform relaxed the grip of the state in many realms. An exception was birth control. Hebei had pioneered in reducing birth rates from 32.9 per thousand in 1965 to 26.7 in 1970 and 15.5 by 1977. In 1978 the state made birth control a national priority. With fewer people, there would be more wealth per capita. By fall 1979 nearly 1,500 couples in Raoyang had pledged to have no more than one child, and the county was recognized as a pacesetter.[23] Wugong was cited twice in late 1979 by the national women's association for its birth control work.[24]

In 1980, 27-year-old Wang Pengju became chair of the Wugong women's association. Her daughter Junji was born on March 24, 1980. A few weeks later, Pengju was back administering birth control and day care. Like all village households who had their first child in 1980, save four strong-willed holdouts among the 67 targeted families, Pengju pledged to honor the one-child family.

Wugong provided incentives. Couples who agreed not to exceed one child received a bonus of five work points per month for the health care of the child, as well as an adult's grain ration and preference in schooling, housing, and medical care. When new homes were built, one-child families were allocated the same amount of space as two-child families. Families whose single child was a girl panicked. Only a son could be counted on to care for parents in old age in a rural society that lacked pensions. Only a son continued the patrilineal family line, thereby honoring parents and ancestors. Families with no sons sought to evade the one-child limit.

County leaders brutally implemented the 1980 birth control campaign. Fearing their careers would be hurt by too many births, they ordered the most obviously pregnant women — third trimester pregnancies — picked up. Those lacking proof of permission to give birth were subjected to forced abortions at makeshift facilities. All doctors, experienced or not, were compelled to perform the procedure. Dozens of women fled and gave birth in the homes of kin living elsewhere. Villagers described the pregnant women as frightened mice fleeing killer cats. One distraught husband whose wife died in a forced abortion took blood revenge. He stalked the son of the commune party secretary and slashed the boy's throat, killing him. When the wife of a neighboring party leader gave birth to twin sons, the gossip mill insisted that the privileged had access to fertility drugs. Even though villagers agreed that China had a population crisis, arbitrary implementation made people feel like victims.

By 1983 all women of childbearing age had to have regular pregnancy checkups. Raoyang routinely aborted any unauthorized pregnancy and sterilized every woman who gave birth to a second child. Of the 1,712 women of childbearing age in Wugong commune, fully 752 (and 14 men) were sterilized.

New Models

Raoyang began to search for domestic markets, foreign investment, and foreign markets. Despite its proximity to the port of Tianjin, ties to conservative leaders had long combined with a weak productive base and primitive transportation and communication to cause Raoyang to lag. But the county finally shut down its inefficient state chemical fertilizer and silk thread factories in late 1981 and contracted to export 100 tons of peanuts a year to Japan in late 1982. The local press bragged that Japanese were addicted to Raoyang roasted peanuts.[25]

In the early 1980s Wugong village began to tout people like mink breeder Qiao Qingshan of the east end and chicken king Li Qingji from the west end as new-style models of business success. Ironically, economic model Qiao, a 37-year-old party member and army veteran, was in the political doghouse. His wife, Bai Kui, had already borne a daughter, but the couple desperately wanted a son. In February and April 1981 Bai did not show up for the bimonthly pregnancy test. The authorities insisted that the pregnancy end. Bai denied she was pregnant. Two months later she again missed her test. When officials demanded an abortion, she fled to her mother's home in another village. In early autumn she gave birth to a boy. Over time, the state came to accept a tacit two-child policy for households without a son. Still, those whose second child was a girl resisted the birth control police.[26]

Despite his political problems, in August 1981 Qiao Qingshan got a 1,700-yuan loan from the Agricultural Bank to buy 15 minks, three male and 12 female. It was the kind of opportunity that his kinsman, humiliated Qiao Yong, was denied in the 1960s when Tigress Xu degraded him. By late spring 1982, Qingshan's breeder minks had 58 offspring. Net income in year 1 was 600 yuan. Raising minks was a smelly but profitable business.

In 1981 Qiao also started making rope at home like his father and grand-father before him. He earned 100 yuan from rope in 1981 and 300 yuan in 1982. Because their second child broke birth control limits, the Qiaos for-feited land. It seemed a small price to pay. Indeed, after the fall harvest, Qiao stopped farming to concentrate on business. The state's grain quota was met by market purchases.

With reform came travel and knowledge, previously blocked by controls that locked rural people within their villages. When he started his rope busi-ness Qiao searched for raw material as far off as Tianjin and Jinan, the capital of Shandong. He read, inquired, and visited a successful mink farm 100 miles away. Travel, openness, exchange, and knowledge joined to expand wealth. In once destitute Yanggezhuang, they led to a transfer of suitable seeds for their salty and alkaline soil that produced bumper crops of peanuts and water-melons. The resurgence of market and mobility brought wealth.

Qiao's furs were purchased by a Hengshui state enterprise and sold abroad. Success brought imitators. In 1982 Qiao sold six breeder minks to Zoucun villager entrepreneurs, five in Anping county and four in Shenxian county. Wugong's Li Zhigan also started raising minks. Li's household income sky-rocketed from under 1,000 yuan in 1981 to 2,300 in 1982 and 4,000 yuan in 1983. Other villagers soon left farming for furs. The surge in mink farming, however, posed the problem of market glut and falling prices.

Another new-style model, Li Qingji, who graduated from junior high in 1958, became Wugong's premier chicken farmer. In 1983 his net profit on eggs was 5,000 yuan based on sales of 500 eggs per day. Li started with a state production loan of 1,800 yuan in April. He contracted to sell the eggs to the county and the local supply and marketing coop rather than risk the market. The produce went to Raoyang in a rented village truck.[27]

In the Li household, like most others, women farmed, with the men pitch-ing in during the busy season. Otherwise men concentrated on sidelines or were on the road seeking better-paying jobs. Li planned to abandon agricul-ture altogether by 1984. There was too much money to be earned in business to waste time in the fields. He pulled his young daughter out of junior high to work in a plastic bag factory. He would train her to take on a household business. School enrollments dropped as parents put children to work.

When Li's oldest son married in 1982, the father spent 400 yuan for ban-quet food. It was again possible to celebrate life's important moments without fear of being branded feudal. Weddings, holidays, and family gatherings took on renewed joy. In summer 1983 Li built a four-room home. Li said he was a middle peasant. Others jibed, "But now he is a rich peasant!" Chicken king Li retorted, "My living standard now is much higher than the landlords and rich peasants in the old days."

Hard-drinking Li Lu, another successful local entrepreneur, was rarely in Wugong. A builder by trade, Li had been forced back to the countryside after the Leap famine. Hired by a construction company in 1981, Li first worked on a project in Taiyuan, Shanxi province, and then went off to Tianjin for several months. From his 1982 construction earnings of 8,000 yuan, Li invested in a candle-making sideline, an important Wugong craft before collectivization. Li then designed an almost lavish 4,000-yuan home with five rooms and a graceful overhang supported by wooden pillars. It was his second home, built to avoid inheritance disputes between his two sons. In 1983 most villages enjoyed a construction boom. More than 50 Wugong homes went up that year, as well as new sideline enterprises, shops, and restaurants.

Although life improved for "landlord" Li Maoxiu, he exercised caution. While others displayed wealth on fancy courtyard gates, Li did not even rebuild his run-down house. His clothes remained tattered, his bedroom dominated by a yellowing poster of Mao. But stacks of regional newspapers on the bedroom floor revealed his inquiring bent of mind. In 1982 and 1983 Li made two trips south to Guangdong province to find high-quality cloth. He bought 500 yards of nylon where prices were lower, selling it back in the north before and during the lunar New Year, when prices peaked. Then he stored what remained until after the autumn harvest, when demand and prices would rise again.

Starting in the early 1980s, villagers traveled freely, whether for business or holidays. Honeymoons became popular. One person described them to us as a new Chinese invention. Villagers furnished homes, buying television sets, washing machines, baby strollers, and motorbikes.

Markets and money created demands for new services. When counties in Hebei were told to identify a legal specialist, a teacher from Liuman village was informed that he was now an attorney on the payroll of the court. He subsequently opened his own practice in Raoyang and prospered. Wugong had no beauty parlor before reform. By 1982 there were four, all thriving. Imported shampoo replaced brown soap, and women surveyed magazines featuring styles from Hong Kong and Japan. Young rural women began to feel more equal to urbanites. Restaurants, inns, and repair shops flourished.

Transportation exploded. Products and people were trucked in and out. The buses were run-down but inexpensive. Passengers and packages were jammed in. Goods were piled high on the roof. In 1982 Wugong's daily northbound bus schedule offered direct access to Beijing, Tianjin (both six hour trips), and Baoding, as well as regular service to the county seat. The southbound schedule offered routes to Shijiazhuang and Hengshui, as well as to neighboring Shenxian county. But major train lines did not run through Raoyang. Villagers merely had access starting in January 1981 to a new narrow-gauge rail line connecting the Raoyang county seat to Shenxian county to the south.[28] Southbound passengers could connect at Shenxian with the large-gauge railway that ran east-west between Dezhou in Shandong and the Hebei capital Shijiazhuang, a link to major north-south lines. Freight was substantial.

The Raoyang platform was seasonally stacked with bales of crude cotton cloth. It was a far cry, however, from the rich prize that Geng was lobbying for, a stop on the Beijing–Kowloon railroad.

Critics of the New Order

Modernization enhanced life. Grandmothers used running water proudly to clean grandchildren before bedtime. Elderly widows or the ill could turn a spigot and get water for tea instead of having to trek to a well in inclement weather. Yet material gain was accompanied by popular anger. Pork production, which grew rapidly following the end of collective pigsties, was limited by a lack of cold-storage facilities. State electric power shortages hurt the enterprises. Small Japanese-style walking tractors were in short supply. Households quarreled over access to scarce water. Inevitably some felt cheated, especially because political connections made pervasive corruption seem like the source of winning and losing. Villagers seethed.

Welfare beneficiaries, the old, the sick, and the vulnerable felt threatened. In 1983 Wugong had given subsistence minimums to 11 households of revolutionary martyrs, 30 army-dependent households, and eight households that were short of labor, guaranteeing 420 catties of grain and 35 yuan in cash for the old or infirm. But no expenditure was needed in that first year of da baogan. The old had land. They got others to work it and lived on a portion of the product or received family support. Villagers agreed that a socialist country should guarantee subsistence and dignity for its elderly.

In 1983 Wugong closed its unpopular nursery school. Preschoolers accompanied parents to the fields. Elder villagers did not place a high value on schooling. A young woman who passed the college entrance examination was kept in the fields by parents who could see little gain in paying tuition for a daughter who would marry into another family.

Heavily subsidized village clinics disbanded. The paramedic, on his own, had so few patients that he had to resume field work. Traditional medicine revived. But having to pay for everything made some villagers nostalgic for revolutionary-era minimal guarantees.

Medical personnel responded to the market. A woman doctor left the county hospital and set up an office in Yincun, quickly earning 2,000 to 3,000 yuan a month. A physician from the China-Japan Friendship Hospital in Beijing opened an air-conditioned clinic in Guanting. Some doctors made house calls. Smaller health stations provided nursing services. Still, the changes frightened the poor and elders accustomed to the old system. The cost of serious illness could devastate a family.

The Hebei government claimed that work in capitalist Hong Kong was inhuman. But for many youngsters, Hong Kong was China's future. After Raoyang's new movie theater opened in late 1981, residents flocked to Hong

Kong movies to dream of a future of Hong Kong–like clothing, furniture, travel, and music.

Geng ignored movies and built political networks. He met with former Hebei party secretary Lin Tie's wife in April 1983 in Shijiazhuang. She presented him with her calligraphy.[29] Geng hung it over his bed, adding pictures on his walls of the rehabilitated President Liu and Premier Zhou. On May 21, 1983, Geng, still smoking heavily, attended, along with others in the Peng Zhen–Lin Tie network, the funeral of 1950s adviser Lu Guang in Handan. Lu had been an early victim of the assault on Peng Zhen, the former Beijing first party secretary who fell at the outset of the Cultural Revolution. Peng was now back at the center of state power. No one, not even Wang Guangmei, President Liu Shaoqi's widow, spoke ill of Geng. Reform leaders sought to win Geng's support.

Still, Wugong remained the most collectivized village in Hengshui. The conservative prefecture had invested so much in it and still believed in its unity, its leaders, their integrity, their capacity, and the ability of Wugong people once again to achieve productive success. Since 1977 Zou Liji, Geng's secretary, had prodded the Boss to do what Hengshui wanted him to do. Zou bullied the old man into line, going with him to key meetings. Zou sang the praises of da baogan and the rich rewards of reform. Zou was made vice chair of the Wugong commune in mid-1982.[30] But Wugong resisted further reform and fell behind in wealth and production. The Mao-era slogan in the Wugong party headquarters courtyard was "serve the people" (wei renmin fuwu). In the new era, many people placed hope on the market and on merchants who claimed to be "serving you" (wei nin fuwu).

Forty Cheers for Reform

By 1983 Wugong could be presented as a model of reform. In early September, *Hengshui Daily* praised the "pioneering advances" of Geng and Wugong in the "new era."[31] September 10 ushered in a multiday gala commemorating the 40th anniversary of the founding of the original Wugong coop of four households. It was larger than the celebrations of 1973 and 1978. The featured speaker was Hebei governor Zhang Shuguang, a Raoyang native who had assumed the top provincial post in 1982. The special guest of honor was Lin Tie, now a member of the prestigious Central Advisory Committee. A generous Lin Tie presented Wugong as a model of reform. Fifty dignitaries, including representatives of model reform units, honored Wugong at the festivities. More than 2,000 people attended the opening ceremony. A provincial Hebei *bangzi* opera troupe entertained the celebrants, an expansive "science and technology" exhibit was staged, and exciting cultural performances attracted crowed in excess of 10,000.

Hebei Daily claimed that Wugong had moved beyond the "leftist strait-

jacket of the past" (guoqu "zuo" de kuangkuang) and boldly e
reform agenda of the "new age."[32] As with the 1953 and 196:
national publications heralded the "new developments" in Wu
the past, a book, this one entitled *The Fortieth Spring*, showed a
tion between Wugong's present course and the village's orient
early 1940s. The narrative emphasized village harmony and a diversified ccc.
omy that respected the market and household enterprise.[34] Pleasing patrons
won rewards.

A Wugong Agro-Industrial-Commercial Association with Geng as the honorary chairman and articulate Li Zhongxin the top administrator was inaugurated in October. Governor Zhang Shuguang, a close associate of reformist Vice Premier Wan Li, promoted it. It was a way to train local technical personnel to advance mechanization, commodification, and division of labor. Six association-run service companies took charge of water supply and marketing, agricultural machinery, agricultural technology, industrial sidelines, and irrigation and electricity.

Although Wugong had resisted reform for more than 20 years, on October 31 *People's Daily* hailed the 40th anniversary of the wartime coop. Geng and the new Wugong Agro-Industrial-Commercial Association were now proclaimed pacesetters in reform worthy of national emulation.[35] Wugong was still blessed by its network of backers.[36] Political networks still facilitated economic success.

15 ❖ REFORM
AND ITS
DISCONTENTS

Despite reform, many institutional dynamics persisted. Wugong continued to benefit from a thick network of political ties, while Hebei authorities continued to shackle reform. Villagers made the most of opportunities to improve life while coping with an economically polarizing and corrupt system.

To loyal party conservatives in Hebei, reform turned things topsy-turvy. Losers waxed nostalgic about revolution, hoping for morality and selflessness as the antidote to a system in which money turned into power and power into money, with greed in the saddle.

Reform seemed to alter everything. The dynamic role of the south was now openly acknowledged. As reflected in the 1963 flood relief from the south, in Mao-era standards of grain success, and in Geng Xiufeng's southern odyssey into an awe-inspiring richness of water, the south symbolized wealth long before Deng Xiaoping reignited reform during a 1992 tour of the reformist and economically dynamic coastal south.

To many North China plain villagers, the south seemed alien, an impossible ideal. Others saw it as China's future. By 1990 Raoyang villagers tapped two fingers as a thank you when tea was poured, emulating a Cantonese custom sweeping the country in the wake of Guangzhou's emergence as the capital of China's then richest province, emblematic of reform success. By 2000, southern-style dog breeding was ubiquitous in Raoyang. Dog meat was served in restaurants all over the north. Village women in Raoyang who marketed homemade garments often sewed on a brand name associated with the south.

Regional identities intensified. Tianjin people moved to stake out a leading place in an expansive northeast Asian international economy. New enterprises in Raoyang now sought to tap Tianjin's links to a global economy. People sought a better life by seizing reform opportunities in their region.

Education Failures and Achievements

Villagers who had been in junior or senior high school when the Cultural Revolution blocked mobility through education constituted a "lost generation." Hopes for careers in medicine, hydrology, engineering, education, and the arts were dashed. The losses were magnified by awareness of Raoyang's earlier successes in education. The waste of a generation has been obscured by urbanites who view villagers as an inferior and superstitious breed whose horizons end at the mud walls of isolated communities, as "dumb," "lice-ridden" creatures who "lived with outmoded customs that could not be uprooted."[1] Such biases scapegoat village victims for the hardships imposed on rural China by the sophisticated holders of urban power.

The Raoyang countryside is populated by outstanding talents. The daughter of former Wugong party secretary Yang Tong, Yang Yuexin, a scientist and physician residing in Beijing, who completed a Ph.D. in nutrition at Wageningen University in Holland, entered into a joint venture with a firm in Lyon and presented papers at international conferences. In the late 1990s Dr. Yang worked with the World Health Organization on nutrition projects, using money she earned to buy a new television set for her ailing father. Li Jinying, a nuclear physicist living in Beijing, conducted atomic energy research in Paris. The son of a Wugong teacher, he rose to the top of his government unit and led a nuclear energy delegation to Moscow in 2001. Cheng Tiejun, a native of Zhangcun, earned a Ph.D. in sociology from Binghamton University and taught at Macau University. While building institutional links with researchers throughout China, he drafted a book on the Cultural Revolution. Li Qingchang, a University of Wisconsin engineering graduate, whose mother hailed from Fanyuancun, managed a joint venture in Shenzhen.

Some Raoyang villagers of the lost generation became technological innovators at successful local factories and enterprises. But most never recovered from a revolutionary war on education that made villagers seem stupid. Locked into their villages by policies hostile to autonomous activities, to education, and to the market, denied physical and career mobility, kept ill informed by a system premised on secrecy, censorship, propaganda, and paternalism, rural people found that safety lay in feigning ignorance. Wugong's leaders shrewdly invited the writing team from Nankai University to explain the spring 1976 campaign against reformer Deng Xiaoping, just as they had requested guidance from every group of urban intellectuals to visit the village. Locals were wise to treat the torrent of policies hurled down from on high, including the denunciation of Mao's successor Lin Biao as another Confucius, as so unfathomable that it was prudent to seem dumb.

Rural education in the reform era remains crippled by massive under funding as a result of the plunder of money earmarked for education, while the prospects of poorer students are dashed by the imposition of fees that deprive them of educational access. At one point in 2000 the Raoyang government declared bankruptcy. It stopped paying the salaries of teachers and workers for months at a time, a pattern widespread in poorer communities. Five out of six teachers were soon absent from school, seeking ways to earn income and leaving students in the charge of caretakers, not educators. Public education declined as top teachers left for private schools or to go into business. Despite new opportunities opened by reform, other doors closed, and escape from rural poverty remained a challenge. Government budgets still privileged the urban, the exam system still discriminated against rural students, and residential controls still kept villagers locked out of opportunity.[2]

Water and Waste

Revolutionary-era economic irrationality was apparent in water policies. The state had prioritized power production over transportation and commercial linkages and urban over rural interests. The annual corvée labor deployed to control the Hai River would end the threat of flood to Tianjin and guarantee a reliable water supply to industry. The Hutuo, a Hai River tributary that had once linked Raoyang to Tianjin, was dammed in the 1950s and dried up. Extreme water shortages plagued much of the north by 2000.

Mao-era claims of self-reliant Dazhai miracles had much to do with huge state investments providing the national model village unique access to abundant water.[3] Wugong leaders never believed that water-blessed Dazhai had anything to teach villagers in the parched plains where the well drilling campaigns of the 1970s and subsequently had required ever-deeper and costlier wells. In the reform era, Wugong and others began to learn how to tap multiple aquifers and above all to conserve precious water.

Still, owing to the short-term economic thinking of enterprising households, a lack of effective regulation, and state unaccountability, the water crisis intensified. Throughout North China water use skyrocketed, while the state continued water subsidies.[4] In Raoyang county, floods damaged crops from 1997 through 1999, and 2000 brought drought.

Death and Cultural Rebirth

In spring 1983 Wugong east-ender Wang Wencong, a Red Army veteran, died. Wang was mourned by family members, many of them key players in Geng's network. But in line with the new openness, the family rejected revolutionary burial practices.

Wang's family history encapsulated a Wugong saga. In 1941, Wencong's father, rope maker Yuzhang, borrowed 40 yuan to open a store. It became a gathering spot for patriots, the place where Geng Xiufeng first heard rose-colored descriptions of Soviet collectives. By the 1943 famine, debt threatened the survival of the Wang family. An uncle fled to the Japanese-occupied northeast for work. In 1944 hungry Wencong joined a communist-led anti-Japanese guerrilla force in Raoyang.

On the eve of the 1946 lunar New Year, Yuzhang persuaded Half-Ripe Li Dier not to drop out of Geng Changsuo's fledgling coop. "Next year," Yuzhang said, "I wonder if you'll again be able to eat dumplings," suggesting that a miserable fate resulted from not having a coop. Li then stuck with the coop, which flourished under Boss Geng's leadership, winning support from Lin Tie, later the village's patron.

After the Communist Party came to power, son Wencong returned from the army. Families reknit. Geng made Yuzhang's son team secretary. Another son became secretary of the village youth league and eventually a state official. Wugong party insiders married into the family networks running the county.

Wang Wencong, a father of four, had suffered from debilitating diabetes since 1974. In fall 1982, when he was 62, his family sought treatment, first in Beijing and then in Shijiazhuang. Still Wencong declined. The family prepared for the end. Our request to observe mourning rites was honored. The access reflected China's reform openness.

Wencong's oldest son and youngest daughter still lived in Wugong. His oldest daughter returned from nearby Gaoqiao village to help the youngest son, who worked in a Raoyang office and returned to Wugong a month before his father's death. The two daughters-in-law, one a Wugong commune hospital employee, were also on hand. A doctor visited daily in the final week. On April 19, 1983, Wang Wencong slipped into a coma. The women took charge. His older sister insisted on an appropriate funeral. A coffin was purchased five days before the end.

Upon their father's death, his children washed his face, hands, and feet, then summoned a specialist to dress the corpse in a new shirt, trousers, an old-fashioned coat, and shoes. Granddaughter Wang Pengju, born in 1953, who had excoriated "superstition" in the revolutionary era, participated fully. The body was kept at home for three days. Friends and relatives paid respects. More than 150 visited. Women wailed; men offered words of condolence.

On the first evening, the body was placed in a brightly painted coffin. A large embroidered silk cloth, a *menglian,* covered the body. It was decorated with eight elegantly garbed white-faced female figures to accompany the old soldier to the afterworld. The coffin was then sealed and placed in a slightly elevated position against the north wall of the kitchen.

The room held 15 female relatives in mourning attire, for some a thick white headband, for others a white hood covering the head, white pants made of coarse cotton cloth, and white strips of cloth covering the shoe tips. Mourners knelt and bowed to the coffin. Some lay prostrate, emitting spine-chilling cries. Others chanted rhythmically: "You can put your heart at rest; you may go with your heart at rest." Their faces were swollen and contorted. A small fire was fed with spirit money for use in the afterlife. The rooms on both sides of the one with the coffin held visibly frightened children. A meal feted 40 relatives at noon on the third day.

On day 3 nearly 200 onlookers gathered to watch two young men drive four-foot hollow metal pipes into the ground in the center of a dirt path. Every 30 seconds or so a skyrocket was lit and dropped into the pipe. A muffled explosion sent the rocket on its way. A few seconds later, as the rocket reached several hundred feet, a thunderous boom echoed across the village. Hundreds were fired to scare evil spirits and notify villagers of the impending burial.

After lunch, the coffin was placed on a log rack. Burly men, primarily neighbors, carried the load and led a half-mile procession to the cemetery. Female relatives followed in two wagons drawn by draft animals. More than 100 villagers trekked to an open pit dug that morning by neighborhood volunteers. Crying and chanting continued. As the coffin was lowered, women collapsed. Funeral wreaths sent by Wencong's factory, the work units of his oldest son and other relatives, and team 1 were placed on the coffin. Then it was covered with earth.

Three days after the funeral, close relatives built a five-foot-high cone-shaped dirt mound and a small brick fireplace to burn more spirit money. Mourning continued for a month, with daughters-in-law wearing black armbands and women related by blood to Wang wearing white cloth on shoe tops to ward off misfortune. At the end of the month mourners returned to the grave to burn paper and weep.

Funeral expenses exceeded 400 yuan, far more than the average annual per capita village income. The coffin, purchased in Shenxian county, cost 220 yuan. Burial garments cost 100 yuan, rockets 40, the silk burial cloth 12, and food for family and friends more than 20. Villagers hungered for community and meaning in an era of corruption and lawlessness. With health care unreliable, they sought a healthy, moral life and turned to those close to them in search of self-defense and mutual aid. The revolution against what was sacred to Chinese families waned.

The Death of a Revolutionary

The death of 85-year-old Boss Geng Changsuo in 1985 communicated a very different message. During the 1985 lunar New Year, Geng had difficulty swallowing food. He ate less and less. On August 12 he was rushed to Shijiazhuang in a county-owned Japanese car and was admitted to the Senior Cadres Medical Complex (Gao gan bing fang), a unit attached to the provincial hospital. It had Hebei's best staff and equipment. A specialist from Beijing diagnosed Geng, a chain smoker, with terminal lung cancer. Our request to say farewell was granted, another sign of reform openness.

Geng had wasted away to almost nothing. He was too weak to stand, yet

unable to lie down because fluids collected in his lungs. Attended
son, Delu, he was propped up in bed. He slept for two or three n
time. Breathing was labored. His hearing was almost gone, his v
per. But his eyes remained bright, and his mind was still sharp. Sii
tears streaming down his face, he recalled our last visit, joked about our whit
hair and pot bellies, pored over our family photos (taking several for his
hospital mirror), and insisted that we eat some of his fruit. We embraced and
said a final goodbye.

Officials had already begun funeral arrangements as if Geng were state
property. He would be cremated, with his remains interred at a site for revolutionary heroes outside Shijiazhuang. Family members were aware of the plan
but were not included in the discussions.

In November, as Geng neared the end, he asked to go home. A dispute
arose among his children about where to spend his last days. Some contended
that a state unit should be seen caring for him. But Geng insisted on remaining
at home. Borne in a donkey-drawn cart, he surveyed Wugong's crops one last
time. Doctors from the bare-bones clinic in Raoyang attended him almost
daily. Geng Changsuo passed away at home on November 26, 1985.

A county memorial meeting was held at the Raoyang Revolutionary Martyrs Cemetery on November 28. All seven children and their families gathered
to grieve. There were no sky rockets, no mourning garments, no menglian, no
burning of ritual money, no painted coffin, and no chants. Revolutionary
sobriety prevailed. Potted plants and official funeral wreaths surrounded the
body. A soldier stood guard as hundreds of mourners paid respects.

Following the austere ceremony, Geng was cremated in Shijiazhuang.
Provincial authorities then held rites on December 7. Governor Zhang Shuguang spoke. Condolence letters and mourning wreaths came from national
leaders, including conservative modernizer Chen Yun, Hebei resistance leader
Lu Zhengcao, and former Beijing party secretary Peng Zhen, the patron of the
Lin Tie network in Hebei that for decades had supported Wugong. Geng was
remembered as a village leader of high integrity, deeply committed to nation
and socialism. *People's Daily* ran a brief obituary.

Family members pleaded for Geng's ashes. But it was not until 1991 that
Zhang Mandun, his grandson and political heir, received some remains. The
ashes were divided between the Shuangfeng Mountain state cemetery in the
provincial capital and the lineage burial ground in the natal village. Some
relatives worried that the ashes they received were not the patriarch's remains.
In death as in life, Geng was pulled between state and village. Economic
reform had not changed everything. In vital matters, the party still dictated.

Raoyang and Wugong leaders used Geng's reputation to legitimate their
opposition to all-out reform. It was said that he had embraced material gain,
but in as collective a way as possible. The slogans plastered around the county
and village about the need to emulate Geng's spirit buttressed the Wugong

party's desire to hold on to as many tasks as possible done by the village government, referred to as the collective. The village party bragged that it was the collective that could machine harvest wheat in three days instead of three weeks and thereby end stoop labor. Male officials boasted that collective work kept daughters at home — not in distant factories — where they could be monitored to live in moral ways, by conservative mores, not an aping of alien looseness.

The Party Clings to Power

In the 1980s popular desires for political reform grew. People complained bitterly about party corruption. Many educated citizens saw democracy as the way forward. The death of previously disgraced party reformer Hu Yaobang on April 15, 1989, provided a focus for long-simmering rage at a selfish and despotic regime. Protest spread across the country, even in conservative Hebei, especially in urban Shijiazhuang and Baoding.

Hebei students joined the 1989 nationwide democracy movement whose epicenter was Beijing's Tiananmen Square. In Shijiazhuang, all the colleges joined. Even teachers and hospital staff participated. Units of the 27th Army in the city stayed away when democracy demonstrators marched to demand the removal of top officials and an end to corruption.

On April 24 a poster went up at Hebei University in Baoding, once the province's heartbeat of revolutionary fundamentalism. Students, complaining that dictatorship made them ignorant and therefore incapable of contributing to China's promising scientific future, presented themselves as patriots trying to end a dark epoch.[5] College officials tried to suppress the burgeoning movement. By the end of April, however, Baoding colleges were bursting with prodemocracy activity.

College administrators tried to keep Baoding students from going to Beijing to join the struggle. They also attempted to block emissaries from Beijing who carried news about the popular movement. On April 26 a party editorial denounced the demonstrators as counterrevolutionaries. The next day Deng Xiaoping approved the deployment to Beijing of 500 troops from the 38th Army at Baoding.[6] Full of patriotism, the demonstrators and their supporters were furious at being labeled enemies of the people. Their protests had broad popular support. The 27th Army in Shijiazhuang informed the party center that the military too wanted corruption ended, inflation curbed, and job assignments made fair.[7]

On April 30 more than 400 students from Hebei University joined the demonstrators in Beijing.[8] The democracy movement won even broader popular support from citizens by announcing a hunger strike on May 13. The news reenergized people, and protest marches spread.

A demonstration involving 150,000 protesters and onlookers in Shijiazhuang on May 18 brought out government employees, researchers, high school students, medical personnel, and others. Calling for democracy and an end to corruption, the crowd insisted that reformer Zhao Ziyang and conservative Li Peng engage in dialogue and called on Deng Xiaoping to resign.[9]

On May 19 students blocked the movement of the 27th Army to Beijing.[10] By May 20 rumors circulated that Deng Xiaoping had demanded swift action and that a military crackdown was imminent. Activists in Baoding urged supporters not to go to Beijing but to prevent units of the army stationed in Baoding from marching to Beijing. The commander of the 38th Army was rumored to be resisting orders for a crackdown. Students surrounded hundreds of 38th Army trucks. Some mocked the encirclement, arguing that the people's army could never fire on the people.

Following a declaration of martial law on May 20, the 27th Army in Shijiazhuang and the 38th in Baoding moved into Beijing that night, though some were blocked in the suburbs of Beijing by villagers.[11] In Shijiazhuang students seeking to avert bloodshed petitioned the Hebei People's Congress, demanding that the National People's Congress gather to dismiss Li Peng, who was seen as willing to use bloody means to block political reform.[12]

The 38th Army received orders on June 3 to clear Tiananmen Square. The 27th Army followed. Met by bus blockades, the army used deadly force. On June 4, tanks and troops, including the 38th Army from Baoding and the 27th from Shijiazhuang, crushed the democracy movement in Beijing, killing many hundreds, perhaps a few thousand.[13] Demonstrators found that the 38th helped get wounded to hospitals, while the 27th killed wildly.

By the time of the June 4 massacre, more than 10,000 urban Hebei people had gone to Beijing. Anger and anxiety swept through Baoding and Shijiazhuang. On June 5 more than 8,000 demonstrators carried wreaths to the North China Martyrs' Mausoleum, to the Shijiazhuang Liberation Monument, to the gate of the provincial party committee, and the headquarters of the 27th Army.[14] Early on the morning of June 6, more than 3,000 students and residents attacked the headquarters of the 27th Army, shouting, "27th Army butchers!" "The 27th Army suppresses the people," and "The 27th Army kills the elderly, students, and children." On June 7 approximately 3,000 Shijiazhuang students abandoned their campuses.[15] More than 300 students and residents gathered at the headquarters of the 27th Army, where seven began a sit-in.[16] Aware of the popular outrage, the army worried that soldiers of the 27th Army and their kin might be shunned, taken hostage, or targeted for violence.[17]

Raoyang soldiers serving in Shanxi province participated in the massacre. When they returned home on leave, they boasted about restoring order and portrayed the democrats as aliens. The Wugong township government viewed the democracy movement as yet another sign of moral decay that should be rooted out. Young people seemed to their conservative elders to fight, watch television, tattoo their bodies, shoot pool, join gangs, steal, loiter, and hardly ever work. Raoyang doggerel verse mocked teenagers for their long hair. After the Beijing massacre, when central party authorities required heavy doses of socialist education for students to counter bourgeois liberalization, senior Hebei rural leaders felt vindicated. Law and order were popular. Beijing University students were sent to a military base in Shijiazhuang. The military's disciplining of students ended only after Deng Xiaoping's 1992 southern tour reignited economic reform.

Political reform, however, could not be ignored. As early as 1987, rulers in Beijing, led by conservative reformers Peng Zhen and Bo Yibo, opted for village elections because local party branches were moribund or self-serving. Villagers responded to official abuses by evading taxes, getting around population limitation policies, and withholding compulsory grain deliveries. Beginning in 1990, the Ministry of Civil Affairs tried to set up elections and sought to prevent local power holders from manipulating them.[18] Hengshui, the prefecture that encompassed Wugong, would not allow the central ministry in to organize elections. Democracy was seen by Hengshui officials as non-Chinese. Even where Hebei prefectural and county leaders pressed elections, lower-level party functionaries often resisted. Hengshui prefecture and Raoyang county remained pure party kingdoms.

Wugong Commercializes

Wugong stressed industry and commerce, hoping to become a conglomerate with an industrial sector, periodic market, modern transportation, and permanent shops. A conglomerate of astonishing proportions rose in Daqiuzhang village outside Tianjin. It was promoted as a national model of reform success. The leaders of Dazhai (Mao's model revolutionary village) and Xiaojinzhuang (Jiang Qing's model village) were among the many who visited, seeking ways to get ahead.[19] In 1985 and 1986 Raoyang sent delegations. It emulated Daqiuzhuang by promoting small factories throughout the county and helping them exhibit at the Guangzhou trade fair in 1987. By 2000, Raoyang factories produced logo items for ten American universities. But progress was halting, and in the end conservative Raoyang failed to match the dynamism of neighboring Shenxian county to the south. Raoyang officials said Shenxian enjoyed special advantages. Raoyang denizens, however, blamed useless local officials.

In January 1984 Wugong was officially designated a "market town" (zhen), one of three in the county. Wugong took land from agriculture for township enterprises and commercial offices, most run by party insiders. Many soon failed; a few sunk roots.

At first the Wugong "market" was a handful of peddlers and half-empty state-run shops. By the mid-1980s, however, a consumer revolution had swept the village. A hundred new homes were built in 1985, and villagers soon owned 188 television sets (including 18 color sets), 512 sewing machines, 97 washing machines, more than 1,500 bicycles, 26 small tractors, 9 motorbikes, and three four-ton trucks worth 40,000 yuan each. Standards of living began to suggest "town" rather than "village."

By the early 1990s the Wugong market challenged Zoucun's. Meeting on the fourth and ninth days of the market cycle, the Wugong fair attracted more than 10,000 people. The village leased out stores. With permanent shops open daily, with numerous restaurants, and an array of manufactured goods, the "town" market in Wugong was less oriented to agriculture and handicrafts than the "country" market in Zoucun. Some mothers purchased calligraphy books to help their children learn to write better. Other parents bought science fiction comic books to inspire their children.

Soon one-fifth of the store owners were not locals. Some team 3 households moved to a new market street. New buildings featured a shop on the main floor and a residence above, with steam heat for winter and overhead fans for summer. The old village crossroads featured herbal medicine specialists and other health care providers.

Pop music and sensational magazines, some pornographic, were popular. One lurid account was entitled "The Tragedies That Befall Virgins," while another described the gruesome tortures supposedly inflicted on some rural brides whose bedding was not bloodstained after the first night of marriage. Some 200 prostitutes came to Raoyang in the mid-1990s. Notices pasted on Wugong walls warned of sexually transmitted diseases. Elders shook their heads at moral decay. In the provincial capital, taxi drivers boasted that White Russians were back as whores, proof positive of the superiority of China's reforms over Russia's failed agenda.

In the early 1990s the Wugong factory with the largest payroll, 300 workers, was tied to the local party. It produced towels in the abandoned Geng Changsuo museum, using 1920s vintage machines. But in 1992, under articulate Li Zhongxin, although flush with state bank loans, subcontracts from state-owned enterprises, and contracts for sales in the northeast, it went bankrupt. With village government support, it resumed some production in 1994, this time run by Zhang Dadong, a son of party secretary Zhang Mandun, Boss Geng's heir. Li Zhongxin became an official.

In the mid-1980s state aid facilitated the construction of a huge cottonseed-oil factory run by Yang Tong, former village party secretary, and Macho Li Shouzheng, also a retired party leader. With a simple process, a monopoly position, and an assured market in the state sector, the factory was long kept afloat. After a few years, Yang and Li were replaced by younger, technically trained people. Yang and Li were kept on the payroll. But increasingly, state waste yielded to enterprises that operated on hard budget constraints, that is, profit or die. Management was taken over by Geng Xiufeng's grandson, Geng Jianzhi.

Most Raoyang families tried to escape being locked into farming grain and cotton where the state still dictated quotas and prices. Raising animals for fur expanded. By 2000 more villagers raised foxes. Fruit orchards, especially peaches, spread.

One of the richest villagers in the mid-1990s, heir to the west-end factory manufacturing paper string for cigarette packs, feared that Beijing's antismoking campaign would hurt business. To tap into the construction boom, he reconfigured his machines to produce the molding for the inside of windows. When business soared, he built a veritable mansion, a three-story fortress, outfitted with up-to-date electronic gadgetry.

One Raoyang industry gained ground in the 1980s and 1990s by exporting to Asia and North America. In 1974 a snuff bottle craftsman came to Hengshui and set up a workshop run by the prefecture. Apprentices were trained to hand paint the inside of tiny snuff bottles. The Hengshui Art Factory attracted the best county-level painters with higher salaries and urban registrations for multiple family members eager to leave the countryside. The factory won contracts with the Imperial Palace and the Friendship Store in Beijing. In 1981 two Raoyang apprentices set up a factory in Guocun village. By 1993 the factory employed 90 skilled workers and exported to Thailand, Singapore, and Japan. Everyone worked on a piece-rate basis, earning 1,000 to 2,000 yuan per month. The factory owner became the Guocun village head in 1993. Wugong's own snuff bottle factory expanded customary motifs to include Jesus, Mary, and Joseph. Wugong also mounted an effort to export Christmas tree ornaments. By 2000 it had opened two outlets in the south, one in Shenzhen and one in Guangzhou.

Expansive markets encouraged technological innovation. The Five Star Brewery set up a division in Hengshui using German equipment. It prospered. In 1999 Raoyang's grain bureau opened a carrot juice factory with 240 workers. It bought machinery from Honeywell in Minneapolis to meet the quality standards of potential importers in Australia and New Zealand. Geng Xiufeng's grandson was enticed to move from the cottonseed-oil factory to manage the expanding Raoyang operation. Ads on Shijiazhuang television featured Ge You, star of the popular movie *To Live.* His Raoyang-born father had been a guerrilla fighter. One Raoyang village pioneered greenhouse vegetable farming and refrigeration. Farmers monitored urban prices closely before choosing to dispatch produce to Tianjin and even as far away as Shanghai.[20] The county government took interested farmers on inspection tours of greenhouse successes so that knowledge could be transferred. Wealth expanded for many in the 1980s and 1990s.

A sports clothing factory started in 1986 by a Wugong family with one sewing machine kept upgrading skills and flexibly adapting to popular styles. It won a market and added to its work force. By the 1990s it was producing more than 1,000 sports suits a day. Orders poured in from as far away as Xinjiang province. These entrepreneurs freely "borrowed" the labels of many world-famous brands, more as an effort to gain status than to mislead customers attracted to the cheap garments. By 2001 the factory had reinvested 600,000 yuan to become the largest in Wugong. The machines were deafening, but women workers were not given earplugs.

Throughout the 1990s, well-connected Wugong residents received the largest share of bank loans in the county. In 1997 Geng's grandson, Zhang Mandun, was made chair of the Wugong township assembly. Nepotistic political networks remained intact. With the closure of the money-losing Hengshui steel plant in Handan, built in the revolutionary "third-front" campaign, prefectural party networks plundered the unit to advance private fortunes. Scandals and gossip about corrupt leaders were legion.

The rural economy kept growing, but in regions without political connections it developed less rapidly than in the fat years of 1978–84. There were cycles of boom and bust. There were also large layoffs when state-related units suffered subsidy reductions or went broke. Wealth still expanded, though less quickly, perhaps, than anger about those in power who benefited disproportionately or corruptly. Nonetheless, by the end of the century, telephone and electric power lines crisscrossed Wugong. The main street had night lights, and many homes had telephones.

The Train to the Future

In 1990 it was announced that the Beijing–Kowloon railroad would be routed through Raoyang. Geng Changsuo's lobbying had delivered. Stretching 1,585 miles, the railroad was China's longest and most expensive. There would be three stations in Raoyang: in Guanting in the north, in the county seat, and in Wugong — even though Wugong was just 12 kilometers south of Raoyang. Hengshui would be a regional center for the project with its administrative reach extending beyond provincial borders. But the statist system was structured to benefit itself. Fearful that construction materials would be stolen and taking care of their own units, the national builders hired little local labor.

The province funded a five-day 50th-anniversary celebration of the founding of the original Wugong coop. It began on November 26, 1993. Retired Hebei governor Zhang Shuguang, a long-time Wugong backer, delivered the keynote speech. Dignitaries came from Shijiazhuang, Hengshui, and Raoyang. A top Hebei bangzi opera troupe entertained the throng. The gala legitimated setting up 50 permanent telephone lines into Wugong.

Boss Geng's heir, Zhang Mandun, expressed appreciation for the "concern and help of the party and government at every level." Wugong, he boasted, now employed more than 700 workers in 16 enterprises, each with gross

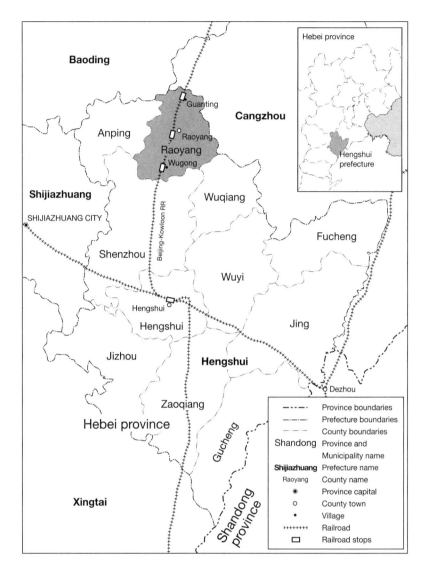

Raoyang county in Hengshui prefecture and
the Beijing-Kowloon Railroad, 1995

annual incomes of 500,000 yuan or more. Virtually every household had a television set and a washing machine. Most owned a color television set, a refrigerator, and a stereo. A few had cars, motorcycles, air conditioners, and microwave ovens. A handful lived in new foreign-style houses (xiao yang lou). Per capita income was 1,700 yuan in 1992. Almost 50 households were in the 10,000-yuan income category. With the railroad, heir Zhang predicted, Wugong would keep on growing.

A project embodying revolutionary values, the Beijing–Kowloon line ran through poor and mountainous regions, especially former revolutionary-base areas, to help loyal regions that had stagnated in the Mao era. The Wugong station, finished in 1995, featured a bronze bust of Boss Geng. Cargo trains began to roll through Raoyang in 1995; regular passenger service started in 1996. Nine trains stopped each day in Raoyang. Although designated the railroad's first cargo management station south of Beijing, Raoyang was bested by neighboring Shenxian in attracting services. Almost all freight in and out of Raoyang went on newly paved highways that energized commerce.

Only a few local trains stopped at Wugong. As in other small stations in poverty areas, the economic impact of the railroad was minimal. Geng Changsuo's success in rerouting the north-south line to tie it to the Raoyang county seat, thereby linking the county to the east-west route that connected inland Xi'an and coastal Tianjin, was not at century's end the hoped-for bonanza. Some see the Wugong station as the last gasp of economic irrationality. Observers in Beijing, however, insisted that it was the power group in Hebei province and Hengshui prefecture who resisted reform that had kept local people from benefiting fully from the transportation breakthrough.

Among China's coastal provinces, Hebei was perhaps the most resistant to reform. As a gap grew both with the richer south and with the neighboring Beijing and Tianjin metropolises, nativism rose among those who found the success of the globalized south and nearby modernizing cities to be alien, even a fruit of neocolonialism. Models of success seemed tied to special privileges for the south, a reversal of fortunes that previously subsidized northerners found unjust. It also seemed unfair that Hebei had lost its two most powerful engines of growth and revenue when Beijing and then Tianjin were taken from the province and set up as independent "municipalities" that reported directly to the national government. After Guangxi in the south, Hebei was the poorest, least urbanized, and most backward coastal province. In 1995 it ranked last among coastal provinces in ratio of trade to gross domestic product and in foreign loans and direct investment. With little immediate gain from the Beijing–Kowloon line, Raoyang people railed at worthless regional leaders. Citizens credited themselves, not the government, for rising standards of living, even while cursing the authorities as an obstacle to that rise. Wugong, however, again drew on its political capital to gain designation as a "special economic zone."

Agonies

Resentments grew. People were angry about expanding income gaps, rapacious taxation, the government's failure to pay pensioners, and county refusal to pay teachers for months on end. Industry and income raced ahead far faster in neighboring Shandong province, which had an active reformist leadership.

In the revolutionary era, privileged people monopolized material perquisites behind closed doors. In the reform era, wealth was flaunted, outraging those left behind, left out. While most lived far better than before, many felt humiliated by the insufferable new rich. In 1993 Raoyang county authorities built a new set of superior apartments for themselves, to the displeasure of many.

People complained that the county government overpriced scarce items, burdened villagers with fees, and stole from them. Officials insisted that villagers did not pay taxes and used every wile to evade state regulations, from family planning to crop requisitions. In the ongoing struggle over revenues, the county used electric cattle prods on resisters and resorted to seizures of property. In 2000 the county jailed and fined by the day those unable to pay additional taxes. Many villagers had to borrow wherever they could to survive and to avoid time in jail. Seething at corrupt county officials who drove Volkswagen Santanas, villagers chose not to fill potholes, hoping instead to see "Mr. Santana" break an axle in a village ditch.

Rural people fixated on what was immoral. A bitter rhyme about social stratification pointed to the plight of those at the bottom of the heap, an imaginary tenth level, below the level assigned to cruelly targeted intellectuals of the Cultural Revolution era, known as "the stinking ninth." The tenth level was comprised of those workers, peasants, and soldiers who were still foolish enough to be honest and rely on revolutionary selflessness. The regime seemed like hypocrisy personified. Those with values lost out in the state's corrupt games. Villagers looked elsewhere for ethical bonds.

According to a popular doggerel on stratification, those on top, taking care of friends and family, eating, drinking, gambling, and whoring, while keeping concubines in Shenzhen, a southern export hub, were officials, subcontractors from state-owned enterprises, and security forces. In the middle, cheating as best they could to get some crumbs, were doctors, newsmen, entrepreneurs, and local officials. Dedicated teachers, according to the rhymed gossip, were almost as badly off as honest tillers, never tasting the sweet richness of the new wealth.

An aging but still independent-minded Geng Xiufeng, while continuing bitterly to attack the horrors of revolution, also lambasted the reform state as run by plunderers and tribute seekers, a system of "relying on power to get one's bread" (kao quan chifan), fascism. In the early 1990s he wrote a protest letter to Jiang Zemin, the heir to Deng Xiaoping. In 1992, shortly after allowing us to film him talking about the Leap catastrophe for a documentary movie, Xiufeng was struck by a debilitating stroke. His writing days were over. Although hardly able to walk, let alone pose a further threat to the powerful, he was again the target of character assassinations.

Just before dying in 1999, Xiufeng hoped for an end to "blind obedience," the unwillingness of leaders to take criticism, bureaucratism, and worship of leaders — the mentality of doing only what one is told to do. As he declined, Xiufeng held fast to his critique of the abuses of the state, both those of the Mao era and after. In his view, the reformers had failed to deliver promised gains to the rural poor, widened inequality, and expanded official corruption.

Articulate Li Zhongxin, now back in party leadership, showed us his new eight-room house, costing 70,000 yuan. Wugong leaders were part of a network knit by marriage and blood. Party secretary Zhang Mandun continued to tap political connections. Boss Geng's heir married his daughter to one of the leaders of Raoyang county.

But villagers increasingly found the party elites of blood inheritance to be parasitic, an anachronism, not helping people benefit from openness and reform, mainly just taking care of their own. In 1994 heir Zhang, now known by some as Lao Bao, the lord of justice, built a large residence, complete with the village's first indoor shower, to receive family members of his parents' generation who, after retirement, stayed in Wugong a couple of months a year, coming from Beijing, Tianjin, and Baoding, where they had long held jobs on the state payroll. Neighbors murmured that Geng Changsuo, who had lived modestly, cared too well for his children. The residence was upgraded and refurbished in 1998.

Discontented villagers saw the nouveau riche as undeserving, seldom earning wealth from hard or expert work. Tensions between prospering and poor, along with localized violence, continued to rise. Order felt fragile. While driving just outside Raoyang in the late 1990s, we were the targets of hold-ups on four occasions. One was life-threatening, while the others featured villagers wielding daggers, staves, and bricks to exact a toll from all outside vehicles.

Many blamed leaders by complaining about their foreign friends, especially Americans and Japanese. Nationalism intensified, promoting a racialized notion of Chineseness going back to the Yellow Emperor, a tale of more than 4,000 years of blood continuity. One Raoyang verse that mocked all groups ribbed elders for spouting "my country right or wrong." But another rhyme popular among Raoyang villagers, long a patriotic source for military and security recruits, was more nativistic:

Mao Zedong was a stupid emperor; he didn't treasure the loyal.
He loved traitors.
The founding fathers were driven out; all that remains are flatterers.
Don't fight foreign enemies! Instead we killed each other.
The world turned upside down.

278 REFORM AND ITS DISCONTENTS

Popular chauvinism demanded rulers who would stand up for China and end humiliations imposed by Japan, America, and Taiwan. Villagers fantasized what they would do if a corrupt official driving a Japanese car got stuck in their mud:

> He'd call on peasants to pull it out; we'd just turn it upside down.
> Open it and look inside; find a bastard.

In the 1990s Raoyang merchants traveled north to the Russian border and south to Hong Kong and overseas in all directions in search of deals. But in 1995, when a potential Japanese investor was hosted at the county's first karaoke hall, local listeners, patriotic heirs of those victimized by Japan's invasion half a century earlier, had mixed reactions. The investment was never made.

The patriotism that had supported Mao was more powerful than ever. In 1993, when the International Olympic Committee awarded the 2000 Olympic Games to Sydney over Beijing, a national campaign targeted the United States for China's loss of international dignity. Some party leaders in Wugong then blamed America for all China's problems. In 2001, three months after a Chinese air force jet smashed into an American reconnaissance flight in international air space, we were surrounded at a huge vegetable market in rural Raoyang by angry young males demanding to know why America had invaded China's air space.

Bankruptcies, unemployment, brownouts, violence, theft, and unaccountable power fed resentment. Since business needed party protection, corruption was rife. A typical enterprise was run by a few Lis and one Wang, that is, an enterprising family and a party connection. A nostalgia grew for the final years of the Cultural Revolution when vigilante violence had ebbed. It was remembered as pure, equal, and altruistic. Cultural Revolution songs revived. Amnesia infused nostalgia. Elders recalled revolution as moral compared to a reform era in which girls, supposedly made immoral by foreign influences, wore summer clothing that was light and skimpy.

Concern about disorder caused by those falling behind led to efforts to raise the poorest. Beginning in the mid-1980s, reformers channeled infrastructural resources to hard-core poverty regions. In 1993, with 13.8 percent of the rural population officially below the poverty line, Hebei had the largest population of the poor of any coastal province.[21] A 1995 campaign, centered on mountain counties, sought to boost 1.5 million people to a 200-yuan per capita annual income through workfare for road-building and water improvements projects. However, no resources reached the Raoyang poor.

The Raoyang county party secretary was ousted in 1997 for failing to respond to a life-threatening water crisis when a flash flood followed heavy snows. The party did little to help villagers. A military unit was sent in. Its commander, finding the party leader useless, burst into his house where he lolled in pajamas watching television. The commander beat the party secretary and demanded he be replaced. The secretary was transferred to the Hengshui prefectural administration, a promotion. Party officials laughed at the power-lessness of their detractors. The new county party secretary did not appear to villagers to be an improvement. The turnover of officials came ever faster. Offices were said to be for sale.

Raoyang power brokers saw it differently. They felt themselves trapped, while villagers were free. They had to implement unfunded mandates from the center and brave villager anger at the miscellaneous taxes imposed for the projects. Villagers could come and go, no longer subject to the discipline of the collective era and no longer bound to the village. Nonofficial families could have more than one child by paying fines that in 2000 ranged from 500 yuan for a second child in a poor village to 8,000 yuan for a third child in a rich village. By contrast, people on urban payrolls and party members risked a loss of job if they had a second child. Rural rulers felt discriminated against.

In Hengshui, Wugong's prefectural center, the state-run department store expanded and modernized in the late 1990s with the help of a large bank loan to the daughter of the retiring state enterprise manager. Locals commented that connections and corruption unfairly enriched the families of the power-ful. The political system seemed hardly to have changed at all. In Wugong, a rising young leader, Li Yongli, was a grandson of a marriage of the families of old east-end leader Macho Li Shouzheng and the capable west-end leader, Li Wer. Yongli was sharp, but villagers increasingly viewed the party elite of blood inheritance as living off the backs of people.

While major agonies of the Mao era had ended, the political system experi-enced by Wugong villagers showed few signs of change for the better. People saw that the networks once tied to the Mao-era factional struggle between reformer Lin Tie and revolutionary Liu Zihou still secured positions, per-quisites, and power for the privileged. How were villagers to see any improve-ment in the appointment of Niu Maosheng as Hebei governor at the start of the new millennium when he was transferred from Beijing after disclosure of massive corruption in the Water Resources Ministry he headed?[22] A few years later he was imprisoned on new corruption charges.

Army connections were a way for villagers to get things done. Retired senior officers who held party and government jobs were hubs of connections. Villagers sought them out and recounted which were most helpful. Some fixers sold their services for a fee, arranging better jobs and facilitating urban registrations.

Villagers in hinterland Hebei and other northern provinces did not regard themselves as great beneficiaries of the ocean-going openness enjoyed by southern coastal regions. They felt unfairly marginalized by reform. Increas-ingly in this heartland (what some saw as central China — neither the coastal region to the east, infused with foreign money and culture, nor the hinterland minority nationality region to the west), locals believed that their region, the supposed origin of the Han "race," was poor because it had sacrificed over the millennia, long ago resisting invading nomads from the steppe and recently resisting Japanese militarists, offering a northern sacrifice that protected the autonomy of the undeserving south, allowing that soft region to flourish while the martyred north suffered and stagnated. This northern "center" saw southerners as promoting disorder and selfishness (that is, openness, diversity, and decentralization), while people of the northern hinterland found that what China needed was a powerful state center to maintain order and redistribute riches to their still suffering people. In contrast to an imagined state socialist equality of the past, the present reality seemed like an unfair polarization that marginalized villagers of the northern center.

The northern center was conservative not because it was intoxicated by revolution, but because reform seemed not to serve its deepest interests. By arguing against openness and foreign pollution and opposing a supposed loss of independence caused by alleged economic dependence on so-called capitalist imperialism, people loyal to Monarch Liu Zihou's old network attempted to conserve much of the old order. They saw themselves as standing up for Hebei, for socialist egalitarianism, and for the heroes and martyrs who fought a revolution to win justice for China. To them, all that was good about revolution was threatened by reform.

Religion

Religion and spiritualism of all kinds spread. Among these were officially sanctioned forms of Christianity and also independent house churches and heretical sects. With Hebei the historical home to nearly half of China's Roman Catholics, Catholicism quickly revived. Periodic crackdowns, including one in the late 1990s, led to arrest, torture, forced labor, and death for numerous priests and bishops. Revolutionary Baoding was a hotbed of religion.

Raoyang leaders had long told us that villagers were not interested in religion. But in 1990 a large Catholic church was erected in Zoucun, walking distance from Wugong. The 40,000-yuan structure was built (without state funds) to replace a late 19th-century church demolished in the Cultural Revolution. A smaller Catholic church went up in Gaoqiao, just north of Wugong. Equipped with six large ceiling fans, neon lights, an elaborate altar (replete with plastic flowers placed in sorghum whiskey bottles), and a foot-powered organ, the Zoucun church held 200 worshippers. There were morning and evening prayers each day, with four masses on Sunday. A small dwelling attached to the church was reserved for regularly visiting priests from Shenxian county to the south. Prayer books were printed in Cangzhou city. The church was so crowded on Christmas Day that many of the faithful had to stand outside in the freezing cold.

The Zoucun church functioned as an informal community center. Children raced around the courtyard and played in the steeple. When we s, unannounced to attend mass, people eagerly told us that their pa grandparents had been educated in Catholic schools.[23] Persecution of ful had contributed to a sense of martyrdom.[24] All 14 paintings in the church treated the crucifixion of Christ. The underground Catholic (nity that flourished in Xianxian county east of Raoyang remained tie(Vatican despite party repression.[25] Nonbelievers in Raoyang gossipeu that Catholics were a bit too close. They participated in incestuous marriages, it was rumored, and had as many children as possible to increase their numbers.

A Buddhist temple was built in the early 1990s in the market town of Yincun in northeast Raoyang. The Shengxiandao secret society, which authorities had tried to wipe out in the early 1960s, spread all over Hebei. Its members pledged to do good works and won respect. Hebei was also a center of the Falungong spiritual group of *qigong* practitioners that was banned in 1999. When Xu Xinmu, former director of personnel in the Hebei provincial government, was sentenced to four years for warning fellow Falungong practitioners of government plans to outlaw the group, more than 13,000 protested in an open letter to President Jiang Zemin.[26]

Human bonds that were weakened during a generation of revolution, village isolation, and wars on culture struggled to come back to life. But the ethos of dominant villagers was not humanizing for all.

The Gender Gap

Young village women seldom felt nostalgia for Mao-era clothing when, even on sweltering summer days, decorum dictated a thick band of elastic across the breasts, a cotton T-shirt, and a heavy army uniform buttoned up to the neck and down to the wrists. For youth, reform was liberating. Raoyang had changed since the 1930s, when it was the most conservative spot in the region, a place where men kept their women from leaving the walled-in family courtyard. By the 1980s, television, travel, and magazines had brought modern fashions in clothing, music, films, and ideas to the countryside.

A generation and gender gap grew, pitting freedom against constriction, openness against tightening, progress against reaction. It was captured for us in a tableau of an elderly man garbed in traditional dark blue shuffling slowly to the fields, a hoe balanced effortlessly on a shoulder. Suddenly a teenager on a mountain bike wearing a fuchsia athletic shirt swept past, a pirated Sony Walkman sound system pounding out musical rhythms. Many of the young had modernized mentalities.

However, a backlash against Jiang Qing, Mao's wife, and against socialist gender policies in general, reinforced misogynist tendencies. Steps would be taken to assure that women fulfilled their patriarchally subordinated roles. In the early 1990s women were pressured to leave industrial, commercial, and

service jobs and return home. With large-scale layoffs of state industrial workers and with erratic cycles of boom and bust in the state enterprise sector,
women bore the brunt of the erratic transition from an economy monopolized
by state and collective enterprise.

The vicissitudes of change were manifest in the marriage of Li Meidu. Her
parents arranged for her to marry into prosperous Wugong in 1993. A native
of nearby Nanguanzhuang, she was tall, attractive, and well educated. Even in
better-off Wugong, her gold ring, gold necklace, and fashionable clothing set
her apart. Village women explained that Meidu's new family was among the
richest in Wugong, her father-in-law having run a factory for a decade.

While we were chatting, a short and plain young man appeared. Meidu,
three months pregnant, snapped at her husband, Nine Happinesses, "Who
told you to come?" He mumbled, "Mother told me to bring you home."
Meidu replied, "Get out! I'm not going with you!"

Nine Happinesses, the oldest son of the wealthy Wei family, was believed
to be retarded. An earlier marriage had quickly ended in divorce. The Weis,
accusing the first wife of being barren, promptly approached Meidu's parents
to arrange a second marriage. Meidu's father, an accountant who earned only
200 yuan a month, was desperate to support a son studying in a professional
school. The Weis agreed to pay not only a handsome bride price for Meidu but
also the entire cost of her dowry and a monthly allowance for her parents.

Meidu protested the arrangement right up to the wedding day. In the end,
however, she complied. Once married, Meidu made no secret of her distaste
for her husband, and villagers predicted that she, too, would seek a divorce.
Meidu's in-laws showered her with money, and Meidu seemed determined to
make them pay dearly. Her father-in-law donated 10,000 yuan to the village
primary school so Meidu could be hired as a part-time teacher. He also paid
the 9,000-yuan tuition bill for the teacher-training certificate she hoped to
earn. Meidu seemed a capable negotiator empowered by the dynamics of
commercialization, but like many women she was trapped in sometimes brutal patriarchal inheritance relations.[27]

The complex plight of women was also visible in the fate of aspiring writer
Shi Guiying, the wife of the surly ex-soldier Li Mengjie. He awoke one night
in the early 1980s to observe her in a corner working on the novel that he had
ordered her to drop. Noting where she hid the manuscript, he waited to strike.
As Guiying was finishing her book, Mengjie burned the manuscript. She was
furious. So was he. Mengjie beat Guiying badly.

Mengjie had grown fond of a Caozhuang school teacher whose husband, a
commune official, brutalized her. Guiying's son told his mother that he saw
Mengjie and the paramour in an embrace. Guiying swallowed the bitterness
until the day when Mengjie followed her to work and then kicked and cursed
her in view of her co-workers. She wanted to divorce Mengjie. But if she

moved out of the home built with her savings and moved in with her parents, she would become the miscreant who had abandoned the family. She would lose all claim to house and children and might even be compelled to pay damages. Guiying had to remain with her husband, vulnerable to further beatings, while seeking divorce.

Guiying's friends, led by Geng Huijuan, Boss Geng's political daughter, urged forgiveness and compassion. Mengjie was a good provider and supposedly a faithful husband. He did not gamble or squander wealth. Besides, as an orphan, Mengjie had experienced a rough childhood. And he had brought honor to the village as a soldier and party member. Should not Guiying continue to help him? After all, family harmony was best for the children. Geng Xiufeng, recognizing the difficulties faced by divorced women, warned Guiying that she would be pressured to leave the village if she divorced.

The aspiring writer still filed for divorce. The case dragged on while the authorities sought reconciliation. Eventually Guiying found a cultural worker with whom she shared intimacies. He promised he would get divorced when she did. Their secret could not be kept. Gossip spread that Guiying had betrayed Mengjie and taken up with a married man. The Geng family treated a cuckolded Mengjie as the victim in need of emotional support. Guiying was isolated and damned. The night before the divorce was final, Mengjie beat her one last time, telling Guiying he would leave her a memory she would never forget. The settlement gave Mengjie the house built with Guiying's money. He also took the boy. As locals saw it, she was left with the girl. The court ordered Mengjie to pay ten yuan per month toward child support.

Mengjie immediately married his lover, the now divorced school teacher who was 12 years his junior. Guiying faced a socially stigmatized life. She raised her daughter and helped support, educate, and find urban work for the children of her brother and sister. And she wrote. In 1989, when visiting Tianjin to find a publisher for her fiction, she met again her love from a few years past, only to discover that, although he had divorced when she broke with Mengjie, he had remarried. She broke down, sobbing that the fates were eternally against her. She repeated Buddhist phrases learned from her grandmother, blaming herself for her suffering, since "good is rewarded with good and evil with evil."

Friends helped Shi Guiying find a job with the Hengshui prefectural cultural bureau. She moved into its dormitory, forced to leave her daughter in Wugong with her mother. Mengjie cut off child support. In Hengshui, she rose to department head and eventually chaired the municipal culture and art association. She continued to write, bringing out a book of short stories, *Dreams of a Sandy Shore* (Shanan menghuan). Her son eventually rejoined her. After her daughter married and had a child, Guiying retired in the mid-1990s and raised funds from girl friends to start an arts kindergarten, the Sunshine

School (Yangguang), in Hengshui, a beautiful oasis passing on the Chinese cultural forms Guiying had studied in her youth.

Another school opened in Shenxian county, south of Raoyang, in response to the crisis of rural education. The private high school attracted the best teachers in the region with salaries far higher than those paid to Raoyang public school teachers. It reflected the growing economic polarization. Early in the 21st century, younger and more technically oriented Raoyang officials tried to upgrade education, using every connection to get computers into the public schools. Despite inadequate funding, a majority of Raoyang high school graduates won entrance to tertiary education through competitive examinations. A better future for villagers awaited more state funding for education.

The Eternal Local

As the millennium ended, a reflective "landlord" Li Maoxiu looked beyond the decades of pain brought by revolution. Saddened by the death of his son, Li Wei, Maoxiu grew more tender toward his aging wife and more loving with his grandchildren.

In 1994 local people asked us to stop using the Beijing dialect and start speaking as they do. Little children then stopped throwing stones. Upon hearing a greeting spoken in the local argot, children skipped happily with us and introduced their friends.

Lineage bonds intensified. In Wugong, the Li lineages have revived as mutual help ventures. The division between the northern Li and the southern Li began to heal. A southern Li from the village center, Li Daduo, became head of the village government. Party leaders enjoyed eating out at a restaurant across from the abandoned Geng Changsuo museum, an eatery run by another southern Li. Ethical bonds were restored. During the 1996 lunar New Year, articulate Li Zhongxin led his children to bow (bainian) to lineage seniors in 28 households.

Soon after collectives returned land to households, lineages reconstructed burial mounds that had been destroyed in the Cultural Revolution. The party apparatus, however, kept inveighing against sacred burial mounds, emblematic of the resurgence of lineage life, as a superstition that hurt production by reducing arable acreage. In 1996 Hebei called for the elimination of ten million grave mounds on arable land.[28] The party touted cremation; villagers resisted.

Against the revolution's demand for class ties above all, families held together. Han Peng, Boss Geng's granddaughter who grew up in Beijing, visited Wugong after her grandmother Xu Shukuan, Geng's wife, had been buried. Geng was especially proud of Peng, the first college graduate in the family. But he also liked to tease her, quoting Mao on how intellectuals were not as clean as peasants. Han Peng had not accompanied her mother to Geng's funeral in 1985.

Han Peng graduated from a branch school associated with Beijing Normal University and became a supporter of Deng Xiaoping's reform policies, but also an advocate of more thoroughgoing change. In visiting Wugong, she found herself embroiled in squabbles with conservative villagers and put off by the problems faced by women. "To me, honestly, Wugong is another world," she observed. "I grew up in Beijing, and my family situation did not allow me to gain knowledge of country life. From the limited experience I had, I cannot imagine that I could ever cope with the physical harshness of life as a villager."

Han Peng was dismayed by the power of the "old feudalism." Culture, as everywhere, held ambiguous promise for the future. Raoyang's people took great pride in their ancient history and culture, in the development of martial arts, traditional crafts, local opera, fireworks, and food specialties, all of which seemed crude to urban sophisticates.

Patriots were delighted when a 2,300-year-old map was unearthed in an imperial mausoleum in Pingshan county, 50 miles west of Raoyang. Archeologists describe the map, carved into a copper plate, "not only as the oldest map ever found in China, but the oldest map noted with numerals in the world."[29] Ancient glories, modern patriotism, contemporary agonies, and hopes for a better future were complexly and passionately mixed.

In 1990 Han Peng, after a sojourn in the open southern port of Shenzhen, went to Australia, took the name Jennifer Han, and married an Australian. We could chat with the granddaughter of revolutionary hero Geng Changsuo in her home outside Sydney or by e-mail. Jennifer's mother, Geng Duo, Boss Geng's fourth daughter, a retired widow, went to live for a while in the grandiose new home of heir Zhang Mandun. She also visited Jennifer in Australia to help after the birth of a first child, then returned to Wugong. Twins followed. The mother flew back to Australia and again returned to the village. At the turn into the new millennium, the village was increasingly connected to an ever-smaller planet.

Before leaving China, Han Peng was invited to visit her grandmother's burial mound. Unenthusiastic about participating in a "superstitious" rite, she nevertheless joined her relatives to pay respects on a windy and desolate day. "We took out the food we had brought and placed it in front of the burial mound. My younger uncle started to cry very sadly. My cousins set off some firecrackers. The noise was deafening. My uncles burnt paper, providing money for the dead. The smoke got in my eyes, making tears run down. My older uncle pointed out other grave mounds. He told me that the one at the end belonged to my great grandfather and the neighboring one belonged to an uncle who was killed by the Japanese. He described many others. I started to feel there were very deep roots under this piece of land. I could feel the harshness of village lives. They lived and died after struggling with poor land, natural disasters and local toughs. They never had modern education or comforts. Oh, I felt deep respect for these people who had the strength to deal with hard lives and who provided the seed for later generations to grow. I felt I was a part of them. And I was proud of it."

APPENDIX
OF TABLES

Table 1   Crop area, yields, and output in Wugong village (brigade), 1961–1982 (area in mu; yields in catties per mu)

Year	Corn		Millet		Sorghum		Wheat		Sweet potatoes	
	Area	Yield	Area	Yield	Area	Yield	Area	Yield	Area	Yield
1961	1,300	360	456	273	210	248	850	215	250	602
1962	1,451	403	500	389	292	287	932	232	257	525
1963	1,440	205	500	449	150	167	1,000	356	250	196
1964	1,550	271	300	399	50	272	1,600	161	200	213
1965	1,250	528	350	527	400	569	1,150	301	100	716
1966	1,376	515	230	549	289	610	1,400	352	125	374
1967	1,377	373	401	398	422	549	1,508	298	149	501
1968	1,488	428	298	504	310	652	1,357	223	137	527
1969	1,243	445	319	443	659	540	1,481	377	122	648
1970	1,628	460	322	361	239	920	1,752	424	145	649
1971	1,725	476	317	330	110	968	1,866	468	148	600
1972	1,534	492	254	371	427	634	1,850	610	0	0
1973	1,041	555	273	370	812	734	2,300	546	0	0
1974	1,005	632	325	409	1,028	715	2,200	691	0	0
1975	754	570	194	509	1,237	635	2,000	714	16	630
1976	963	514	200	355	1,114	677	2,206	726	0	0
1977	900	433	200	208	1,300	622	2,050	552	0	0
1978	900	578	200	178	1,300	490	2,200	813	0	0
1979	1,416	618	174	346	810	574	2,400	761	0	0
1980	3,000	733	160	400	300	434	2,500	572	0	0
1981	1,700	762	160	485	290	522	3,150	502	0	0
1982	1,852	776	160	494	135	610	2,150	319	0	0

* Grain-sown area exceeds the area listed as all grain as a measure of double cropping.

Five-Year Averages

	1961–65	1966–70	1971–75	1976–80
Total grain (1,000 catties)	1,116	1,662	2,808	3,061
Per capita grain output (catties)	541	721	1,112	1,206
Grain yield (catties per mu)	492	722	1,175	1,288
Total cotton (catties)	40,182	66,056	95,689	60,651
Per capita cotton output (catties)	19	29	38	24
Cotton yield (catties per mu)	64	110	121	91

Oil (sesame and peanuts)		Cotton		All grain		Grain-sown Area*	Total grain (1,000 catties)	Per capita grain output (catties)	Cultivated area all crops	Irrigated area
Area	Yield	Area	Yield	Area	Yield					
260	191	850	62	2,296	457	3,144	1,051	552	3,701	1,550
200	307	558	76	2,600	482	3,532	1,254	615	3,701	1,700
400	148	600	45	2,300	410	3,300	942	453	3,701	1,700
600	18	600	47	2,100	370	3,700	776	364	3,701	1,800
280	316	550	92	2,100	740	3,250	1,555	719	3,701	2,000
382	207	360	54	2,020	768	3,420	1,552	719	3,201	2,000
364	254	520	96	2,349	608	3,857	1,429	644	3,401	2,000
219	228	650	137	2,233	611	3,589	1,369	593	3,643	3,020
213	257	662	131	2,531	708	4,012	1,762	750	3,585	3,585
222	288	650	131	2,404	915	4,438	2,199	906	3,699	3,699
259	313	846	110	2,300	1,005	4,751	2,312	936	3,650	3,505
322	95	705	89	2,470	1,108	4,856	2,734	1,096	3,664	3,664
243	260	780	152	2,310	1,147	4,746	2,764	1,091	3,664	3,664
251	268	800	145	2,400	1,327	4,793	3,184	1,249	3,662	3,662
239	169	830	108	2,370	1,287	4,571	3,049	1,188	3,662	3,662
195	243	757	58	2,350	1,330	4,707	3,126	1,236	3,657	3,657
220	319	650	87	2,450	1,119	4,990	2,741	1,088	3,657	3,657
226	274	650	82	2,450	1,329	4,900	3,255	1,265	3,657	3,657
260	249	650	72	2,450	1,363	4,900	3,003	1,185	3,657	3,657
260	365	650	158	2,450	1,299	4,900	3,180	1,254	3,657	3,657
260	210	1,000	118	2,150	1,512	4,300	3,250	1,273	3,657	3,657
260	89	1,000	135	2,150	1,407	4,300	2,950	1,141	3,657	3,657

Table 2   Population and labor utilization in Wugong village (brigade), 1961–1982

Year	Total population	Male population	Female population	Total labor[1]	Full male labor	Full female labor
1961	1,904	890	1,014	701	346	356
1962	2,040	1,029	1,011	650	390	260
1963	2,080	1,049	1,031	650	390	260
1964	2,131	1,074	1,057	680	400	280
1965	2,163	1,096	1,047	680	400	280
1966	2,185	1,098	1,087	700	410	290
1967	2,218	1,104	1,114	785	440	345
1968	2,309	1,113	1,196	785	440	345
1969	2,349	1,084	1,265	785	440	345
1970	2,426	1,143	1,283	1,110	589	521
1971	2,471	1,185	1,286	1,114	646	468
1972	2,496	1,189	1,307	1,090	564	426
1973	2,533	1,216	1,317	1,090	564	426
1974	2,549	1,224	1,325	1,285	714	571
1975	2,567	1,224	1,343	1,151	641	510
1976	2,534	1,226	1,308	1,186	522	664
1977	2,552	1,230	1,322	1,215	542	673
1978	2,573	1,211	1,362	1,197	527	670
1979	2,534	1,185	1,349	1,297	606	671
1980	2,536	1,142	1,352	1,321	610	711
1981	2,553	1,196	1,357	1,330	620	710
1982	2,586	1,206	1,380	1,347	629	718

[1] This figure includes individuals rated as partial labor power so that two half-labor power individuals are counted as a full labor power.

% of labor force male	Labor in industrial sidelines in teams and brigades	Labor working outside the team	Labor working in brigade	Labor working in commune	Labor working in county
49	45	60	60		
60	139	60	60		
60	118	50	50		
59	113	50	50		
59	131	50	50		
59	118	60	60		
56	78	50	50		
56	118	70	70		
56	119	70	70		
53	122	83	70	13	
58	125	92	80	12	
52	136	102	100	2	
52	135	113	110	3	
56	132	133	120	13	
56	152	131	125	6	
44	158	173	134	5	34
45	198	197	154	15	28
44	235	210	165	20	25
46	225	223	170	11	42
46	450	208	160	10	38
47	430	189	145	9	35
47	410	162	121	7	34

Table 3   Collective income and income distribution in Wugong village (brigade), 1961–1982

Year	Gross crop income (1,000 yuan)	Gross sideline income (1,000 yuan)	Percent of income from sidelines	Gross income total (1,000 yuan)	Net income total (1,000 yuan)	Total income distributed (1,000 yuan)
1961	174	27	13	199	146	129
1962	264	164	38	428	334	252
1963	193	81	30	274	199	177
1964	160	57	26	217	167	130
1965	246	73	23	319	227	197
1966	242	67	20	309	227	192
1967	264	53	17	317	228	194
1968	302	72	19	375	278	238
1969	350	85	19	436	321	265
1970	387	105	21	492	350	292
1971	435	129	23	564	400	313
1972	476	161	27	597	431	324
1973	530	149	22	680	402	329
1974	657	157	19	814	586	421
1975	547	204	27	747	489	400
1976	403	273	36	777	548	404
1977	463	407	47	870	614	426
1978	503	437	46	940	691	484
1979	606	420	41	1,025	533	522
1980	793	264	33	1,057	798	632
1981	739	291	39	1,030	769	656
1982	852	127	14	923	641	622

Note: Income figures include the value of income paid in kind as well as in cash.

Percent of gross income distributed	Cooperative membership (people)	Per capita distributed income (yuan)	Per capita income paid in cash (yuan)	Per capita grain allocation (catties)	Value of labor day (yuan)
76	1,904	79	15	362	.59
68	2,040	130	34	500	1.42
64	2,080	85	19	374	.87
63	2,131	61	5	297	.64
62	2,154	91	21	417	.74
62	2,185	85	18	420	.70
60	2,309	89	18	400	.74
67	2,373	105	22	420	.47
65	2,413	115	26	410	.48
59	2,426	120	31	410	.48
56	2,471	127	38	420	.86
55	2,494	130	28	420	.83
48	2,533	142	43	420	.88
52	2,549	165	61	440	.96
52	2,567	156	67	440	.85
52	2,534	159	71	420	.87
49	2,538	168	75	440	.99
51	2,521	188	84	460	.98
51	2,533	206	102	487	1.00
60	2,516	251	127	498	1.10
64	2,518	256	126	657	1.10
67	2,545	298	131	673	1.25

Table 4   Crop sales to the state in Wugong village (brigade), 1961–1982 (sales figures in 1,000 catties)

Year	Wheat	Coarse grains	Total grain	% of grain sold	Per capita grain sales (catties)	Cotton	Oil
1961	30	40	70	7	37	47	10
1962	30	43	73	6	36	33	1
1963	40	45	85	9	41	15	0
1964	40	17	57	7	27	23	8
1965	40	161	201	13	93	45	42
1966	60	178	238	15	104	17	61
1967	62	84	146	10	63	44	80
1968	86	58	144	11	61	83	110
1969	128	108	236	13	134	81	94
1970	300	261	561	26	231	79	85
1971	350	213	563	24	228	87	65
1972	351	450	801	29	321	57	52
1973	501	471	972	35	384	113	103
1974	550	483	1,033	32	405	109	102
1975	602	490	1,092	36	425	83	66
1976	650	450	1,100	35	434	37	35
1977	650	450	1,100	40	433	52	31
1978	700	130	830	25	329	44	8
1979	727	142	869	29	343	34	4
1980	590	156	746	23	296	97	3
1981	401	237	638	20	254	112	4
1982	351	405	756	26	297	100	2

Five-Year Averages

	1961–65	66–70	71–75	76–80
Wheat sales (1,000 catties)	36	127	471	663
Total grain sales (1,000 catties)	97	265	892	929
Percent of grain sold	8	15	31	30
Per capita grain sales (catties)	47	118	353	367
Cotton sales (1,000 catties)	33	61	90	53
Oil sales (1,000 catties)	12	86	78	16

Table 5   Collective accumulation in Wugong village (brigade), 1961–1982

Year	Total circulating funds (100 yuan)[1]	Fixed assets (cumulative capital) (100 yuan)[2]	Total accumulation (100 yuan)	Per capita accumulation (yuan)[3]	Percentage of accumulation by teams
1961	70	1,230	1,300	68	
1962	145	1,284	1,429	70	27
1963	135	1,345	1,480	71	26
1964	141	1,660	1,801	85	37
1965	140	928	1,068	50	70
1966	98	648	746	34	12
1967	90	1,095	1,185	51	7
1968	130	1,671	1,801	76	13
1969	130	2,578	2,708	112	13
1970	170	2,904	3,074	127	22
1971	116	3,689	3,805	154	29
1972	215	6,427	6,642	266	54
1973	101	9,166	9,267	366	70
1974	156	10,938	11,094	435	71
1975	70	7,600	7,670	299	61
1976	454	12,223	12,677	500	68
1977	626	13,060	13,686	539	67
1978	982	13,897	14,879	587	70
1979	2,631	13,753	16,384	647	81
1980	3,342	14,747	18,089	713	78
1981	3,056	16,875	19,931	780	77
1982	2,954	17,145	20,099	780	77

[1] Circulating funds include funds annually replenished for such purposes as welfare and production expenses.

[2] Fixed assets is the value of machinery, equipment, and other physical assets possessed by teams and brigades, with the exception of land, the most valuable asset, which is not assigned a monetary value.

[3] All accumulation was in the hands of the villagewide coop prior to 1962, thereafter the accumulation process took place both at the team and at the brigade levels, as indicated in the changing percentages shown in team accumulation.

Five-Year Averages

	1961–65	1966–70	1971–75	1976–80
Total circulating funds (100 yuan)	126	124	132	1,607
Fixed assets (100 yuan)	1,289	1,582	7,564	13,536
Total accumulation (100 yuan)	1,416	1,903	7,696	15,143
Per capita accumulation (yuan)	69	80	304	597
% of accumulation by teams	40	13	57	73

Table 6   Agricultural machinery in Wugong village (brigade), 1955–1982

	Total machinery		Machinery used in agriculture							Irrigation and drainage machinery			
			Large and medium tractors[1]		Small tractors		Threshers		Sprayers/dusters		Diesel engines		Electric motors	
							Lg. and Med	Small	Mechanical	Manual				
	No.	HP	No.	HP	No.	HP	No.	No.	No.	No.	No.	HP	No.	HP
1955	2	24									2	24		
1968	8	24									2	24		
1969	11	44									4	44		
1970	80	341	1	55			3			51	4	44	37	198
1971	137	363	1	55			4	2		79	4	44	40	220
1972	226	925	2	110			5	2	1	97	43	464	53	295
1973	259	1,061	2	110			5	2	1	97	59	592	53	295
1974	267	1,186	3	165			6	1	3	105	62	619	55	306
1975	300	1,646	3	165			6		4	102	71	732	81	613
1976	320	1,693	3	165	4	48	6		3	96	56	606	55	424
1977	322	1,734	3	165	6	72	6		3	84	61	658	50	392
1978	259	2,100	3	165	6	83	6		3	82	71	1,060	111	707
1979	265	2,136	3	165	7	70	5		3	84	75	1,066	75	407
1980	267	2,142	3	165	6	84	5		2	85	75	1,151	75	407
1981	377	2,044	3	165	7	84	6	1	3	147	75	1,083	75	397
1982	377	2,044	3	165	7		6	1	3	147	75	1,083	75	397

Note: Totals may exceed components, since a small number of machines are not included in these tables. There were no changes recorded between 1955 and 1967.

[1] Wugong had access to state-owned tractors from 1954. It bought its own tractors for the first time in 1970.

Power machinery				Agricultural processing machinery					Animal husbandry machinery	
Engines		Electric motors		Rice mill	Flour mill machine	Cotton gin	Cotton beater	Oil press	Crusher	Fodder cutter
No.	HP	No.	HP	No.	No.	No.	No.	No.	No.	No.
										6
					3					7
4	44			3	6	5	4	1	6	5
4	44			4	6	5	3	1	6	5
2	24	7	32	4	6	3	3	1	8	6
4	32	7	32	3	3	3	3	1	8	6
10	88	2	8	3	6	3	3	1	6	5
5	60	15	77	3	6	3	4	1	9	7
18	212	31	238	2	7	3	4	1	6	9
13	202	39	245	1	7	3	4	1	10	10
0	0	30	210	1	7	3	4		7	11
				3	7	1	4		9	11
				3	4	1	4		12	11
				3	4	1	4		9	9
				3	4	4	4		9	9

Table 7   Per capita collective income distributed in teams 1, 2, and 3, Wugong brigade and Wugong commune, 1960–1982 (in yuan)

Year	Team 1	Team 2	Team 3	Wugong brigade	Wugong commune
1960	57	50	49	52	
1961	71	70	88	79	
1962	126	110	147	130	
1963	85	76	94	85	
1964	57	55	71	61	
1965	93	85	95	91	
1966	87	78	97	85	42
1967	84	78	97	89	
1968	106	91	111	105	
1969	117	103	122	115	
1970	122	105	134	120	
1971	123	110	143	127	
1972	125	112	184	130	
1973	140	117	167	142	
1974	170	128	191	165	80
1975	134	95	188	156	
1976	140	120	207	159	
1977	144	137	214	168	
1978	177	159	223	188	
1979	201	168	242	206	109
1980	249	195	297	251	95
1981	261	208	304	256	107
1982	269	188	274	298	221

Note: The brigade figure is weighted by team size with team 3 the largest team. The figures include the value of income in kind as well as cash.

Five-Year Averages

	1960–64	1965–69	1970–74	1975–79	1980–82
Team 1 (yuan)	79	97	136	159	260
Team 2 (yuan)	73	73	114	136	197
Team 3 (yuan)	90	104	164	215	292
Wugong brigade (yuan)	82	97	134	175	268

Table 8 Collective income, value of the labor day, and accumulation in the villages (brigades) of Wugong commune, selected years 1964–1978

	1978 population	Total collective income per capita (yuan)			Per capita collective income distributed (yuan)					Value of labor day (yuan)					Per capita accumulation			
		1966	1974	1978	1964	1968	1972	1975	1978	1964	1966	1968	1972	1975	1965	1971	1977	1978
Wugong	2,533	136	318	676	61	105	130	156	190	.64	.70	.47	.83	.85	133	307		548
Zoucun	2,839	72	210	564	23	32	65	86	126	.35	.21	.43	.50	.70				301
Nanguan-zhuang	836	74	158	249	41	43	46	49	83	.23	.28	.29	.31	.32				220
Dongsong	761	77	109	168					66									110
Yangge-zhuang	1,977	66	104	264					96									213
Wangqiao	1,208	59	163	215	30	35	57	61	99	.30	.35	.45	.47	.50				189
Songqiao	1,137	63	140	262					66									184
Gaoqiao	1,837	95	156	306					112									311
Yuanzi	641	94	92	174	50	54	35	40	72	.37	.37	.30	.37	.42				177
Gengkou	2,154	66	164	270					84									290

✣ ABBREVIATIONS

CVSS	Edward Friedman, Paul G. Pickowicz, and Mark Selden, *Chinese Village, Socialist State* (New Haven: Yale University Press, 1991)
FBIS	U.S. Foreign Broadcast Information Service
GMRB	*Guangming ribao*
GXF: 1979	Geng Xiufeng, "Nongcun chu bian," unpublished manuscript, 6 vols., 1979
GXF: 1988	Geng Xiufeng, "Renjian zheng dao," unpublished manuscript, 1988
GXF: 1992	Geng Xiufeng, "Renjian zheng dao," unpublished manuscript, 1992
HBRB	*Hebei ribao (Hebei Daily)*
Huakai, 1963	*Huakai di yi zhi* (Tianjin: Tianjin renmin chuban she, 1963)
JJDSD	*Zhonghua renmin gongheguo jingji da shi dian* (Changchun: Jilin renmin chuban she, 1987)
JJDSJ	Fang Weizhong, ed., *Zhonghua renmin gongheguo jingji dashi ji* (Beijing: Zhongguo shehui kexue chuban she, 1984)
JPRS	Joint Publication Research Service
NCNA	New China News Agency
QZWG	*Qingzhu Wugong renmin gongshe jitihua ershi zhounian dahui huibian* (Hengshui, 1963)
RMRB	*Renmin ribao (People's Daily)*
SCMP	*Survey of the China Mainland Press* (Hong Kong)
WGRM	Nankai daxue lishi xi, Wugong dadui cun shi bianxie zu, eds., *Wugong renmin de zhandou licheng* (Beijing: Zhonghua shuzhu, 1978)
XZGJS	Zheng Derong, Shao Pengwen, Zhu Yang, and Gu Min, eds., *Xin Zhongguo jishi, 1949–1984* (Changchun: Dongbei shifan daxue chuban she, 1985)

ZGXT   Zhongguo Hebei sheng wei zuzhi bu, Zhonggong Hebei sheng wei dangshi ziliao zhengji bianshen weiyuanhui, Hebei sheng dang'anju, eds., *Hebei sheng zhengchuan xitong zuzhi shi ziliao, Hebei sheng difang junshi xitong zuzhi shi ziliao, Hebei sheng tongyi zhanxian xitong zuzhi shi ziliao, Hebei sheng qunzhong tuanti xitong zuzhi shi ziliao, 1949–1987* (Shijiazhuang: Hebei renmin chuban she, 1990)

ZNDJ   Nongye chuban she, ed., *Zhongguo nongye dashi ji, 1949–1980* (Beijing: Renmin chuban she, 1980)

ZRDJ   Zhonghua renmin gongheguo jingji dashi ji bianxuan zu, ed., *Zhonghua renmin gongheguo jingji dashi ji, 1949 nian shiyue–1984 nian jiuyue* (Beijing: Beijing chuban she, 1985)

ZZSZL   *Hebei sheng Raoyang xian zuzhi shi ziliao, 1924–1987* (Shijiazhuang: Hebei renmin chuban she, 1991)

❧ NOTES

2 Back from the Brink

1   Our earlier volume, CVSS, assesses the social costs of the party's decision to move rapidly to collectivization of agriculture and nationalization of industry from 1953, reaching a crescendo in the years 1955–56. See the careful analysis of the new democracy in Mao's thought and the decision to abandon it in Wang Haibo, "A Study of Mao Zedong's 'On New Democracy,'" *Jingji yanjiu* 12 (December 1993), pp. 16–25, in JPRS-CAR-011, February 16, 1994, pp. 3–10.

2   CVSS.

3   Nicholas Lardy, "The Chinese Economy under Stress, 1958–1965," in Roderick Mac-Farquhar and John K. Fairbank, eds., *The Cambridge History of China: Volume 14, The People's Republic, Part 1: The Emergence of Revolutionary China, 1949–1965* (Cambridge: Cambridge University Press, 1987), pp. 378–83.

4   Kenneth Lieberthal, "The Great Leap Forward and the Split in the Yenan Leadership," in MacFarquhar and Fairbank, eds., *The People's Republic, Part 1*, p. 318.

5   ZZSZL, pp. 90, 92, 107–14, 118–19.

6   ZZSZL, p. 183; Hebei sheng diming bangong shi, ed., *Hebei zheng qu yan ge zhi* (Shijiazhuang: Hebei kexue jixu chuban she, 1985), pp. 324–26.

7   Material in this and the following four paragraphs draws on GXF: 1988, pp. 62–69.

8   Geng Xiufeng quoted Zhang during an interview that appears in the documentary film *The Mao Years*, Sue Williams (producer and director), Paul G. Pickowicz (associate director), Ambrica Productions, New York, 1994. Also see GXF; 1988, pp. 67–68.

9   ZZSZL, pp. 114, 213.

10 GXF: 1979, vol. 4, pp. 12, 77–78.

11 GXF: 1979, vol. 4, p. 121.

12 Jia Wenping, *Zhenli yu mingyun* (Beijing: Renmin chuban she, 1995), pp. 139–63.

13 The letter is in GXF: 1979, vol. 4, pp. 81–89. For a discussion of Geng Xiufeng's political thought see Paul G. Pickowicz, "Memories of Revolution and Collectivization in China: The Unauthorized Reminiscences of a Rural Intellectual," in Rubie S. Watson, ed., *Memory, History, and Opposition under State Socialism* (Santa Fe: School of American Research Press, 1990), pp. 127–47.

14 GXF: 1988, pp. 72–74.

15 Lardy, "The Chinese Economy," p. 385. Hebei grain yields dropped from 153 catties per mu in 1958 to 113 in 1961, the lowest level in a decade. CVSS, pp. 259–60.

16 Lieberthal, p. 322; Dali Yang, *Calamity and Reform in China: State, Rural Society and Institutional Change Since the Great Leap Famine* (Stanford: Stanford University Press, 1996), pp. 73–81; Lardy, pp. 381–82. The text of the "Twelve Articles on People's

Communes" of November 1960 is in Mark Selden, *The People's Republic of China* (New York: Monthly Review Press, 1979), pp. 516–17.

17   Roderick MacFarquhar, *The Origins of the Cultural Revolution: Volume 3, The Coming of the Cataclysm, 1961–1966* (New York: Columbia University Press, 1997), pp. 41–42.

18   Lieberthal, pp. 323, 325; Yang, pp. 78–79. A partial translation of Mao's "Sixty Articles on People's Communes" is in Selden, *The People's Republic of China.*

19   XZGJS, p. 298; JJDSJ, p. 339; MacFarquhar, pp. 48–49.

20   This paragraph and the following two paragraphs draw on Lardy, "The Chinese Economy," pp. 388–90; Yang, pp. 81–89.

21   XZGJS, pp. 295–97; Yang, pp. 81–89.

22   GXF: 1979, vol. 4, p. 169.

23   ZZSZL, pp. 111–13, 118–19.

24   This paragraph and the following paragraphs are based on GXF: 1979, vol. 4, pp. 134–38.

25   On the popularity of Hengshui White Lightning see *Beijing dagong bao,* June 26, 1963.

26   WGRM, pp. 104–05.

27   This paragraph and the following four paragraphs are based on GXF: 1979, vol. 4, pp. 162–64.

28   GXF: 1979, vol. 4, p. 164.

29   The full text of the letter dated August 20, 1962, is in GXF: 1979, vol. 4, pp. 161–68.

30   Lieberthal, pp. 329–33; Yang, pp. 88–89.

31   ZZSZL, p. 213.

32   ZZSZL, p. 113.

33   Uradyn Bulag, *The Mongols at China's Edge: History and the Politics of National Unity* (Lantham: Rowman and Littlefield, 2001), pp. 134–35.

34   GXF: 1979, vol. 4, pp. 151–52. Also see WGRM, pp. 103–04.

35   MacFarquhar, pp. 220–21, 226, 278.

36   GXF: 1979, vol. 4, pp. 152–57.

37   Lardy, p. 383; XZGJS, p. 301; JJDSD, p. 317.

38   FBIS, March 19, 1980 (supplement), p. 23; RMRB, January 8, 1979; MacFarquhar, pp. 41–42. On the reduction of state workers see JJDSD, pp. 351–52; XZGJS, pp. 299–300.

39   Ma Hong and Sun Shangqing, eds., *Studies in the Problems of China's Economic Structure,* Beijing, 1981:JPRS-CEA-84-064-I.

40   Huakai, 1963, p. 275.

41   Jonathan Unger, *Education under Mao: Class and Competition in Canton Schools, 1960–1980* (New York: Columbia University Press, 1982), pp. 49–53.

42   XZGJS, pp. 305, 319.

43   HBRB, April 27, 1963.

44   Lieberthal, pp. 337–38.

45   The Li Huiying and Shi Guiying material is in Huakai, 1963, pp. 281–97.

46   Ibid., pp. 203–18.

47   See Wolfgang Kubin's reference to Shu Ting in "Images of Subjugation and Defiance: Female Characters in the Early Drama of Tian Han," in Tani Barlow, ed., *Gender Politics in Modern China* (Durham: Duke University Press, 1993), p. 139.

48   CVSS, p. 294; see statistical appendixes in this volume.

49   Jia, pp. 193–204.
50   HBRB, September 1, 1977, and March 13, 1978.
51   HBRB, September 23, 1962.
52   HBRB, November 24, 1962, and December 19, 1962. Also see HBRB, March 5, 1963.

3   Memory and Myth

1   GXF: 1979, vol. 4, p. 171.
2   HBRB, November 22, 1963.
3   Huakai, 1963, p. 182.
4   Huakai, 1963, pp. 100–01.
5   This and the next paragraph draw on GXF: 1979, vol. 4, p. 17; GXF: 1988, pp. 77–78.
6   GXF: 1979, vol. 4, p. 177.
7   Roderick MacFarquhar, *The Origins of the Cultural Revolution: Volume 3, The Coming of the Cataclysm, 1961–1966* (New York: Columbia University Press, 1997), pp. 220–21.
8   XZGJS, pp. 332, 335.
9   HBRB, November 22, 1963; RMRB, December 7, 1963.
10   HBRB, December 7, 1963. The second principle dictated that Wugong would market its rope exclusively through state channels.
11   GXF: 1992, p. 259.
12   GXF: 1979, vol. 4, pp. 178–79.
13   *Geng Changsuo zouguo de daolu* (Tianjin: Hebei renmin chuban she, 1966).
14   HBRB, November 25, 1963.
15   Vaclav Smil, *China's Environmental Crisis: An Inquiry into the Limits of National Development* (Armonk: M. E. Sharpe, 1993), p. 39.
16   RMRB, December 28, 1963; Judith Shapiro, *Mao's War against Nature* (Cambridge: Cambridge University Press, 2001).
17   QZWG, p. 53.
18   GXF: 1979, vol. 4, p. 179.
19   Yields of approximately 550 catties of unhusked grain per person are adequate to provide self-sufficiency in the range of 1,700–1,900 calories. Kenneth Walker, *Food Grain Procurement in China* (Cambridge: Cambridge University Press, 1984), p. 15.
20   FBIS, December 11, 1963, DDD 7.
21   Huakai, 1963, p. 151.
22   Huakai, 1963, pp. 346–47.
23   Huakai, 1963, p. 357.
24   This account of the celebration draws on interviews and GXF: 1979, vol. 4, pp. 179, 188, 207.
25   QZWG contains a number of photos that display the slogans.
26   GXF: 1979, vol. 4, pp. 180–84, provides details on the exhibition. Some production figures displayed at the exhibit were far higher than those later given to us by the brigade accountant. The accountant's 1962 figures were 45 catties per mu of ginned cotton (equivalent to 135 unginned catties) and 148 catties per mu of peanuts.
27   QZWG, pp. 14–16, provides the text of Lin's speech.

28   QZWG, pp. 19–20.
29   GMRB, December 7, 1963.
30   QZWG, pp. 53–55.
31   HBRB, November 22, 25, 27, 30 and December 3, 1963.
32   GXF: 1979, vol. 4, pp. 206–07.
33   GMRB, December 8, 1963; HBRB, November 30, December 3, 1963; *Beijing dagong bao*, December 7, 1963; *Zhongguo qingnian bao*, December 12, 1963.
34   RMRB, December 7, 1963.
35   HBRB, November 27, 1963.

4   Socialist Education

1   GXF: 1979, vol. 4, pp. 208–09.
2   In November 1962 Mao exhorted the party's Tenth Plenum "Never forget class struggle." In May 1963 the party launched the "learn from Lei Feng" campaign and initiated a five-anti movement taking class struggle as its theme. XZGJS, pp. 332, 335–36; Richard Baum, *Prelude to Revolution: Mao, the Party, and the Peasant Question, 1962–66* (New York: Columbia University Press, 1975), pp. 1, 11–42; Li Zhisui, *The Private Life of Chairman Mao* (New York: Random House, 1994), p. 398.
3   Byong-jun Ahn, *Chinese Politics and the Cultural Revolution* (Seattle: University of Washington Press, 1976), p. 94.
4   Kenneth Lieberthal, "The Great Leap Forward and the Split in the Yenan Leadership," in Roderick MacFarquhar and John K. Fairbank, eds., *The Cambridge History of China: Volume 14, The People's Republic of China, 1949–1965* (Cambridge: Cambridge University Press, 1987), pp. 337–38.
5   Baum, p. 20.
6   ZZSZL, pp. 113–14.
7   Barry Naughton, "The Third Front: Defense Industrialization in the Chinese Interior," *The China Quarterly* 115 (September 1988), pp. 351–86; Yabuki Susumu, *China's New Political Economy: The Giant Awakens* (Boulder: Westview, 1995), pp. 38–40.
8   Huakai, 1963, p. 219.
9   ZZSZL, p. 291.
10   CVSS, p. 60.
11   Geng Huijuan, "Jianjue zou yu gong nong xiang jiehe de daolu," RMRB, September 11, 1968.
12   Roderick MacFarquhar, *The Origins of the Cultural Revolution: Volume 3, The Coming of the Cataclysm, 1961–1966* (New York: Columbia University Press, 1997), pp. 338–39.
13   ZNDJ, p. 117.
14   Nicholas Lardy, "The Chinese Economy under Stress," in MacFarquhar and Fairbank, eds., pp. 396–97.
15   Ibid., p. 381.
16   GXF: 1992, pp. 258–59, 274–79. The following paragraphs draw on this memoir.
17   Huakai, 1963, pp. 194–99.
18   Huakai, 1963, pp. 172–73.
19   Geng Changsuo, "Chun jie hua jin xi," RMRB, February 10, 1964.

20   CVSS, p. 104.

21   Ibid., p. 212.

22   *The Great Cultural Revolution in China* (Hong Kong: Asia Research Committee, 1967), p. 77.

23   Li Zhisui, p. 405.

24   *Zhongguo yishu yingpian bianmu, 1949–1979* (Beijing: Wenhua yishu chuban she, 1981), vol. 2, pp. 696–97.

25   *Zhongguo da baike quanshu: dianying* (Beijing, Shanghai: Zhongguo da baike quanshu chuban she, 1991), p. 437.

26   Paul Clark, *Chinese Cinema: Culture and Politics Since 1949* (Cambridge: Cambridge University Press, 1987), p. 131.

27   *Zhongguo wenxuejia cidian* (Beijing: Beijing yuyan xueyuan, 1978), pp. 129–31.

28   QZWG, p. 126.

5   A Whiff

1   Richard Baum, *Prelude to Revolution: Mao, the Party, and the Peasant Question, 1962–66* (New York: Columbia University Press, 1975), pp. 84–89.

2   Roderick MacFarquhar, *The Origins of the Cultural Revolution: Volume 3, The Coming of the Cataclysm, 1961–1966* (New York: Columbia University Press, 1997), p. 401.

3   ZZSZL, p. 114.

4   Dali Yang, "Surviving the Great Leap Famine: The Struggle over Rural Policy, 1958–1962," in Timothy Cheek and Tony Saich, eds., *New Perspectives on State Socialism in China* (Armonk: M. E. Sharpe, 1997), pp. 283–89.

5   Kenneth Lieberthal, "The Great Leap Forward and the Split in the Yenan Leadership," in Roderick MacFarquhar and John K. Fairbank, eds., *The Cambridge History of China: Volume 14, The People's Republic of China, 1949–1965* (Cambridge: Cambridge University Press, 1987), pp. 343–48; Baum, pp. 125, 208.

6   ZZSZL, p. 114.

7   MacFarquhar, pp. 408–09.

8   Huakai, 1963, pp. 189–94.

9   HBRB, September 2, 1983.

10   Baum, pp. 84–87; Byong-jun Ahn, *Chinese Politics and the Cultural Revolution* (Seattle: University of Washington Press, 1976), pp. 94, 106; MacFarquhar, pp. 401–02.

11   MacFarquhar, p. 406.

12   Lieberthal, p. 349; MacFarquhar, p. 410.

13   Lieberthal, p. 350.

14   ZZSZL, p. 114.

15   GXF: 1992, p. 318.

16   GXF: 1979, vol. 4, p. 222; WGRM, pp. 117–18. This account of the campaign in Wugong relies principally on interviews with Wugong officials, 1995 interviews with Cang Tong and former members of the Beijing Experimental Drama Troupe, and the 1979 memoir of Geng Xiufeng, vol. 4, pp. 222–27.

17   WGRM, p. 119.

18   GXF: 1979, vol. 4, p. 226.

19   WGRM, p. 119.

20   Huakai, 1963, pp. 73–86.

21   GXF: 1992, p. 319.

22   Craig Dietrich, *People's China: A Brief History* (New York: Oxford University Press, 1986), p. 156.

23   Ahn, p. 108; Baum, p. 124.

24   Baum, pp. 125–26.

25   Lieberthal, p. 350; Baum, pp. 125–26.

26   ZZSZL, p. 114.

27   GXF: 1979, vol. 4, p. 227.

6   Riding High

1   WGRM, p. 120.

2   GXF: 1979, vol. 4, pp. 242–43.

3   Ho Chin, *Harm into Benefit: Taming the Haiho River* (Peking: Foreign Languages Press, 1975), p. 10.

4   Judith Shapiro, *Mao's War against Nature* (Cambridge: Cambridge University Press, 2001), p. 107.

5   We are grateful to Lillian M. Li for drawing our attention to the vast, but frequently abortive, efforts of the Qing state to bring North China waters under control. See her forthcoming book, *Fighting Famine in North China: State, Market and Ecological Crisis, 1698–1998.*

6   Jun Jing has published a number of seminal studies of water-related relocation and resistance traumas, including "Villages Dammed, Villages Repossessed: A Memorial Movement in Northwest China," *American Ethnologist* 26, no. 2 (1999), pp. 324–43, "Population Resettlement: Past Lessons for the Three Gorges Dam Project," *The China Journal* 38 (1997), pp. 65–92, and "Environmental Protests in Rural China," in Elizabeth Perry and Mark Selden, eds., *Chinese Society* (London: Routledge, 2000), pp. 143–60.

7   WGRM, p. 120.

8   On intravillage marriage in Wugong and rural North China, see Mark Selden, "Family Strategies and Structures in Rural North China," in Deborah Davis and Steven Harrell, eds., *Chinese Families in the Post-Mao Era* (Berkeley: University of California Press, 1993), pp. 152–57.

9   Geng Changsuo, "Xiang shehuizhuyi da dao qianjin: jinian 'Guanyu nongye hezuohua wenti' fabiao shi zhounian," *Zhongguo qingnian bao,* July 29, 1965.

10   GXF: 1979, vol 4, pp. 247–48.

11   CVSS, pp. 52–132.

12   Labor models were explicitly urged to learn from Wugong in late 1963 in the chapter entitled "Ban Wugong shi de dadui, dang Geng Changsuo shi de shezhang" in QZWG, pp. 53–56.

13   Geng Changsuo, "Xiang shehuizhuyi da dao qianjin."

14   WGRM, pp. 120–21.

15   *Hengshui ribao,* March 13, 1978.

16   Geng Changsuo, "Shenma chang dusai ziji de erduo?" RMRB, October 25, 1965.

17   GXF: 1979, vol. 4, p. 251.

18   The country appears to have been divided into northern and southern regions with respect to agricultural policy at least since 1961. MacFarquhar, pp. 41–42.

19   HBRB, July 6, 1978.

20   ZZSZL, p. 118.

21   Geng Changsuo, "Shenma chang dusai ziji de erduo?"

22   Hebei sheng, Raoyang xian, Wugong gongshe, Wugong dadui wenxue chuangzuo zu, "Xie xianjin renwu, zuozhe bixu xianjin," *Da gong bao* (Beijing), December 13, 1965.

7   The Stench

1   The locus classicus for seeing the Cultural Revolution as including village China is Richard Baum, "The Cultural Revolution in the Countryside: Anatomy of a Limited Rebellion," in Thomas W. Robinson, ed., *The Cultural Revolution in China* (Berkeley: University of California Press, 1971), pp. 367–476. See also the important statistical survey by Andrew Walder and Yang Su, "The Cultural Revolution in the Countryside," *The China Quarterly* 173 (2003), pp. 74–99. For a collection including several essays on the Cultural Revolution in the countryside See Joseph Esherick, Paul G. Pickowicz, and Andrew Walder, eds., *The Cultural Revolution as History* (Stanford: Stanford University Press, forthcoming).

2   ZGXT, pp. 103–05; Kenneth Lieberthal and Bruce Dickson, *A Research Guide to Central Party and Government Meetings in China, 1949–1966* (Armonk: M. E. Sharpe, 1989), pp. 185–87; XZGJS, pp. 398–400; Harry Harding, "The Chinese State in Crisis, 1966–69," in Roderick MacFarquhar, ed., *The Politics of China, 1949–1989* (Cambridge: Cambridge University Press, 1993), pp. 165–72.

3   Hebei sheng diming bangongshi, ed., *Hebei zheng qu yan ge zhi* (Shijiazhuang: Hebei kexue jixu chuban she, 1985), p. 16; ZCXT, p. 104

4   FBIS, October 27, 1978, K1–2.

5   HBRB, December 26, 1981; FBIS, January 20, 1982, R6.

6   William Hinton, *Hundred-Day War: The Cultural Revolution at Tsinghua University* (New York: Monthly Review Press, 1972), pp. 134–37.

7   Feng Jicai, "Voices of Madness," in Zhang Lijia and Calum McLeod, eds., *China Remembers* (New York: Oxford University Press, 1999), p. 137.

8   This account of the Cultural Revolution in Raoyang draws on ZZSZL, pp. 114, 225, and interviews with officials, villagers, and red guards.

9   ZZSZL, p. 225.

10   This discussion of the Cultural Revolution in Wugong draws on interviews with participants and victims, and GXF: 1979, vol. 5, pp. 2–38.

11   Christina Gilmartin analyzes the issues surrounding the rise and fall of women leaders in terms of their husbands and the general difficulty of women securing and maintaining leadership positions in the party from the 1920s forward. "Gender in the Formation of a Communist Body Politic," *Modern China* 19, no. 3 (July 1993), pp. 299–329. A rare Chinese reflection on this issue is provided by Liu Binyan in his political reportage "The Fifth Man in the Overcoat," in Perry Link, ed., *People or Monsters? And Other Stories and Reportage from China after Mao* (Bloomington: Indiana University Press, 1983), pp. 79–97.

12   Wu Mingshi describes the identical torture in his labor camp novel *Red Sharks*. See Yenna Wu, "Expressing the 'Inexpressible': Pain and Suffering in Wu Mingshi's *Red Sharks* (Hong sha)," in Philip F. C. Williams and Yenna Wu, eds., *Doing Time Behind the Great Wall: Prisoners in Contemporary Chinese Literature and Social Science Research* (London: Routledge, forthcoming).

13   *Di sishi chuntian* (Shijiazhuang: Huashan wenyi chuban she, 1983), p. 138.

14   Anita Chan, Richard Madsen, and Jonathan Unger, *Chen Village: The Recent History of a Chinese Community* (Berkeley: University of California Press, 1984), pp. 169–70; Liang Heng and Judith Shapiro, *Son of the Revolution* (New York: Knopf, 1983), pp. 122, 140.

15   This exchange is quoted in GXF: 1979, vol. 5, pp. 30–36.

16   FBIS, January, 1977, K2.

8   Whatever Chairman Mao Says

1   "Jianjue anzhao Mao Zhuxi de ganbu zhengce banshi," HBRB, March 29, 1967.

2   This and subsequent paragraphs draw on GFX: 1979, vol. 5, pp. 22–40.

3   GXF: 1979, vol. 5, pp. 12–21. The text is "Kang Sheng tongzhi tan Liu Shaoqi ruhe pohuai Zhongguo zou shehuizhuiyi daolu."

4   Lin Tie, "Wo yu Geng Changsuo tongzhi he ta chuangban de Wugong dadui, Wugong gongshe de guanxi he jidian kanfa," unpublished memoir prepared for the authors, December 1979.

5   For this and subsequent paragraphs compare CVSS, chapters 2–4.

6   See *Hengshui ribao*, November 29, 1979; CVSS, pp. 122–23.

7   Frederick Teiwes and Warren Sun, eds., *The Politics of Agricultural Cooperativization in China: Mao, Deng Zihui, and the "High Tide" of 1955* (Armonk: M. E. Sharpe, 1993), pp. 8–9. Mark Selden, *The Political Economy of Chinese Development* (Armonk: M. E. Sharpe, 1994), pp. 26–82.

8   Geng Changsuo's 1967 charges about the crimes of Liu Shaoqi and Lin Tie in Hebei virtually mirrored propaganda generated by the New China News Agency in Baoding in the city's final days as temporary provincial capital. See "Hebei sheng shixian liangshi zigei," RMRB, January 28, 1968.

9   ZZSZL, p. 226.

10   The army, no less than other organizations, was of course scarred by infighting and purges as indicated by the fall of Luo Ruiqing and subsequent conflicts throughout the Cultural Revolution, such as those pitting Lin Biao against the old marshals.

11   Geng Huijuan, "Jianjue zou yu gong nong xiang jiehe de daolu," RMRB, September 1968.

12   Andrew Walder and Gong Xiaoxia, "A Red Guard's Memoir of Traitor Hunting, Compiled by the Office of the Party Committee, Shijiazhuang Region, and the Office of the Party Committee, Hebei," *Chinese Sociology and Anthropology* 26, no. 1 (fall 1993).

13   ZZSZL, p. 131.

14   GXF: 1979, vol. 5, pp. 22–25.

15   RMRB, February 5, 1968.

16   ZGXT, p. 104.

17   William Whitson, *The Chinese High Command: A History of Communist Military Politics, 1927–1972* (New York: Praeger, 1973), pp. 359–403. Whitson posits a conflict in Hebei politics pitting North China Field Armies associated with the fallen Peng Zhen, Lin Tie, Bo Yibo, and Nie Rongzhen against the Second Field Army associated with Li Xuefeng and Liu Zihou, on the one hand, and Lin Biao's 38th Army, on the

other. See Jurgen Domes, "The Role of the Military in the Formation of Revolutionary Committees, 1967–68," *The China Quarterly* 44 (October–December 1970), p. 123.

18   GXF: 1979, vol. 5, p. 41.

19   "Hebei de chuan guo zhuming laodong mofan zai wenhua da geming zhong li xingong," RMRB, February 6, 1968.

20   GXF: 1979, vol. 5, p. 42.

21   Heng Rui and Ji Ren, "Xi kan nongcun da hao xingshi: fang Hebei sheng, Raoyang xian, Wugong dadui," *Zhongguo xinwen,* February 7, 1968.

22   "Hebei de chuan guo zhuming laodong mofan," RMRB, February 6, 1968.

23   "Xikan nongcun," *Zhongguo xinwen,* February 7, 1968.

24   See Anita Chan, Richard Madsen, and Jonathan Unger, *Chen Village: Under Mao and Deng* (Berkeley: University of California Press, 1993), on the 1968–69 campaign of Chen Boda and Lin Biao to level income by moving to brigade accounting.

25   David Zweig, *Agrarian Radicalism in China, 1968–1981* (Cambridge: Harvard University Press, 1989), p. 56.

26   David Zweig, "Agrarian Radicalism as a Rural Development Strategy, 1968–1978," in William Joseph, Christine Wong, and David Zweig, eds., *New Perspectives on the Cultural Revolution* (Cambridge: Harvard University Council on East Asian Studies, 1993), p. 67.

27   Geng Changsuo, "Laoji Mao Zhuxi de jiaodao henzhua jieji douzheng," RMRB, May 19, 1968.

28   RMRB, March 31, 1968.

29   FBIS, June 5, 1968, p. F1.

30   NCNA, Shijiazhuang, July 24, 1968.

31   Geng Changsuo, "Jianjue suqing zichanjieji silingbu de duhai," RMRB, August 5, 1968.

32   Geng Changsuo, "Renmin gongshe wansui," *Zhongguo xinwen,* August 28, 1968.

33   This information draws on fieldwork by University of Toronto anthropologist Li Ge. This is a rare area of Dazhai experience that was *not* presented for provincial or national emulation.

34   Geng Changsuo, "Women ping xiazhong nong relie huanying he gong nong jiehe de zhishifenzi," RMRB, September 6, 1968.

35   FBIS, September 5, 1968, p. F5.

36   See Chan, Madsen, and Unger, *Chen Village,* and Jung Chang, *Wild Swans: Three Daughters of China* (New York: Simon and Schuster, 1991).

37   Geng Huijuan, "Jianjue zou yu gong nong xiang jiehe de daolu," RMRB, September 11, 1968.

38   ZZSZL, p. 229.

39   RMRB, October 2, 1968.

40   *Zhoumo bao* (Hong Kong), October 12, 1968.

41   Geng Changsuo, "Yongyuan genzhe Mao Zhuxi nao geming," *Hongqi,* no. 4, October 14, 1968.

42   Harry Harding, "The Chinese State in Crisis," and Roderick MacFarquhar, "The Succession to Mao and the End of Maoism," in Roderick MacFarquhar and John K. Fairbank, eds., *The Cambridge History of China: Volume 15, The People's Republic of China, Part 2: Revolutions Within the Chinese Revolution, 1966–1982* (Cambridge: Cambridge University Press, 1993), pp. 196–99, 306–12.

9   War Communism

1   Thomas Robinson, "China Confronts the Soviet Union: Warfare and Diplomacy on China's Inner Asian Frontiers," in Roderick MacFarquhar and John K. Fairbank, eds., *The Cambridge History of China: Volume 15, The People's Republic of China, Part 2: Revolutions Within the Chinese Revolution, 1966–1982* (Cambridge: Cambridge University Press, 1991), p. 262; Frederick Teiwes and Warren Sun, *The Tragedy of Lin Biao: Riding the Tiger During the Cultural Revolution* (Honolulu: University of Hawaii Press, 1996), chapter 4.

2   Teiwes and Sun, pp. 119–20, state that the military budget increased by 34, 13, and 16 percent in the years 1969, 1970, and 1971, respectively.

3   Wang Nianyi, *1949–1989 nian de Zhongguo: da dongluan de niandai* (Henan: Henan renmin chuban she, 1994), p. 391; Teiwes and Sun, p. 117.

4   Roderick MacFarquhar, "The Succession to Mao and the End of Maoism 1969–82," in *The Politics of China, 1949–1989* (Cambridge: Cambridge University Press, 1993), pp. 249–51.

5   Vaclav Smil, *China's Environmental Crisis* (Armonk: M. E. Sharpe, 1993), pp. 44–45.

6   HBRB, August 17, 1969.

7   ZZSZL, p. 226.

8   Jonathan Pollack, "The Opening to America," *The Cambridge History of China*, vol. 15, part 2, p. 413; Teiwes and Sun, pp. 103–4, 111–15. Teiwes and Sun reject the view that Lin issued Order Number 1 behind Mao's back. See Zhang Yunsheng, "True Account of Maojiawan: Reminiscences of Lin Biao's Secretary," *Chinese Law and Government* 26, no. 3 (March–April 1996); XZGJS, p. 470.

9   Barry Naughton, "The Third Front: Defense Industrialization in the Chinese Interior," *The China Quarterly* 115 (1988), pp. 351–86.

10   *Hengshui ribao,* March 4, 1969.

11   *Hebei minbing geming douzheng gushi* (Shijiazhuang: Hebei renmin chuban she, 1970).

12   See Thomas P. Bernstein, *Up to the Mountains and Down to the Villages: The Transfer of Youth from Urban to Rural China* (New Haven: Yale University Press, 1977), for a detailed discussion of the youth to the countryside movement.

13   Michael Schoenhals, "The Central Case Examination Group, 1966–79," *The China Quarterly* 145 (March 1996), pp. 87–129.

14   Data on Raoyang prison life are based on a series of interviews with former prisoners Zhang Langlang, Zhou Qiyue, and Fung Guo Chiang, and with historian Marianne Bastid Brugière. Portions of a filmed interview of Zhang Langlang are included in a documentary entitled *The Mao Years,* Sue Williams (producer and director) and Paul G. Pickowicz (associate producer), Ambrica Productions, New York, 1994.

15   HBRB, February 24, 1970.

16   For discussions of Cultural Revolution deaths see Harry Harding, "The Chinese State in Crisis, 1966–9," in Roderick MacFarquhar, ed., *The Politics of China, 1949–1989,* pp. 243–44; *A Great Trial in Chinese History: The Trial of the Lin Biao and Jiang Qing Counter-revolutionary Cliques* (Beijing: New World Press) p. 21. For one source on Hebei see ZGXT, p. 696. This official estimate made in 1987 put the toll of injured and dead at just 6,600.

17   This paragraph and the following paragraphs draw on GXF: 1979, vol. 5, pp. 56–65.

18   For the text of the poster see GXF: 1979, vol. 5, pp. 59–65.
19   HBRB, May 21, 1969.
20   As early as July 1971 Zhou Enlai was making public remarks that pointed to a political
      gap separating Mao and Lin Biao. See Committee of Concerned Asian Scholars,
      China! Inside the People's Republic (New York: Bantam Books, 1972), pp. 338–39. On
      Mao's late 1970 statement to Edgar Snow implying a gap between Lin Biao and
      himself, see Chen Jian, *Mao's China and the Cold War* (Chapel Hill: University of
      North Carolina Press, 201), pp. 256–57.

10   Sprouts of Reform

1   Roderick MacFarquhar, "The Succession to Mao and the End of Maoism, 1969–82,"
      in Roderick MacFarquhar, ed., *The Politics of China, 1949–1989* (Cambridge: Cam-
      bridge University Press, 1993), pp. 259–62.
2   For differing views on Lin Biao's politics, see Frederick Teiwes and Warren Sun, *The
      Tragedy of Lin Biao: Riding the Tiger During the Cultural Revolution* (Honolulu: Uni-
      versity of Hawaii Press, 1996).
3   RMRB, September 27, 1977.
4   RMRB, September 17, 1971, in FBIS, September 22, 1971, pp. B1–9; NCNA,
      September 17, 1971, in FBIS, September 17, 1971, pp. F1–2; RMRB editorial,
      December 23, 1976; RMRB, June 30, 1977.
5   The three central points, recalled 26 years later by senior agricultural official Zheng
      Zhong, provide a guide to the thinking of Zhou Enlai and his associates. The State
      Council's report of October 5, 1970 on the North China Agricultural Conference was
      ratified by the Central Committee on December 11, 1970. Both the document and the
      ratification are printed in *Jian guo yilai nongye hezuohua shiliao huipian* (Beijing:
      Zhonggong dangshi chuban she, 1992), pp. 831–33. The document, a paean to class-
      struggle versions of Mao Zedong thought, illustrates the difficulties confronting con-
      servative reformers. While the meeting constituted a breakthrough for conservative
      modernizers, Maoist class-struggle imperatives limited reform possibilities. The con-
      servative modernizers' agenda did not call for expansion of the household economy or
      private marketing, key elements of the reform agenda.
6   Wolfgang Bartke and Peter Schier, *China's New Party Leadership: Biographies and Anal-
      ysis of the Twelfth Central Committee of the Chinese Communist Party* (Armonk: M. E.
      Sharpe, 1985), p. 171; JJDSD, p. 418.
7   The conference was subject to diverse interpretations. Another summary provided by
      a senior Raoyang official in 1987 emphasized the following three points: hard work,
      self-reliance, and suitability to local conditions. Others decided to hew to the class-
      struggle rhetoric of the conference document.
8   Barry Naughton, "Industrial Policy During the Cultural Revolution: Military Prepa-
      ration, Decentralization, and Leaps Forward," in William Joseph, Christine Wong, and
      David Zweig, eds., *New Perspectives on the Cultural Revolution* (Cambridge: Harvard
      University Council on East Asian Studies, 1993), pp. 155, 167.
9   Chris Bramall, "Origins of the Agricultural 'Miracle': Some Evidence From Sichuan,"
      The China Quarterly 143 (1975), pp. 731–55.
10   David Zweig, *Agrarian Radicalism in China, 1968–1981* (Cambridge: Harvard Uni-
      versity Press, 1989), pp. 58–62.

11 David Zweig, "Agrarian Radicalism as a Rural Development Strategy," in Joseph, Wong, and Zweig, eds., *New Perspectives on the Cultural Revolution,* p. 72; Zweig, *Agrarian Radicalism in China, 1968–1981,* pp. 41–42.

12 Nicholas Lardy, *Agriculture in China's Modern Economic Development* (Cambridge: Cambridge University Press, 1983), p. 127. In 1970 capital construction in the state sector soared to 29.5 billion yuan, twice the average of the preceding four years. Nobuo Murayama, "The Investment Cycle in China: Why Overexpansion of Investment Persists," *China Newsletter* 45 (July–August 1983), p. 12.

13 Township industry grew even faster, 29.6 percent per year between 1970 and 1978. Rizwanul Islam, "Growth of Rural Industries in Post-reform China," *Development and Change* 22 (1991), pp. 687–724.

14 HBRB, December 21, 1981, p. 1; FBIS, January 12, 1982, p. R4.

15 Geng Changsuo, "Zai douzheng zhong xue, zai douzheng zhong yong, *Hong qi,* September 1970, pp. 14–16.

16 Hebei sheng Raoyang xian Wugong dadui dang zhibu, "Yong Mao Zhuxi zhexue sixiang jielu maodun jiejue maodun jixu geming," RMRB, November 20, 1970.

17 GFX: 1979, vol. 5, p. 82. The record of Geng's travel is based on pp. 82–116 of this source.

18 Xiaoming Wei, "A Study of a Production Team in North China in 1969 and 1970," M.A. thesis, University of Montana, 1992, pp. 49–50.

19 RMRB, November 20, 1970.

20 Geng Changsuo, "Zuo shishi qiushi de mofan," RMRB, October 24, 1977.

21 Geng Changsuo, "Be a Leader in Consciously Implementing Chairman Mao's Revolutionary Line," NCNA, January 29, 1971, in FBIS, February 8, 1971, p. F3.

22 XZGJS, p. 488.

23 ZZSZL, pp. 132–33.

24 ZGXT, p. 104.

25 See GXF: 1979, vol. 5, pp. 129–39, for the full text of the letter.

26 See GXF: 1979, vol. 5, pp. 66–78, for the full text of the letter.

27 ZZSZL, p. 133.

28 GXF: 1979, vol. 5, pp. 147–49.

29 JJDSD, p. 420.

30 Wolfgang Bartke, *Who's Who in the People's Republic of China* (Armonk: M. E. Sharpe, 1981), pp. 122–23.

31 RMRB editorial, April 4, 1978, p. 1.

32 FBIS, September 8, 1971, p. 3.

33 GXF: 1979, vol. 5, p. 172.

34 GXF: 1979, vol. 5, p. 173.

35 Edward Rice, *Mao's Way* (Berkeley: University of California Press, 1972), pp. 504–05.

36 Michael Kau, *The Lin Biao Affair* (White Plains: International Arts and Sciences Press, 1975, p. 76.

37 MacFarquhar, "The Succession to Mao," pp. 268–78.

38 Geng Changsuo, "Zuo zijue zhixing Mao Zhuxi geming luxian de daitou ren," RMRB, January 15, 1972. This reform-oriented article had the same title as Geng's fundamentalist article of January 29, 1971, "Be a Leader in Consciously Implementing Chairman Mao's Revolutionary Line."

11   Stalemate

1   Kristin Parris, "Local Initiative and National Reform: The Wenzhou Model of Development," *The China Quarterly* 134 (June 1993), pp. 242–45.

2   *Zhongguo yishu yingpian bianmu, 1949–1979* (Beijing: Wenhua yishu chuban she, 1981), vol. 2, pp. 864, 976.

3   RMRB, August 21, 1973, p. 2.

4   *Hongqi*, no. 5, 1973.

5   On intravillage income differentiation in Wugong, and more generally in the Chinese countryside, see Mark Selden, "Income Inequality and the State in Rural China," in Mark Selden, *The Political Economy of Chinese Development* (Armonk: M. E. Sharpe, 1993), pp. 137–60; on family patterns and income differentials, see Mark Selden, "Family Strategies and Structures in Rural North China," in Deborah Davis and Stevan Harrell, eds., *Chinese Families in the Post-Mao Era* (Berkeley: University of California Press, 1993), pp. 139–64.

6   *Hebei wenyi*, no. 4, 1973, pp. 25–27.

7   FBIS, November 22, 1972, p. F2–3.

8   HBRB, April 8, 1982, pp. 1, 3.

9   JJDSD, p. 422.

10 ZZSZL, p. 226.

11 HBRB, October 20, 1973.

12 Geng Changsuo, "Zuzhiqilai de daolu yue zou yue kuanguang," RMRB, August 18, 1973.

13 *Di sishi chuntian* (Shijiazhuang: Huashan wenyi chuban she, 1983), pp. 162–66.

14 Commentator, HBRB, December 21, 1981, p. 1, in FBIS, January 12, 1982, p. R4.

15 NCNA, Taiyuan, 16 February 1972, "The Agriculture and Forestry Sciences and Technical Service Group in Tachai," in FBIS February 24, 1972, p. B3.

16 "An Intellectual Enthusiastically Welcomed by the Poor and Lower-Middle Peasants," RMRB, June 13, 1971, in FBIS, July 7, 1971, p. B11.

17 "Advances in Anti-Hail Experiments in Xiyang," *Kexue shiyan*, October 1977, in JPRS 71477, July 17, 1978, p. 59.

18 RMRB, September 21, 1970.

19 The quotation is from an unpublished manuscript which contends that Dazhai never received any large amount of free aid from the state. William Hinton concludes: "What they did get and put to use, like the spray irrigation system, Dazhai people paid for in installments over many years."

20 Dwight Perkins, ed., *Rural Small-Scale Industry in China* (Berkeley: University of California Press, 1977), p. 76.

21 FBIS, August 19, 1975, p. K1.

22 *Di sishi chuntian*, pp. 45, 165.

23 WGRM, p. 131.

24 GXF: 1979, vol. 5, p. 207.

25 Zhang Zaixin, "Raoyang xian canjia di shiyi jie Ao yun hui Wang Runlan," *Raoyang xian wen shi ziliao*, vol. 1, pp. 143–45.

26 Wang Zhilan, "Wo de fuqin yi dai wushi Wang Shaoxian," *Raoyang xian wen shi ziliao*, vol. 1, pp. 146–52.

27 Ji Xuede and Liu Yuhao, "Chang Xiangting de 'gai jing nan' Chongqing xi ban," *Raoyang xian wen shi ziliao*, vol. 1, pp. 130–36.

28   Zhu Guangxun, "'Hu guan gong' Tian Zhenqing," *Raoyang xian wen shi ziliao*, vol. 1, pp. 139-42.

29   Cui Cunzheng, "Lishi ming yi Sun Minqin," *Raoyang xian wen shi ziliao*, vol. 1, pp. 128-29.

30   GXF: 1979, vol. 5, p. 213.

31   GXF: 1979, vol. 6, p. 27.

32   GXF: 1979, vol. 5, p. 214.

33   HBRB, November 28, 1973; *Hengshui ribao*, November 29, 1973; RMRB, December 7, 1973.

34   FBIS, January 8, 1974, pp. B4-6.

35   William Joseph, *The Critique of Ultra-Leftism in China* (Stanford: Stanford University Press, 1984), pp. 136, 140. For the subsequent critique of Zhang see *Beijing Review*, no. 8 (1977), pp. 14-16.

36   *Zhongguo yishu yingpian bianmu, 1949-1979* (Beijing: Wenhua yishu chuban she, 1981), vol. 2, pp. 1022-23.

37   The Central Committee approved the reopening and enrollment of worker-peasant-soldier students at Beijing and Qinghua Universities on June 27, 1970. Most other universities remained closed for several more years. JJDSJ, p. 418.

38   XZGJS, p. 555.

39   Roderick MacFarquhar, "The Succession to Mao and the End of Maoism, 1969-82," in Roderick MacFarquhar, ed., *The Politics of China, 1949-1989* (Cambridge: Cambridge University Press, 1993), pp. 290-91.

40   GXF: 1979, vol. 5, p. 236.

41   FBIS, February 27, 1974, pp. F1-6.

42   FBIS, November 18, 1974, pp. K3-4.

12   Tremors

1   Roderick MacFarquhar, "The Succession to Mao and the End of Maoism, 1969-82," in Roderick MacFarquhar, ed., *The Politics of China, 1949-1989* (Cambridge: Cambridge University Press, 1993), pp. 286-93; David Zweig, *Agrarian Radicalism in China, 1968-1981* (Cambridge: Harvard University Press, 1989), pp. 62-66.

2   ZZSZL, p. 139. Jun Jing chronicles the long and tumultuous history of a branch of the Kong family in Gansu province and its complex relationship to Confucius in *The Temple of Memories: History, Power, and Morality in a Chinese Village* (Stanford: Stanford University Press, 1996).

3   Kay Johnson, *Women, the Family, and Peasant Revolution in China* (Chicago: University of Chicago Press, 1983), pp. 193-207.

4   See Jeremy Brown, "Staging Xiaojinzhuang: The City in the Countryside, 1974-1976," in Joseph Esherick, Paul Pickowicz, and Andrew Walder, eds., *The Chinese Cultural Revolution as History*, (Stanford: Stanford University Press, forthcoming), for a detailed discussion of how urban elites stage managed the Xiaojinzhuang model in ways that revealed their contempt for rural people.

5   Roxane Witke, *Comrade Chiang Ch'ing* (Boston: Little, Brown, 1977), pp. 460-61, 476; Ross Terrill, *The White-Boned Demon: A Biography of Madame Mao Zedong* (New York: William Morrow, 1984), pp. 331-37; GMRB, Oct. 10, 1974.

6   *Hebei sheng zhongxue shiyong keben: yingyu*, 1975, vol. 2, lesson 7.

7   On marital patterns see Mark Selden, "Family Strategies and Structures in Rural North China," in Deborah Davis and Stevan Harrell, eds., *Chinese Families in the Post-Mao Era* (Berkeley: University of California Press, 1993); William Parrish and Martin Whyte, *Village and Family in Contemporary China* (Chicago: University of Chicago Press, 1978), pp. 139–64.

8   RMRB, December 27, 1975.

9   "Jianku fendou de zhengzhi bense yong bu bian," RMRB, June 4, 1975.

10   RMRB, May 19, 1975.

11   RMRB, December 27, 1975.

12   Tiejun Cheng and Mark Selden, "The Construction of Spatial Hierarchies: China's *Hukou* and *Danwei* Systems," in Timothy Cheek and Tony Saich, eds., *New Perspectives on State Socialism in China* (Armonk: M. E. Sharpe, 1997), pp. 23–50; E. B. Vermeer, "Income Differentials in Rural China," *The China Quarterly* 89 (1982), pp. 1–33.

13   FBIS, September 17, 1975, p. E2; Zweig, *Agrarian Radicalism in China*, pp. 66–67.

14   See Qin Huailu, *Ninth Heaven to Ninth Hell: The History of a Noble Chinese Experiment* (New York: Barricade Books, 1995), pp. 447–69, for a vivid account of the clash at the conference as seen by Chen Yonggui and his supporters.

15   FBIS, September 29, 1975, pp. E1–5.

16   FBIS, September 29, 1975, pp. E1–5; MacFarquhar, "The Succession to Mao," pp. 294, 300.

17   FBIS, October 16, 1975, pp. E3–5; October 20, 1975, pp. E7–9; MacFarquhar, "The Succession to Mao," p. 294. The text of Hua Guofeng's speech, "Build Dazhai-type Counties Throughout the Country," is in Mark Selden, *The People's Republic of China: A Documentary of Revolutionary Change* (New York: Monthly Review Press, 1979), pp. 675–81.

18   FBIS, October 27, 1975, p. E2.

19   Selden, *The People's Republic of China*, pp. 674–80.

20   FBIS, November 5, 1975, pp. K1–2; November 20, 1975, pp. K2–3; December 2, 1975, pp. K1–2.

21   GXF: 1979, vol. 6, pp. 64–67.

22   The text of the letter is in GXF: 1979, vol. 6, pp. 67–72.

23   MacFarquhar, "The Succession to Mao," p. 297.

24   MacFarquhar, "The Succession to Mao," pp. 299–301; and Kenneth Lieberthal and Bruce Dickson, *Research Guide to Central Party and Government Meetings in China, 1949–1986* (Armonk: M. E. Sharpe, 1989), pp. 234–35.

25   HBRB, December 11, 1981, p. 1, in FBIS, December 29, 1981, pp. R3–4.

26   Paul G. Pickowicz, "People, Politics, and Paramedicine in China," in Guenter Risse, ed., *Modern China and Traditional Chinese Medicine* (Springfield: Charles C. Thomas, 1973), pp. 124–46.

27   *Di sishi chuntian* (Shijiazhuang: Huashan wenyi chuban she, 1983), pp. 80–81.

28   Xiao Lan, *The Tiananmen Poems* (Beijing: Foreign Languages Press, 1979); MacFarquhar, "The Succession to Mao," pp. 301–05.

29   "Quarterly Chronicle and Documentation," *The China Quarterly* 67 (September 1976), pp. 661–62; Roger Garside, *Coming Alive! China after Mao* (New York: McGraw-Hill, 1981), pp. 115–36; MacFarquhar, "The Succession to Mao," pp. 301–05.

30   FBIS, Nov. 27, 1978, p. K1.

31   RMRB, June 10, 1977, p. 3.

32   FBIS, July 21, 1976, p. K2.

33   *Issues and Studies* 15, no. 1 (January 1979), p. 101.

13   Earthquakes

1   See Chen Yong et al., eds., *The Great Tangshan Earthquake of 1976: An Anatomy of Disaster* (New York: Pergamon Press, 1988); Cheng Yongdi, ed., *Tangshan dizhen jishi: Xingcun chedi zishu* (Taiyuan: Shanxi renmin chuban she, 1991); Liu Huixian, ed., *Tangshan da dizhen zhenhai* (Beijing: Dizhen chuban she, 1985–86), 4 vols.

2   XZGJS, p. 589.

3   RMRB, November 26, 1976.

4   RMRB, December 5, 1976.

5   Kuo Feng-lien, "How Chiang Ch'ing Tried to Undermine Tachai," *China Reconstructs* nos. 26, 2–3 (February–March 1977), p. 36.

6   FBIS, September 23, 1976, pp. K1–2.

7   RMRB, November 26, 1976.

8   Joseph Fewsmith, *Dilemmas of Reform in China: Political Conflict and Economic Debate* (Armonk: M. E. Sharpe, 1994), pp. 19–21.

9   See Fewsmith, *Dilemmas of Reform in China;* Daniel Kelliher, *Peasant Power in China: The Era of Rural Reform, 1979–1989* (New Haven: Yale University Press, 1992); Louis Putterman, *Continuity and Change in China's Rural Development* (New York: Oxford University Press, 1993); David Zweig, *Freeing China's Farmers: Rural Restructuring in the Reform Era* (Armonk: M. E. Sharpe, 1997); Kate Xiao Zhou, *How the Farmers Changed China: Power of the People* (Boulder: Westview, 1996); Barry Naughton, *Growing Out of the Plan: Chinese Economic Reform, 1978–1993* (Cambridge: Cambridge University Press, 1995); Mark Selden, *The Political Economy of Chinese Development* (Armonk: M. E. Sharpe, 1993).

10   GMRB, September 5, 1977.

11   RMRB, June 10, 1977.

12   *Hengshui ribao,* September 1, 1977, and March 13, 1978; *Hongqi,* August 1977.

13   XZGJS, pp. 600–02; Kenneth Lieberthal and Bruce Dickson, *A Research Guide to Central Party and Government Meetings in China, 1949–1986* (Armonk: M. E. Sharpe, 1989), pp. 249–50; Roderick MacFarquhar, "The Succession to Mao and the End of Maoism," in MacFarquhar, ed., *The Politics of China, 1949–1989* (Cambridge: Cambridge University Press, 1993), pp. 314–16.

14   Wolfgang Bartke, *Who's Who in the People's Republic of China* (Armonk: M. E. Sharpe, 1981), p. 431.

15   *Hengshui ribao,* August 8, 1978.

16   *Zhongguo qingnian bao,* February 8, 1978.

17   Di sishi chuntian (Shijiazhuang: Huashan wenyi chuban she, 1983), p. 116.

18   HBRB, March 27, 1978.

19   *Hengshui ribao,* May 2, 1978.

20   RMRB, April 17, 1978.

21   GXF: 1979, vol. 6, pp. 82–87. Geng's letter is dated December 31, 1977.

22   HBRB, August 13, 1978.

23   RMRB, October 5, 1978.

24   HBRB, December 15, 1978, in FBIS, December 20, 1978.
25   XZGJS, p. 625.
26   JPRS 71, 881, September 18, 1978, p. 27.
27   RMRB, November 3, 1978.
28   FBIS, October 27, 1978, pp. K1–2.
29   FBIS, October 31, 1978.
30   *Hengshui ribao,* December 4, 1978.
31   *Hengshui ribao,* December 4, 1978.
32   HBRB, December 11, 1981, in FBIS, December 29, 1981, p. R4.
33   GMRB, December 9, 1978.
34   WGRM.
35   ZZSZL, p. 160.
36   RMRB, December 25, 1978.

14   Reform

1   *Hengshui ribao,* January 21, 1981.
2   *Hengshui ribao,* March 28, 1979.
3   HBRB, July 3, 1979.
4   Geng Changsuo, "Zhi you shehuizhuyi nenggou jiu Zhongguo," *Hengshui ribao,* May 26, 1979; Geng Changsuo, "Yao an bianzhengfa ban shi," HBRB, June 9, 1979.
5   ZGXT, pp. 134, 743.
6   HBRB, October 23, 1981, April 16, 1982, June 21, 1982.
7   HBRB, April 17, 1983.
8   HBRB, April 24, 1983; Office of the United Nations Disaster Relief Co-ordinator, China, *Case Report: Drought and Floods in Hebei/Hubei Provinces, 1980/81,* Case report no. 011 (May 1982), especially pp. 28–30 (Geneva: United Nations, 1982).
9   HBRB, April 5, 1983; *Case Report,* Annex 1, "Drought and Floods in the People's Republic of China: Delivery of International Famine Relief."
10   *Hengshui ribao,* October 22, 1979.
11   HBRB, December 29, 1979.
12   HBRB, November 7, 1979; *Chinese Women,* no. 1, 1980.
13   *Hengshui ribao,* June 13, 1981 (reprinted from HBRB).
14   *Zhengming* 2, 1983, p. 20. Joseph Fewsmith, *Dilemmas of Reform in China: Political Conflict and Economic Debate* (Armonk: M. E. Sharpe, 1994), p. 107.
15   Mark Selden, *The Political Economy of Chinese Development* (Armonk: M. E. Sharpe, 1993), p. 33.
16   HBRB, January 30, 1981.
17   *Hengshui ribao,* October 22, 1981.
18   *Gongchandang yuan,* no. 10, October, 1980.
19   *Hengshui ribao,* September 11, 1981.
20   The politics of decollectivization are discussed in detail in David Zweig, *Freeing China's Farmers: Rural Restoration in the Reform Era* (Armonk: M. E. Sharpe, 1997); Joseph Fewsmith, *Dilemmas of Reform in China: Political Conflict and Economic Debate* (Armonk: M. E. Sharpe, 1994).
21   Selden, *The Political Economy of Chinese Development,* pp. 18–22.
22   Kenneth Pomeranz, *The Great Divergence: China, Europe, and the Making of the Modern*

World Economy (Princeton: Princeton University Press, 2000), pp. 9–107. Also, see his "Beyond the East-West Binary: Resituating Development Paths in the Eighteenth-Century World," *Journal of Asian Studies* 61 no. 2 (May 2002), pp. 539–90, and his critics in the same issue, Philip C. C. Huang, Robert Brenner, and Christopher Isett.

23 *Hengshui ribao,* December 10, 1979.

24 *Hengshui ribao,* September 24, 1979, October 24, 1979.

25 *Hengshui ribao,* December 11, 1982.

26 Tyrene White, "Domination, Resistance, and Accommodation in China's One-Child Campaign," in Elizabeth J. Perry and Mark Selden, eds., *Chinese Society: Change, Conflict, and Resistance* (London: Routledge, 2000), pp. 102–19.

27 Paul G. Pickowicz, "Peasant Family Tries New Pursuits," *China Daily,* June 6, 1983, p. 6.

28 *Hengshui ribao,* December 16, 1980.

29 HBRB, April 24, 1983.

30 ZZSZL, p. 272.

31 *Hengshui ribao,* September 2, 1983.

32 HBRB, September 11, 1983.

33 *Zhongguo nongmin bao,* September 29, 1983.

34 *Di sishi chuntian* (Shijiazhuang: Huashan wenyi chuban she, 1983).

35 RMRB, October 31, 1983.

36 *Hengshui ribao,* October 21, 1983.

15   Reform and Its Discontents

1   Zhai Zhenhua, *Red Flower of China* (New York: Soho Press, 1993), pp. 171–72. Also see Dorothy Solinger, *Contesting Citizenship in Urban China: Peasant Migrants, the State, and the Logic of the Market* (Berkeley: University of California Press, 1999).

2   On rural discontent during the reform era see Solinger, *Contesting Citizenship in Urban China;* Thomas Bernstein, "Farmer Discontent and Regime Responses," and Dorothy Solinger, "China's Floating Population," in Merle Goldman and Roderick MacFarquhar, eds., *The Paradox of China's Post-Mao Reforms* (Cambridge: Harvard University Press, 1999), pp. 197–240; and chapters by David Zweig, Jun Jing, Stephan Feuchtwang, Peter Ho, Tyrene White, Sing Lee, and Arthur Kleinman in Elizabeth Perry and Mark Selden, eds., *Chinese Society: Change, Conflict, and Resistance,* 2nd edition (London: Routledge, 2003).

3   For three different critiques of China's water strategies see Vaclav Smil, *China's Environmental Crisis: An Inquiry into the Limits of National Development* (Armonk: M. E. Sharpe, 1993); Judith Shapiro, *Mao's War against Nature: Politics and the Environment in Revolutionary China* (Cambridge: Cambridge University Press, 2001); and Gavan McCormack, "Water Margins: Competing Paradigms in China," *Critical Asian Studies* 33, no. 1 (March 2001), pp. 5–30. Doubts about Dazhai miracle numbers persist. One investigator found on returning to Dazhai that food numbers he had been given in 1971 were fraudulent. John Gittings, *China through the Sliding Door* (New York: Simon and Schuster, 1999), p. 92. Others concluded that with state subsidies gone, Dazhai had again become a "dirt-poor village." See George Black and Robin Munro, *Black Hands of Beijing* (New York: John Wiley and Sons, 1993), p. 118. An article by Jin Zhong in *China Daily,* January 31, 2000, however, proclaims the village's re-

surgence under the entrepreneurial leadership of Guo Fenglian. By 1998 agriculture accounted for just 7 percent of Dazhai income, and most villagers work in factories or services.

4   Lorien Holland, "Running Dry," *Far Eastern Economic Review*, February 3, 2000, pp. 18–19.

5   This account of Baoding in 1989 draws on information provided by Ann Fessenden, a former teacher at Hebei University; and Timothy Brook, *Quelling the People: The Military Suppression of the Beijing Democracy Movement* (Toronto: Lester, 1992), pp. 29, 71–72.

6   Zhang Liang (pseud.), compiler, *The Tiananmen Papers* (New York: Public Affairs press, 2001), p. 81.

7   Ibid, p. 79.

8   Ibid., p. 104.

9   Ibid., p. 215.

10   Brook, *Quelling the People*, p. 71.

11   Zhang, *Tiananmen Papers*, p. 227.

12   Ibid., p. 291.

13   Michel Oksenberg, Lawrence Sullivan, Marc Lambert, eds., *Beijing Spring, 1989: Confrontation and Conflict: The Basic Documents* (Armonk: M. E. Sharpe, 1990); Tony Saich, ed., *The Chinese People's Movement: Perspectives on Spring 1989* (Armonk: M. E. Sharpe, 1990); Roger Des Forges, Luo Ning, and Wu Yen-bo, eds., *Chinese Democracy and the Crisis of 1989: Chinese and American Reflections* (Albany: State University of New York Press, 1993). The most rigorous attempt to document the deaths at Tiananmen may be Timothy Brook, *Quelling the People*, pp. 151–69. Brook notes Beijing's acknowledgment that close to 300 were killed and more than 8,000 wounded; the Red Cross report based on surveys of Beijing hospitals in the immediate aftermath of the massacre that 2,600 had been killed; and estimates in the range of 3,000 to 10,000 by activists. While recognizing that the numbers are problematic given official attempts to conceal casualties, Brook finds the Red Cross estimate plausible.

14   Zhang, *Tiananmen Papers*, p. 399.

15   Ibid., p. 404.

16   Ibid., p. 407.

17   Ibid., pp. 407–08.

18   Lianjiang Li and Kevin O'Brien, "The Struggle over Village Elections," in Goldman and MacFarquhar, eds., *The Paradox of China's Post-Mao Reforms*, pp. 129–44, and Daniel Kelliher, "The Chinese Debate over Village Self-Government," *The China Journal* 37, January 1997, pp. 63–90, provide informed discussions on village elections drawing on interview data from Hebei and other provinces.

19   Bruce Gilley, *Model Rebels: The Rise and Fall of China's Richest Village* (Berkeley: University of California Press, 2001), pp. 41, 106, 110.

20   Frank Pieke, "Networks, Groups, and the State in the Rural Economy of Raoyang, Hebei," in Edward Vermeer, Frank Pieke, and Woei Lien Chong, eds., *Cooperative and Collective in China's Rural Development* (Armonk: M. E. Sharpe, 1998); Pieter Brandjes et al., "Vegetable Boom and the Question of Sustainability in Raoyang County, North China," International Centre for Development Oriented Research in Agriculture, Wageningen, the Netherlands, 1994.

21   "Hebei Drive Reduces Poverty," *China Daily,* June 29, 1995; Shaoguang Wang and Angang Hu, *The Political Economy of Uneven Development in China* (Armonk: M. E. Sharpe, 1999).

22   Craig Smith, "Graft in China Flows Freely, Draining the Treasury," *New York Times,* October 1, 2000.

23   See Richard Madsen, *China's Catholics: Tragedy and Hope in an Emerging Civil Society* (Berkeley: University of California Press, 1998).

24   See Richard Madsen, "The Catholic Church in China: Cultural Contradictions, Institutional Survival, and Religious Renewal," in Perry Link, Richard Madsen, and Paul G. Pickowicz, eds., *Unofficial China: Popular Culture and Thought in the People's Republic* (Boulder: Westview Press, 1989), pp. 103–20.

25   *New York Times,* June 7, 1998.

26   "Fighting Falungong," *China Rights Forum* (spring 2000), p. 53.

27   On domestic violence in rural China during the reform era see Paul G. Pickowicz and Liping Wang, "Village Voices, Urban Activists: Women, Violence, and Gender Inequality in Rural China," in Perry Link, Richard Madsen, and Paul G. Pickowicz, eds., *Popular China: Unofficial Culture in a Globalizing Society* (New York: Rowman and Littlefield, 2002), pp. 57–87.

28   *China Daily,* October 22, 1996.

29   *China Daily,* November 26, 1997.

❈ INDEX

Page numbers in *italic* indicate tables and maps

Gender inequality, 200–201, 281–282

Geng Changsuo: at Agricultural Work Conference, 27; at anniversary celebrations, 42, 130, 191; anti-corruption campaign and, 65, 68; awards and honors, 248; Chen Yonggui's visit to, 209–210; on collectivization, 75–76; as coop leader, 2, 24, 40; during Cultural Revolution, 90, 93–96, 103–108; Dazhai visit of, 71; death of, 266–268; documentary film on, 30; economic policy of, 112–113; on educated youth, 76–77; family network of, 180, 194–196, 284–286 (See also Geng Huijuan); flood relief and, 33, 34–35, 44; during four cleanups campaign, 61; honesty of, 15, 56, 102, 184, 195; housing project and, 79, 80; land reclamation and, 31; Lin Tie and, 2, 4, 27, 28, 37–38, 40, 103–104, 114, 249; Mao, letter to, 114; marriage of (See Xu Shukuan); mechanization and, 167, 168; modernization and, 237, 244; at National Day ceremonies, 78, 130; at National People's Congress, 63; at Party Congresses, 131, 181, 229; patronage ties of, 26, 58, 71, 122, 157, 169–170, 232; polemical writings of, 124–127, 130, 156–157, 172–173, 182, 206, 220–221; railroad lobbying by, 209, 210, 231–232, 259, 273; at Raoyang Party Congress, 163; in reform era, 260; resistance to Leap excesses, 7, 9, 12–13; resistance to reform, 16–17, 18–19, 31, 32, 115, 156–157, 163, 175, 206, 229, 231, 237, 244; revised history of Wugong, 113–115, 187, 188; on revolutionary committee, 116, 121, 127; revolutionary successors and, 48–49; socialist education work of, 52–53; visits to model villages, 45; well-drilling and, 73, 119; in Wugong Agro-Industrial Commercial Association, 261; on Wugong model, 78–79

Geng Delu, 195

Geng Duo, 195, 285

Geng Huijuan: in Beijing, 116–117, 136–

137; during Cultural Revolution, 93, 94–95, 97, 98; mediator in Li Chunyu-Geng Xiufeng feud, 166; militia and, 136, 139; at Raoyang Party Congress, 163; as revolutionary successor, 49–50; rise of, 122, 171–172, 181, 239; sent down to village, 76–77, 83; wedding of, 128–129; women friends of, 51, 283

Geng Jianzhi, 271

Geng Jinxiang, 193, 195

Gengkou, 108, *251*

Geng Sujuan, 195

Geng Xiufeng: on anti-corruption campaign, 64; archive compiled by, 5; book project and, 217, 221, 233; as critic, 2; criticism of reform state, 276–277; criticism of Wugong commune, 43; during Cultural Revolution, 95, 96, 102; on Dazhai model, 214; during famine, 12–13; harassment by Xu lineage, 149–150, 158, 161; in housing project plan, 79, 80; -Li Chunyu feud, 164, 166, 190–191; Mao, letter to, 164–166; retirement of, 67–68; travels of, 158–161; at 20th anniversary celebration, 41; on unsuitable crops, 197; in vegetable contract controversy, 18; Wugong coop, role in, 30, 187–188

Geng Xueren, 180, 194–195, 199

Geng Zhuanluo, 195

"Get Organized" speech (Mao), 30, 43, 187

Ge Wen, 29, 30

Ge Yu, 272

Government, county. See Raoyang county

Government, provincial: Great Leap famine and, 6, See also Hebei province

Grain: distribution system, 16, 18–19, 25–26; exports, 6; for flood relief, 35; forecasts of yields, 7, 9, 33–34, 39–40, 164; high-yield varieties, 152; illegal sales, 106; in ill-suited conditions, 197, 208, 214; imports, 13; prices, 20, 78, 126, 179, 238; production, 17, 25, 35, 39, 52, 74, 78, 118–119, 168, 175, 179–180, 227, 245, 250, *288–289*; quotas, 13, 14, 16, 165; ration, 10, 12,